Microsoft® SharePoint® 2010: Deploying Cloud-Based Solutions

Phillip Wicklund

Published with the authorization of Microsoft Corporation by:
O'Reilly Media, Inc.
1005 Gravenstein Highway North
Sebastopol, California 95472

ISBN: 978-0-7356-6210-0

2 3 4 5 6 7 8 9 10   LSI   6 5 4 3 2 1

Printed and bound in the United States of America.

Microsoft Press books are available through booksellers and distributors worldwide. If you need support related to this book, email Microsoft Press Book Support at mspinput@microsoft.com. Please tell us what you think of this book at http://www.microsoft.com/learning/booksurvey.

Acquisitions and Developmental Editor: Kenyon Brown
Production Editor: Holly Bauer
Editorial Production: Octal Publishing, Inc.
Technical Reviewer: Wayne Ewington
Copyeditor: Bob Russell
Indexer: Julie Hawks
Cover Design: Twist Creative • Seattle
Cover Composition: Karen Montgomery
Illustrator: Robert Romano

I would like to dedicate this book to the Lord, Jesus Christ,
for "from Him and through Him and to Him are all things.
To Him be the glory forever"
(Romans 11:36).

Contents at a Glance

Table of Contents

What do you think of this book? We want to hear from you!

Microsoft is interested in hearing your feedback so we can continually improve our
books and learning resources for you. To participate in a brief online survey, please visit:

microsoft.com/learning/booksurvey

Part II   Deploying SharePoint in the Public Cloud

4   Administering SharePoint Online. 157

5   Identity Management and Authentication 197

Part III Deploying SharePoint in the Private Cloud

What do you think of this book? We want to hear from you!

Microsoft is interested in hearing your feedback so we can continually improve our
books and learning resources for you. To participate in a brief online survey, please visit:

microsoft.com/learning/booksurvey

Introduction

This book is about Microsoft SharePoint in the cloud. This might entail SharePoint in a public cloud, such as SharePoint Online, or SharePoint in a private cloud, such as your own data center. It also can mean SharePoint in a hybrid cloud, where you deploy SharePoint to both the public and private clouds for various reasons.

So, why do you need a book on SharePoint in the cloud? Isn't cloud-based SharePoint the same as on-premises SharePoint? It's commonly understood that the cloud offers significant benefits over standard data centers. These benefits include being highly available and scalable. They also include robust automation and the ability to be self-healing, bringing the average server-to-administrator ratio from 50:1 all the way up to 500:1. But what about SharePoint in the cloud specifically? Well, the differences between on-premise SharePoint and SharePoint in the cloud are probably more numerous than you'd think. In one obvious sense, this book will help you learn various techniques for migrating to the cloud, but the book goes well beyond that.

Consider how the administration effort is quite different between on-premises and public cloud-based administration tools such as the Office 365 Administration Center. Additionally, licensing varies dramatically, along with authentication and authorization (identity management). Cloud-based customizations are also quite different, and rely heavily on sandboxed solutions, for example.

From a private cloud perspective, SharePoint is a unique animal. It benefits from the technologies that provide the foundation, namely Hyper-V for virtualization and System Center for automation. But it also relies on multitenancy capabilities to support tenant isolation—a key pillar for any private cloud.

All of these topics, and more, comprise the scope of this book. Come, learn, and see the powerful capabilities of SharePoint in the cloud. After all, the cloud is the future!

Who Should Read This Book

This book is primarily for IT professionals, IT architects, and IT decision makers who want to understand the capabilities of SharePoint in the cloud, and want to know what it takes to either get their on-premises SharePoint deployments into the public cloud or build their own private cloud—or perhaps a little of both.

The earlier chapters paint a broad picture and can appeal to a wide audience of readers who are simply interested in what it means to have SharePoint in the cloud. However, as the book progresses, the chapters become increasingly technical.

Assumptions

The book focuses on the technologies, techniques, and planning that is required to support SharePoint in the cloud. This means background information on SharePoint is not provided in great detail in earlier chapters, and is not provided at all past Part I of the book. It is assumed that you have a general idea of what SharePoint is, and how it is used from an end-user perspective. As the book progresses, you'll see that the chapters become more technical and discuss topics such as those in the following list (note that previous knowledge of these topics isn't required, but is helpful):

- Out-of-the-box SharePoint capabilities, such as site collections, sites, document libraries, pages, content types, workflows, and so on.
- Remote PowerShell.
- Identity management, such as user accounts, Active Directory, and identity federation.
- Networking concepts such as DMZs, NLBs, DNS, reverse proxies, and so on.
- Customizations with Visual Studio and SharePoint Designer.
- Infrastructure technologies such as Hyper-V and System Center.
- Lots more PowerShell!

Who Should Not Read This Book

This book is meant to introduce SharePoint in the cloud to you at a high level. There are certain areas of the book that are intended to be introductory, because to exhaust those areas would require multiple books in and of themselves. Chapter 7 ("Introduction to Customizing and Developing in SharePoint Online") and Chapter 8 ("Introduction to Creating a Private Cloud") are good examples of this. As you read through the book, you'll see references to other books that cover the particular area in more depth. So, if you're looking for broad strokes, this book is for you. If you're looking to go deeper because you already have a solid understanding of these cloud concepts, than this book is not for you.

Organization of This Book

The book is organized into three parts. Part I, "Introducing SharePoint in the Cloud," explains what it means to have SharePoint in the cloud. Part II, "Deploying SharePoint in the Public Cloud," focuses on SharePoint in the public cloud. Part III, "Deploying SharePoint in the Private Cloud," focuses on SharePoint in the private cloud.

It is helpful to read Part I in its entirety before moving on to the rest of the book. Thereafter, some of you might jump to Part III—for example, if you're not interested in the public cloud—or you might skip Part III if you're only interested in SharePoint in a public cloud. Many of you will want to learn about both the public and private clouds, because you will need to support some sort of hybrid deployment.

Note that Chapters 2 and 7 are more or less "swing" chapters in that they are relevant to both public and private cloud models. Chapter 2 focuses on planning, and Chapter 7 covers customizing SharePoint Online. While both of these chapters reference SharePoint Online (Microsoft's public cloud), they are highly relevant to on-premises deployments as well.

The following are brief chapter descriptions to help you understand the contents of the book.

Part I, "Introducing SharePoint in the Cloud"

Chapter 1, "Introducing SharePoint Online" opens by explaining what the cloud is and why SharePoint works so well in it. The chapter moves on to discuss the core features of SharePoint in general, followed by a discussion around various cloud models that SharePoint fits into, such as SharePoint in the public, private, and hybrid clouds.

Chapter 2, "Office 365: Feature and Overview" takes concepts surrounding the public cloud a bit further by introducing you to Office 365, Microsoft's SharePoint public cloud offering, as well as the umbrella offering for other products such as Exchange Online, Lync Online, and Office Professional Plus.

Chapter 3, "Planning for SharePoint Online" rounds out Part I of the book by introducing you to all the considerations around planning for SharePoint Online. This includes planning for the core capabilities of SharePoint as well as defining your information architecture. The chapter concludes with a discussion of governance in SharePoint Online.

Part II, "Deploying SharePoint in the Public Cloud"

Chapter 4, "Administering SharePoint Online" highlights techniques for administering SharePoint Online sites. This comprises global administration through the Office 365 Administration Center, including creating and managing sites, site quotas, user profiles, and managed metadata.

Chapter 5, "Identity Management and Authentication" explores the different identity provider options and the pros and cons of each. The chapter focuses heavily on identity federation, the technology whereby your users can achieve a single sign-on experience between their on-premises sites and SharePoint Online. The chapter concludes with details on managing identity with Remote PowerShell.

Chapter 6, "Migrating to SharePoint Online" explains how to migrate SharePoint on-premises to SharePoint Online. It compares the different migration approaches between SharePoint Online Standard and Dedicated editions.

Chapter 7, "Introduction to Customizing and Developing in SharePoint Online" concludes Part II with an introduction to customizing SharePoint Online to meet your company's unique needs. This includes a discussion about building your own custom sandboxed solutions and using SharePoint Designer to brand your sites, as well as a brief discussion on how to integrate SharePoint Online with Windows Azure.

Part III, "Deploying SharePoint in a Private Cloud"

Chapter 8, "Introduction to Creating a Private Cloud" introduces the concept of a private cloud. In one sentence, a private cloud is the intersection of virtualization and automation. However, as you'll learn when reading this chapter, a lot of technologies help to make this marriage work, including Hyper-V, the System Center suite, and the Opalis workflows.

Chapter 9, "Introducing Multitenancy in SharePoint 2010" walks you through the fundamentals of multitenancy in SharePoint. You'll see examples that show how multitenancy keeps tenant data and customizations isolated from one another, a key element of SharePoint in a private cloud.

In Chapter 10, "Configuring Tenant-Aware Service Applications," you'll learn that creating your service applications is the first logical step when configuring SharePoint for a private cloud. This chapter walks you through the less obvious process of configuring your service applications in a tenant-aware fashion using PowerShell.

Chapter 11, "Configuring Tenant-Aware Site Collections" builds on the foundation set in Chapter 10 by showing you how to create tenant site collections and features. You'll also see how to associate your tenants to popular service applications such as the user profile and managed metadata services. PowerShell again plays a significant role in configuring these multitenancy capabilities.

Code Samples

Five chapters in the book feature example scripts written in PowerShell. You will benefit from downloading these scripts separately so that you don't need to manually enter them, and thereby risk introducing typos and other errors. Additionally, since scripts can change over time as a result of feedback or changing cmdlets, downloading them ensures that you're always working with the most up-to-date content.

Introduction   **xix**

You can download the scripts from this book's website, at:

http://go.microsoft.com/FWLink/?Linkid=227001

You can also check for additional information and updates at:

http://sharepoint-in-the-cloud.com

Acknowledgments

Wow—I'm finally here! It's so great to be at the finish line with my second book!

However, I'll be the first to acknowledge that this book would not have been possible without some serious help. First I want to thank my wife Sarah, who stood by me and encouraged me every step of the way. I can't stress enough how much of an impact her support had on my ability to complete this book. Thanks, babe—I love you!

I also want to thank my technical editor Wayne Ewington (Microsoft), and my development editor Kenyon Brown (O'Reilly). You guys were awesome to work with, and you provided great feedback and help! This book would've looked like Swiss cheese without your watchful eyes!

There were also four extraordinary contributing authors who helped me write some key chapters. Eric Hanes (Chapter 2), Brian Wilson (Chapter 3), Faraz Khan (Chapter 7), and Brian Neilson (Chapter 8) all chipped in and deserve MAJOR kudos! I also want to thank Adam Grocholski (Azure MVP). Adam generously wrote the section "What Is the Cloud?" in Chapter 1. This book was under tight deadlines right from the start, and I'll be the first to admit that I wouldn't have stood a chance flying solo. THANKS SO MUCH, GUYS! I very much appreciate the help that you gave and your contributions to this great book!

All five contributing authors are colleagues of mine at our employer, RBA Consulting, which also deserves some accolades. The management staff at RBA has been so generous. They helped carve out a role that gave me some freedom to write during business hours. Also, on several occasions, I had to dip into emergency PTO to make my deadlines. Some of you might not know it, but I also have five children at home, so the great work/life balance that I have at RBA had a significant impact on the book as well as on my ability to maintain a sane personal life. It's to this end that I want to extend my sincerest thanks to RBA Consulting.

And last, but not least, I want to thank the great folks at O'Reilly Media/Microsoft Press. I'm so thankful to have been given this amazing opportunity to write for such a prestigious publishing brand. It's truly incredible! I feel humbled, and I hope I can live up to the great legacy they've built.

—Phil Wicklund

Errata and Book Support

We've made every effort to ensure the accuracy of this book and its companion content. Any errors that have been reported since this book was published are listed on our Microsoft Press site at oreilly.com:

http://go.microsoft.com/FWLink/?Linkid=227003

If you find an error that is not already listed, you can report it to us through the same page.

If you need additional support, email Microsoft Press Book Support at *mspinput@microsoft .com*.

Please note that product support for Microsoft software is not offered through the addresses above.

We Want to Hear from You

At Microsoft Press, your satisfaction is our top priority, and your feedback our most valuable asset. Please tell us what you think of this book at:

http://www.microsoft.com/learning/booksurvey

The survey is short, and we read every one of your comments and ideas. Thanks in advance for your input!

Stay in Touch

Let's keep the conversation going! We're on Twitter: *http://twitter.com/MicrosoftPress*.

Part I
Introducing SharePoint in the Cloud

Part I is an introduction to Microsoft SharePoint in the cloud. Chapter 1 opens by explaining what the cloud is and why SharePoint works so well in the cloud. With that primer under your belt, you will then learn about the core features of SharePoint in general as well as various cloud models into which SharePoint fits, such as SharePoint in the public, private, and hybrid clouds.

Chapter 2 takes the concept of the public cloud a bit further by introducing you to Microsoft Office 365, Microsoft's SharePoint public cloud offering, as well as the umbrella offering for other products such as Exchange Online, Lync Online, and Office Professional Plus.

Chapter 3 ends this part of the book by introducing you to the considerations around planning for SharePoint Online. This includes planning for the core capabilities of SharePoint, as well as defining your information architecture. The chapter concludes with a discussion on governance in SharePoint Online.

Chapter 1
Introducing Microsoft SharePoint Online

In this chapter, you will learn about:

- Why people are rapidly deploying SharePoint into the cloud
- Comparing the public, private, and hybrid cloud models
- An overview of customizing SharePoint in the cloud
- An overview of migrating to the cloud
- How security and authorization is handled in the cloud
- Navigating the SharePoint Online administrative pages

If you follow the technology industry, you have probably noticed that everyone suddenly seems to be "going to the cloud" these days. Is cloud computing some new concept? The short answer is, no. Cloud computing has been around much longer than you might realize. In fact, you more than likely have been using cloud computing for some time but were not even aware of it. If you use an online service for email, such as Hotmail, Gmail, Yahoo, and so on—and it's highly likely that you are using at least one of these—you are already in the cloud.

In recent years, the buzz around the cloud has grown immensely. Every company in the world is looking for proven ways to increase the return on investment (ROI) on the technologies that they use, and the cloud is proving that it can do just that.

SharePoint in the cloud is no exception. Microsoft is pouring a lot of resources into its SharePoint cloud offering because they know that not only will it bring them significant revenue, it will also save their clients a lot of capital, as well. It's an incredible win-win situation!

This is because SharePoint can be tough to deploy and maintain, primarily because significant expertise and experience is required to do so successfully. Many companies can't afford or (for other reasons) are unable to recruit the necessary talent. Because of this, taking SharePoint to the cloud is especially appealing to them. When in the cloud, they can essentially outsource that costly, time-consuming administrative overhead.

It's out of this cloud-based value proposition that Microsoft released a new offering called Microsoft Office 365, and therein, a child product called SharePoint Online. Office 365 is actually a suite of four cloud-based technologies: Microsoft Exchange Online for email, Microsoft Lync Online for presence and messaging, SharePoint Online for collaboration, and Microsoft Office Professional Plus paired with Office Web Apps for browser-based document authoring.

Although SharePoint Online is very similar to its on-premise cousin, SharePoint Server, it has some very unique aspects that warrant focused study. Some of these unique complexities include licensing, user and identity management, and user authorization. Also, there are differences in administering SharePoint Online sites versus SharePoint Server sites. Moreover, there are considerable complexities with respect to migrating to SharePoint Online as well as customizing SharePoint Online.

Beyond SharePoint Online, the Microsoft product, you might elect to create your own SharePoint Online-esque experience by deploying SharePoint into your own private cloud. You see, SharePoint can reside in either the public cloud or your own private cloud (and sometimes both). By creating your own private cloud, you benefit from all the automation, scalability, reliability, and self-healing that any great cloud ought to provide.

But before you delve into the depths of public and private clouds, let's focus for a bit on what the cloud actually is, the ROI that the cloud is designed to provide, and why you ought to deploy SharePoint into the cloud. Following this look into cloud fundamentals, it's important to see the unique implementation that SharePoint Online takes with cloud technologies, including looking at the various SharePoint cloud-based models, features of SharePoint Online, an overview of how to customize SharePoint Online, how to migrate to the cloud, and how to navigate the Office 365 administration pages. With these core fundamentals under your belt, you'll be ready to begin planning, administering, and deploying your cloud-based SharePoint solutions.

What Is the Cloud?

So what really is the cloud? To answer that question, you need to take a step back and look at the different approaches and paradigms that have appeared during the history of the computer industry. Back in the 1960s and 1970s, most computing was done on very large, very expensive mainframe computers. In the 1980s, the personal computer (PC) was introduced. This made computing more affordable and accessible to a wider audience. However, there was a drawback to the PC: it simply did not have the computing horsepower of the mainframe. Thus, in the late 1980s and early 1990s, the client-server model was introduced.

Using the client-server model, PCs could connect to and take advantage of the power of bigger computers on the same network. This model continued through the mid 1990s (and continues even today) and has matured into exposing the functionality of servers via the Internet in the form of web services. These services could be consumed by applications within and outside of the network.

During this entire progression, companies bought more and more hardware and built bigger and bigger data centers. Companies built out multiple data centers in attempt to handle increases in traffic as well as to be able to handle disaster recovery scenarios. This approach has become incredibly expensive and has resulted in information technology (IT) and business patterns that slow innovation while simultaneously dramatically increasing total cost of ownership. The cloud computing paradigm focuses on the need to break out of these costly and growth inhibiting patterns.

The goal of cloud computing is to enable organizations to consume existing services and increase their speed to market by eliminating the tasks of creating the required infrastructure and skill set to adopt technology. This consumption-based cost model shifts the organization's investment from an up-front capital expenditure to an operating expense, which brings with it on-demand capacity flexibility as well as flexible licensing structures.

Cloud computing is really about managing the different components required for solutions. There are basically four cloud models, and you'll notice a pattern with regard to benefits and tradeoffs as you compare each model. These tradeoffs are illustrated in Figure 1-1. As a solution moves from a complete on-premises implementation to cloud implementation, organizations see a lower total cost of ownership, which results, in large part, from the fact that organizations are giving up control of various aspects of their solutions.

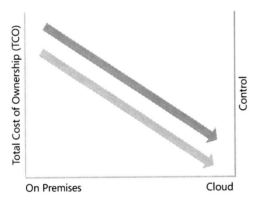

FIGURE 1-1 Total cost of ownership typically goes down when you migrate to the cloud; however, so does control and flexibility.

Running Applications On-Premises

To truly understand what cloud computing is and what the various models provide, you first need to understand what it takes to run applications on-premises. Specifically, you need to understand what IT does so that the business can run its applications. You can organize the tasks that IT performs into five logical groupings. The first grouping is infrastructure. This grouping includes procuring the physical location for the data center, securing the location, ensuring that the location has proper utilities (electrical, water, heat, Internet connectivity, and so on), and procuring the required hardware (servers, switches, and so forth). Once the tasks in the first grouping have been completed, IT can focus on the second grouping, which is installing and configuring the operating system(s) required for the business. Once the operating system(s) are successfully installed and configured, IT can move on to the third logical grouping: services. Tasks in this group include getting the network configured to handle inbound and outbound traffic, messaging, and load balancing. Besides networking tasks, IT also needs to put into place the management, scaling, security, update, and backup services that are required to keep the business running. Once the services are in place, IT can perform any required development tasks, which is the fourth logical grouping. This includes putting the necessary runtimes and development platform tools in place as well performing any custom application development tasks. Once all of the required tasks have been completed, the business can then run its applications, which is the fifth logical grouping. Cloud computing offloads these tasks from the organization onto the provider. Figure 1-2 helps you to visualize these tasks and how they support the business applications.

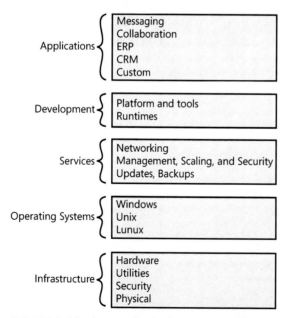

FIGURE 1-2 A business application is comprised of five layers of technologies, ranging from the application itself, all the way down to the physical hardware.

Application Service Provider

The Application Service Provider (ASP) model is a model with which you might already be familiar. You might be using an ASP to host a database or web server right now. The ASP takes care of the data center and its networking and utilities, as well as acquiring and maintaining the necessary hardware. The organization that employs an ASP is responsible for everything else, from the operating systems installed on the servers to the applications required for its businesses to run. Table 1-1 presents an overview of these differences.

TABLE 1-1 Differences Between On-Premises IT Deployments and the ASP Cloud Model

On-Premises	ASP
Applications	Applications
Development	Development
.NET Runtime	.NET Runtime
Databases	Databases
Security	Security
Management	Management
Load Balancing	Load Balancing
Scaling	Scaling
Backup	Backup
Logical Servers	Logical Servers
Storage	Storage
Virtualization	Virtualization
OS	OS
Server Hardware	Server Hardware
Networking	Networking
Utilities	Utilities
Physical	Physical

Managed by organization

Managed by provider

Infrastructure as a Service

The Infrastructure as a Service (IaaS) model builds upon the ASP model, abstracting and managing additional solution components. In this model, which is described in Table 1-2, the vendor manages the operating system (including installation and patching), virtualization, storage, and logical server configurations. Amazon's Elastic Compute Cloud (EC2) is one example of an IaaS offering. You can place your solution components on top of pre-built server configurations that are defined and managed by Amazon.

TABLE 1-2 IaaS Abstracts Even More from the Organization

On-Premises	ASP	IaaS
Applications	Applications	Applications
Development	Development	Development
.NET Runtime	.NET Runtime	.NET Runtime
Databases	Databases	Databases
Security	Security	Security
Management	Management	Management
Load Balancing	Load Balancing	Load Balancing
Scaling	Scaling	Scaling
Backup	Backup	Backup
Logical Servers	Logical Servers	Logical Servers
Storage	Storage	Storage
Virtualization	Virtualization	Virtualization
OS	OS	OS
Server Hardware	Server Hardware	Server Hardware
Networking	Networking	Networking
Utilities	Utilities	Utilities
Physical	Physical	Physical

Managed by organization

Managed by provider

Platform as a Service

The Platform as a Service (PaaS) model abstracts and manages even more solution components than the IaaS model. In a PaaS scenario (see Table 1-3), the vendor handles everything
from backups, scaling, and load balancing, to security, databases, and development platforms. PaaS facilitates quicker time to market by requiring the organization to only focus on
its applications and services rather than the underlying infrastructure. Microsoft's Windows
Azure product is a PaaS offering. Organizations create their service and applications and
deploy them to Windows Azure. Microsoft handles the rest, from creating virtual machines,
to enabling the organization to quickly scale up or down, out or in, based on need.

TABLE 1-3 PaaS Allows Organizations to Build Applications Without Concern for Underlying Infrastructure

On-Premises	ASP	IaaS	PaaS
Applications	Applications	Applications	Applications
Development	Development	Development	Development
.NET Runtime	.NET Runtime	.NET Runtime	.NET Runtime
Databases	Databases	Databases	Databases
Security	Security	Security	Security
Management	Management	Management	Management
Load Balancing	Load Balancing	Load Balancing	Load Balancing
Scaling	Scaling	Scaling	Scaling
Backup	Backup	Backup	Backup
Logical Servers	Logical Servers	Logical Servers	Logical Servers
Storage	Storage	Storage	Storage
Virtualization	Virtualization	Virtualization	Virtualization
OS	OS	OS	OS
Server Hardware	Server Hardware	Server Hardware	Server Hardware
Networking	Networking	Networking	Networking
Utilities	Utilities	Utilities	Utilities
Physical	Physical	Physical	Physical

◼ Managed by organization

◻ Managed by provider

Software as a Service

Unlike the previously discussed models, the Software as a Service (SaaS) model removes all management responsibility of the solution from the organization, as shown in Table 1-4. The SaaS vendor develops, deploys, and maintains the solution. The organization simply consumes the solution as a service and configures it to meet its specific needs. The Office 365 product suite (including SharePoint Online) is a prime example of the SaaS model. You don't need to buy any servers or software licenses. You simply sign up and configure the services that you want your organization to use.

TABLE 1-4 SaaS Allows Organizations to Use and Configure Software with Little Concern for Custom Development or Infrastructure

On-Premises	ASP	IaaS	PaaS	SaaS
Applications	Applications	Applications	Applications	Applications
Development	Development	Development	Development	Development
.NET Runtime	.NET Runtime	.NET Runtime	.NET Runtime	.NET Runtime
Databases	Databases	Databases	Databases	Databases
Security	Security	Security	Security	Security
Management	Management	Management	Management	Management
Load Balancing	Load Balancing	Load Balancing	Load Balancing	Load Balancing
Scaling	Scaling	Scaling	Scaling	Scaling
Backup	Backup	Backup	Backup	Backup
Logical Servers	Logical Servers	Logical Servers	Logical Servers	Logical Servers
Storage	Storage	Storage	Storage	Storage
Virtualization	Virtualization	Virtualization	Virtualization	Virtualization
OS	OS	OS	OS	OS
Server Hardware	Server Hardware	Server Hardware	Server Hardware	Server Hardware
Networking	Networking	Networking	Networking	Networking
Utilities	Utilities	Utilities	Utilities	Utilities
Physical	Physical	Physical	Physical	Physical

▨ Managed by organization

▧ Managed by provider

Why Deploy to the Cloud?

Now that you're familiar with what the cloud is, it will be helpful to see some specific reasons why people are choosing to deploy SharePoint there rather than on-premises. Some of these reasons include variable load, capacity, costs, business agility, and business stability.

Handling Variable Load

Variable load has been the bane of on-premises self-hosting since the dawn of computing, and SharePoint is no exception. Consider a company that deploys SharePoint into its enterprise and then sends a communication to 20,000 employees. Those employees all hit the home page at the same time, and performance grinds to a halt, resulting in a negative impression of the IT department. This is called bursting.

On and Off Again

On and off again is an example of variable load. Consider a service that an IT department wants to enable, but only for a short duration. Tax season or budgeting time are examples of events within a year that IT might need a service available for only a short period of time.

The problem with on and off again is the procurement of resources (such as infrastructure) that are needed to support the service. Services in the cloud, such as infrastructure as a service, can support spinning up a set of new servers, and then turning them off again after they're no longer needed. What's even better is most providers only charge you for the time the servers are on; they don't charge for the procurement process or storing the servers when they're not in use.

Disposable Computing

Disposable computing is similar to on and off again, with the exception that when it's turned off, it's also thrown away. There's no emotion involved in killing off resources that are cloud-based. You set up the infrastructure when you need it, and you throw it away when you're done.

Growing Fast

Growing fast is a common trouble spot for new SharePoint deployments. Many companies simply "spin up" a SharePoint site and see adoption take off like wild fire. One example might be users quickly loading up thousands of documents, and you finding yourself rapidly running out of storage as a result. Another example might simply be increased user load, leaving you stranded with too few web front-ends or other system resources to properly handle the traffic. This is where SharePoint in the cloud has a significant advantage. There's no need to worry about procuring new hardware. All you need to do is allocate more virtual resources and spin up new virtual servers to accommodate the load. You'll never need to worry about what's physically on a rack in a data center. In fact, for SharePoint Online editions such as Standard, you don't even need to worry about resources at all, because Microsoft guarantees a certain level of responsiveness and availability at all times.

Unpredictable and Predictable Bursting

Bursting is when you experience a sudden influx of load on the system. Perhaps an organization sends a company-wide announcement, linking readers to an article in SharePoint. All at once, 100,000 people browse to that page and the responsiveness of the system drops rapidly. This would be an example of predictable bursting. A benefit of the cloud in this case would be that you can spin up new infrastructure to support the influx of load, perhaps just for eight hours. After the influx has tapered off, you could dispose of that infrastructure.

However, bursting is oftentimes unpredictable, and it's with unpredictable bursting that cloud computing really shines. For example, many infrastructure cloud providers allow you to specify events for which the system will automatically scale out to handle the demand. You could specify an event where, if the CPU of the servers are all averaging over 50 percent utilization, a new server will be automatically added into the farm to help with the increasing load. With regard to bursting, the farm would automatically scale out to handle the load, and then scale back again after the levels die off.

Excess or Inadequate Capacity

Similar to variable load, managing the right capacity is not easy when SharePoint is not in the cloud. For example, you want to buy enough hardware and bandwidth, but not too much. Not enough means bad performance, but too much means wasted resources and dollars spent. This is a fine line to walk when on-premises, but in the cloud, it is much easier to change capacity as your needs change.

Cost of Ownership

Cost is very much more fixed when not in the cloud. If your company's leadership tells you to cut costs, this is much harder on-premises. This is because of all the fixed costs associated with maintaining data centers as well as hardware costs and personnel expenses.

The Fixed-Cost Dilemma

The fixed-cost dilemma is common across industries. Essentially, the dilemma is that your business owns an asset, such as SharePoint infrastructure. What comes with that asset is fixed costs to maintain it. In the case of SharePoint, these costs are many, including:

- Bandwidth
- Hardware, data center space
- Storage
- Software/Licensing
- Electricity, building costs, and so on
- Personnel, such as:
    - Network administrators
    - Storage administrators
    - SQL database administrators
    - SharePoint administrators

As you can see, there are many costs associated with SharePoint. The key benefit to the cloud is greater flexibility in changing capacity, and thereby having control on costs.

Three-Year Hardware Life Cycles

Physical pieces of hardware have limited life cycles. Most servers are rotated out of production every three years. Procuring new hardware so frequently is a significant cost to a business. With the cloud, you never need to procure hardware—ever—and thus, you'll typically realize a considerable costs savings.

Personnel Costs

Probably the most expensive SharePoint expense isn't the application itself, hardware, or networking—it's people. SharePoint requires highly-skilled resources to install, deploy, configure, and maintain it. And the truth of the matter is these resources are scarce. Most companies have a hard time recruiting experienced SharePoint professionals; the cloud largely offsets most of these resource needs by providing their services for you. Consider the following roles that would likely be less necessary to your organization if SharePoint were in the cloud:

- SharePoint architect
- SharePoint farm administrator
- SQL database administrator
- Network architect
- Security architect
- Storage architect

Instead, you could focus your dollars on business-focused resources. The goal of these resources is to take business requirements and map them to SharePoint functionality, thus improving the ROI for your SharePoint investment. The following roles are needed no matter whether SharePoint is in the cloud or not, but when in the cloud, you'll have more capital to make larger investments in these ROI generating resources:

- SharePoint information architect
- Enterprise librarian/taxonomy architect
- SharePoint search architect/discoverability architect
- SharePoint program, product, and project manager(s)
- SharePoint business analyst
- SharePoint governance controller
- Creative designer (branding)
- SharePoint developer

Business Agility

Of all the great benefits of SharePoint in the cloud you've seen thus far, business agility might be the most compelling cloud driver yet. Consider time-to-market. With SharePoint in the cloud, you can literally have a cloud-based collaboration site spun up and ready for use within an hour of reading this sentence. Stop what you're doing, put down the book, go to *www.office365.com*, and then enter your information and start collaborating. It's that easy. Obviously, that's an oversimplification, but it's more true than not. And when compared with the process of building a SharePoint server farm from scratch, it's an incredible proposition for deploying to SharePoint Online.

Another agility concept plays off the adage, *Scale fast or fail fast*. Certain business models literally live or die based on their ability to be flexible in their offerings. A six-month reaction time will bankrupt the business, whereas six hours is closer to what's needed, if not an instantaneous reaction to changing needs. This concept is similar to scaling and capacity management that was discussed in previous sections.

It's obvious that there is a significant business market that stands to benefit most clearly from deploying SharePoint to the cloud. That business market is small businesses. Why would a small business spend literally hundreds of thousands of dollars building an infrastructure and buying expensive software licenses when it can get SharePoint Online for USD $5 per user, per month? If you have 25 employees who need to collaborate with each other and customers, what sounds more palatable, USD $125/month or USD $100,000? Clearly, the former wins the day, and Office 365 is seeing staggering adoption rates for small businesses because of this obvious low entry cost advantage.

Business Stability

Companies are building their businesses on SharePoint. SharePoint helps their employees collaborate, store business-critical documents, and supply real-time information and products to their customers. It's no wonder that uptime and high availability are critical.

Achieving a highly available SharePoint farm is no trivial task. Consider the following technologies that need to be in place to accommodate greater than 99 percent uptimes and short disaster recovery time objectives:

- Multiple web front-ends, load balanced and redundant
- Redundancy of SharePoint service applications, such as Search
- Network redundancy, such as switches, network interface cards, reverse proxies, and load balancers
- Redundancy of domain controllers

- SQL redundancy, such as clustering, mirroring, and/or log shipping

- Storage redundancy, such as storage area network (SAN) replication and disk striping (RAID)

- Data center redundancy, meaning all of the above in a second, failover data center

SharePoint Online offers a 99.9 percent uptime Service Level Agreement (SLA), multiple data center redundancy and failover, with less than 24-hour recovery time objectives (RTO), all for USD $5 per month, per user. Now that's a good deal!

SharePoint in the Cloud

We've just finished discussing what the cloud is and why businesses are choosing to deploy SharePoint to it. Now it's time to take things a little deeper and investigate what exactly SharePoint looks like when it's in the cloud. There are three primary deployment models when SharePoint is considered cloud-based. The first model is SharePoint in a *public cloud*, wherein 100 percent of your SharePoint deployment is hosted externally to your company. This model has all the main benefits of being cloud-based that were described in the previous section. From a SharePoint perspective, the only downside might be fewer available features and less flexibility with regard to customization, because you don't have access to the underlying infrastructure. However, the offset to that is typically a much reduced cost of ownership. Office 365 and SharePoint Online Standard and Dedicated editions are the best examples of SharePoint in a public cloud.

The second model is called the *private cloud*. The private cloud model takes public cloud services, such as SLAs, anywhere access, disaster recovery, and so forth, and brings them into an on-premises solution. Many enterprise companies take this approach when they have a chargeback model, where they sell IT services to their business units. The main advantage of this model is utmost flexibility in features and customizations, because SharePoint is controlled internally. However, that flexibility comes with greater cost of ownership because you can't outsource the administrative effort.

The third model is oftentimes called a *hybrid cloud*, or perhaps a better name is the *combined cloud*. The idea behind this third model is that often when a company transitions to the cloud, it starts with on-premises SharePoint deployments that gradually migrate to the public cloud. Most companies will take this approach if they are currently on premises, but desire to move to the cloud incrementally.

Figure 1-3 shows how these three models, as well as Microsoft's SharePoint Online, are paired with flexibility, administrative effort, and cost of ownership.

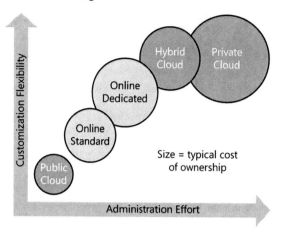

FIGURE 1-3 SharePoint in the cloud can be deployed into three typical models: the public cloud, the private cloud, and a hybrid cloud. Each approach affords various degrees of administrative effort, flexibility, feature availability, and cost.

Figure 1-3 demonstrates that the private cloud offers the most control but at considerable cost. As you slide down and to the left, you trade cost for less control. To determine if flexibility is something you even need, read Appendix A, "Server, Online SharePoint, and Online Dedicated Compared," and Chapter 7, "Introduction to Customizing and Developing in SharePoint Online." You'll probably be surprised that on-premises and the cloud are very close to parity, which makes this Figure 1-3 a bit over pronounced.

SharePoint in the Public Cloud

SharePoint has many providers of cloud-based hosting. The biggest name in the game is obviously Microsoft Online Services. Microsoft provides SharePoint cloud services through its Office 365 program, where SharePoint Online comes in two flavors, Standard and Dedicated (with many smaller variations within each). Other than Microsoft, there are other public SharePoint cloud providers. Because of innumerable differences, Microsoft Online Services and Office 365 will be the focus throughout this book.

Office 365 Overview

Office 365 takes the office experience of email, document management, collaboration, and digital communication to the cloud. Office 365 is comprised of four of Microsoft's core products, including SharePoint Online, Exchange Online, Lync Online, and the Office Professional Plus suite.

> **Note** Office 365 can be purchased in one of three versions: Office 365 for Professionals and Small Businesses, Office 365 for Midsized Businesses and Enterprises, and Office 365 for Education. For more details on the features of Office 365 and how these three models compare, read Chapter 2, "Office 365 Feature Overview."

SharePoint Online   SharePoint is integral to the Office 365 experience, and in many ways it acts as the hub for a company's cloud computing experience. Businesses can create sites and share documents with their employees. They can also open up their sites to their partners and easily create partner and client collaboration sites, something that is notably more difficult on premises. SharePoint Online also integrates with Lync and Office. This means that employees can easily author, share, and discuss documents.

Public-Facing Internet Sites in SharePoint Online

As an alternative to intranet/extranet-like collaboration, a new feature with SharePoint Online 2010 is the ability to create public-facing websites. You can register your own domains with Microsoft and manage your SharePoint Internet sites in SharePoint Online, alongside your intranet and extranet sites. See Chapter 4, "Administering SharePoint Online," to learn how to create these sites and register domains.

SharePoint Online comes in two flavors, Standard and Dedicated. Standard means that you share hardware with other Office 365 clients. With Dedicated, your sites run on your own dedicated physical equipment. There are many more differences, such as the various features that do and do not work between Standard and Dedicated versions. Refer to Appendix A for a detailed comparison.

> **Note** In addition to features that are or are not available between the Standard and Dedicated versions, there are many customizations that vary in availability. See Chapter 7 to learn how customizations such as custom Web Parts and branding differ.

Exchange Online   Email has been running in the cloud for dozens of years. With Exchange Online, a business can forgo the administrative effort around what can easily be viewed these days as a commodity service. Exchange Online is usable by default via browser access to Outlook Web Access, Microsoft's browser-based Exchange email service. If the business purchases Office Professional Plus, either packaged with Office 365 or separately, it can use the Outlook client to connect to Exchange Online in the cloud. Figure 1-4 shows the new Outlook Web Access browser interface that comes with Office 365.

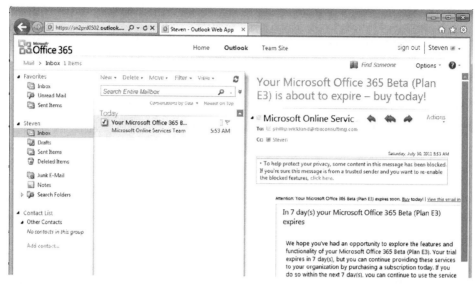

FIGURE 1-4 Exchange Online can either be used in the browser through Outlook Web Access or in the Outlook client application (shown here).

Lync   Lync connects people across a business by providing functionality such as presence and availability, instant messaging (IM), audio and video conferencing and calling (via voice over IP [VOIP]), and online meeting abilities. Within SharePoint Lync, *presence* is throughout team sites, bringing an important social aspect to document collaboration. Figure 1-5 demonstrates some of the meeting functionality, where a rudimentary instant messaging session can easily turn into an online meeting presentation, complete with audio and video conferencing.

FIGURE 1-5 Lync facilitates business communication by providing voice and video conferencing, instant messaging, presence, and, as shown here, online meetings.

Office Professional Plus   Documents remain part and parcel to business collaboration, and this is no different in the cloud. The only thing changing is where documents are authored and published. New with Office 365 is browser-based creation and editing of documents, such as Microsoft Word, Microsoft Excel, and Microsoft PowerPoint documents. With this new browser-based functionality in Office 365 and SharePoint 2010, multiple users can author documents from anywhere, anytime, without a dependency on a locally installed application. If a company still wants the ability for its employees to take these cloud-based documents offline, it can add the full Office Professional Plus client suite to its Office 365 experience for an additional monthly fee. Figure 1-6 presents an example of editing a PowerPoint presentation in the browser that is uploaded into an Office 365 SharePoint site.

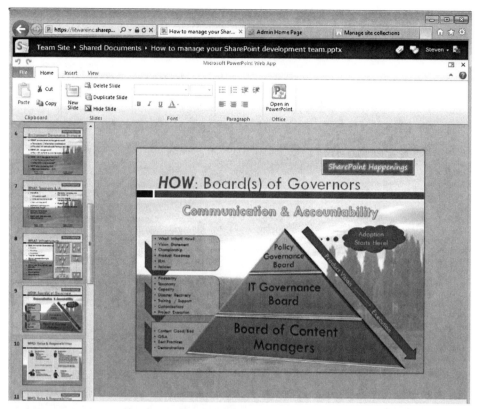

FIGURE 1-6 Office documents can now be authored and edited directly within SharePoint and the browser, as with the authoring of this PowerPoint presentation.

Other SharePoint Cloud Providers

There are more cloud providers than Microsoft. There are dozens of smaller cloud shops that offer SharePoint in the cloud, and large providers such as Amazon that offer infrastructure as a service where you can host your own private SharePoint cloud and still take advantage of a lot of cloud benefits.

Smaller SharePoint cloud providers include popular brands such as fpweb and Rackspace. Both companies provide similar models to Microsoft's SharePoint Online Standard and Dedicated editions. This book does not provide a detailed comparison between Microsoft Online Services and other cloud providers.

SharePoint in the Private Cloud

If the SharePoint servers in your data center are all virtualized, does this mean you're in a private cloud? No, it doesn't. Virtualization is only the first step in the processes. The premise behind the cloud is that you have technologies in place that act on behalf of the human administrator in an automated fashion. It's this automation that makes the cloud highly available, scalable, and even self-healing. It's this automation that makes the cloud so powerful! Automation to this degree is a paradigm shift from the typical data center model to what's now being coined as the "private cloud."

In addition to infrastructure automation, SharePoint 2010 has built-in features that help maintain hundreds or thousands of *tenants* (or clients, customers, and so on). It is very important for SharePoint in the cloud to be *tenant-aware*. Tenant-aware means that SharePoint can support isolated groups of people, whereby one group cannot see the data of another group, nor can one group negatively impact the performance or availability of a different group. Without the multitenancy capabilities of SharePoint, it would be near impossible to make SharePoint a holistic cloud solution. It's the combination of infrastructure automation and the multitenancy features of SharePoint that define what it means for SharePoint to be deployable to a private cloud.

Comparing the Typical Data Center with the Private Cloud

The private cloud is a paradigm shift away from the archaic data center model. Companies spend millions of dollars and countless hours of labor in red tape procuring new hardware, fire fighting performance issues, managing production outages, and so forth. There are technologies today that can greatly increase the efficiency of resources and increase the availability of services. Consider the following series of technologies and how they are reshaping today's data centers:

Hyper-V Cloud Virtualization   Hyper-V allows the flexibility to scale out (add new servers) or scale up (increase dedicated resources) on the fly, without necessarily requiring new physical components. As the demand for a given service expands, those services can easily accommodate the load without the need for lengthy hardware procurement processes.

Systems Center Operations Manager   Systems Center Operations Manager (SCOM) is a monitoring technology that watches environments for issues and then notifies individuals or other services when a problem occurs. An issue might be as big as a server going down, or a lower-level problem such as a particular service reaching capacity.

Systems Center Opalis   Opalis is an automation platform that responds to events in a data center and knows how to handle those events. You could say that Opalis is the brains of the private cloud. Opalis might instruct Virtual Machine Manager to spawn a new server, or it might have rules that necessitate the creation of a change ticket in Service Manager that must be approved before the scale event can occur.

Systems Center Service Manager   Service manager helps your IT department react to events by providing incident and problem resolution, change control, and configuration management. Service Manager can receive automated change requests from Opalis, or manual, day-to-day change requests submitted by IT professionals.

Systems Center Virtual Machine Manger   Systems Center Virtual Machine Manger (SCVMM) is a technology with which IT professionals can centrally administer all their virtual machines in the data center and rapidly provision and optimize new and existing virtual machines. SCVMM also allows for the dynamic scaling of resources through management packs that have resource optimization enabled.

It's clear that the private cloud is very different from the traditional data center model. It all revolves around automation, high availability, and self-healing. Hyper-V provides the flexibility, and Systems Center provides the monitoring and automation. For more detail, see Chapter 8, "Introduction to Creating a Private Cloud," and Chapter 9, "Introducing Multitenancy in SharePoint 2010."

Multitenancy in SharePoint 2010

The concept of a tenant in SharePoint is similar to how an apartment building views its tenants. A given tenant only has access to its own space; he can't go into other tenant's rooms and take their furniture. However, all the tenants of the apartment share the same building and common infrastructure such as hallways and parking garages. Multitenancy capabilities in SharePoint 2010 follow a similar paradigm.

Figure 1-7 depicts a SharePoint web application with five site collections. Supporting the web application are two service applications (such as Search or managed metadata). Multitenancy isolates the data of both the web application as well as the service application. A web application can have thousands of tenants, with multiple site collections in each tenant. There could even be thousands of site collections in a tenant if the tenant has enabled My Sites for its users. Then the data stored in SQL is horizontally partitioned in the database, further isolating it from other tenants.

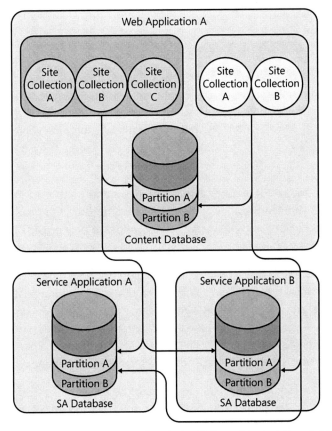

FIGURE 1-7 Multitenancy in SharePoint 2010 provides isolation of data, services, and customizations on a tenant-by-tenant basis.

There are essentially two ways to house tenants in SharePoint: give them each their own web application, or give them one or more site collections. The problem with web applications is scalability. If you have 100 tenants, it's inadvisable to have 100 web applications. However, you can have hundreds or thousands of site collections. In SharePoint 2007, this was possible, but with multitenancy in 2010, you can realize the following benefits that weren't easily possible in 2007:

- Site subscriptions
- Feature packs, granular feature availability
- Host header site collections
- Tenant administration sites
- Isolation of services (profiles, managed metadata, search, and so on)
- Isolation of customizations

Chapter 10, "Configuring Tenant-Aware Service Applications," has a more thorough overview on multitenancy in SharePoint 2010.

Site Subscriptions   A site subscription is nothing more than a globally unique identifier (GUID), or simply a unique ID, that is associated with one or more site collections. Every site collection that is associated with the same GUID is what makes up the tenant. Site subscriptions can only be created in Windows PowerShell when on the SharePoint server. First, the IT professional creates the subscription (tenant), and then begins creating site collections associated with that subscription.

Feature Packs   A feature pack is similar to site subscriptions in that it is another GUID, but this time each GUID has a collection of features associated with it and is assigned to a tenant. You can use feature packs to trim features out of the tenant UI. Often, a cloud provider or IT department uses feature packs along with their chargeback model to only provide functionality to tenants after they have paid for it.

Host Header Site Collections   Host header site collections aren't actually a new feature with SharePoint 2010, but it is a critical feature when it comes to multitenancy. Using header site collections, an IT professional can assign multiple "vanity domains" to a given web application. You can use this to give each tenant in the web application its own root-level domain. For example, if the web application has a URL of http://intranet.contoso.com, a site collection at http://intranet.contoso.com/sites/sales can be accessible via http://sales.litwareinc.com.

Tenant Administration Sites   Tenant administration sites are site collections associated with a given tenant (subscription ID). The tenant administration site is used to perform central administration such as configurations, but isolated to the tenant. For example, from the tenant administration site, you can create new site collections, manage user profiles, configure My Sites, configure Search, manage the metadata term store, and so forth.

Isolation of Services   As with the tenant administration site, service applications can be deployed in *partitioned mode*. When a service application is in partitioned mode and is associated with a web application that contains tenants, each tenant sees its own administrative interface to configure the service application. This is especially powerful with service applications such as managed metadata, user profiles, and Search. Table 1-5 shows the full list of service applications and their tenant abilities.

TABLE 1-5 Service Applications That Can Be Partitioned and Store Tenant Data

Service application name	Can be partitioned	Stores tenant data
Access Services	No	No
BCS	Yes	Yes
Excel Calculation	No	No
FAST for SP	No	No
Managed Metadata	Yes	Yes
Performance Point	No	No
PowerPoint	No	No
Project Server	Yes	Yes
Usage and Health	No	No
User Profiles	Yes	Yes
Search	Yes	Yes
Subscriptions Settings	Yes	Yes
State	Yes	No
Web Analytics	No	Yes
Word Conversions	Yes	No
Word Viewing	Yes	No
Visio Graphics	Yes	No

Isolation of Customizations   It wouldn't be possible to have a fully-functional, multitenant application if the application didn't allow for customizations on a tenant-by-tenant basis. The basic premise here is if a tenant decides to paint her living room, this shouldn't cause the power to go out in her neighbor's apartment. SharePoint 2010 allows for many tenant-by-tenant customizations through site collection–scoped tools such as SharePoint Designer. Another great new feature in SharePoint 2010 is the concept of *sandboxed solutions*. Sandboxed solutions allow a tenant to deploy partially trusted code (Web Parts, event handlers, and so on) into its site collections, where that code cannot access or negatively impact other tenants. This is accomplished through code/process isolation as well as resource quotas such as CPU cycles and memory utilization.

Chapter 7 offers a complete guide to customizing SharePoint Online as well as a very detailed explanation of sandboxed solutions, including what does and does not work in the sandbox.

SharePoint in a Hybrid Cloud

There's no doubt that neither the public cloud nor the private cloud models are going to fit the needs of all SharePoint deployments perfectly. There must be a middle ground, and that middle ground is what's often called a *hybrid cloud*. A hybrid cloud is when you combine both the use of a private cloud with the use of the public cloud. From a SharePoint perspective, a hybrid cloud can be beneficial when you want to move to the public cloud, but you want to move incrementally. Perhaps you want to move to the public cloud, but some of your sites are heavily customized and the migration process for them is significantly more complicated. The compromise here is to move the sites with very few customizations to the public cloud but keep the others in the private cloud while you work on resolving the customization issues.

Note Single sign-on is possible between your on-premises SharePoint, and SharePoint Online. This is accomplished by using Active Directory Federation Services 2.0 to federate user authentication to the cloud.

Another common use for a hybrid cloud is collaboration with partners or customers. Often, a company won't want to open up its internal infrastructure to the outside world. The public cloud is the perfect solution for this, because it is hosted externally, and your employees, partners, and customers can access the cloud from anywhere, anytime, without the need for Virtual Private Network (VPN) or anything similar.

Table 1-6 lists some common ways businesses structure their hybrid SharePoint deployments (focus on keeping components that are not supported by SharePoint Online, on-premises).

TABLE 1-6 Some SharePoint Features Are Best Left On-Premises, Whereas Others Are a Great Fit for the Cloud

Common for on-premises	Common for Online
Insights	Sites
Content	Content
Composites	Communities
FAST Search	SharePoint Search
Internet Sites	Basic Composites

Note Search currently cannot federate between an on-premises search service application and SharePoint Online.

SharePoint Online Features Overview

It doesn't matter whether you choose the Standard or Dedicated edition, SharePoint is still SharePoint. Both editions are on the SharePoint 2010 platform, which means you get all the latest and greatest features that SharePoint has to offer. SharePoint Online still has all the main features of the "SharePoint wheel," including Sites, Communities, Content, Search, Insights, and Composites, as illustrated in Figure 1-8.

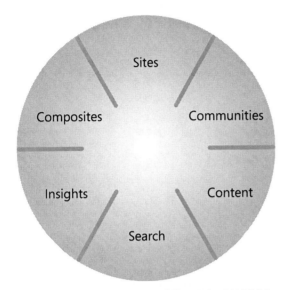

FIGURE 1-8 The main features of SharePoint 2010 fall into six categories: Sites, Communities, Content, Search, Insights, and Composites.

Sites

You can use SharePoint Online to create collaboration sites where your users can share information with each other and partners or clients. These sites can be accessed by a wide range of devices and browsers, from anywhere in the world. Sites can also be taken offline through SharePoint Workspace 2010.

In addition to collaboration spaces, you can also create public-facing websites in SharePoint Online. If you own a domain, you can configure the domain with your domain registrar to point to your SharePoint Online site collection(s). This domain registration also affords you the opportunity to have a SharePoint Online site that does not use the default sharepointonline.com domain as the site's URL.

Figure 1-9 shows the Administration Center interface with which your SharePoint Online administrator can manage the site collections. When the administrator prepares to create a new site collection, she has most of the templates available to her as if it were an on-premises solution (see Figure 1-10). As a result, businesses can quickly create intranet and extranet sites in just minutes. Once these sites are created, users can add countless out-of-the-box Web Parts onto their sites to build out their content. These Web Parts include calendars, tasks, document sharing, discussion boards, and so forth. Users can also place specific audiences on Web Parts to secure or hide content that is only relevant to certain groups of users. Additionally, content can be tagged and searched to facilitate faster discovery of information.

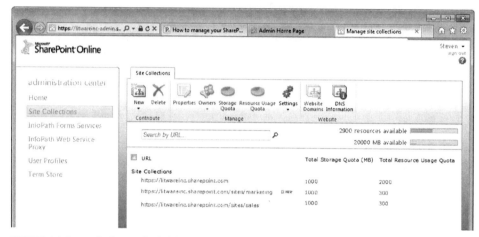

FIGURE 1-9 Instead of central administration access, SharePoint Online Standard edition provides an Administration Center interface with which you can create new site collections, manage users, set quotas, and so on.

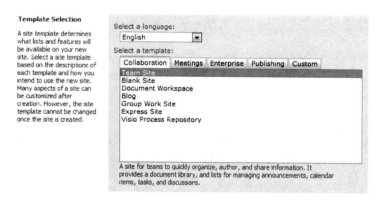

FIGURE 1-10 The majority of site templates that are available in an on-premises deployment of SharePoint are also available in SharePoint Online.

Before the name Office 365 was coined, SharePoint Online 2007 used to fall into the Business Productivity Online Suite (BPOS). Since the introduction of Office 365, SharePoint Online 2010 offers these new site templates that were not available in BPOS:

- Group Work Site

- Express Site

- Visio Process Repository

- Document Center

- PowerPoint Broadcast Site

- My Sites and My Site Host

- Search Center

- Publishing Portal

- Enterprise Wiki

Note Records Center templates are not available in SharePoint Online.

With the introduction of these site templates and features, SharePoint Online has made significant strides toward feature parity when compared to the 2007 BPOS version.

Note WCM Workflow and approval, along with Variations, are not available in SharePoint Online for Internet sites.

Reference Chapter 4 for specifics on how to create sites in SharePoint Online.

Communities

Communities is SharePoint's take on Web 2.0, or perhaps more accurately, enterprise social collaboration. In BPOS with SharePoint Online 2007, this was a nearly non-existent feature, but with Office 365, there is a lot more "social" available in SharePoint Online. The three most important social features in Office 365 are:

- The inclusion of My Sites
- The inclusion of Profiles
- Integration with Lync

My Sites were not available in BPOS, but they are available today. This inclusion alone offers significant advances in cloud-based SharePoint social capabilities. My Sites in SharePoint Online provide users with the ability to create their own personal sites. A user can then upload personal documents to the site, create a blog, and use it as a social platform similar to Facebook but for the enterprise instead. This includes features such as statuses, tagging content across the portal and surfacing those tags on My Site, rating content, and viewing other employees' tags and information.

Note My Sites are only available to licensed E1–E4 plan users. They are not available for Kiosk or Partner users. See Chapter 2 for more information about available plans and licensing.

This is all possible with the inclusion of Profile features into SharePoint Online 2010. Each user can have his own profile (see Figure 1-11), in which he can enter his interests, skills, and other personal information that he wants to share. Profiles are either created when a new user is created, or a business can set up a profile import from its current Active Directory domain.

To learn more about profile importing, see Chapter 4.

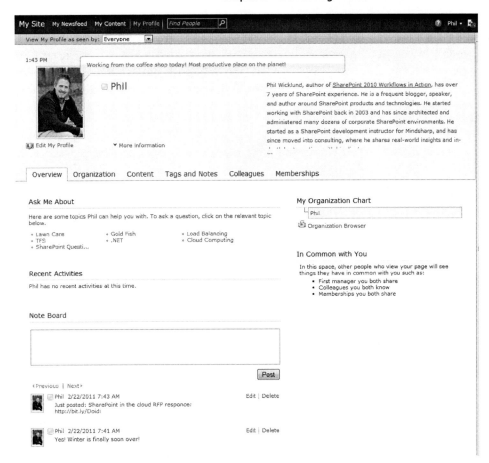

FIGURE 1-11 Profiles in SharePoint Online foster a social and collaborative spirit in your sites, similar to popular social networking sites such as Facebook.

Content

Content and document management is one of the core features of SharePoint Online. The content features of SharePoint Online can be placed into two main categories: web content management and document management. Web content management features provide an easy method to create and manage pages and web content. These features include drag and drop Web Parts for easy page administration as well as rich text editing of page content directly in the browser. Also, a sophisticated workflow engine is available for approval of content changes. New with SharePoint Online 2010 is the availability of the publishing portal. In BPOS, you could only engage in basic collaboration when in SharePoint Online 2007. Today, businesses can use SharePoint Online as their enterprise intranet and extranet solutions, and publish important news, announcements, and events to their employees in the same fashion they would if on premises.

> **Note** WCM workflow and approval is not available for SharePoint Online for Internet Sites.

Document management in SharePoint Online includes a host of features, including versioning of documents, check-in/check-out, publishing, routing of documents with the content organizer, as well as the document ID service, which assigns a document a unique ID and allows users to find a document no matter where it is in SharePoint. The document ID service and content organizer are also new features with SharePoint Online 2010.

> **Note** SharePoint Online does not provide integration with Information Rights Management or Records Center.

A significant new feature in SharePoint 2010 is the ability to have a managed metadata term store. When a document is uploaded into SharePoint Online, this document can be tagged with metadata. By tagging a document with metadata, you can increase the ease with which a user can find and identify the document, because the user can see how the document is classified without the need to open it. Also, from a search perspective, users receive more accurate search results when documents are tagged. This is especially true if your site contains thousands of documents.

The managed metadata term store is a centralized location in which all of your metadata terms reside. With the tags centralized, it's easier for you to define your organizational taxonomy and then push that taxonomy down to your users. Additionally, managed metadata helps an organization enforce consistency in term usage such as department names and product names. Figure 1-12 shows an example of a term store in SharePoint Online with a term hierarchy mapped to political geographies.

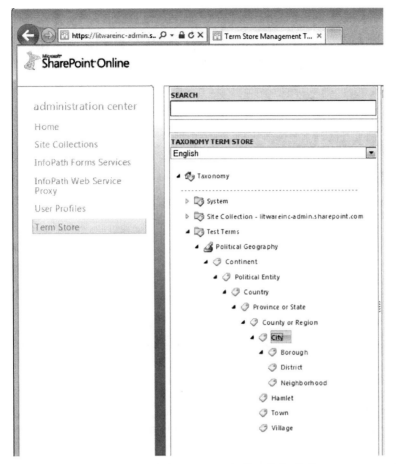

FIGURE 1-12 A business can use the term store in SharePoint Online to create a central location from which it can manage its business terms. These terms can then be added to documents to help classify them and improve discoverability.

With the term store in place, when you upload a document into SharePoint Online, you can tag that document with a tag from the term store. After the tag is added, you can then sort, filter, and group all the documents in the library based on the tags, even if there are tens of thousands of documents.

Search

With Search in SharePoint Online, you can search across all your SharePoint sites that reside in the cloud. All search results are security trimmed, which means that when a user performs a search, he sees only that content for which he has permissions. The following are some additional search features that you can take advantage of when searching in SharePoint Online:

- Boolean query syntax for free-text queries and property queries
- Prefix matching for search keywords and document properties
- Suggestions while typing in the search box
- Suggestions after the initial search is performed
- Federated search results when searching from Windows 7

Standard vs. Dedicated Search?

Both Standard and Dedicated editions of SharePoint Online provide search results across multiple SharePoint sites in a given site collection. The primary difference between the two editions is that Dedicated searches can also be across multiple site collections.

Content outside of SharePoint Online can also be indexed if you're using SharePoint Online Dedicated. For example, you can index Internet websites, other SharePoint sites, and Microsoft Exchange public folders, as well as other systems through third-party protocol handlers or Microsoft .NET connectors. All of this can be done if the search crawler's service account has access to the content source that is being crawled, and that content is available over the wide-area network (WAN).

Enterprise Search and Search Service Application Federation

Currently, Search in the Dedicated edition can only crawl WAN content. This prevents corporations from viewing results across their enterprise—both on-premises and cloud content. It is anticipated that in future versions of Office 365, you'll be able to federate search results between an on-premises search service application and SharePoint Online, thus providing one set of results, regardless of whether the content is cloud-based or based on premises.

Insights

Insights in SharePoint Online are features with which a business can see and make decisions regarding critical operational data via the business intelligence (BI) features of SharePoint 2010. SharePoint Online puts many of these BI features at your disposal, including Web Parts with which you can chart and graph SharePoint list data. Also, there are other BI Web Parts that you can use to create key performance indicators (KPIs).

> ## Business Intelligence Features That Are Not Available in SharePoint Online
>
> Microsoft Office PerformancePoint services and PowerPivot are not available in any form of SharePoint Online. The best option for BI in SharePoint Online is to use Excel Services, Visio Graphic Services, and the KPI Web Parts.

Another very popular BI feature in SharePoint Online is Excel Services. With Excel Services, you can render an Excel document in the browser when it is stored in SharePoint. It would be easy to create charts in that Excel workbook and simply upload the book into SharePoint for user consumption. A user can take this even further if she uses the Representational State Transfer (REST) features of SharePoint Online. Essentially, you can access any data in SharePoint Online via REST web services. If there's an Excel document with a chart in it, for example, you can access that chart via its REST URL and then render it on the home page of the company's portal.

Composites

Composites in SharePoint Online are the combination of a number of features that when assembled can create compelling business applications. The main composite features include InfoPath Forms, Workflow, Visio Graphics, Access Services, Excel Services, and Business Connectivity Services (BCS).

With InfoPath Forms, you can create rich client or browser-based forms with an intuitive design tool, similar to Word. You can then publish these forms into SharePoint, from which users can fill out the forms and submit the data to business applications, or simply to a document library in SharePoint. Sometimes when a user submits a form, a workflow starts. Workflows facilitate the progression of a business process from start to finish. SharePoint workflows can handle human interaction and automate the delegation of tasks and other resources.

> **Note** When building your composite applications, be aware that no full-trust code is permitted in SharePoint Online Standard. Only the Dedicated edition permits full-trust code. For more information, see Chapter 7.

Other kinds of composites are technologies such as Visio Graphics, Excel Services, and Access Services. These composites bring business applications that are a part of Office products into SharePoint and the browser, making them more widely findable and available to end users of those systems. BCS is a technology that allows users to connect to and render Line of Business (LoB) data in SharePoint. Consuming and manipulating data in SharePoint has never been easier.

> **Note** BCS is only supported for the Dedicated edition of SharePoint Online, and the scope of the external data that can be accessed is rather limited (for example, you can't access data in Azure). For more details about what is possible, see Chapter 7.

Configuring and Customizing SharePoint Online

SharePoint Online ships with a number of out-of-the-box features that you can configure, but even so, many companies find that they need to customize their cloud-based SharePoint sites. What's great about SharePoint Online is that for the most part, the customizations available to you when you're in the cloud are nearly the same as when you're on premises. There are some important differences, but consider the following examples where parity exists:

- Browser-based configuration
    - ❑ Change the theme of a site
    - ❑ Add/remove Web Parts and author pages
    - ❑ Sort, filter, and group with custom list view data
    - ❑ Query data across a site collection with content query Web Parts
    - ❑ Apply metadata and tagging on documents by using content types and a central term store
    - ❑ Take advantage of the out-of-the-box workflows

For detailed information on how to customize SharePoint by using the browser, read SharePoint 2010 Foundation Step by Step, *by Olga Londer and Penelope Coventry (2011, Microsoft Press; ISBN: 978-0-7356-2726-0).*

- SharePoint Designer-based customizations

    ❑ Create custom master pages for advanced site branding

    ❑ Build custom Data Form Web Parts

    ❑ Create connectable Web Parts showing master/detail views

    ❑ Create custom workflows for your business processes

For a detailed guide on SharePoint Designer, read SharePoint Designer 2010 Step by Step, *by Penelope Coventry (2010, Microsoft Press; ISBN: 978-0-735-62733-8).*

- InfoPath-based customizations

    ❑ InfoPath Forms Services (InfoPath client not needed because forms are rendered in the browser)

    ❑ Create custom list and library edit views directly from the ribbon

    ❑ Create custom workflows forms (initiation, association, and task edit forms)

    ❑ Create custom business forms deployed into form libraries

    ❑ Add custom .NET code behind an InfoPath Form

The preceding list demonstrates that you can build pretty advanced applications in SharePoint Online, and the process remains very consistent with on-premises customizations. The biggest changes from on-premises to cloud-based customizations are around customizations created in Microsoft Visual Studio. Visual Studio is a tool used by programmers to write custom-coded applications that meet only the most complicated business requirements. In SharePoint Online, these customizations must be deployed into that sandbox as a sandboxed solution rather than a typical full-trust farm solution.

Sandboxed Solutions

Sandboxed solutions are a new concept for SharePoint Online. Described basically, sandboxed solutions are custom-coded solutions deployed into a site collection's solutions gallery—also known as the "sandbox." When Visual Studio SharePoint projects are compiled, they generate a file with a .wsp extension. This file is called a *solution package* that can be uploaded into a solution gallery in a SharePoint Online site collection. The solution gallery is an important new feature for SharePoint Online, because in previous versions, you could not upload your custom-coded resources. Those resources, such as Dynamic Link Libraries (DLLs), were only permitted on the SharePoint servers themselves. Now, with sandboxed solutions, you can deploy packages containing customizations into the solution gallery and make them available across the site collection. The following are common examples of solutions built in Visual Studio for the sandbox:

- Custom .NET Web Parts in either C# or VB.NET

- Custom SharePoint features that can add or remove custom functionality

- Event Receivers that can respond to items or documents being created, edited, and so on

- Custom-coded actions for SharePoint Designer workflows

- Silverlight applications

- List definitions, instances, site columns, and content types that are created upon feature activation rather than manually through a browser

When you create a new Visual Studio project, a dialog box opens, asking you to choose if the application will be a sandboxed solution or a farm solution. If you choose sandboxed solution, you can upload that solution into the solution gallery after you compile it and generate the .wsp package. Figure 1-13 shows a solution gallery that contains five sandboxed solutions.

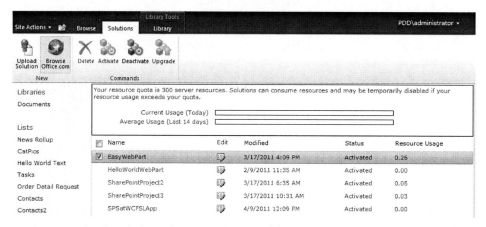

FIGURE 1-13 Using the solution gallery, site collection administrators can upload custom solutions into their site collection. After the solution is uploaded and activated, the functionality therein is available for end users to utilize.

Note After you upload a package, you need to activate the solution before your customizations are enabled and available to users. To do so, on the ribbon, on the Solutions tab, click the Activate button. Conversely, to remove functionality, click the Deactivate button.

Up to this point, you've seen examples of solutions that work well in the sandbox. Well, what about those that don't work in the sandbox? There are certain customizations that are not allowed in SharePoint Online. The following are a few examples of customizations that are not permitted. The basic premise is that the influence of the code cannot extend past the boundaries of the current site collection, such as:

- A Web Part that tries to query outside of the sandbox—for example, attempting to call a Windows Communication Foundation (WCF) service (the exception being a Silverlight Web Part)

- A Web Part that queries a different site collection, even if the Web Part's site and the other site collection are both hosted in SharePoint Online

- Visual Web Parts that use an ASCX user control for its view (because the ASCX file must be deployed on the server)

- Custom-coded Visual Studio workflows (because Visual Studio workflows must be deployed into the Global Assembly Cache [GAC] on the server)

Resource Usage While in the Sandbox

It's important to remember when working with sandboxed solutions that SharePoint Online limits you to a certain level of system resources; therefore, you need to be aware of how many of those resources your customizations might consume. For example, if you have a Web Part or two that do complex queries across your site collection, those Web Parts will likely utilize a lot of the server's CPU. Microsoft needs to ensure that your customization won't negatively impact the performance of other customer's site collections, and because of this, each customer is allotted a certain amount of server resources. If you reach your resource quota, those Web Parts or other customizations will stop functioning until the next day.

Note Each SharePoint Online customer receives a pool of resources that can be divided up among each site collection. You can therefore allocate more resources to your more critical site collections, and less to site collections that are not as critical or perhaps where no customizations exist.

User Management and Security in SharePoint Online

Security in SharePoint Online is an important concept to understand before you get started. This is because changing directions after leaving the gate isn't necessarily an easy thing to do. For example, in the beginning, you might start by using Office 365 user accounts, but later you decide to switch gears and use your on-premises Active Directory accounts. That transition isn't an easy one, because you'll need to redo the permissions in SharePoint, which can take a considerable amount of time.

It is important to plan out how your users are authenticated to SharePoint Online, and subsequently, what they are authorized to do after logon. From an authentication perspective, there are essentially four options:

- None—anonymous
- Cloud-based identity—Office 365 accounts (@onmicrosoft.com)
- Identity federation with on-premises Active Directory domain
- Partner Access via external invites

Anonymous Users

A new feature with SharePoint Online 2010 is the ability to create public-facing websites. You can buy a domain at a local domain registrar and point it to Microsoft's Office 365 IP Address, and subsequently provision site collections from that domain. You can configure these websites to allow anonymous access to the site, which is typical for Internet-facing sites. The site owners can configure what those anonymous users are allowed to do.

Cloud-Based Identity and Synchronization

The most common way to manage users in SharePoint Online is to create accounts in Office 365. These accounts have an onmicrosoft.com domain suffix, such as @[*mycompany*].onmicrosoft.com. While in the Office 365 Admin Overview page, click the Users link to see all of your users. Next, click the New drop-down list (see Figure 1-14), and then select User to create a new user account.

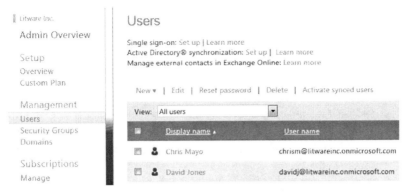

FIGURE 1-14 You can create new users right from the Office 365 Admin Overview page. These users will have a onmicrosoft.com logon.

After you create the new account, you need to assign a license to the new user in order for him to access Office 365 functionality, including SharePoint Online. To do this, on the same Admin Overview page, in the navigation pane, click Licenses. Next, click the Assign Now link to assign a license to the new user. See Chapter 2 for more details on what licenses are available and how they compare.

The trouble with creating users manually is that it is tedious. And what if you have 30,000 users in your company? Then it's simply impractical. One capability that you can take advantage of is the Active Directory synchronization tool. Using this tool, you can synchronize all of your users in your on-premises Active Directory domain with Office 365.

The Active Directory synchronization tool will crawl your domain(s) and create copies of your users in Office 365. By default, it synchronizes every 3 hours, so if you add new users or update the properties of an existing user, it can take up to 3 hours for those changes to be reflected. You can either register your own domain with Office 365, or your users can use the onmicrosoft.com domain, for example, jdoe@contoso.onmicrosoft.com.

Passwords Are Not Synchronized

Active Directory synchronization simply replicates users; it does not accommodate single sign-on. This means that your users will effectively have two accounts and need to manage two passwords. The next section shows you how to enable your users to log on with their corporate credentials and take advantage of single sign-on if they're already logged on to your on-premises domain.

To learn more about how to setup Active Directory synchronization, see Chapter 5, "Identity Management and Authentication."

On-Premises Identity and Single Sign-On

If you have an on-premises Active Directory domain already in place that is not being disabled and move exclusively to the cloud, you might want to consider a single sign-on approach to identity management. The obvious reason is that it's easier for users to be able to log on to SharePoint Online resources with a single set of credentials, namely their corporate domain credentials that they use on a daily basis. Also, if their personal computer is on the domain, the users will not get a second logon prompt when they connect to SharePoint Online because they already logged on to the domain when they signed in to their computer.

This is all made possible through an Active Directory federation trust via Active Directory Federation Services 2.0 (ADFS 2.0). If you configure an ADFS 2.0 server in your domain, you can ask Microsoft's ADFS 2.0 server to trust the credentials received from your server.

Active Directory synchronization is also necessary to enable single sign-on. After the ADFS 2.0 trust is configured, the federated identities are mapped to accounts in the directory services domain of Microsoft Online Service. Those accounts can be created via synchronization from your on-premises domain, but because of the federation, your end users won't even know there are actually two accounts behind the scenes.

To see more details on how to set up single sign-on with ADFS 2.0, *see Chapter 5.*

Partner Users and External Access

It's not always reasonable to manage all of the users that access your SharePoint Online sites yourself. You might want to invite your customers or partners to have access to some of your sites so that your employees can more effectively collaborate with them. A new feature in SharePoint Online called Partner Access makes this external access easy. Using Partner Access, your site collection administrators can invite external users into their sites by simply typing the external user's email address and sending an invitation, as shown in Figure 1-15.

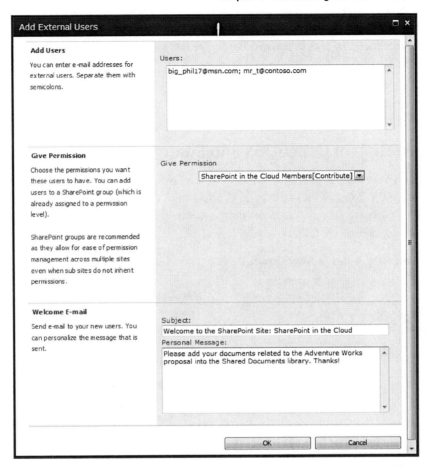

FIGURE 1-15 You can send invitations to external users to log on and collaborate with you in SharePoint Online. All they need is a Hotmail account (hotmail.com, live.com, or msn.com), and they don't need to be a user in Office 365 to obtain access.

The recipient of the email receives an invitation that links her back to the SharePoint Online site. At this point, she is prompted to log on—currently only live.com, hotmail.com, and msn.com accounts work. However, if the recipient does not have a Hotmail account, she can create one, and thereafter her new account will be mapped to the original email address, even if it was not a Hotmail address. This way, the user can have immediate access after she creates her new Hotmail account, and the individual who issued the invitation won't need to send a new one.

Note External users are free in SharePoint Online L plans. For K and E plans, external users will be licensed below the K cost, sold in packs of 50. See Chapter 2 for more information about plans and licensing.

To learn more about how to set up single sign-on with ADFS 2.0, *see Chapter 5.*

Authorization in Office 365 and SharePoint Online

Once a user authenticates to SharePoint Online, the next step is authorization. Authorization specifies what the user can and cannot do in SharePoint Online. Typically, permissions in SharePoint Online are very similar to on-premises SharePoint. Table 1-7 shows the different out-of-the-box roles in SharePoint Online.

TABLE 1-7 Security Roles in SharePoint Online

Role	On-premises equivalent	Permissions
Office 365 global administrator		Has full control across all Office 365 services and features
		Create users and assign licenses
		Reset passwords
		Create global security groups
		Create support tickets
		And more
SharePoint Online service administrator	Farm administrator	Create new site collections
		Manage quotas
		Assign site collection administrators
		Enable/disable partner access
		And more
Site collection administrator	Site collection administrator	Full control to all sites in the site collection, plus manage site collection–scoped settings, such as:
		Features and Solutions
		Search settings
		Master pages and layouts
		Recycle bin
		SharePoint Designer settings
		And more

Role	On-premises equivalent	Permissions
Site owner	Site owner	Create subsites
		Manage lists and libraries
		Manage permissions and security
		Change themes and branding
		And more
Contributor	Contributor	Author pages
		Add items and documents
		And more
Visitor	Visitor	View content

These roles can be modified or you can create your own roles to meet unique requirements. The only exception is the SharePoint Online service administrator or the Office 365 global administrator, because those roles are not configurable.

In addition to roles, there are several ways to accommodate security groups to assign permissions to more than one user at a time. Table 1-8 outlines the various group methods that are available.

TABLE 1-8 Security Group Options in SharePoint Online

Method	Description	When to use...
Office 365 global security groups	These groups are created by the Office 365 global administrator and can be used across all of your SharePoint Online site collections.	If you have many users (more than 50) and/or those users need to have permissions across more than one SharePoint Online site collection.
	Additionally, if Active Directory synchronization is configured, those synchronized groups are mapped as Office 365 global groups. Group memberships for synchronized groups are updated every three hours, or on demand.	
SharePoint groups	Whenever you create a new site collection, you'll get a few of these groups automatically. By default, they map to the common roles, such as site owners, site contributors, and site visitors. However, you can create your own custom groups.	If you have many users (more than 10) and those users need to be uniquely permissioned across many lists or subsites within a given site collection.

Migrating from On-Premises to SharePoint Online

Migrating an on-premises SharePoint deployment into the cloud entails two main stages:

1. Migration planning

2. Actual migration of the content

The planning seems trivial, but it shouldn't be overlooked or underestimated. Customizations provide a great example that demonstrates the importance of migration planning. If you don't survey your customizations up front, you might go through all the migration effort only to realize that your users are unable to perform the actions that they could on-premises, and you need to roll back the migration as a result.

The actual migration of the content is a bit easier to grasp, but is no less complicated. There are many approaches to migration. Some are out-of-the-box mechanisms such as taking a SQL backup. Other popular approaches involve third-party migration tools that move documents from on-premises to the cloud, one document at a time. Most of those third-party tools use the SharePoint web services to accomplish this.

Getting Ready for Migration

There is a lot that needs to occur before you move to SharePoint Online. It is important to perform a full analysis of your on-premises SharePoint deployment and formulate a strategy that will successfully get you into the cloud. You need to consider authentication and authorization, versions of your databases, how large your content is, and determine what customizations won't work in the cloud. If you don't go through this rigorous analysis, you're likely to hit a lot of bumps along the road and possibly incur unforeseen downtime. Chapter 6, "Migrating to SharePoint Online," lays out this strategy in more detail, but the following sections present some of the key points for which you'll need to plan.

Planning for Authentication and Authorization

As described in the previous section, it's important to think through how your users will log on to SharePoint Online, and what mechanisms you'll use to grant them permissions once they're logged on. The following are some questions to consider:

- Where will your user accounts be stored?

- How many accounts do you have? Are they manually or automatically provisioned?

- Do you need single sign-on with on-premises directory services?

- What security groups do you need?

- Where will your security groups be scoped?

The answers to these questions have considerable infrastructure implications, so sorting them out well ahead of time is crucial.

Version Compatibility

Depending on what mechanism you use to migrate your content, you'll need to check if that mechanism has dependencies on the current SharePoint version, Service Pack, and cumulative update. For example, SharePoint Online Dedicated often utilizes a SQL content database backup/restore to migrate SharePoint content. When attaching a SharePoint content database, the source's SharePoint version must be identical to the destination's version number. With respect to the Dedicated edition, you'll want to confirm with Microsoft what version number you'll need to update SharePoint and SQL to before you migrate.

Capacity Compatibility

It is important to survey the capacities of your databases and site collections as you prepare to migrate. The reason for this is that Microsoft has clear supported guidelines around capacities that must be resolved before it will allow you to migrate. For example, a site collection cannot exceed 100 GB. Before you're able to migrate, you'll need to move content around in your on-premises deployment to manage to these capacities.

Planning for Downtime

Downtime is a significant factor that you need to consider when planning a migration. There are ways to minimize downtime, and it's even possible to experience none at all. One common approach is to make the on-premises farm be read-only during migration, and disabling the farm completely after the migration is complete (perhaps even change the Domain Name System [DNS] to point to SharePoint Online, thus automatically redirecting users to the new site).

Customization Compatibility

Customizations made on-premises will not necessarily work when they arrive in the cloud. This is especially true for customizations developed in Visual Studio, but there are instances with SharePoint Designer, such as BCS, in which no-code customizations will no longer function either. The basic idea is to survey all the customizations in all of your sites and determine what will and will not work in the cloud. A common strategy is for all Visual Studio customizations to be repackaged as sandboxed solutions before migration commences. However, this may or may not be possible, depending on the customization.

Chapter 7 includes details on which customizations are and are not permissible in Standard and Dedicated editions of SharePoint Online.

Content Migration Options

The first question to ask yourself when considering a migration technique is whether you're migrating to SharePoint Online Standard or Dedicated edition. The two models entail very different approaches to migration. For example, since Standard is shared hardware in a multi-tenant configuration, you cannot restore a SQL backup of a SharePoint content database. One database in Standard likely contains the data for hundreds of customers. For that reason alone, SQL backups are only applicable to the Dedicated edition, where your databases will retain their individuality. Table 1-9 shows a few of the migration options with their pros and cons. See Chapter 6 for more details on these options as well as other common approaches.

TABLE 1-9 Migration Paths from On-Premises to SharePoint Online

Option	Description	Standard vs. Dedicated	Pros/Cons
Manual via browser	Manual migration using the browser by re-creating sites, pages, libraries, and so on, and then uploading the content.	Both	Pros: free, easy if only a small amount of content needs to be migrated Cons: slow, costly in person hours
SQL backup	Straight SQL backup/restore. The backup is placed on an external hard drive and typically mailed to Microsoft Online's data center where it's taken off the drive and restored.	Dedicated	Pros: fastest approach, bulk migrate hundreds of sites in one restore Cons: only works for SharePoint Online Dedicated
Farm backup	Backup using the Central Administration user interface.	Neither	Not supported because of source farm-specific references in backup
PowerShell backup	Uses the *Backup-SPSite* PowerShell command to migrate a single site collection.	Dedicated	Pros: easy to migrate single site collection Cons: limited to 15 GB
PowerShell export	Uses the *Export-SPWeb* PowerShell command to migrate a single site, list, or library.	Neither	Not supported
Third-party migration tool	Uses SharePoint Online web services to send data from the source to the destination site.	Both	Pros: Easy to use, and significantly faster than manual move via browser Cons: cost. **Note:** Ensure that the third-party supplier is on Microsoft's supported vendor list before purchase.

Getting Around in SharePoint Online

For the most part, end users will work in their SharePoint Online sites exactly the same way they would as if SharePoint were deployed on-premises. This includes performing actions such as creating subsites, document libraries, lists, views, working with Web Parts, and managing security. The goal of this section is not to delve into the out-of-the-box user interface administration of SharePoint in general, but rather to discuss how SharePoint Online is different, and specifically how to administer your SharePoint Online deployment. This is represented in Figure 1-16, where the circle labeled *SPO-S Admin Center* represents the SharePoint Online Administration Center, and the other circles represent your SharePoint sites.

The *SPO-S Admin Center* circle is essentially the equivalent of the on-premises SharePoint Central Administration user interface. The primary and most obvious difference is that in the SharePoint Online Administration Center, you have significantly fewer administrative actions that you can perform. The reason is that all the core SharePoint administration is done on your behalf by Microsoft; the SharePoint Online Administration Center is the remainder of the actions that you can tailor to the specific needs of your business, such as creating site collections and managing your user profiles.

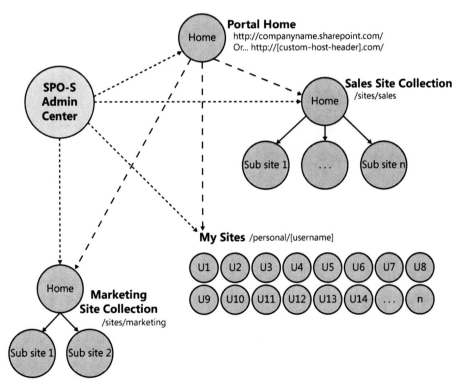

FIGURE 1-16 The Administration Center is the hub of all administrative actions and is similar to the on-premises Central Administration site.

From the SharePoint Online Administration Center, you can create one or more site collections—up to 300 total (not including My Sites). Information architecture is different from one business to another, but in general, most organizations create site collections that more or less map to their business units, departments, teams, projects, and groups. In addition to these sites, most businesses incorporate a portal whereby users can navigate to the respective department sites as well as view cross-department information such as news and events.

Note You can only have one site collection at the root; for example, http://litwareinc.sharepoint.com/. All additional site collections need to be deployed under the "sites" managed path, with My Sites being the exception.

As far as URLs are concerned, you have two options: either you can use the sharepoint.com domain, such as litwareinc.sharepoint.com, or if you own your own domain, you can use that, instead. Standard and Dedicated editions allow for the use of host header site collections, which means that you could use a URL such as http://portal.litwareinc.com/sites/sales even though it is deployed into SharePoint Online. This latter approach is very popular because it offers seamless continuity between your on-premises domains as well as anything you have in the cloud.

Note Custom managed paths are not allowed in SharePoint Online. All of your sites must either be deployed in the root (only one) or in the "sites" managed path.

The SharePoint Online Administrative Center is actually nested within the Office 365 user interface, as shown in Figure 1-17. All users of Office 365 have access to the Office 365 Home page. From this page, you can go to the browser-based email, install and use Lync and navigate to the home SharePoint portal, as well as browse resources to help ramp up the various products within Office 365.

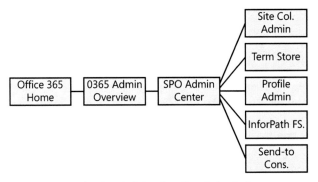

FIGURE 1-17 To begin administering SharePoint Online, you must go to the Administration Center, which is on the Admin Overview page.

If you have the proper administrative privileges, on the Office 365 Home page, you can click the Admin link to open the Office 365 Administrator Overview page, as illustrated in Figure 1-18.

FIGURE 1-18 If you have administrative privileges, you'll see the Admin link at the top of the Office 365 Home page. Click the link to go to the Admin Overview page.

From the Office 365 Admin Overview page, you can configure settings across all four of the Office 365 products, including SharePoint Online, Lync Online, Outlook Online, and Office Professional Plus. You can also create new users and groups, buy more user licenses, and access more administrator-specific Help information.

The Services section contains each of the four Office 365 products, each of which has a Manage link (see Figure 1-19). When you click the Manage link, you're taken to the SharePoint Online Administration Center (see Figure 1-20). The Administration Center is where you can manage your SharePoint Online site collections, such as creating new site collections as well as managing site collection administrators and quotas. Other things you can do in the Administration Center are configure send-to connections, InfoPath settings, user profiles, and the term store. Each of these configuration topics is discussed in detail in Chapter 4.

FIGURE 1-19 Click the Manage link in the Services section of the Admin Overview page to go to the SharePoint Online Administration Center.

FIGURE 1-20 From within the SharePoint Online Administration Center, you can create, edit, and delete site collections. You can also view the term store and manage profiles, among other tasks.

Chapter 2
Office 365 Feature Overview

In this chapter, you will learn about:

- Exchange Online
- Lync Online
- Office Professional Plus (Office Web Apps)
- Licensing and Purchasing Office 365
- Administering Office 365

If you are like most people working in practically any type of business these days, you use a computer to create and collaborate on documents, as well as software to create and edit those documents. You probably use an email program to send those documents to your customers and partners. And like many workers today, you are tied to your mobile phone, bouncing from one meeting to the next in a never-ending quest to get caught up on a never-ending list of tasks. If there were a tool to help make those days more organized and efficient, you probably wouldn't hesitate to use it.

Microsoft Office 365 is that tool.

Office 365 is a new way for users to consume the familiar Microsoft Office applications while moving the framework and infrastructure to the cloud where you can access it from just about anywhere. Office 365 provides a scalable, elastic solution that can grow as demand grows, but it can do so on a much smaller cost scale than when you need to support hardware and an IT team to manage it.

Office 365 for professionals and small businesses is a subscription service that combines the familiar Microsoft Office Web Apps with a set of web-enabled tools that are easy to learn and use. These tools work with your existing hardware and come backed by the robust security, reliability, and control that you need to run your business without the huge infrastructure. To put it another way, Office 365 gives you and your partners—no matter where they're located—access to feature-rich productivity tools while helping to relieve the burden of managing and maintaining business systems. This frees up IT departments and businesses to focus on initiatives that can deliver true competitive advantage.

But not everyone needs everything that Office 365 has to offer. There are those who need some capabilities now, but other capabilities later. Office 365 has different licensing plans that can be tailored to meet vastly different needs and let you add the features that you need when you need them. With some Office 365 plans, you have access to familiar Office applications such as Microsoft Word and Microsoft Excel. These applications are installed locally on a user's computer but are downloaded and licensed from the cloud. Office 365 service plans expand this Office experience by combining those applications with the latest versions of Microsoft's cloud productivity services: Exchange Online, SharePoint Online, and Lync Online.

Office 365 includes the most compelling elements of Microsoft Office Live Small Business (the Internet-based service designed to assist non-technical users with the creation of professional-looking websites), such as email, public websites, and much more. These users will benefit from better functionality and integration with Microsoft Outlook and other Office products, better collaboration with documents, and an improved mobile experience.

In this chapter, you will learn about the different ways that Office 365 can be licensed as well as the differences between the Enterprise, Small business, and Education versions. You will also learn about the four products that make up the Office 365 suite, and how to administer and support the different features and functions.

Office 365 Overview

Before you go too deep exploring the four products that make up Office 365, it's helpful to first consider it from a high level. This section provides a brief overview of Office 365, such as how the four products—Exchange Online, Lync Online, SharePoint Online, and Office Professional Plus—can help you do your work better. You'll also be introduced to fundamentals, such as system requirements, availability service level agreements (SLA), single sign-on, desktop configuration, and much more.

Introducing the Four Key Products of Office 365

Office 365 offers many of the same important features with which you're already familiar and use every day with Microsoft SharePoint 2010, Office Professional Plus 2010, Microsoft Exchange 2010, and Microsoft Lync 2010. Office 365 offers users nearly unlimited access to these tools, which you need to get through your busy workday. These are the tools that will help you:

- Master your inbox and calendar with the latest advanced management tools in the latest version of Outlook.

- Collaborate simultaneously with coworkers on documents in real time with the new coauthoring functionality.

- Take advantage of the power of instantly sharing slideshows with just about anyone, anywhere, with the new Broadcast Slide Show feature available in Microsoft PowerPoint.

- Use the latest video and photo editing tools in PowerPoint to easily create brilliant, professional-looking presentations that will help you stand out above the rest.

- Transform enormous amounts of data into meaningful information and compelling dashboards by using the latest features of Excel and Excel Services with SharePoint Online.

- Access your documents from just about any place and from any device with Office Web Apps, and be able to perform lightweight editing on those documents from any device with a browser.

- Virtually meet with your coworkers online via voice and video anywhere in the world and share your desktop with them.

These are just some of the ways that Office 365 is designed to make your office experience more flexible and much more efficient. The section "Four Products in One," later in this chapter, covers each of the four products in greater detail.

Office 365 System Requirements

Office 365 is built on the latest server software and on a rearchitected identity infrastructure. To ensure a great user experience, you will need to ensure that you meet the minimum requirements on your clients, as listed in Table 2-1:

TABLE 2-1 Office 365 System Requirements

Operating system requirements

Windows 7 (Windows 7 Professional or Enterprise recommended)

Windows Vista SP2 (Windows Vista Business or Enterprise recommended)

Windows XP Pro SP3 (Windows XP Home and
Media Center edition only for managed identity deployment)

Mac OS X, 10.5 (Leopard), 10.6 (Snow Leopard)

Windows Server 2003 and Windows Server 2008

System software

Microsoft .NET Framework 3.0 (for Windows XP)

Java client 1.4.2 (for Macintosh OS X)

Browser software—Microsoft Online Portal

Internet Explorer 7 or above

Mozilla Firefox 3.x or higher

Apple Safari 4 or higher

Goggle Chrome 3 or higher

Downloads

A service connector application that will replace the Sign in application.

Office client requirements*

Office 2010 (Professional Plus recommended)

Office 2007 SP2 (reduced functionality)

Office 2008 for Mac and Entourage 2008 Web Services Edition

Office 2011 for Mac and Outlook 2011 for Mac

.NET 2.0 or later

Lync 2010

Browser software—Outlook Web Apps

Internet Explorer 7 or later

Mozilla Firefox 3.x

Apple Safari 3.x

Google Chrome 3 and later versions

Outlook Web App also has a lite version, which supports a reduced set of features across almost any browser.

* Not required for browser-only users.

99.9 Percent Availability

Availability and reliability are crucial when it comes to accessing your most important documents. Office 365 services boast a 99.9 percent scheduled uptime by using redundant network architecture that is hosted at geographically-dispersed Microsoft data centers. Data centers act as backups for each other: If one fails, the affected customers are transferred to another data center with limited interruption of service.

Recovery Time Objective/Recovery Point Objective

Two measurements commonly used in service uptime management are recovery time objective (RTO) and recovery point objective (RPO). RTO is the measurement of the time between a service failure and when the service is available again. RPO is the measurement of the time between the latest backup and the point at which the service failed. This instant in time represents the nearest historical point from which the service can be recovered. Office 365 has a set RPO and RTO in the event of service failure:

- **12-hour RPO**   Microsoft protects an organization's data and has a copy of that data that is equal to or less than 12 hours old.
- **24-hour RTO**   Service resumes within 24 hours after service disruption.

The Microsoft System Center Operations Manager (SCOM) is the backbone of the Office 365 services environment. It is designed to maximize the reporting of security events from the operating system and applications. The Office 365 services operations team uses the latest technology and optimized processes to harvest, correlate, and analyze information as it is received.

Proactive monitoring continuously measures the performance of key subsystems of the Office 365 services platform against the established boundaries for acceptable service performance and availability. When a threshold is reached or an irregular event occurs, the monitoring system generates warnings so that operations staff can address the threshold or event.

International Availability

Office 365 is currently available in the following countries/regions: Australia, Austria, Belgium, Canada, Colombia, Costa Rica, Cyprus, Czech Republic, Denmark, Finland, France, Germany, Greece, Hong Kong, Hungary, India, Ireland, Israel, Italy, Japan, Luxembourg, Malaysia, Mexico, Netherlands, New Zealand, Norway, Peru, Poland, Portugal, Puerto Rico, Romania, Singapore, Spain, Sweden, Switzerland, Trinidad and Tobago, the United Kingdom, and the United States.

Provided that licenses are purchased in approved countries/regions, users can still use their licenses in most countries. However, be aware that exceptions to this can occur and availability of some features can vary in different countries.

Service Administration

Even though you are relying on Microsoft's data center to handle all the back-end infrastructure components, you still have access to some administrative functionality that you need to configure to use Office 365. The administration page of Office 365 gives the administrator access to all of the online control panels that are needed to manage the Microsoft Online Services to which your company has subscribed.

The Admin page (see Figure 2-1) can be accessed by clicking the Admin tab of the main Office 365 Home page. In addition to accessing the various individual control panels, this is where Administrators manage Users, Licenses, and handle support issues.

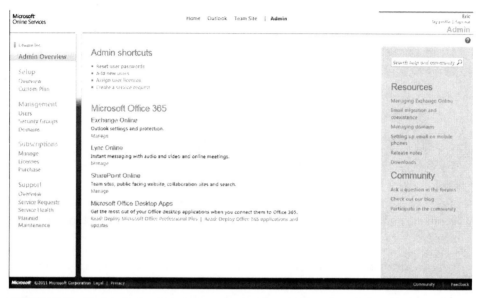

FIGURE 2-1 Use the Admin page to manage users, security groups, and the four products that make up Office 365.

Federated Identity and Single Sign-On

As an administrator, you can use a single sign-on approach to authenticate your users to Office 365. To achieve this, you can configure an on-premises Active Directory Federated Services server and proxy (a Microsoft Windows Server 2008 service) to federate identities with the Office 365 Federation gateway. After Active Directory Federated Services is configured, all Office 365 users whose identities are based on the federated domain can use their existing corporate logon to automatically authenticate to Office 365. Chapter 5, "Identity Management and Authentication," covers federated identity in detail. Among the key benefits to using this service are the following:

- Users don't need to log on to Office 365 if they've already authenticated to your domain.

- Users don't need to remember two sets of credentials and passwords.

- More Active Directory (AD) infrastructure is required to support single sign-on, but much less administration overhead is needed for creating and managing user accounts.

Identity federation is dependent upon Active Directory synchronization (DirSync) being configured properly. DirSync provisions copies of on-premises identities in Microsoft Online's user store. Exchange Online and Lync Online require a local identity to which to attach mailboxes, which is why DirSync is required. However, the federated identity is simply mapped to this credential and is not actually used for authentication. Authentication takes place on the trusted on-premises identity provider. For more information on how to configure DirSync, see Chapter 5.

> **Note** DirSync can only synchronize a single forest. If you have more than one forest in your Active Directory, you'll want to pick the forest with your user accounts or plan on a forest consolidation.

Microsoft Office 365 Desktop Setup

Office 365 Desktop Setup is an installer service that checks for and provides important software updates to keep you synchronized with Office 365. These updates are required for successful client connection to, and operation with Office 365. Office 365 Desktop Setup uses Windows Server Update Services (WSUS) and Windows Update to identify, download, and install required software updates.

Office 365 Desktop Setup checks for the following Office 365 requirements:

- **Windows**   Windows XP SP3 with Internet Explorer 7; Windows Vista with SP2; Windows Server 2008 R2; or Windows 7
- **Office versions**   2007 Office system SP2; Office 2010 RTM

Office 365 Desktop Setup also installs software updates that are required by Office Professional Plus clients for connecting to Office 365 services. After you've signed in to the Office 365 portal for the first time, you should run the Desktop Setup on your computer. To set up your desktop for Office 365, perform the following steps:

1. Sign in to the Office 365 portal. In the right pane, under Resources, click Downloads.

2. Under Set Up And Configure Your Office Desktop Apps, click Set Up.

   The Microsoft Office 365 Desktop Setup tool starts.

3. Sign in using your Microsoft Online Services ID.

   Office 365 Desktop Setup will check your system configuration.

4. After you have selected the applications that you want to configure, click Continue, review the service agreements, and then click I Accept to begin installing updates and configuring desktop applications.

After you run the Office 365 Desktop Setup, a shortcut to the Office 365 portal is added to the Start menu on your desktop.

Anywhere Access

Office 365 makes it easy to access and interact with your email, documents, and data from just about anywhere and from most Internet-connected devices that support the Internet Explorer, Firefox, or Safari browsers, including your phone, computer, or tablet. Not all functionality (such as creating new documents or editing existing ones) is available via the browser, because some features require that you install Microsoft Office Mobile 2010. You use Office Mobile 2010 to share, edit, and comment on documents with the same familiar Office experience to which you're accustomed, but via a mobile device.

 Note The Office Mobile 2010 application is not included in Office Professional Plus 2010 or as part of Office Web Apps.

More and more business people are working from their mobile devices. No matter where you work from today, you can use Office 365 to keep you connected. Whether in the office, down the street, or across the country, you can stay connected with people, collaborate on your documents, participate in meetings, and have access to your data. Office 365 delivers a consistent Office experience from just about any device and any location.

Users who are remote and using their laptops can take advantage of SharePoint Workspace 2010, which they can use to work with important SharePoint documents offline.

You may not always have access to your computer that has Office Professional installed, but you still need to work with your documents. For those times, you can use Office Web Apps to view your documents and perform light editing from within a web browser.

Document Coauthoring

Being able to easily communicate and share ideas is important to all of your collaborative projects. Whether it is writing a proposal, creating a presentation, or analyzing data, Office Professional Plus helps you to work better with customers and partners by providing new and enhanced features such as coauthoring and presence information.

Coauthoring allows you to collaborate with multiple users on an Excel spreadsheet, Word documents, or a Microsoft OneNote notebook at the same time by using web-based collaboration. You can now work simultaneously with your customers and partners no matter where they are located.

 Note Coauthoring capabilities are also possible in the on-premises version of SharePoint.

When collaborating via email, you either need to wait for each member of the team to make changes, or you must work in parallel and merge the changes by hand. With a SharePoint Team Site, everyone can access the latest version of the document in a central location so that they're always viewing and responding to the exact same document. You can also send a link to someone outside your company, such as an editor, consultant, or customer so that they can edit the document, too.

You now know what you can do with Office Web Apps working through most web browsers or in tandem with the locally installed Office client on your computer. You can see your documents in full fidelity and make edits with the confidence that the original formatting and structure of the document will be preserved.

But what if you know that you are not going to have Internet access, and you need to work on your documents offline? Using SharePoint Workspace client, you can synchronize a SharePoint document library with your computer. Changes you make offline are synchronized to the original the next time you connect to your libraries and SharePoint Team Sites.

Mobile Access

With Office Web Apps, you can view Word, Excel, and PowerPoint files on most mobile devices. For Office Web Apps on SharePoint, the following mobile browsers are supported:

- **Internet Explorer**   Windows Mobile 6 through 6.5 and Windows Phone
- **Safari 4**   iPhone 3G, 3GS, or 4
- **BlackBerry**   5.x and later
- **Nokia**   S60, S60 5.0, 3.x, or later
- **Android**   1.6, 2.1, and 2.2

The Apple iPad is not officially supported for viewing Word and PowerPoint files, but you can achieve a pretty high level of fidelity by using it nonetheless.

Note   To access pages by using mobile devices, you enter the same URL that is used by browsers running on computers. However, this is a little clunky and hard to manage in many cases; therefore, it is recommended you click E-Mail A Link on the Share And Track tab of the ribbon in SharePoint Online to receive the address in an email message. After you have the site open on your mobile device, you can save it as a browser favorite for easier access later.

Real-time mobile device access to your email, calendar, contacts, and tasks is provided via Exchange ActiveSync to a wide range of mobile devices, including Windows Phone, Nokia E and N series devices, Palm devices, Apple iPhone and iPad, and certain Android phones. Blackberry devices are also supported on certain plans.

Online Meetings

No matter what you do or what business you are in, you have most certainly attended online meetings and conference calls. With Office 365, you can easily schedule and host meetings online without the need for a large IT staff or sophisticated support hardware and software. Office 365 takes the complication out of the software and focuses on keeping it information worker–friendly. You can still take advantage of all of the power of an expensive online meeting service, but with Office 365, it is much easier and cheaper.

Office 365 puts all of your critical applications in one place for easy access and an immersive Office experience no matter where you are. Office 365 reduces the number of clicks it takes to access your email, contacts, calendar, and online meetings. You can schedule meetings without the need to leave the email thread. When you don't have to bounce around several applications trying to set up a meeting or checking if someone is available, it saves you time and helps to keep you focused on the task at hand.

When you use Lync Online, your concept of what a meeting is will change. When you collaborate, share information, and communicate in real time from your computer, whether it is a scheduled meeting or an ad-hoc meeting, you will start to see meetings in a whole new way. You no longer need to be at your desk and use your phone to connect to your meetings. Lync Online supports an integrated conferencing experience, enabling users to join the same conference from the computer (via the Lync 2010 client) or from a phone (this requires a separate public switched telephone network audio conferencing service).

Lync Online provides Lync-based, multiparty audio conferencing capabilities. Using Lync Online, you can experience high-quality audio, visual call and roster controls, network quality indicator, and other powerful user management features.

In addition to audio, you can use Lync Online to connect via high-quality video sessions. With Lync Online, you can easily schedule an online meeting with video or seamlessly escalate a chat to a video call.

> **Note** Lync Online does not support interoperability with third-party, room-based conferencing systems.

Like many popular online meeting applications that you're already used to, not only can you connect by using video and audio with Lync Online, you can also share content, your desktop, applications, presentations, and virtual whiteboard. Lync Online meetings even support standard online meeting functionalities, such as annotations and polling.

Four Products in One

Office 365 is Exchange Online, Lync Online, SharePoint Online, and Office Professional in a cloud-based solution. This means that with Office 365, you can access your favorite features of Exchange, Lync, SharePoint, and Office Professional in a solution that can be accessed from just about anywhere and from most mobile devices.

As discussed earlier, not all features of these products are available via the browser, but most features you count on day-to-day are present and look almost exactly the same as their on-premises versions. This section takes a closer look at these four products individually. Since most features are the same as those of their on-premises equivalent, the focus will be mostly on what is different or new with the cloud offering.

Exchange Online

Exchange Online gives you the functionality and reliability with which you're already familiar in on-premises Exchange, delivering email, calendar, and contacts while protecting users against viruses and spam. Exchange Online provides the core features of Exchange Server, so your users get the same robust and reliable capabilities they are used to from on-premises Exchange, including:

- **Large mailboxes**   Each user has a standard mailbox storage of 25 GB (except for kiosk workers, who get only 500 MB) and the ability to send attachments up to 25 MB.

- **Antivirus/anti-spam**   Forefront Online Protection for Exchange is included, providing multiple filters and virus-scanning engines to help protect your organization from spam, viruses, and phishing scams.

- **Web-based access**   For web-client access, Outlook Web App provides a premium browser-based experience that matches the look and feel of the full Outlook client.

- **Mobility**   Mobile access is available from all phones that are capable of receiving email, including Windows Phone, iPhone, Android, Palm, Nokia, and Blackberry devices.

- **Shared calendar and contacts**   Users can compare calendars to schedule meetings with Exchange Online and have access to collaboration features, such as shared calendars, groups, global address list, external contacts, tasks, conference rooms, and delegation.

It can be too time consuming and complex for most organizations to deploy, manage, and maintain an on-premises Exchange infrastructure. With Exchange Online, there is often little or nothing to deploy—you simply "turn it on." You do not need to pay an IT team for maintenance, security, and endless upgrades, because they are all included with the online service. You won't lose control over the most important aspects, including policies, services, and features that can impact your business. The service handles the back-end infrastructure. You still get the control you need.

Exchange Online User Subscriptions

Each user who accesses the Exchange Online service requires a User Subscription License (USL), which can be purchased separately as an individual component. This section focuses on the plans that apply to Office 365. Exchange Online Kiosk aligns with the Kiosk Worker licensing plans (K1, K2), and Exchange Online matches up with what is offered by default with the other Office 365 plans.

Table 2-2 provides a detailed comparison of the features and their limitations.

TABLE 2-2 Feature Comparison Between Kiosk and Standard Editions of Exchange Online

Feature	Exchange Online Kiosk	Exchange Online
Mailbox size	500 MB	25 GB
Outlook Web App (regular and lite versions)	Yes	Yes
POP	Yes	Yes
IMAP	No	Yes
Outlook Anywhere (MAPI)	No	Yes
Microsoft Exchange ActiveSync	No	Yes
Exchange Web Services	No	Yes
Inbox rules	No	Yes
Delegate access	No (cannot access other users' mailboxes, shared mailboxes, or resource mailboxes)	Yes
Instant messaging interoperability in OWA	No	Yes (requires Lync Online or Microsoft Lync Server 2010)
SMS notifications	No	Yes
Personal archive	No	Yes
Voice mail	No	E4 Plan
Legal hold	No	E4 Plan

Message Size Limits

Large messages can negatively impact system performance and can slow down delivery for all users; thus, message limits are imposed to prevent this from happening. The basic message size limit for Exchange Online is 25 MB. This value cannot be adjusted up or down, but an administrator can create transport rules that limit the maximum size of any individual attachments, which would effectively limit the size of the email, because most of the size is usually the attachment. Messages larger than 25 MB are not delivered; the sender will receive a Non-Delivery Report (NDR).

Recipient Limits

An Exchange Online mailbox can only send messages to a maximum of 500 recipients per day. This is intended to discourage users from sending unsolicited bulk messages on purpose or by accident. Exchange Online has additional restrictions that are designed to prevent users and applications from sending large volumes of email that will slow down the system for everyone. Users can address a maximum of 100 recipients in each email message. These limits apply to both emails sent within an organization as well as to messages delivered to external organizations.

Deleted Item Recovery in Exchange Online

With Exchange Online, users can restore deleted items from their email folders. When an item is deleted, it is kept in a user's Deleted Items folder until it is manually removed by the user or automatically removed by set retention policies.

After a user removes an item from the Deleted Items folder, the item is kept in the Recoverable Items folder for 14 days before being permanently removed. Users can still recover these items without contacting an administrator by using the Recover Deleted Items feature in Outlook Web Access or Outlook.

Microsoft Outlook

Microsoft Outlook is the rich "thick client" email program that includes the same support for calendars, contacts, and tasks as its online version. Exchange Online supports Outlook 2010 and Office Outlook 2007. Key features of Outlook include:

- **Outlook Web Access**   You can use Outlook Web Access (OWA) to connect to Exchange Online over the Internet with no need for a Virtual Private Network (VPN) connection. Communication between Outlook and Exchange Online occurs via a Secure Sockets Layer (SSL) tunnel.

- **Exchange Autodiscover Service**   For users who prefer a locally installed Outlook client, the Exchange Autodiscover service automatically configures your locally installed version of Outlook to work with Exchange Online. With Autodiscover, you can receive your required profile settings directly from Exchange Online the very first time you sign in with your email address and password.

- **Cached Exchange Mode**   Using Cached Exchange Mode, you can access a local copy of your Exchange mailbox when you are not connected to the Internet. Cached Exchange Mode maintains a client-side copy of your Exchange mailbox in Outlook and automatically synchronizes this copy with the appropriate email server. In addition to providing offline access, this also makes for a faster user experience when you do not have a very good Internet connection or resources are limited.

> ## Offline Address Book
>
> When a user is working offline, she can still access her Outlook address book because the Global Address List is cached locally. The offline version of the address book is a snapshot of the AD information available in the Global Address List.

Outlook 2010

Outlook 2010 supports many of the latest Exchange Online features, including:

- Conversation view and conversation actions (for example, Ignore, Always Move)
- MailTips
- Personal archive
- User-assigned retention policies
- Alerts for users on legal hold
- Meeting room finder
- Voice mail preview

> **Note** Outlook 2007 has limited support for use with Exchange Online, and Outlook 2003 is not supported at all.
>
> Exchange Online supports Outlook for Mac 2011.

Instant Messaging and Presence

Outlook Web App can interoperate with Lync Online and on-premises Lync Server 2010 to provide users with instant messaging (IM) and presence within the Outlook Web App interface and SharePoint Online. This capability is available in most plans, but it is not available to users with Kiosk subscriptions, even if they have accounts in Lync Online or Lync Server.

Remote Device Wipe

If you lose your mobile device, you can wipe all data off of the device remotely, preventing it from being accessed the next time the device connects to Exchange Online. You can trigger the remote wipe through the Outlook Web App Options page from any browser, or an administrator can log on to the Outlook Web App Settings page and trigger the device wipe on your behalf. A confirmation message is sent to your Exchange account when the mobile device acknowledges the remote wipe request. Figure 2-2 shows the mobile administration screen, in which you can select a phone and delete all the Exchange content off of that phone.

FIGURE 2-2 If you lose a mobile phone or it is stolen, you can delete all the Exchange content from it remotely through the user's Outlook Web App interface.

Delegate Access (Send on Behalf Permissions)

Many times, a manager needs his assistant to manage his calendar, email, or contacts. For circumstances such as this, Send on Behalf Permissions is a perfect feature. When another user is delegated to send emails on your behalf, he can put your name in the from field so that it looks as if the email came from you, but it will also note that it was sent on behalf of you.

> **Note** The ability to access other mailboxes via delegate access is not available to users with Exchange Online Kiosk subscriptions.

Inbox Rules

Just as with on-premises Exchange, you can create inbox rules that automatically perform specific, criteria-based actions on messages as they arrive. However, this feature is not included in all plans.

> **Note** Inbox rules are not available to users with Exchange Online Kiosk subscriptions.

Information Rights Management

Exchange Online does not provide hosted Information Rights Management (IRM) services, but administrators can use on-premises Active Directory Rights Management Services (AD RMS) in conjunction with Exchange Online. If an AD RMS server is deployed, Outlook can directly communicate with the AD RMS server, enabling you to compose and read messages protected by AD RMS. There is no need for interoperability between the AD RMS server and Exchange Online in order to use the AD RMS features of Outlook.

To enable the advanced AD RMS features introduced in Exchange 2010, administrators can import the Trusted Publishing Domain from their AD RMS server to Exchange Online by using Remote PowerShell. After this one-time import, the following features become available:

- Support for IRM in Outlook Web App
- Support for IRM in Exchange ActiveSync
- IRM search
- Transport protection rules
- Protected voice mail
- Journal report decryption
- Outlook Protection Rules

Size of the Personal Archive

Each user's personal archive can only be used for storage of their messaging data. A user on the any of the E1–E4 and P1 plans receives 25 GB of total storage, which the user can apportion across her primary mailbox and personal archive. This means the total allocation of 25 GB includes the mailbox and the personal archive. Details of what is included with each plan will be detailed later in this chapter in the section "Licensing and Purchasing Office 365."

Directory Synchronization

The Microsoft Online Services Directory Synchronization tool is provided to simplify management of the Microsoft Online Services environment and to help synchronize a company's local AD data with Exchange Online, SharePoint Online, and Lync Online. The tool is available free of charge. This is a rather significant topic and is covered in greater detail in Chapter 5.

Rolling Legal Hold (Single Item Recovery)

Some organizations need to preserve the contents of users' mailboxes for archiving and eDiscovery purposes, but only for a specific amount of time, such as one year. You can use the Single Item Recovery feature in Exchange Online to meet this need by providing rolling legal hold capabilities.

eDiscovery (Electronic Discovery) Defined

eDiscovery is the term used to describe the process of discovering electronic information, such as documents or emails, during a civil litigation. A "legal hold" is when a lawyer identifies an email or document as a piece of evidence for his case/litigation. When placed on legal hold, emails and documents cannot be deleted.

Single Item Recovery is enabled by default on all mailboxes in Exchange Online with a 14-day retention period. This is done to facilitate recovery of deleted items. By extending the Single Item Recovery retention period, organizations can ensure that mailbox items are preserved for a specified amount of time. Single Item Recovery uses the same mechanisms as legal hold to preserve original copies of items that have been modified or deleted.

To change the Single Item Recovery period for a mailbox, an administrator must contact the Office 365 help desk. If the desired Single Item Recovery period is longer than 30 days, the mailbox must have an Exchange Online (Plan 2) subscription.

Migration and Coexistence

Microsoft provides tools to help migrate from an existing email environment to Exchange Online. Using these tools, administrators can migrate to Exchange Online from:

- IMAP-based email systems
- Microsoft Exchange Server 2003
- Microsoft Exchange Server 2007
- Microsoft Exchange Server 2010

At a high level, organizations have the following options:

- **IMAP cutover migration**   Migrate data from IMAP-based email systems to Exchange Online with a single cutover migration.
- **Exchange cutover migration**   Migrate data from Exchange 2003, Exchange 2007, Exchange 2010, and Hosted Exchange systems to Exchange Online in a single cutover migration.

- **Exchange simple coexistence**   Perform a staged migration from Exchange 2003, Exchange 2007, and Exchange 2010 with web-based migration tools and minimal changes to on-premises infrastructure.

- **Exchange rich coexistence**   Add an Exchange 2010 Service Pack 1 server to the on-premises Exchange 2003 or Exchange 2007 environment, and use the Exchange Management Console to move mailboxes to Exchange Online.

Lync Online

Microsoft Lync Online is a next-generation cloud communications service that connects people virtually from just about anywhere. Lync Online provides many intuitive communications capabilities across presence, IM, audio/video calling, and a rich online meeting experience, including PC-audio, video, and web conferencing.

Using Lync Online, you can determine whether your colleagues are available without the need to send an email, walk over to their office, or place a phone call. With Lync Online, it's much easier for you to collaborate on important decisions and documents with your colleagues—whether they are in the same building, across the street, or sitting in a hotel in another country. Lync Online also gives you the ability to make computer-to-computer audio or video calls, not just IM.

Lync Online provides a set of tools with which you are already familiar and most likely already use today. With Lync Online and Office 365, you get integrated presence and real-time collaboration capabilities with the Office Outlook messaging and collaboration clients.

Within SharePoint Online, the Members Web Part takes advantage of integration between Lync Online and SharePoint Online. The Web Part provides the same presence and IM capabilities that you get in the Lync client but from within your Team Sites. You do not need to leave the SharePoint Online site, where you might already be working and collaborating with other colleagues, just to have an ad-hoc meeting.

 Note Using Lync Online, users can connect with Windows Live Messenger contacts via IM, audio, and video calls directly from Lync.

Lync Online Features

Lync online works very much like the Lync Server 2010, so this section will not explore all of Lync's functionality in depth. Rather, this section looks at the features at a very high level and takes a look at some features that are not present in the online version.

> **Note** To access and use the Lync Online service, you must install the Microsoft Lync 2010 client. Currently, there isn't a browser-based version of Lync (except through Outlook web access).

Instant Messaging   IM is the method of communicating between two or more people in real time by using text-based messages over an Internet connection or internal network.

Presence   Presence is the ability to see another user's online status. With Lync Online, you can set your status to indicate whether you are Available, Busy, or Away so that coworkers can quickly determine your status (Figure 2-3).

FIGURE 2-3 Presence gives your coworkers a way to see your status.

With most IM clients, you have to add your contacts one at a time or import them, or you may even have to search the list of another application to create your contacts. Once you have integrated Lync Online with the Global Address List, you do not need to add all of your coworkers to your contacts; you are already connected to them and just have to search for them or type in a name to ascertain presence information.

Office Outlook and SharePoint Online   Integration with Outlook and SharePoint Online is very important for creating a seamless and rich online work experience. When Microsoft Lync Online is properly set up, you can instantly find and communicate with people from within Office Outlook, just as you would with the Lync client, as shown in Figure 2-4.

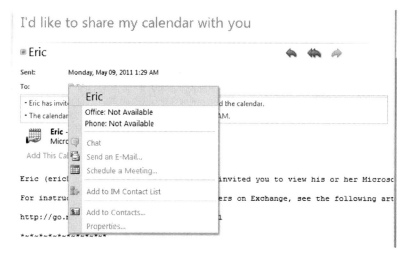

FIGURE 2-4 You can see your coworker's presence information directly from Outlook and Outlook Web Access.

Just as when you're using your locally installed version of Microsoft Outlook, you see a colored presence indicator that represents a person's status. You can then click the presence icon and initiate a chat, email the person, or schedule a meeting by using Lync 2010 and the interactive Office 2010 contact card, all without ever leaving Outlook Online.

Like Outlook Online, Lync Online integrates with SharePoint Online sites by using the same presence indicator that is displayed in Outlook Online and the Lync client. You can initiate a chat, send an email, or schedule a meeting seamlessly from within SharePoint Online.

For presence information to work correctly within Outlook Online and SharePoint Online, the Lync desktop client must be installed. Lync Online works with Exchange Online to retrieve presence status updates, based on existing Exchange calendar information; out-of-office messages in Lync 2010; and presence status from Outlook.

Lync-to-Lync Audio and Video Calls   One of the key features of Lync Online—which is only available to the highest-tier plans—is the ability to use your Lync client to make computer-to-computer audio and video calls via your computer and a web camera. Person-to-person audio and video communication can be routed between your computer and another computer within the same Lync online organization (within or outside the corporate firewall) or between any permitted federated domains.

File Transfer   You can easily transfer files among your colleagues by using Lync Online thanks to the built-in peer-to-peer file transfer capabilities, without the need to leave the Lync client.

Remote Access   Lync Online lets you to use the service directly over the Internet, without requiring you to connect to your corporate network through a remote access service or VPN.

> **Note** File transfer is not available on remote access connections.

Distribution Lists   Easily add email distribution lists to your contact lists by using your Lync client. Lync Online makes it easy for you to send instant messages to individual members of a distribution list or the entire distribution list. Similar to Outlook, you can expand distribution lists to see the individual members within it.

> **Note** For all versions of Lync, the contact list is limited to 250 contacts, and a distribution list counts as one contact against that limit.

Lync External Connectivity   You can use Lync Online to connect with users in other organizations that are also using Lync Online, as long as you are federated with them. Once you are federated with another organization, you can see that organization's contacts and presence information. Lync Online external connectivity requires that you have the consent and coordinate proper configuration of both parties of the federation relationship. Once the federation is set up by the administrators of both sides, users in each organization can see presence, communicate with each other via IM, and make Lync-to-Lync audio and video calls, as if they were working in a single organization.

In addition to Lync-to-Lync federation, Lync Online users can also connect with their contacts from the Windows Live Messenger. All federated communications are encrypted between the IM systems by using access proxy servers. Service administrators can set up certain domains to allow chat only or audio only. Administrators control which domains and services are allowed to communicate with Lync Online users by using *allow lists* and *block lists*.

> **Note** File transfer is not available with federated connections.

Lync Online/Lync Server On-Premises

Lync does not support cloud and server coexistence between Lync Online and Lync Server using a single domain. This means that using a single domain name, it is not possible to deploy a subset of users in Lync Online simultaneously with other users on-premises. Lync federation should be used to enable users to communicate between Lync Online and Lync on-premises deployments by using different domain names, just as you would with two different organizations.

It also is not possible to split different Lync workloads between the cloud and on-premises. It is not possible to deploy IM and meetings in the cloud with voice on-premises for a single user or vice versa.

Lync Online with Exchange and SharePoint On-Premises

Lync Online supports presence with an on-premises deployment of Exchange Server 2007 and Exchange Server 2010. The Lync Online service provides presence updates that are based on calendar information and Out of Office details that appear in Lync 2010.

Lync Online also works seamlessly with on-premises SharePoint Server for presence and click-to-communicate in your local SharePoint sites. As with all features of Lync, this also requires that you install the Lync 2010 client and run it on your desktop.

Administration: Lync Online Control Panel

From the main Admin page, you can access the Lync control panel (see Figure 2-5). In the control panel, you can perform actions related to service administration and Lync Online, which include:

- Enable or disable Lync Online
- Create users and assign licenses that enable use of Lync Online
- File support tickets
- Access online help
- Manage Lync user's settings and policies
- Lync Federation (on/off, open federation/specific domains)
- Audio/video (Lync-to-Lync and multi-party are controlled together)
- File transfer
- Lync with Windows Live

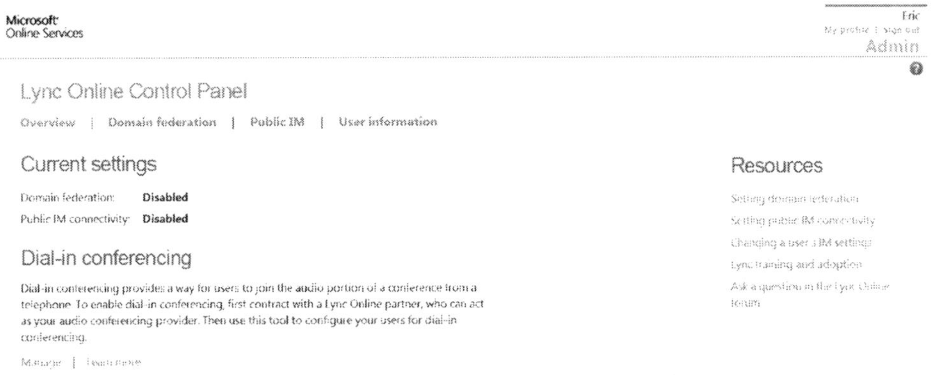

FIGURE 2-5 You can manage Lync Online from the Lync Online Control Panel within the Office 365 administration interface.

SharePoint Online

Using SharePoint Online, a company can easily create and manage custom team-focused and project-focused sites for collaboration. In addition, it is possible to deploy a company-wide intranet portal for use in disseminating information and news across the organization. Chapter 1, "Introducing SharePoint Online," described the main features of SharePoint Online (Sites, Composites, Search, Insights, Communities, and Content), so this section won't rehash all that. The key is to understand all the differences between feature availability with SharePoint Server and SharePoint Online, Standard and Dedicated. To view a detailed table comparing the availability of features between these versions of SharePoint, see the Appendix, "Server, Online SharePoint, and Online Dedicated Compared."

Microsoft Office Professional

Office and SharePoint Online work better together; in fact, better than ever before. In addition to document collaboration and management, features light up when Office is used with SharePoint Online. New coauthoring capabilities are available in which two or more users can simultaneously edit the same document. With the lighter-weight Office Web Apps, you can work with Office documents directly in a browser when you are on the go or at a shared PC. You can now access your documents anywhere you have Internet access—on your mobile device, your browser, and your computer.

Some highlights of the new functionality in Office 2010 that work with SharePoint Online include:

- **The Backstage view**   Introduced in Office 2007, the Backstage view gives you a way to manage your documents and related data—from this view, you can create, save, and send documents; inspect documents for hidden metadata or personal information; set options such as turning on or off AutoComplete suggestions; and more.

- **Outlook alerts**   Stay up to date with changes to documents and list items in your SharePoint Online sites by receiving notifications of changes as alerts and Really Simple Syndication (RSS) feeds.

- **Use SharePoint Workspace to manage documents offline**   Users can synchronize SharePoint Online libraries and lists to their computers with just a few clicks. You can easily update documents and lists offline and be confident that everything will automatically synchronize to the server when you go back online.

- **Document Coauthoring**   Use Office Professional Plus to collaborate on the web with colleagues to edit Excel spreadsheets, build reports or documents in Word, and annotate OneNote notebooks in real time online. With these capabilities, you can effectively conduct brainstorming sessions, update data, and create compelling customer presentations from different locations, simultaneously and on an ad-hoc basis.

- **PowerPoint Broadcast Slide Show**   You can share your PowerPoint 2010 presentations live with anyone who has access to an Internet connection and a web browser. With the Broadcast Slide Show feature, you can broadcast presentations online as you deliver them. Presenters can also create high-quality videos of their presentations with just a few clicks to deliver the information to those who can't attend the event.

- **Outlook Social Connector**   With the Outlook Social Connector, you can expand your social networks, stay up to date, and get additional information about other users without the need to leave Outlook.

SharePoint Online can be used with the following Office desktop programs:

- Access 2010
- Excel 2007 or 2010
- InfoPath 2010
- Outlook 2007 or 2010
- PowerPoint 2007 or 2010
- SharePoint Designer 2010
- SharePoint Workspace 2010
- Microsoft Visio 2010
- Word 2007 or 2010

With Outlook 2010 or 2007, you can view or edit calendars and contact lists that are stored on your SharePoint sites, and create and manage sites for organizing your meetings. Together, Outlook 2010 (or 2007) and SharePoint Online support the following capabilities:

- Read/write access to SharePoint Online items (for example, calendars, tasks, contacts, and discussions)

- Synchronization and offline support for document libraries and lists

- Roll-up views of calendars and tasks across different lists and sites

- Unified view of your personal tasks and your SharePoint tasks

Office Web Apps vs. Office Professional

Office Web Apps provides a lightweight version of the Office product via a browser-based interface. Although you can read and perform some editing with Office Web Apps, many features discussed in this chapter are not available. Table 2-3 provides a high-level overview of the differences between each product.

TABLE 2-3 **A Comparison of Functionality Between Office Web Apps and Office Professional**

Functionality	Client	Web Apps
Coauthoring	Yes	*
Editing	Yes	Limited
Broadcast Slideshow	Yes	No
Outlook Social Connector	Yes	No
Presence Information	Yes	No
Document Templates	Yes	No

* Coauthoring capabilities are also available for use with Office Web Apps provided with Windows Live SkyDrive.

Licensing and Purchasing Office 365

Office 365 is designed to be the most comprehensive productivity solution, while at the same time offering the reliability and security that you are used to from Microsoft. With Office 365, Microsoft also introduces a new subscription-based licensing model that lets you pay for just what you need and easily add services as you require them. Office 365 can be licensed in one of three models: Office 365 for professionals and small businesses, Office 365 for midsized businesses and enterprises, and Office 365 for education.

While Office 365 for small businesses is fairly straightforward, with only one plan (P1) under that model, enterprise and education have several licensing plans that at first glance can appear confusing and overly complicated. Office 365 for small businesses was created to provide an effective model for small organizations and individuals. Office 365 for midsized businesses and enterprises has a number of plans that are designed not for individuals but for large organizations; the plans are equally sophisticated in their offerings. This section will help you to understand the differences between the plans and also eliminate the apparent complexity.

Office 365 Pricing Is Subject to Change

Pricing is typically never set in stone. The subsequent sections detail the licensing plans in Office 365. However, you should be aware that there's an opportunity for this information to fall out of date.

Office 365 for Professionals and Small Businesses (P1)

Microsoft Office 365 for professionals and small businesses, also known as the P1 licensing plan (Figure 2-6), is a pay-as-you-go, easy-to-use set of web-enabled tools with which you can access your email, important documents, contacts, and calendar from just about any-where and from almost any device. It is intended for individuals or organizations with fewer than 25 employees that do not have an IT support staff. It is easy to set up and use and is perfect for consumers who are not technical.

Office 365 is engineered to provide tools for collaboration, messaging, document sharing, and online meetings. This plan works seamlessly with the programs that you might already use, such as Outlook and Office. All Office 365 plans provide powerful security to protect your data.

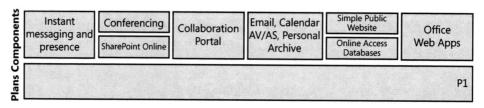

FIGURE 2-6 Small Business Licensing Plan.

Plan P1 includes the following set of features:

- IM and online meetings
- Email and calendar with personal archiving
- Office Web Apps (lite versions of Word, Excel, PowerPoint, and OneNote)

- Collaboration portal via SharePoint Online sites

- Simple public website

- Online Access databases

Office 365 for Midsized Businesses and Enterprises

This version of Microsoft Office 365 is also a pay-as-you-go, easy-to-use set of web-enabled tools with which you can access your email, important documents, contacts, and calendars from just about anywhere and from almost any device. Enterprise has additional features, however, that many larger organizations need, such as Active Directory Synchronization; email archiving for legal holds; Blackberry enterprise server; phone support 24 hours a day, seven days a week; and voice capabilities. Enterprise is also ideal for organizations that need more control over deployments of Office Professional Plus or that want to take advantage of existing on-premises infrastructure.

The enterprise tier also has plans for low-touch users that just need a kiosk interface because they do not use a computer as a major part of their day. Oftentimes, these users share a computer with others. These plans, called Kiosk plans, are designed to give a user the ability to access email and a company portal as well as the ability to read documents. Before we get too far into the different enterprise plans, let's look at the fundamental differences between the kiosk worker plans (K1, K2) and the other enterprise plans (E1–E4), also known as information worker plans.

Kiosk Plans (K1 and K2)

Figure 2-7 illustrates that the Kiosk plans offer a much lighter version of Office 365, as evidenced by the smaller mailboxes, no SharePoint storage capabilities, a web-only version of Outlook, and web-only versions of Office.

Information Worker vs. Kiosk Worker

	E1-E4 Plans	K1-K2 Plans
Mailbox Size	25GB	500MB
SharePoint Storage	500MB	None
Outlook	Full Client (MAPI/MAPI)	Web Access Only
Office	Office Professional Plus	Office Web Apps
Lync	Full Client	None

FIGURE 2-7 An overview of the differences between kiosk and information worker enterprise plans.

In addition, the Kiosk plans are grouped into three tiers: Hosted Exchange, plan K1, and plan K2, as shown in Figure 2-8.

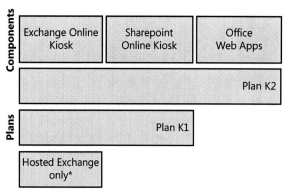

FIGURE 2-8 Kiosk worker plans are composed of three tiers.

The Kiosk plan provides a lower cost model for those workers who need basic functionality. At its very base level is an option to have only a hosted version of Exchange. This lowest-level plan doesn't have a "K#" associated with it; it is simply referred to as a component called Hosted Exchange.

The K1 plan adds to the online version of Exchange with a limited version of SharePoint online. Under this plan, the end user does not have most of the functionality that is part of the full SharePoint Online offering. Kiosk workers use SharePoint Online to access to a corporate portal; they have read-only capability and cannot collaborate.

For workers who need a little more, including reading and light editing of documents, the K2 plan builds on the K1 plan by adding the browser-only Office Web Apps. Office Web Apps gives the kiosk worker access to lite versions of Word, Excel, PowerPoint, and OneNote.

Kiosk plans are intended for an online, limited-access, low-touch worker at an affordable price point and represent the low-end version of the enterprise plans.

Now let's look at the more robust, rich client experience of the E1–E4 plans.

Enterprise Plans (E1–E4)

The enterprise plan is designed for organizations with more than 50 users that need additional functionality, such as advanced archiving, Office Professional Plus, and voice mail. These plans are also designed with current on-premises Microsoft customers in mind, helping them to move some or all functionality to the cloud.

The first level of the E plans is E1 (see Figure 2-9), which offers a basic collaboration portal and messaging. The user can use SharePoint Online for collaboration as well as the added functionalities of instant messaging, presence, email, and calendar. This plan also includes conferencing, with which the user can make computer-to-computer calls and share desktops.

Building upon the E1 plan, the E2 plan adds the Office Web Apps (see Figure 2-9). In addition to collaboration, users can read and do some light editing of Word, Excel, PowerPoint, and OneNote files. This is an ideal low-cost solution for information workers who do not need the full functionality of Office Professional or more advanced SharePoint functionality.

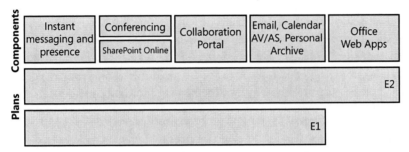

FIGURE 2-9 Enterprise plans E1 and E2.

The E3 plan (see Figure 2-10) includes advanced SharePoint functionality of SharePoint services for Excel, Access, Visio, and forms; this is an ideal solution for advanced users of SharePoint. In addition to the added SharePoint functionality, this plan introduces advanced email archiving, which is required for legal compliance. Other features included in the E3 plan are unified messaging, integrating voice mail with email, calendars, and contacts. Finally, the E3 plan also introduces Office Professional Plus and a number of different ways IT administrators can control deployments of Office to their users. Office Professional Plus is fully integrated with Office 365 and provides a seamless Office experience.

The most complete plan available is the E4 plan (see Figure 2-10). This plan includes everything offered by the other E plans, but also adds full functionality of Lync Online with the ability to make audio calls through Office 365 via Dial-in Audio Conferencing. The E4 plan is ideal for an organization that wants to have full integration with its existing private branch exchange (PBX) solution (business telephone system) or that is building out a new PBX solution and wants to take advantage of the lower-cost, more efficient solution of Office 365 and Lync Online.

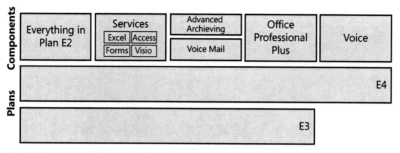

FIGURE 2-10 Enterprise plans E3 and E4.

While the enterprise tier with its various plans provides a number of customizable and robust solutions for just about any type of worker, there is still a need for another tier that is not for kiosk workers, individual professionals, or information workers. That tier is targeted toward students and educators. The education plans for Office 365 offer an extremely cost effective way of placing cutting-edge technology into the hands of students and educators.

Office 365 for the Enterprise (E Plan) is ideal for organizations with at least 250 users or devices that want to license software and cloud services for a minimum of a three-year period. The Microsoft Enterprise Agreement (EA) gives you the best overall pricing based on the size of your organization, along with the full benefits of Microsoft Software Assurance and simplified licensing management through the company-wide option. The EA also provides the best way to license Microsoft's on-premises software and online services, such as Office 365, within the same agreement.

Licensing Office 365 Enterprise with an EA

Keeping pace with the expanding array of Microsoft cloud services, the EA gives you the flexibility to choose among on-premises software and cloud services to best suit your needs and help you optimize your technology expenditures. When you choose to transition aspects of your IT organization to the cloud, your EA helps you to:

- Transition to cloud services at your own pace.
- Move users back and forth between on-premises software and cloud services.
- Match and adjust online service plans to meet user needs.
- Easily add and adjust new online service users above your EA commitment.

You can choose to purchase your software licenses via EA Enrollments or subscribe to licenses through the Enterprise Subscription programs. These programs are based on a three-year term with the ability to add and adjust products and online services over time. The Enterprise Enrollment offers pricing advantages beyond standard license and subscription pricing. Should you add new users or devices during your enrollment, you can equip them with software and cloud services that you are already using and then account for these changes through an annual reconciliation process known as "True Up."

This ability to grow or downsize subscription counts might be attractive, especially if you expect significant fluctuations in workforce size and IT requirements. However, unlike the EA Enrollments, wherein you retain perpetual use rights for the licenses that you purchase, with subscription programs, you have access to Microsoft software and cloud services for as long as you maintain your subscription.

Office 365 for Education (EDU)

Office 365 for education is based on the live@edu service that Microsoft has been offering for many years, with the addition of all the new capabilities offered with Office 365. Office 365 for Education will provide cloud-based services for educational institutions that are priced to save money and give students affordable access to familiar, next-generation pro- ductivity tools while helping educational institutions free up resources.

Everything in Office 365—with the exception of Office Professional Plus—is free to students and available at a low per-user, monthly cost to educators and staff (see Figure 2-11). A stu- dent can gain access to Office Professional Plus and enjoy the same benefits of collaboration and seamless Office integration as enterprise users.

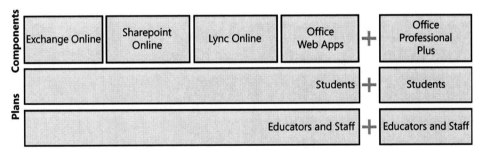

FIGURE 2-11 Office 365 Education plans.

Currently, educators and staff can also license Office Professional Plus for an additional cost per person, per month over the basic plan that includes Office Web Apps. Office 365 for Education is an affordable way for students to take advantage of the benefits of SharePoint Online as an online learning environment with integrated social-networking to enhance col- laboration—all within the familiarity of a classroom environment with extensible boundaries.

Students also receive large 25-GB mailboxes and the ability to send attachments up to 25 MB from virtually anywhere by using their mobile devices. They will also be able to access email, important documents, contacts, and calendars on nearly any device, including Windows and Mac-based computers, Windows Phone, iPhone, Android, and BlackBerry.

Final Overview of Licensing

Licensing can certainly be overwhelming, and there are several differences between the various tiers and plans. Table 2-4 presents those details side by side in an easy-to-consume format. Education is not included in this table; you can assume that whatever is available in the P1 tier, plus the option for Office Professional Plus, is also available to students.

TABLE 2-4 Feature Comparison Between P, K, and E Plans

	For Small Businesses SharePoint Online in P1	**For Kiosk Workers SharePoint Online in K1–K2**	**For Information Workers SharePoint Online in E1–E4**
Team Sites	Yes	Yes	Yes
Simple public-facing website	1 basic public-facing site included	No	1 basic public-facing site included
Site Designer	Yes	Yes	Yes
SharePoint Designer 2010	Yes, for intranet sites	Yes, for intranet sites	Yes, for intranet sites
Custom SharePoint Designer Workflows	Yes	Yes	Yes
Sandboxed Solutions	Yes	Yes	Yes
My Site	No	No	Yes
Enterprise Features (Forms Services, Excel Services, Visio Services)	No	OK to consume	OK to consume
Access Services	Yes	OK to consume	OK to consume
Business Connectivity Services (BCS)	No	No	No
Site collections	Single Site Collection	N/A	Up to 300
Office Web Apps	View & Edit	View-only for K1 View & Edit for K2	View-only for E1 View & Edit for E2
Search (across site collections)	N/A	Yes	Yes
Basic external document sharing	Yes (up to 50 free)	N/A	Yes (first 50 free)
Storage	10 GB + 500 MB per user license	10 GB + 0 MB per user license	10 GB + 500 MB per user license
Buy additional storage	No	Yes	Yes
Maximum number of users	Up to 50	TBD	TBD
Admin	Single Site Collection	No	Yes, tenant level
Support	Community	24 x 7 phone support for Administrators	24 x 7 phone support for Administrators

Administering Office 365

Now that you have a good understanding of what is in Office 365, let's get started with actually using it and performing some first-step tasks, such as creating users and basic administration.

First things first: Only an administrator can create, edit, and delete user accounts. This chapter assumes that you are either a global administrator or user management administrator. If you are not either one of these, you need to contact your administrator and ask to have these rights assigned to you. Administrative tasks are performed by using the Admin Overview page, on which you can manage user accounts, licenses, services, and other enterprise-wide account settings. To open this page, in the header of the main Office 365 Home page, click the Admin link.

Managing Licenses

Your first duty as an administrator is to ensure that your account is setup correctly. This means you have administrator privileges and that you have the right licenses assigned to you. Based on the services your company has purchased, you will have different licensing options. It is essential to ensure that you are setup with access to all the necessary areas of Office 365 before creating other users, or else you will have a difficult time testing and troubleshooting issues. Also, note that each user that you create will also receive a license. Let's look at managing licenses before creating your first user account. There are two general categories of tasks that administrators can perform on licenses:

- **Assigning licenses**   An administrator can assign licenses to new users when creating new accounts, and an administrator can assign licenses to existing accounts. Administrators can also add a particular license or remove it from a user.

- **Resolving conflicts**   The other task you will face as an administrator is resolving license conflicts that occur when there are more users assigned to a service than there are available licenses for that particular service. Administrators can resolve issues by purchasing additional licenses, removing a license from a user, or deleting user accounts.

Not all administrators accounts are created equal, and only certain types of administrators can do all of the above. Table 2-5 (provided by Microsoft) offers a good overview of what each administrator account can do.

TABLE 2-5 Office 365 Administrator Roles

Administrator role	Assign a license	Remove a license	Purchase more licenses	Delete a user
Global administrator	Yes	Yes	Yes	Yes
Billing administrator	No	No	Yes	No
User management administrator	Yes	Yes	No	Yes
Service administrator	No	No	No	No
Password administrator	No	No	No	No

Creating Users

Now that you have verified that you have the rights you need to assign licenses and have the proper administrative access, it's time to create your first user. There are ways to add multiple users at one time with a bulk import, but for now, let's focus on creating your first single user so that you understand the process.

Adding a User

1. In the header of the main Office 365 Home page, click Admin.

2. On the Admin page, in the left pane, under Management, click Users.

3. On the Users page, click New, and then click User.

4. On the Properties page, complete the user information. Click the arrow next to Additional properties to add optional user information, and then click Next.

5. On the Settings page, indicate whether you want the user to have administrator permissions.

   If you select Yes, select an administrator role from the drop-down list. Also provide the user's preferred email address. This email address is used for important notifications, and the user will need to know what this is to log on later.

6. Under Set User Location, select the user's work location, and then click Next.

7. On the Assign Licenses page, select the licenses that you want to assign to the user, and then click Next.

8. On the Send Results In Email page, select Send Email to send the user name and temporary password for the newly created user to yourself and the new user of your choice by email, and then click Create.

   You can enter a maximum of five email addresses.

9. On the Results page, the new user name and temporary password are displayed.

   When you're finished reviewing the results, click Finish.

Editing Users

When you need to edit a user, you will use many of the same screens and commands that you used to create the user.

Editing a User Account

1. In the header of the main Office 365 Home page, click Admin.

2. On the Admin page, in the left pane, under Management, click Users.

3. On the Users page, select the check box adjacent to the user that you want to edit, and then click Edit.

4. Click the Properties, Settings, Licenses, or More tabs, depending on the changes that you want to make. Complete your changes, and then click Save.

More often than not, you will need to edit more than one user account when you add a new service or license or even change one. Office 365 provides an easy way to edit multiple user accounts at one time.

Editing Multiple User Accounts

1. In the header of the main Office 365 Home page, click Admin.

2. On the Admin page, in the left pane, under Management, click Users.

3. On the Users page, select the check box adjacent to the users that you want to edit, and then click Edit.

4. On the Properties page, edit the information as needed, and then click Next.

5. On the Settings page, edit the information as needed, and then click Next.

6. On the Assign licenses page, do one of the following, and then click Submit:

   - If you're not making any changes to the existing license assignments, click Retain Current License Assignments.

   - To replace existing license assignments, select one or more licenses from the list, and then click Replace Existing License Assignments.

   - To add licenses to the existing license assignments, select one or more licenses from the list, and then click Add To Existing License Assignments.

Deleting Users

Not only can you edit multiple user accounts at one time, you can also delete multiple user accounts.

Deleting Multiple User Accounts

1. In the header of the main Office 365 Home page, click Admin.

2. On the Admin page, in the left pane, under Management, click Users.

3. On the Users page, select the check box adjacent to the user or users that you want to delete, and then click Delete.

4. In the Delete confirmation message box, click Yes.

Administering SharePoint Online

You can delegate an individual to be your SharePoint Online Administrator. Since SharePoint Online environments are in a shared environment (multiple tenants within a farm), they have access and control at the tenant level. Microsoft manages the hardware layer, the Window Server layer, the SharePoint Online farm level, and central administration. Lower management overhead is one of the core values of the Office 365 service. However, this does not mean a loss of control or loss of flexibility. It means that you own your tenancy.

You can then create numerous site collections for company portals, individual projects, various business units, or areas delegated for external sharing. You can also create individual subsites for teams. With SharePoint Online administration, customers can delegate at all levels. A company's SharePoint Online administrator can delegate ownership of a site collection to a separate site collection owner, who can then further create subsites and delegate ownership to a site owner.

SharePoint Online administration tasks include:

- Creating or deleting a site collection
- Activating external sharing for individual site collections
- Assigning site collection ownership for individual site collections
- Adding a support partner for a site collection
- Changing storage quota and warning levels of site collections
- Setting a default SharePoint site that all employees can link to from their Office 365 Information Worker portal

- Adjusting user profile settings on behalf of end users

- Managing metadata/taxonomy (to be consumed across site collections)

Chapter 4, "Administering SharePoint Online," covers these tasks in detail.

Administering Exchange Online

Using Office 365, administrators can add users and user domains, manage licenses, create groups, and perform other common administration tasks. From within the console, administrators can follow links to the Exchange Control Panel, where they can manage settings specific to Exchange Online.

Exchange Online Control Panel

Administrators can use the Exchange Online Control Panel to configure and manage the Exchange Online environment from a web browser. The Exchange Control Panel provides several management capabilities, which are organized into four high-level categories:

- **Users and Groups**   Mailboxes, distribution groups, external contacts, and email migration

- **Roles**   Administrator roles, user roles, and auditing

- **Mail Control**   Rules, journaling, eDiscovery, and delivery reports

- **Phone and Voice**   Unified messaging dialing plans, unified messaging gateways, Exchange ActiveSync access, and Exchange ActiveSync device policy

Many of these settings can also be configured via Windows Remote PowerShell. Remote PowerShell is covered in greater detail later in this chapter.

Forefront Online Protection for Exchange Administration Center

The Forefront Online Protection for Exchange (FOPE) Administration Center allows Exchange Online customers to manage advanced settings relating to email flow and email hygiene. Within the FOPE Administration Center, administrators can:

- Access reports and statistics on email hygiene for their domains

- Set advanced policy filters that are not available via Exchange Online transport rules, such as rules that are triggered by the IP address of inbound or outbound servers

- Configure forced Transport Layer Security (TLS) connections for their domains

- Perform advanced message tracing

- Configure organization-level safe and blocked senders

> **Note** Some settings are read-only in the FOPE Administration Center to help prevent administrators from inadvertently causing problems with their organization's mail flow.

Office Professional Plus Deployment Options

Office 365 can deploy Office Professional Plus in one of three methods to Office 365 users. The first, Office 365 Portal deployment, is a "self-service" model implemented directly by employees, which is ideal for organizations that don't have an IT staff or internal company resources dedicated to deployment. A second method, network share deployment, is much more efficient for deploying to more users, especially over a slower connection. This model requires some IT capability on the part of the organization as well as access to a local network share to host the software that will be deployed. Finally, the IT-managed deployment option is ideal for large custom deployments that use group policies and/or a startup script. This model requires IT staff and the use of on-premises tools such as Microsoft System Center Configuration Manager 2010 or Microsoft System Center Essentials 2010.

> **Note** Office Professional Plus for Office 365 does not support the use of Application Virtualization or Remote Desktop Services (formerly known as Terminal Services) for deployment.

Deploying via Office 365 Portal

The default method for installing Office Professional Plus for Office 365 is to use the Office 365 Portal. This scenario is best for organizations that do not have a dedicated IT staff (see Figure 2-12), do not require a deployment plan, and are not using internal infrastructure such as Active Directory or Group policies.

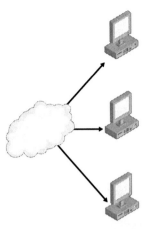

FIGURE 2-12 Users can implement the Office 365 self-service deploy to download and install Office Professional Plus by themselves.

An administrator assigns a license to each user, and then the user signs in to the Office 365 Portal. The user then downloads and configures Office Professional Plus himself.

Downloading Office Professional Plus

1. On the Office 365 Home page, under Resources, click Downloads.

2. On the Downloads page, under Install Microsoft Office Professional Plus, select your language, and then select either the 32-bit or 64-bit version of Office Professional Plus for Office 365.

 Tip Unless you are certain that your computer is operating in a 64-bit environment, it's recommended that you download the 32-bit version of Office Professional Plus.

3. Click Install.

   When prompted, you can choose to run the MicrosoftOffice.exe file directly from the portal, or you can save it to a folder on your computer and then run the file from that folder. It is your choice.

4. After you install Office Professional Plus for Office 365, the Microsoft Online Services Sign In Assistant Required dialog box appears. Click Accept And Install to install it. If you do not install this, you will have problems signing in to Office 365 from your Office applications.

5. When the Sign In dialog box appears, sign in with your Microsoft Online Services ID. If you have a valid subscription, the Subscription Verified dialog box appears. Click Close.

Office Professional Plus is now installed on your local machine and should be synchronized with your Office 365 account and services.

Deploying via Network Share

In this scenario, after creating user accounts and passwords and assigning licenses for all users, the administrator downloads the Office Professional Plus for Office 365 executable file (MicrosoftOffice.exe) to a local network share, as shown in Figure 2-13. This solution is ideal for organizations that want to customize their installations and is less resource intensive, so it is ideal for slower network connections because users can download the software over the local area network (LAN) rather than the wide area network (WAN). This option requires that an accessible network drive be available to the end users who will be receiving the software.

Note To avoid various access and "file not found" errors, it is recommended to set access to the Office Professional Plus source files to read-only and ensure that all users have administrative permissions on their local computers.

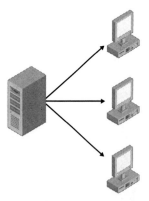

FIGURE 2-13 With Office network share deployment, users download the Office software over the LAN rather than the WAN, which results in faster download times.

You start by creating a network installation point for the Office Professional Plus source files. This is a shared network location from which users will run setup.exe to install Office Professional Plus.

Copy the MicrosoftOffice.exe file to the shared drive, and then extract the files. After setting up the network installation point with the Office Professional Plus source, you can email users the instructions on how to run Office Professional Plus setup.exe from the network installation point and install the product on their local computers.

Deploying via Group Policy Computer Startup Script

This option is ideal for organizations that need to deploy to thousands of users and want to take advantage of Active Directory or Group policies. It also allows for greater control and a centralized model for monitoring and reporting.

In environments that have already installed Active Directory Domain Services, administrators can download the MicrosoftOffice.exe file to a network location, extract the files from the MicrosoftOffice.exe Microsoft Self-Extractor file, and prepare to deploy Office Professional Plus by using a Group Policy computer startup script. With a startup script, you can push customized installs to end users' computers without physically touching each computer, as illustrated in Figure 2-14.

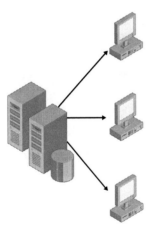

FIGURE 2-14 Office IT managed deployment via managed software deployment tools allows you to push Office out to thousands of users.

In medium and large-enterprise managed environments, IT administrators should download the MicrosoftOffice.exe file to a network share and prepare to use a change and configuration software management tool, such as Microsoft System Center Configuration Manager 2010 or Microsoft System Center Essentials 2010, to deploy Office Professional Plus to users.

An infrastructure that supports software management tools (System Center Configuration Manager 2010 or System Center Essentials 2010) is required for this option.

Remote PowerShell

With Remote PowerShell, you can connect to Exchange Online to perform management tasks that are not available or practical in the web management interface. For example, you can use Remote PowerShell to automate repetitive tasks, extract data for custom reports, customize policies, and connect Exchange Online to existing infrastructure and processes. This is especially useful when you need to perform the same task thousands of times. A procedure that would normally take days through the browser can take only minutes by using a script. The following is a list of common settings that you can configure by using Remote PowerShell:

- User management
- License assignment
- Security group management
- Domain management
- Administrator role assignments

To use Remote PowerShell, your computer must be running the Windows Management Framework, which contains Windows PowerShell v2 and WinRM 2.0. These components are already installed on computers running Windows 7 or Windows Server 2008 R2. You can manually download them for computers that are running other operating systems. You do not need to install any Exchange Server management or migration tools in order to use Remote PowerShell; however, you will need to download and install the Microsoft Online PowerShell Module.

The Microsoft Online PowerShell Module contains core cmdlets for Office 365, such as cmdlets to manage users, groups, and so on. To download the module, use the following links:

- X64: *http://bit.ly/L8LS9z*
- X86: *http://bit.ly/jTqbJW*

To begin, open PowerShell on your computer and run the *Import-Module MSOnline* cmdlet to load the module that you just downloaded and installed. Next, you need to connect to Office 365 by using a set of credentials. Use the *Get-Credential* cmdlet to set your credentials to a variable that you can pass into the *Connect-MsolService* cmdlet. The *Connect-MsolService* cmdlet passes your credentials to Microsoft Online and sets up the secure connection. Once you're connected to Microsoft Online, you can start scripting your administrative actions. Figure 2-15 shows an example of how to connect to Microsoft Online with PowerShell after you've installed the module:

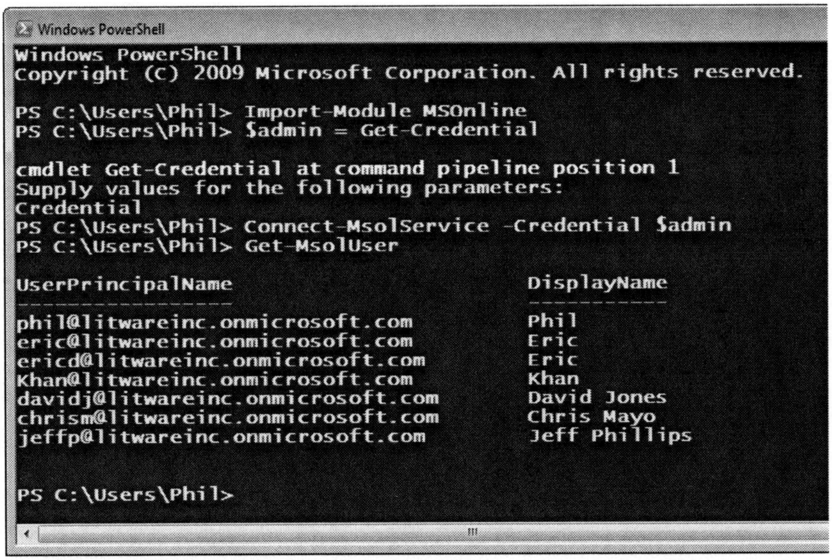

FIGURE 2-15 You can connect to Microsoft Online by passing your credentials into the *Connect-MsolService* cmdlet.

Figure 2-15 shows that the *Get-MsolUser* cmdlet was executed to fetch all the users in Microsoft Online. There are literally hundreds of cmdlets available to an Office 365 administrator. Table 2-6 presents a sampling of some common cmdlets:

TABLE 2-6 Common PowerShell Cmdlets Used for Office 365 Administration

Area	Cmdlets
User management	Add-MsolUser
	Enable-MsolUser
	Get-MsolUser
	Set-MsolUser
	Set-MsolUserPassword
	Remove-MsolUser
License management	Set-MsolUserLicense
Security group management	Add-MsolGroup
	Get-MsolGroup
	Remove-MsolGroup
	Set-MsolGroup
	Add-MsolGroupMember
	Set-MsolGroupMember
Domain management	Add-MsolDomain
	Confirm-MsolDomain
	Get-MsolDomain
	Remove-MsolDomain

Chapter 3
Planning for SharePoint Online

In this chapter, you will learn about:

- How to plan your deployment to SharePoint Online

- Various capabilities of SharePoint Online that need careful planning

- Designing your Information Architecture properly

- How to best govern your SharePoint Online deployment

Planning your Microsoft SharePoint Online environment is a critical step in the process of migrating to the cloud. This chapter is intended to guide you through the planning process and get your organization ready for implementing SharePoint Online.

Some of the core planning activities involve considering the new Administration Center, sites and site collections, languages, user profiles, audiences, social capabilities, InfoPath Forms Services, managed metadata, Microsoft Office Web Apps, and public-facing websites. Each of these capabilities involves a lot of planning and understanding in order to develop a good SharePoint environment.

You also need to understand the information on your sites and how it all fits together. That is why you need to plan out your information architecture. You need to help your end users find the information on your SharePoint Online site; otherwise, user adoption will suffer and your return on investment will be low.

Just putting all of your information into SharePoint Online doesn't mean that it is getting to the right people. Security is important so that sensitive information isn't viewed by those who don't have the appropriate permissions, including those who have access to your environment. You also need a plan on how you'll share information with users outside of your organization, if that happens to be a requirement.

Once you have a plan for securing all your information, you can step back and look at the site to ensure that you have all of the features you need. This might mean that you need to build some custom solutions to meet your unique requirements. Fortunately, with SharePoint Online, you can make custom solutions available. However, it's important to know if there are any restrictions on what can be done as a result of running your site in a hosted environment.

To have a successful SharePoint Online site, you also need a plan for user adoption to be high, but this isn't easy to do with users who are new to SharePoint Online. A big piece of user adoption involves ensuring that all of your users are sufficiently trained and able to succeed. If they don't know how to use SharePoint, they won't use it. There are many different ways to train your users and it is very important to make a good choice. You also need to have guidelines in place so that once your users are trained, they know what they can do with the new SharePoint Online site. Governance plays a significant role in ensuring a successful SharePoint Online deployment. It's important to consider who owns which sites and site collections. Of those owners, what are they charged to do? Do they have the skills to do it, and who holds them accountable to get assigned tasks done? These are all important questions to think through before you release your SharePoint Online sites.

All of this planning is going to give your organization a head start toward implementing the best SharePoint Online site. If you don't plan well, then your investment will become more of an expense. With a successful implementation, you will find that your users are more efficient and effective at their jobs.

Planning SharePoint Online Core Capabilities

Administration of the core capabilities of SharePoint Online is done by using a new interface that contains some of the familiar features of Central Administration, the site used to administer on-premises SharePoint deployments. Site collections, user profiles, and managed metadata are all examples of some of the familiar features that are part of the new Administration Center, which is the name of the site within Office 365 from which you can administer and configure these features.

With SharePoint Online, you will be creating new site collections and sites, so you must design what sites you need, and for what purposes they serve. Within each site, you want a plan for which features are available, and how users will interact with those features.

Languages are another capability that you can configure in SharePoint Online to help deliver content to users in foreign countries. Users can relate to your site better if they don't need to translate it first. With user profiles, you can record what language a user prefers and target content on your site based on that preference. This is a handy tool for getting specific information to a group or audience.

With the new social capabilities of SharePoint Online, you can learn if users like the content you are providing. You can also collect information on the site by using InfoPath Forms Services, which can help capture quality data by validating what users submit. Managed metadata is useful for keeping consistent information throughout your sites, and will help with functions like Search.

Office Web Apps provide you with the capability to deliver Office documents to users who don't have a copy of Office installed on their own computer. This can be a big benefit for your infrastructure team because they don't have to maintain the software as new versions are released.

The final core capability you should plan for is a public website. SharePoint Online allows companies to have up to one public-facing site, which gives your company a quick and easy way to establish a presence on the Internet.

Administration

The administration of SharePoint Online is done by using a new tool. Instead of the familiar Central Administration tool that's a part of an on-premises deployment, SharePoint Online comes with the Administration Center (see Figure 3-1), which the SharePoint Online global administrator can use to set up and configure the new environment. Chapter 4, "Administering SharePoint Online," covers the Administration Center in more detail.

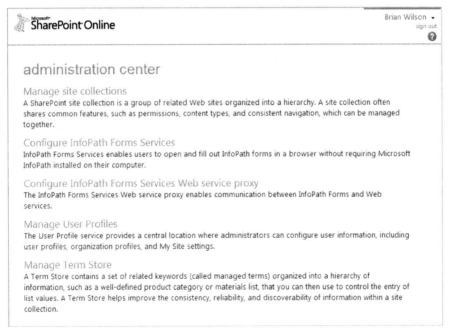

FIGURE 3-1 You can manage SharePoint Online conveniently with the new Administration Center.

SharePoint Online has several administrator roles. The role at the top with the most sweeping privileges is that of global administrator. Next, below that are site collection administrators, and then site administrators/owners (see Figure 3-2). Security will be covered more in the user management and security section later in this chapter. For now, you can start to plan who will fill these core roles in your SharePoint Online deployment.

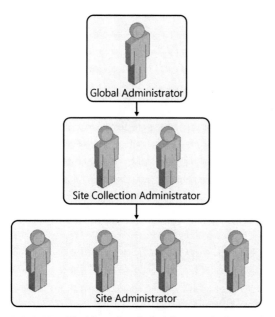

FIGURE 3-2 The hierarchy of administrators in SharePoint Online.

From the Administration Center, you can manage site collections, configure InfoPath Forms Services, configure a web service proxy for InfoPath Forms Services, manage user profiles, and manage the term store.

Chapter 4 goes into great depth on how to use the Administration Center to configure your site collections and settings.

Sites and Site Collections

Before you can open up SharePoint Online for your end users to start using, you need to plan your site collections. Site collections are a hierarchical set of sites that can be managed together. Site collections share many features, such as permissions, templates, content types and a common navigation. Site collections can contain multiple subsites—but not other site collections—that reside below the top-level site. Subsites are provisioned when you create a new site collection.

When you create a new site, you can choose from several site templates that will provide a default set of lists, libraries, and so on that are targeted to the needs of your site. SharePoint Online also has quotas built in for the amount of storage and resources a site collection can use. This prevents sites from using all of the storage that you are allocated with your SharePoint Online account.

Some questions that will help you when planning your site collection are:

- What is the purpose of the content on the site?

  The type of content on your site helps determine which template is right for you. For example, if you're planning for collaboration between colleagues, then a Team Site is a good choice. If you're considering a site that will be hosting a lot of content like news, then a Publishing Site is the better template.

- Who will be accessing the content on the site?

  It's good to know who the audience for your site is so that you can plan permissions accordingly. You want to ensure that sensitive information is accessed only by those who are allowed to access it. You also want to ensure that the content is relevant to the audience that you're targeting.

- Will external users need to access the site?

  External users can access your site when they are invited by using the Share Site functionality on a site. The Share Site feature is called Partner Access; with it, your site owners can invite practically any person in the world to come collaborate with them. This has obvious pros and cons with which you should be acquainted before you enable or disable this functionality.

> **Note** A benefit of Partner Access is not having to worry about managing accounts for your partners and customers. A disadvantage is that it's difficult to control who is invited and if it's appropriate for those individuals have access to your sites.

- Is this site going to be used in other countries that would require different languages?

  When you have users in multiple countries, you might want to look at translating the site by using the Multilingual User Interface (MUI) feature. This feature translates the system-generated text on items such as the menu. The content will still need to be translated manually, but users will still appreciate the effort of providing them with the out-of-the-box text in their local language.

- Will there be large amounts of data stored on your site collection?

  Large amounts of data might mean that you need to purchase more storage space from Microsoft Online Services, so plan to estimate how much content each site will typically use. You can always purchase more storage in the future if it isn't needed now.

- What features will be needed on your site?

  If you plan to have more control over the way navigation works on your site, then you need to activate SharePoint Server Publishing. This also gives you functionality like versioning and check-out. Another feature you might want is Hold and eDiscovery to help track external activities, which are not activated by default. These are just a few of the features you can choose from, so be sure to review and plan what is necessary for your site.

- Is there information to which only certain departments or users should have access?

  Security is important to plan before putting sensitive information on your site. You might have payroll information or contracts whose access you want to restrict to only certain employees. With SharePoint Online, you can set specific group access on a site, list, library, or item.

Site Templates

When creating a new site, you can take advantage of the various templates that are available out-of-the-box with SharePoint Online. The purpose of your site will help determine which site template is the best choice. Different scenarios call for different site templates. Site templates contain lists, libraries, pages, and other features that are designed to give you a good starting point for the type of site you need to use for your organization. Table 3-1 presents a list of the available site templates in SharePoint Online, along with a brief description of each one.

TABLE 3-1 **Site Templates Available in SharePoint Online**

Template name	Description	Service offering
Assets Web Database	Creates a database to track assets, including details and owners.	SharePoint Online for enterprises only
Basic Meeting Workspace	Creates a site to plan, organize, and capture the results of a meeting. It provides lists for managing the agenda, meeting attendees, and documents.	All
Basic Search Center	Creates a site for delivering the Search experience. The site includes pages for search results and advanced searches.	SharePoint Online for enterprises only
Blank Meeting Workspace	Creates a blank meeting site for you to customize, based on your requirements.	All

Template name	Description	Service offering
Blank Site	Creates a blank site for you to customize, based on your requirements.	All
Blog	Creates a site for a person or team to post ideas, observations, and expertise. Visitors to this site can post comments.	All
Charitable Contributions Web Database	Creates a database to track information about fund-raising campaigns, including donations made by contributors, campaign-related events, and pending tasks.	SharePoint Online for enterprises only
Contacts Web Database	Creates a contacts database to manage information about people who your team works with, such as customers and partners.	All
Decision Meeting Workspace	Creates a site for meetings that track status or make decisions. It provides lists for creating tasks, storing documents, and recording decisions.	All
Document Center	Creates a site to centrally manage documents in your enterprise.	SharePoint Online for enterprises only
Document Workspace	Creates a site for colleagues to work together on a document. This template provides a document library for storing the primary document and supporting files, a tasks list for assigning to-do items, and a links list for resources related to the document.	All
Enterprise Wiki	Creates a site for publishing knowledge that you capture and want to share across the enterprise. This template provides an easy content editing experience in a single location for co-authoring, discussions, and project management.	SharePoint Online for enterprises only
Express Team Site	Creates a site for teams to quickly create, organize, and share information. It provides a document library and a list for managing announcements.	All
Group Work Site	This template provides a groupware solution with which teams can create, organize, and share information quickly and easily. It includes Group Calendar, Circulation, Phone-Call Memo, the Document Library and the other basic lists.	All
Issues Web Database	Creates an issues database to manage a set of issues or problems. You can assign, prioritize, and follow the progress of items from start to finish.	All

Template name	Description	Service offering
Multipage Meeting Workspace	Creates a site to plan, organize, and capture the results of a meeting. It provides lists for managing the agenda and meeting attendees in addition to two blank pages for you to customize based on your requirements.	All
Personalization Site	Creates a site for delivering personalized views, data and navigation from a site collection into a My Site. This template includes personalization-specific Web Parts and navigation that is optimized for My Site sites.	SharePoint Online for enterprises only
PowerPoint Broadcast Site	Creates a site with which presenters can broadcast a slide show from Microsoft PowerPoint 2010 to remote viewers who can view it in a web browser.	SharePoint Online for enterprises only
Projects Web Database	Creates a project tracking database to track multiple projects and assign tasks to different people.	SharePoint Online for enterprises only
Publishing Site	Creates a blank site for expanding your website and quickly publishing webpages. Contributors can work on draft versions of pages and publish them to make them visible to readers. This template includes document and image libraries for storing web publishing assets.	SharePoint Online for enterprises only
Publishing Site With Workflow	Only available as a subsite of the Publishing Portal or Enterprise Wiki. A site for publishing webpages on a schedule by using approval workflows. It includes document and image libraries for storing web publishing assets. By default, only sites with this template can be created under this site.	SharePoint Online for enterprises only
Social Meeting Workspace	Creates a site to plan social occasions. This template provides lists for tracking attendees, providing directions, and storing pictures of the event.	SharePoint Online for enterprises only
Team Site	Creates a site for teams to quickly organize, author, and share information. This template provides a document library, and lists for managing announcements, calendar items, tasks, and discussions.	All
Visio Process Repository	Creates a site for teams to quickly view, share, and store Microsoft Visio process diagrams. This template provides a versioned document library for storing process diagrams, and lists for managing announcements, tasks, and review discussions.	SharePoint Online for enterprises only

PowerPoint Broadcast Slide Show

The PowerPoint Broadcast Site uses new functionality in PowerPoint 2010 with which a presenter can broadcast her slide show for remote viewers to watch in a web browser. If you want to take advantage of this functionality in your SharePoint Online environment, you need to create a special site collection that uses the PowerPoint Broadcast Site template. Once it is created, the site provides you with instructions on the home page for setting up your PowerPoint slide show to broadcast. From within PowerPoint 2010, it's as simple as clicking Broadcast Slide Show, selecting the new site or entering the URL from the home page, and then clicking Create Broadcast. For users to access the site, it's important to configure security correctly. To allow specific users to present, you need to place them in the Broadcast Presenters group; viewers need to be put in the Broadcast Attendees group.

Site Collection Space Allocation

SharePoint Online has different levels of storage available to your site collections, based on the number of user licenses and the plan that you purchased. When you create a new site collection, you can decide how much storage to allocate, with the minimum amount being 50 megabytes. You can increase the initial storage amount later if you find that you are getting close to the limit. Email notifications can be configured to inform you when you have reached a predetermined percentage of the site collection's limit. The total amount of storage you have allocated for all site collections is pooled together and shown on the Site Collections page in the Administration Center (see Figure 3-3). When you begin to get close to the total storage quota for your SharePoint Online environment, you can either clean up your site collections by reviewing what content can be removed or purchase more space from Microsoft (or the provider through which you purchased your account).

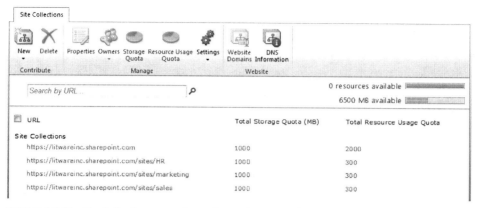

FIGURE 3-3 The Site Collections page shows the total amount of your storage quota used and the total amount of your resources quota used by existing site collections. You can also see the amount of storage quota and resource quota allocated per site collection.

Resources usage quotas are also configurable for each site collection. They specify how many resources your sandboxed solutions can use in a daily period. Once the limit is exceeded, the sandboxed solutions are turned off, which might disable your custom Web Parts. This is done to limit the possibility of negative server performance due to custom user code. You can enable email notifications to notify you when you are getting close to your resource usage quota.

If your organization has a good plan in place for the size of each site collection and quotas set, then you should have plenty of notice before reaching your limits. You should also be able to determine how to best proceed with cleaning up the old content or make a decision to purchase more space.

Sandboxed Solutions and Quotas

Sandboxed Solutions is a feature in SharePoint Online with which site collection owners can deploy code solutions at the site collection level to the solutions gallery. These solutions, once activated, run in a restricted mode that prevents them from destabilizing your farm. Site collections have a quota for the number of resources a sandboxed solution uses. This quota is shared between all of the sandboxed solutions in a site collection, and when the daily quota has been met, all of the sandboxed solutions in the site collection are turned off. Chapter 7, "Introduction to Customizing and Developing in SharePoint Online," explains how to build custom solutions for the sandbox.

Languages

When supporting sites in different countries, most users understandably want the content in their local language. In SharePoint Online, multiple languages are supported, but you need to configure it for site collections and sites. The MUI feature of SharePoint Online can change the language used for the default user interface elements on your site. This includes elements such as menus, navigation items, and other system-generated text. Of course, content owners still need to translate content on the site to the local language. It is important to identify who will be in charge of translating pages for each of the various sites that are in a foreign language.

The following are the different items that can be displayed in a different language by using the MUI feature:

- Site title

- Site description

- Default columns in lists and libraries

- Custom columns in a lists or created as a site column

- Navigation bar links

- Managed metadata

By default, the MUI feature is activated in SharePoint Online, which provides you with two options for configuring and implementing multiple languages. The first option is that your users can enable it for themselves, as shown in Figure 3-4.

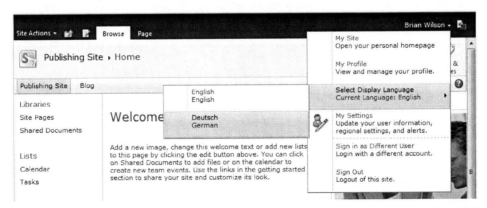

FIGURE 3-4 Users can easily change the display language on a site when the options are made available by a site administrator.

When a user enables this, he only sees the changes to the different user interface elements. To add more options to the available list of languages, a site administrator must select the various languages on the Language Settings page in Site Settings, as illustrated in Figure 3-5.

FIGURE 3-5 Site administrators can choose which languages are available for visitors to view the site.

The second option is that your site collection administrator can enable MUI for an individual site. When you create a new site, switch the view to see all site templates, and then in the Select Language drop-down list, change the language to the one that you want to be the default language for your site (see Figure 3-6). Be sure that the language you choose is the correct one because once the default language is configured, it can't be changed. One last thing to verify is that the sites that are created for you by SharePoint Online—including My Sites, Content Type Hub, and Broadcast sites—have the correct languages configured so that users can change the display language.

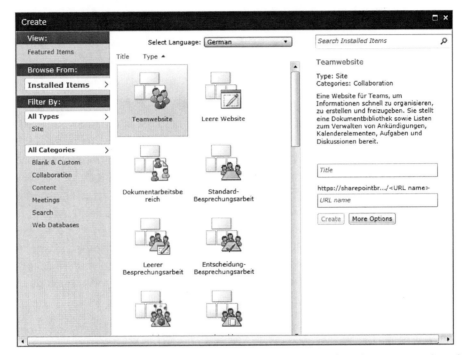

FIGURE 3-6 On the Create page, choose the language of your site in the Select Language drop-down list.

User Profiles

You can use profiles to store metadata about users that can be used for different functions on the sites in SharePoint Online. It also gives users a way to share information about themselves with their coworkers. There are various options for populating the information in user profiles, so it's important to plan accordingly. User profiles are covered in more detail in Chapter 4.

The first and most popular way to import information into user profiles is to synchronize with a data source such as Active Directory (AD). This method gives administrators the most control over what information is available on the SharePoint Online sites and confidence that the information is accurate with other systems they're running. With SharePoint Online, the properties are synchronized with the Office 365 directory services. Office 365 user profiles can be populated with AD information once Active Directory Synchronization (DirSync) has been configured between your on-premises domain and the domain for Microsoft Online. This process is covered in more detail in Chapter 5, "Identity Management and Authentication."

Another method is to allow users to enter information about themselves directly into their profile in SharePoint Online. This information can be overwritten if you are performing synchronization with the Office 365 directory, but if no mapping between fields is created, the user-entered information will remain.

User profile properties are the fields that SharePoint uses to store the information about your users. The user profile policies are the rules put in place to determine the privacy of these user profile properties.

User Profile Properties

User profiles are important to plan out because they hold the information about your users that you determine is necessary. There are two parts to configuring user profile information. There are privacy settings that are set by the owner of the information and the policy settings that are set by the organization. When planning user profile properties, you need to review the default properties provided and determine if there is other information that you want to capture. This information is useful when searching for users in the system, targeting content using audiences, and helping to create relationships between your colleagues and workgroups in your organization. Some examples are searching for someone who works in your department to discuss work topics, displaying the news local to your office location in a targeted Web Part, and finding colleagues who have the same interests as you do. All of this information can be stored in user profile properties.

When you activate directory synchronization, you can synchronize information from AD to the Office 365 directory. Once your information is in the Office 365 directory services, SharePoint Online performs a one-way synchronization on a scheduled interval that is set by Microsoft. You are limited in the properties that you can synchronize to SharePoint Online because it is getting its information from the Office 365 directory services. Here is a list of the out-of-the-box properties:

- First name
- Last name
- Display name
- Job title
- Department
- Office number
- Office phone

Once you have reviewed the default properties and determined that you would like to capture more information, you can add your own custom profile properties. Profile properties can be one of the following types:

- big integer
- binary
- Boolean
- date
- date no year
- date time
- E-mail
- float
- HTML
- integer
- Person
- string (Multi Value)
- string (Single Value)
- time zone
- unique identifier
- URL

Note You can also configure a term store to be used with a new property, which can be useful. Managed metadata is covered in more detail later in this chapter.

You have the option to add the properties that are not visible in the user profile view. This way you can add information that is important but not necessarily useful to the end user. This might be something like an employee ID that is used in an human resource (HR) system, and you want to tie that to information in your SharePoint Online site.

User Profile Policies

User profile policies are rules in SharePoint Online with which administrators can control what information users see when viewing other user's profiles. These rules can be assigned to individual users or groups and help maintain privacy. These policies also allow the default privacy settings to be overridden. You can read more about user profile policies in Chapter 4.

When you are planning out your policies, you should start by looking at the current information that is visible on your user's profiles. Take note of which information you want to make available to users and what information either needs to be added or removed.

SharePoint Online has a set of configurable policies that it provides to help you get started and with which administrators can create custom policies to meet your organization's needs. Here are some questions to help you decide what is right for you organization:

What Information Should Be Required?   SharePoint Online has a set of properties that are required by default. There might be other information that you want available to help with collaboration or building relationships within your organization. There can be many reasons for making a property required, such as the following:

- It is used by key user features.

- It is a key piece of business data used in an application.

- You are using it to create audiences.

- It is information that you want all users to provide.

- If you think the property will rarely be used or will confuse users, than it is suggested to disable the property and not let the user provide information in it.

Any other information that you want to collect can be marked as optional.

What Information Should Your Users Be Allowed to Update?   Some information changes more frequently than other types and might be better left to your users to maintain, especially if it is information that's not essential for your organization to function. Something like a biography or hobbies would be best maintained by a user because he might want to change it frequently.

What Information Should Be Hidden from Other Users?   Some information is more sensitive and your organization's HR policies might dictate what can and can't be shared. Look at the different information items and determine if it would benefit your users if they were able to see it. There are options to set the information so it is visible to everyone, colleagues, or just the profile owner ("just me"). Based on the sensitivity or usefulness to your colleagues, you can select which group can see the information.

Audiences

You can use audiences in SharePoint Online to target information to groups, based on their function or another grouping factor, such as office location. Audiences are created from the User Profiles page in the Administration Center (see Figure 3-7). Before you can create audiences, you have to understand what information on your site you want to target. Documents, links, and Web Parts are some of the most often targeted to a specific audience. Navigation is another area that many organizations like to target. Each of the areas needs to have a good property associated to it that can be used as a filter. For example, if your company wants to allow only HR to see a link to their site, you need to have an associated property (for example, Department) on the user profiles. Then you can create an audience that is built for a specific department, in this case HR. After you create your audiences you need to compile them, and then users who have entered HR in their user profile for the Department property will be allowed to see the link.

FIGURE 3-7 Audiences are managed through the Administration Center on the User Profiles page.

To create or edit an audience, in the Administration Center, click User Profiles, and then in the People section, click Manage Audiences. When you create an audience, you choose if you want it to satisfy all of the rules you add or any of the rules, as shown in Figure 3-8. Rules for audiences in SharePoint Online are broken into two groups: those that are based on a Windows security group, distribution list, or organizational hierarchy, and those that use a user profile property to filter by a value. Once you decide which you want to use, you then provide a value by which users are to be filtered and grouped. After you save your audience, it is compiled on a schedule that is predefined by Microsoft. Then you can use it on your site.

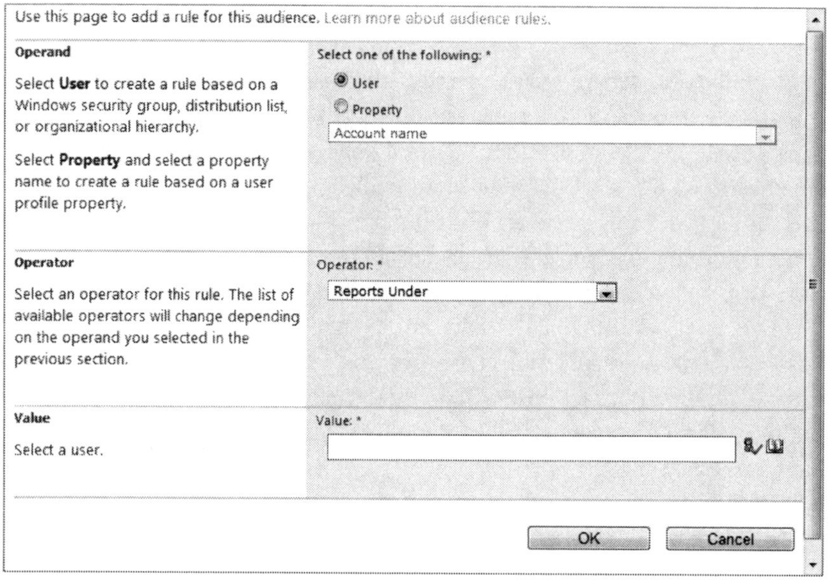

FIGURE 3-8 You can use audience rules to choose either user-based or property-based operands to create a filter on your SharePoint Online users.

Audiences prevents items from being viewed by users who aren't in the audience, but it is not to be confused with security, because if a user has the link to a document or site, he can still access it unless security permissions have been put in place.

Social Capabilities of SharePoint Online

SharePoint Online helps bring social computing into your organization by providing new features such as rating, tagging, and microblogging. With the addition of these features, it is important to understand how they can be used in your environment. Many organizations are embracing more social features, and now you can easily implement some in your organization.

Rating

Ratings in SharePoint Online help bring quality content to the attention of your users (see Figure 3-9). You can create views that highlight the highest rated documents on your site. You can enable ratings to appear in your document library from the library settings. One quick point: SharePoint Online ratings run on a fixed schedule to aggregate new ratings. So when a user rates a document, she might not see her rating take effect immediately.

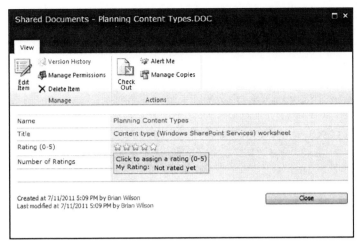

FIGURE 3-9 Ratings are a good way to help inform other users if content is good or bad.

Tagging

Tags and notes is how SharePoint Online provides new social tagging functionality. Tagging content helps other users find relevant information and also share their opinions with other employees. There is also functionality for you to tag external content when you use the script provided by SharePoint Online. There is even a "Like" button with which you can mark content throughout the site. This actually tags the content with the phrase "I like It," as shown in Figure 3-10.

FIGURE 3-10 You can easily add a tag or note to a page with the new functionality provided in SharePoint Online.

The tags that you create are available for viewing on your My Profile page and displayed in a tag cloud, as illustrated in Figure 3-11. Similar to other tag clouds, the more you use a tag, the larger it appears relative to the other tags. The tags that are created also show up in your activity feed, and other users can track this by adding you to their list of colleagues on their profile. If you want to tag something for your own personal use and not allow others to see it, select the Make Private check box.

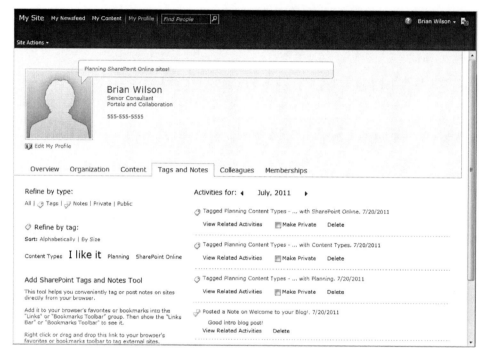

FIGURE 3-11 Using the SharePoint Online social features, you can see an individual's most used tags in the highlighted area on the left and his recent activity from his profile in the highlighted area on the right.

Links can be security trimmed by selecting one of the different options in the Administration Center. Browse to the User Profiles page, and then click Setup My Sites. This is where you will find the various options to security trim links in activity feeds, ratings, social tags, and notes so that they are hidden from viewers who are not authorized to see them. The options are as follows:

- Check All Links For Permission
- Check Only Specified Links For Permission
- Show All Links Regardless Of Permission

By selecting the options to check all links or specific links, there might be some delay with the links appearing on the page. The good thing about checking the links, though, is users won't get to a SharePoint site for which they don't have permission only to be presented with an Access Denied screen. Your best option might be to check only specified links if you know the areas to which you want to prevent or grant users access on your sites. If your sites are going to be more dynamic and users will be creating a lot of sites, then you are probably better with checking all links. Not checking any links can leave your users with a bad experience, particularly if every link they click denies access. It would be better to have a short list that they can access.

> **Note** Tagging of content is stored with the user's profile information in the social database; therefore, you must have My Sites created and configured for tagging to work correctly. Because you don't have control over the database in which the information is stored with SharePoint Online, it's just important to know that you need to have permissions set for users to access My Sites. This is covered in more detail in the next section.

My Sites

My Sites are personal sites on which you can store your documents, blog about topics, and share personal documents and information with peers. You can enter information about yourself, such as particular skills you possess or subjects in which you're interested. This information can be located with SharePoint's search functionality, which means users can connect in a whole new way, and that can help them be more productive. All of these features help to encourage collaboration and social networking within your organization.

Are My Sites Right for Me?

My Sites are a topic of discussion for many organizations as they go through the process of planning out their SharePoint Online implementations. Many organizations choose not to implement My Sites because of concerns that employees will have too much control in these areas, and the company might not be able to monitor it well enough to prevent unwanted content from being posted. These organizations fail to see how useful My Sites can be when governed correctly.

One of the benefits of using My Sites is the ability to share knowledge that might help others in the organization to solve a problem that you've already resolved, or to find other users who might be able to help you to solve a problem. Also, having one's personal documents searchable brings a huge return on investment: if you have hundreds or thousands of documents on your personal file share, it can take a lot of time to find a particular document you're looking for. With your documents in your My Site, you'll benefit from using SharePoint's search capabilities to quickly search across all your documents, thus saving you time.

By default, My Sites are divided into three areas:

- **My Newsfeed**   This is the default page that you see when you access your My Site. Here, you can see recent activities of your colleagues and interests. The colleagues' interests that are displayed are configured through your profile. To modify this list, you can click the My Interests link to open the profile for editing.

- **My Content**   This is your personal site where you can store your personal documents and other files. Content that is added to public lists and libraries here will be visible to other users. If you want to create a personal blog, this is where you access it to add new posts. You can modify this page to add or remove Web Parts.

- **My Profile**   This is where users in the organization can see your personal information that you choose to share. Some examples are a profile picture, "Ask Me About," recent blog posts, and other profile information. A tabbed view of information includes: Overview, Organization, Content, Tags And Notes, Colleagues, and Memberships. The information on these tabs is security trimmed so that private information is not shown if a viewer doesn't have the proper permission.

Other aspects to consider when planning My Sites are:

Which Users Can Create My Sites?   Perhaps your organization wants My Sites only for executive staff. With SharePoint Online, you can assign different users the ability to create a My Site and still allow other social features by setting permissions from the User Profiles page in the Administration Center.

Does the User Have the Ability to Perform Tagging?   With the options available from the User Profile page, you can manage user permissions and select which users can tag content on your sites. Tagging is useful to help with discoverability of content in SharePoint Online, so it's good to allow all users to have access to this feature.

Can the User Add Colleagues?   The ability to add colleagues is available with the Personal Features permission and allows users to keep up to date with what their peers are doing. This helps encourage users to communicate and interact with other users.

The following are the settings that control the functionality just described:

- **Create Personal Site**   All authenticated users can create a My Site by default. You can modify this setting to reduce the number of users that can perform this action.

- **Use Social Features**   All authenticated users have the ability to add ratings and perform tagging by default. This functionality can also be limited to a select group of users.

- **User Personal Features**   All authenticated users can update their profiles and add colleagues by default. You have the option to modify which users have this permission as well.

InfoPath Forms Services

You can use InfoPath Forms Services to open and fill out InfoPath forms in a browser without requiring that Microsoft InfoPath be installed on a computer. To configure InfoPath Forms Services, you need to log on to the Administration Center. The options that are available to configure are whether browser-enabled templates are allowed and an option to deliver an XML file to user agents for indexing purposes.

InfoPath forms are useful in your organization because they allow you to capture consistent information from users that you can use in your business solutions. And you can achieve all of this without writing code because InfoPath is integrated in SharePoint Online. If you intend for your users to create forms themselves, they will need to have the Microsoft InfoPath 2010 client installed on their computers, but it is not required for users who are only filling out the forms in the browser. Users can still add code to their forms and access external data sources in SharePoint lists or by web service calls. The data source has a restriction that it must either be in the same site collection or allow anonymous access because InfoPath Forms Service uses Windows Identity for authentication.

Some benefits to using InfoPath Forms Services are:

- Custom data validation allows you to control what information can be submitted in different entry fields.

- You can use customized layouts to design forms that are intuitive to use and afford easier entry.

- The built-in functionality to show and hide entry fields and the ability to create different views means that the same form can be used for multiple purposes and different audiences.

- You can use data connections to display information from other sources in your form, and you can allow for reusability of information on your site.

When you are ready to deploy your form, you can click the Quick Publish button on the File tab in InfoPath 2010, as shown in Figure 3-12. InfoPath 2010 communicates with your site and publishes your form to the library that you have configured. SharePoint Online doesn't allow you to publish forms that require full trust and also doesn't allow for custom code. Chapter 7 covers InfoPath Forms Services in more detail.

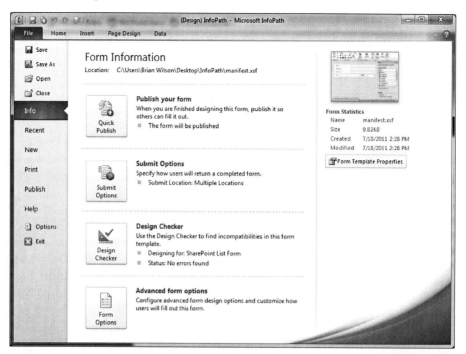

FIGURE 3-12 Use the Quick Publish button to publish your InfoPath form to your SharePoint Online site.

There are two options for filling out InfoPath forms when your environment is configured for browser-enabled forms: you can use the browser, or you can use InfoPath Filler if you have it installed on your desktop. You can configure it so that users must download forms and fill them out offline only by disabling browser-enabled forms in the Administration Center.

Managed Metadata

You can manage SharePoint Online metadata by using a feature called the *term store*, a feature of the enterprise edition of Office 365 (Plans E1–E4). The term store contains a hierarchical set of related keywords (called *term sets*), such as different policy types or office locations, that can be used to control input entry throughout your sites. Term sets help improve the consistency, reliability, and discoverability of information within your site collections. The term store is located in the SharePoint Online Administration Center and also on the Site Settings page.

Suppose that you want to have all of your office locations available as a choice field for different lists on different sites. By using a term set, you can present a consistent list on all sites and prevent disparate information between the sites. It's important to spend time planning out the different fields that you want to offer users so that the data is consistent across your various sites.

Chapter 4 covers managed metadata in more detail.

You can use the term store to organize term sets and the terms they contain from a simple user interface (see Figure 3-13). You can also import a term set if you have a large set of existing terms. However, before you can import a term set, you need to first create a group. You will then have the option to import a term set from the drop-down list on the new group.

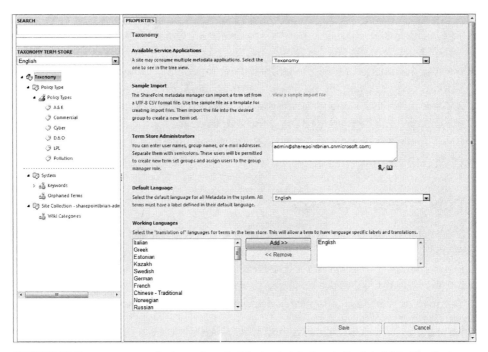

FIGURE 3-13 You can manage the term store via this simple interface in the Administration Center.

Term sets can be configured so that users can enter their own terms when adding items to lists or libraries. You can take advantage of this to collect the most common terms users enter and then clean up the term set so that only quality options are available from which subsequent users can choose. Even though a term set is open and allows for terms to be added by end users, you can change this setting in the future once you have enough of a sample set to start defining subsets or completely different term sets for your lists and libraries. By having users enter the initial set of terms, you also gain a better understanding of how Search might be updated to provide better results by using keywords and search Best Bets.

Office Web Apps

Office Web Apps is a separate offering with Office 365, but you can still use them in SharePoint Online. It is important to plan ahead and determine if you need to purchase the Office Web Apps for your organization. With Office Web Apps, you can view and edit Microsoft Word, Microsoft Excel, Microsoft PowerPoint, and Microsoft OneNote files directly from supported browsers.

To use Office Web Apps, you must first activate the Office Web Apps feature at the site collection level from the Site Settings page. Next, you need to configure your libraries to display the documents in the browser by default for editing. You can do this from the Library Settings page by using the Advanced Settings link. Set the Opening Documents In The Browser property to Open In The Browser. The next time you click one of the documents in the library, it will be presented using the web interface for the corresponding Office application. You have now successfully reduced the requirement for a specific version to be installed on each user's computer.

Public-Facing Websites

SharePoint Online comes with functionality to create a public-facing website for your organization. The website gives your organization the ability to provide content and services to external users. The website is based on SharePoint, but many of the features you have become accustomed to seeing are not available for use on the public view. The site has been designed to provide an optimized environment to host an external website.

Setting up your public-facing website is very easy to do from the SharePoint Administration Center. A special site collection is available as one of the options on the Manage Site Collections page. Once the site collection is created, your site will be ready for you to customize.

Customizing the public website in SharePoint Online is done by using the tools provided on the ribbon. You must go to the member logon area to perform any customizations, which gives you a similar view to your internal SharePoint Online sites. When you are in the member area of the site, you have the ability to add new pages, upload content, and perform other tasks. To modify the pages on your site, select the page in the Web Pages library. The page opens in edit mode and the ribbon presents the tools that you need to begin inserting items, customizing HTML, and performing design tasks.

When you are trying to determine what should be available on your pages, you can look at taking advantage of the gadgets provided with your public website. Table 3-2 lists these gadgets and describes their uses.

TABLE 3-2 Available Public-Facing Gadgets

Gadget	Description
Slide Show	Slide show albums can hold up to 50 images. You can view the images using a timer or you can manually advance through them.
HTML	Inserts custom HTML onto the page.
Map & Directions	Displays Bing Maps on your site for a specific address. You can make the map interactive and show driving directions as well.
Video	Inserts HTML embed code for external videos or inserts a link to a local video.
Contact Us	Website viewers can contact you via email by using the form provided.
PayPal	For an e-commerce site, you can accept payments through Paypal.
Stock list	Displays information about a stock symbol.
Weather	Displays weather information for a specific location.
Date modified	Displays the last date and time at which the page was modified.
Site information	Displays either the Site Title, Site Slogan, or Footer text with this gadget.

Designing the site has been optimized so that you can do all of your customizations through the web interface. The Design tab on the ribbon gives you the ability to change the look and feel of the site. You can move the navigation bar around, change colors, change images, modify the page layout, or apply your own custom cascading style sheet (CSS) to the site. You should spend time reviewing each of the areas in which you can change the design before you get a design team to create a new look for your site. The master page used for the public site has been created specifically for this site, and modifying it with SharePoint Designer might cause the site to stop functioning correctly. It's also important not to change the features that are activated on the site, because this can also destabilize your site.

Domain Name

You can specify a domain name for your public-facing SharePoint Online site through the Administration Center. Before your domain will be available as a selection on the Site Collections page, you must ensure that you own the domain through your favorite domain registrar. You also need to verify it with Microsoft Online Services site through the Office 365 Administration Center.

Planning Your Information Architecture

There are many different schools of thought regarding what Information Architecture (IA) encompasses for a SharePoint Online environment. For the purposes of planning your sites, let's define IA as the organization and presentation of the pages, documents, lists, libraries, and data in your SharePoint Online sites. Technical concepts such as sites and subsites, lists and libraries, content types, and discovery through Search and metadata are the building blocks for actually implementing IA in SharePoint Online.

You use sites and subsites to organize related information together in a single location and present it to your users. You use lists and libraries to organize the information even further, based on whether it's a document, image, textual information, and so on. Inside of those lists and libraries, a content type creates logical groups based on the meaning or purpose of the item, such as different types of cars or hardware. To each of the items in your list and libraries, you assign metadata so that it can be classified and found through Search in SharePoint Online. This metadata is used to tie content types to lists and libraries and assists in presenting quality search results.

IA Basics: Sites and Subsites

To get a good start creating quality IA for you SharePoint Online sites, you should look at your site and answer the following questions:

- How will you divide out the different sites?

    When you are deciding which site to create, you need to think about how you want your site structure to look. You also need to think about who will be using the sites and what content will be on the sites. Some options for dividing up your sites are to look at different departments, what content you will have, how sensitive the information is, and to which project it is related. With an internal Team Site, you can set permissions so that only team members have access to certain areas, and then have a separate public area for information that you want to share with everyone. This gives you flexibility when using a single site. Your other option is to create a separate site for internal teams and one for public information. This would allow you to have a separation of permissions and even allow for easier searching within a site. There might be an area that you forgot to specify permissions for internal users only, thus exposing it to all users.

- Where will you place information on different sites?

    Choosing where to place information is the subject of countless debates, but it's important to be consistent between your sites so that users don't need to remember what data is in which location. Similar sites should have consistent document libraries and lists. You can use content types to allow for storing different documents or list items in the same area. This is a good practice so that you can easily roll up content to parent sites and filter by the metadata in your content types.

■ How will your navigation be presented to the users?

Your top navigation bar should have a link to the different sites or pages to which you want to provide your users easy access. You can add as many links as you want, but the SharePoint navigation control only allows two levels of navigation if you are manu-ally entering links in the navigation page. You can modify your master page to use a different navigation tool if you have requirements for more complex navigation. The stock navigation tool can show more than two levels if you modify your master page by using SharePoint Designer to show more dynamic levels. You would need to use the options to show subsites on the Navigation Settings page and also select the option to display the same navigation items as the parent site.

On the left side of the screen, you have the Quick Launch, tree view, and metadata navigation tools that you can use to provide users with a means to get around the site they're browsing. You can modify the links to point to external sites as well, but it is better to keep these links related to the current site. The Quick Launch is the most widely used tool on most sites because it gives you the flexibility to show the links you want, whereas the tree view shows all of the various lists and libraries on your site with functionality to expand and collapse items. The metadata navigation is used when you are looking at a specific list or library. It provides a way to filter and search them easily, which is really useful on large lists or lists with a large volume of different content types.

■ Will you target information to specific audiences?

By targeting information, you can connect more personally with the users of your site, and using Audiences in SharePoint Online is how you can accomplish this. Content such as weather and local news is a good example of information you can put on Office home pages or a department site. Even though Audiences doesn't provide security to prevent users from getting to the content in another method, it is useful to get the user to see the information you want them to see. Audiences can also be used to display different navigational links on the top bar and in the Quick Launch area. This way you could give links to specific pages for a group-like management so that they don't have to dig to find the areas relevant to them.

■ How will you use managed metadata on your sites?

The information on your site is only as good what the users choose to place on it. You can give the tools to provide quality information by adding metadata to everything. With content types, you can tie metadata to every new document or list item. Metadata is additional information about each of the items. For example, a new docu-ment uploaded to your site is indexed such that when you search for it, you will prob-ably find it. But suppose that you add extra metadata to that document by using a content type, such as department, LoB, or review date. This extra metadata makes it easier still to find your document, create different views based on the data, and per-form different workflows based on the information entered. Metadata is also useful for finding items in large lists via the metadata navigation control that will appear on the left side of the page when it is configured.

■ How will you configure Search to return the best results?

The ability to find content by using Search is very important for a successful SharePoint Online site. If you have thousands of documents in SharePoint Online, being able to efficiently find content with Search is key. Search scopes are a feature with which you search a subset of content, rather than across all your content. This means you enjoy more targeted returns that don't contain thousands of non-relevant results to look through to find what they need.

You can also use keywords and Best Bets to insert specific links at the top of search results when you search on predefined terms. By default, Search is configured to show results on the default search results page and only searches the current site. This limits what information you get back, because it's limited to a single site. If you want to search across all of your sites in a site collection, then a search center will provide you with that functionality. Once you create a search center site, you can direct all of your sites to use it for search results, which ensures that all of your sites use the same search interface.

> **Note** You will need the SharePoint Online Dedicated edition if you need cross-site collection search (search across all your content in SharePoint Online, irrespective of which site collection it resides in).

Storing Information in Lists and Libraries

When you have a better understanding of the content that will reside on your site, you can begin to create lists and libraries to hold your information. There are a lot of options, and understanding your user's needs is essential. Many of the site templates can assist you by creating a useful set of default lists and libraries, but you are not limited to them, by any means. Here is a list of the available out-of-the-box lists and libraries (remember, you can always create your own custom lists and libraries):

Libraries

■ **Asset Library**   Share, browse, and manage rich media assets, such as image, audio, and video files.

■ **Data Connection Library**   Share files that contain information about external data connections.

■ **Document Library**   Store documents or other files that you want to share. Folders, versioning, and check-out is available.

■ **Form Library**   Manage business forms such as status reports or purchase orders. A compatible XML editor (for example, Microsoft InfoPath) is required to edit the files.

- **Picture Library**   Upload and share pictures.

- **Report Library**   Create and manage webpages and documents to track metrics, goals, and business intelligence information.

- **Slide Library**   Share slides from PowerPoint or compatible applications. Special features for finding, managing, and reusing slides are available.

- **Wiki Page Library**   An interconnected set of easily editable webpages, which can contain text, images, and Web Parts.

Document ID Service

There is a new feature in SharePoint Online that will help you with referencing documents in a library. The Document ID Service is a feature at the site collection level that assigns a system-generated ID to every document in the site collection. With the document ID, you have an absolute reference to the document, even if it is moved between folders or libraries. If you have existing documents, you can just check them out and then back in again to receive a new ID. This is a really useful feature that you should consider if your site is going to have a lot of documents on which users will be collaborating.

Lists

- **Announcements**   A list of new items, statuses, and other brief tidbits of information.

- **Calendar**   A calendar of upcoming meetings, deadlines, or other events. The information can be synchronized with Microsoft Outlook or other compatible applications.

- **Contacts**   A list of people your team works with, such as customers or partners. The information can be synchronized with Outlook or other compatible applications.

- **Custom List**   A blank list to which you add your own columns and views. Use this if none of the other lists contain the columns that you need.

- **Custom List in Datasheet View**   A blank list that is displayed as a datasheet to allow for easy data entry. You can add your own columns and view. A compatible ActiveX control such as the one provided in Microsoft Office is required.

- **Discussion Board**   A place to have newsgroup-style discussions. Threads are easily managed and discussion boards can be configured to moderate and approve all posts.

- **Import Spreadsheet**   A list that duplicates the columns and data of an existing spreadsheet. Excel or a compatible application is required.

- **Issue Tracking**   A list of issues or problems associated with a project or item. You can assign, prioritize, and track issue status.

- **Links**   A list of webpages or other resources.

- **Project Tasks**   A place for team or personal tasks. A Gantt chart view is provided and can be opened by Microsoft Project or another compatible application.

- **Status List**   A place to track and display a set of goals. Colored icons display the degree to which the goals have been achieved.

- **Survey**   A list of questions to which you want user to respond. Surveys allow you to quickly create questions and view graphical summaries of the responses.

- **Tasks**   A place for team or personal tasks.

Categorizing Your Information with Content Types

Content types contain site columns, workflows, custom forms, document templates and custom information for solutions, all grouped together for reusability purposes between lists and libraries. Content types are important to plan out so that you can maintain consistent content across sites. An example is a document that should contain the same metadata across departments and follow a consistent workflow. If users in each department create their own rendition of this document library, you will likely end up with inconsistencies, which can lead to complications for the organization down the road.

By using content types, you can store multiple document types, such as Word and Excel, in the same library. Lists provide you with the same functionality to have multiple content types and specify which information is related to each type of list item. Spending time with your content providers for your sites will help you to better understand what content types you might need. Here are some questions you should ask to determine what content types you need:

- What information should be captured for each content type?

  Content types are based on a parent content type such as the document content type or form content type. It contains metadata that all instances of the content type will have. If you want to create a new content type that is different from another, you need to determine what metadata makes it unique. You could have one content type that has office location and another that needs to capture business unit, for example. Each content type serves a purpose and will be available for use in other lists and libraries.

- Does the content type need a retention or audit policy?

  If you have a legal requirement dictating that your organization must retain documents for a period of time, then you can identify these documents and create a content type specific to them. This will help you save storage space by not retaining unnecessary information.

- Will there be workflows tied to the content type?

  You can assign workflows to a content type so that there is a consistent process in place for creating, modifying, or deleting an item. If an employee is changing an important document, you probably want it to be reviewed and approved before it is available for all users.

- Should there be a unique document information panel when the user opens a document content type?

  The document information panel is available once you have opened a document in an Office Web App or your local Office application. It gives you quick access to the metadata that is stored with your document in SharePoint Online. You can modify what is shown on the document information panel by creating a custom view and then applying it to your new content type. This can be useful for capturing metadata from users when they create a new document and save it to SharePoint Online.

- At what level in the site hierarchy should the content type be created?

  The level in the site hierarchy where you create your content type is important to note because the content types will only be available on the current site and any subsites. You might want to create the content type at the site collection level (root) so that all sites can use it. Since the site collection level is the highest at which a content type can be created, you would need to recreate the content type on each site collection on which you need to use it.

  Thanks to new functionality in SharePoint Online, though, you can now share content types across all site collections by using the Content Type Syndication Hub. To access your content type hub, type **http://{rootSiteCollectionURL}/sites/contentTypeHub/** in your address bar, and then press Enter. Next, you begin creating all of your content types on this new site. Once you have the content types created, you need to publish them so that they're available to other sites. To do this, go to Team Site | Site Settings | Site Content Types, and then click your new content type name, as demonstrated in Figure 3-14.

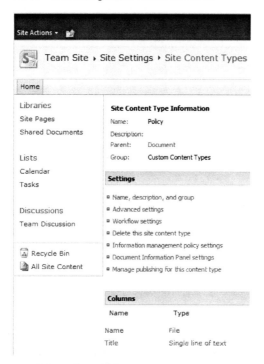

FIGURE 3-14 To publish your content type, go to Team Site | Site Settings | Site Content Types, and then click the content type that you want to make available.

In the Settings section, click the Manage Publishing For This Content Type link. In this section, you can choose to publish, unpublish, or republish your content type, as shown in Figure 3-15.

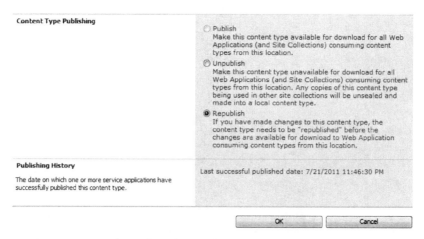

FIGURE 3-15 You can choose from three options for publishing your content type. You can also see the history of the last publishing event.

With the content type published, you can use it on your other site collections by clicking on the Content Type publishing link on the site collection Settings page. You can now refresh all of the published content types so that you can use them on your secondary site collection. Figure 3-16 shows the Content Type Publishing Hubs page, on which you can see the content type hub information as well as which content types are going to be synchronized.

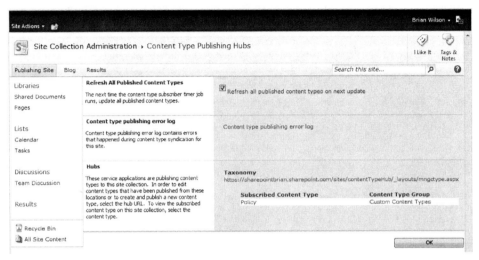

FIGURE 3-16 You synchronize one site collection's content types with the content type hub by selecting the Refresh All Published Content Types On Next Update check box. Notice the content types that are now available for use in the Hubs section.

Discoverability of Information in SharePoint Online

It's important that you provide an easy way to find the different lists, libraries, documents, and colleagues in your SharePoint Online sites. Just putting all of your information into SharePoint Online does not automatically make your users more productive. You must give them easy to use navigation and the ability to successfully find needed content.

SharePoint Online comes with different built-in tools for providing navigation to your users. The tools include top bar navigation (global navigation), Quick Launch navigation (current navigation), tree view navigation, metadata navigation, and Search. Each of these tools provides different methods for displaying navigational items. To modify the links in the global and current navigation areas, you must have Full Control or Design permissions for the site. The commands for changing the navigation are available on the Site Settings page under the Look And Feel section. If you have the publishing feature activated for your site, you will see Navigation; without publishing activated, you will see Quick Launch, top link bar, and tree view. With Search, you can create scopes that help focus the amount of content that is being searched for your terms. You also have the ability to target content with Best Bets and keywords to provide the content that you want users to find when they search for a specific term.

Global and Current Navigation

The global navigation bar, located at the top of the page, is used mostly for navigating to subsites and pages. This helps you get to sites quickly. You can apply audience filtering to the links on the global navigation bar and target the links to a specific group. This doesn't prevent users from getting to the site by a different way, but the links won't be available to them unless they are in the audience. Figure 3-17 shows the Navigation Settings page on a publishing site. Here, you can edit global and current navigation in the same page.

FIGURE 3-17 On the Navigation Settings page, you can edit the global and current navigation in the same location. There are options to show subsites and pages as well.

Current navigation includes links specific, but not limited to, the current site. The Quick Launch tool is used most often to show links to the different lists, libraries, and pages. You should use this area to direct your users to specific areas on the current site that they will be using most often. Figure 3-18 shows where the global and current navigation areas appear on the page.

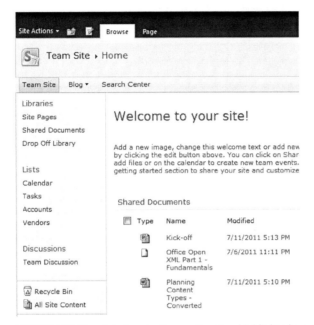

FIGURE 3-18 The global navigation section (top highlighted area) contains links to subsites and pages. The Quick Launch section (bottom highlighted area) has links to areas on the current site.

The tree view navigation (see Figure 3-19) shows the various types of site content that you would normally see on the View All Site Content page, including document libraries, lists, discussion boards, surveys, sites, and workspaces. The tree view also shows the Metadata navigation items that you have configured in your lists or libraries. By default, the tree view is not enabled on your site. To turn it on, on the Site Settings page, click the Tree View link in the Look And Feel section, and then select the Enable Tree View check box.

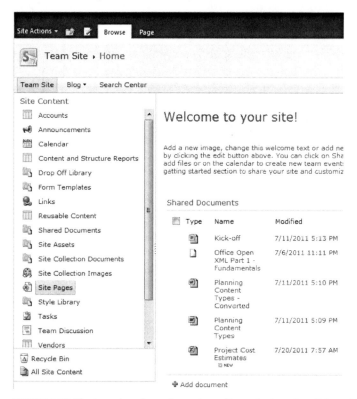

FIGURE 3-19 The tree view shows the various site content, such as lists and libraries, for the current site.

Discovering Information Through Its Metadata

By creating term sets in the term store, you can provide additional metadata navigation on your site that can assist your users in finding content in large lists or libraries (see Figure 3-20). With thousands of items and documents on your site, metadata becomes even more important because it helps distinguish information for your users.

SharePoint Online also has folders that you can use, but this provides nothing more than a visual method to find items in a list or library. When you search for an item, the folder is not going to be able to provide the type of metadata to return quality results. Folders will also not be useful when you are trying to create views of information because a folder can't be used as a property on which to filter.

There are quite a few cons (and some pros) regarding the use of folders instead of metadata. To see a more detailed comparison, see Chapter 4.

Once you create your term set, you must ensure that the Metadata Navigation And Filtering feature is activated for your site if you want to sort and filter based on your terms. You can activate the feature on the Site Settings page. In the settings for your list or library, you have the option to select which navigation hierarchy and filtering to provide to your users. You also have an option to automatically index columns in the list, which further enhances perfor-mance of queries when using metadata navigation. With SharePoint Online, the default list view threshold is set to 5,000 items. By using the metadata navigation, you can filter down the items so that you do not exceed that threshold, as illustrated in Figure 3-20.

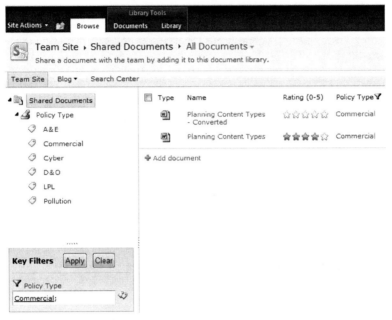

FIGURE 3-20 The metadata navigation appears in lists and libraries when configured and allows quick filtering by using key filters or clicking a tag listed in the navigation hierarchy.

Discovering Information with Search

The ability to search and get quality results for your users is a big determining factor in user adoption of your SharePoint Online site. If information can't be found by searching, then it doesn't really provide a good user experience, especially when you're trying to find one document out of a thousand.

With SharePoint Online, the content on your sites is scheduled to be crawled and indexed every 5 minutes. This means that after an item is uploaded or content is written to your site, it will not appear in the search results until the next crawl is completed. The duration of the crawl depends on other factors, such as the amount of new and updated content or the task load on the site collection at the time the crawl is initiated.

Plan Search and Metadata You can increase the accuracy of search results by using other functions in SharePoint Online, such as content types, managed metadata, search scopes, keywords, and Best Bets. Search in SharePoint Online uses a model that places a high value on the metadata of a document in addition to the contents of a document.

When you view results on the results page in your site, notice the refiners listed on the left side of the page. These refiners are based on the metadata associated with the results returned from a user's search query. These refiners help filter the search results so that users can get more relevant content. This again points to the significance of metadata and document tagging. Without metadata, your users cannot benefit from the refining options and will suffer a poor search experience.

Plan Search Scopes Search scopes are tools to narrow the area of content that is searched by the user's query. Search scopes are created at the site collection level from the Site Settings page. When creating search scopes, you are given the option to add the scope to a display group such as Search drop-down list that will determine when your new scope is available for users to select and use (see Figure 3-21). You can also choose to specify an alternate search results page to which the user is directed when this scope is used. An example of a search scope that you can create is to specify a site such as a department site. You could create a rule that includes all items in that site and below. Your search results will now be narrowed down to only the content on those sites.

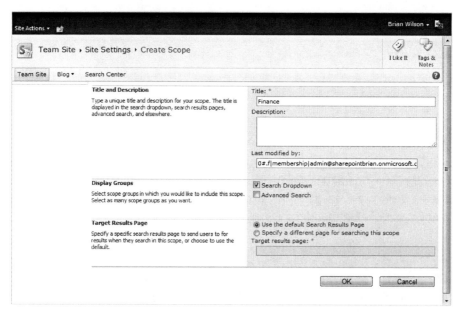

FIGURE 3-21 You can choose in which display group your search scope will appear.

Plan Search Results Look and Feel   You also have the option to target your search results to a custom page if you want to modify what your search results look like for the new scope. For example, perhaps you want to create a custom people search results page that gleans custom profile properties such as phone number and office location. You can edit the out-of-the-box search results Web Parts and tailor the XSL to render your custom properties, and then present the results as you see fit.

Plan Search Keywords and Best Bets   The ability to target a specific document or link to users when they search for a predefined term can be accomplished by using keywords and Best Bets. These tools are useful to pass information to a user any time she performs a search on a term and it is most likely the information she is looking for. For example, when a user searches for the term "calendar" and you always want to provide a link to the corporate calendar, you would add "calendar" as a keyword and set the Best Bet link to point to the corporate calendar. To add keywords, you click the Search Keywords link on the site collection settings page.

It is important to note that the keyword or its synonyms must match the exact term the user entered in the search. The keyword "calendar" will not return the Best Bet if the user searches for "calendars" (plural). In this case, you would want to add a second keyword, "calendars." When search results are returned and they do contain a Best Bet link, it will be at the top of the search results and labeled with a star.

Plan Search Result Security Trimming   Sometimes there is sensitive information that you don't want to be indexed or information that you don't want to dilute your results. To remove this information, you can change the settings for a specific library or list on the Advanced Settings page, as demonstrated in Figure 3-22.

Note If you have permissions configured on a list or library to prevent users from seeing sensitive information, SharePoint Online will automatically remove it from the search results, whether or not you modify the advanced settings on a list or library.

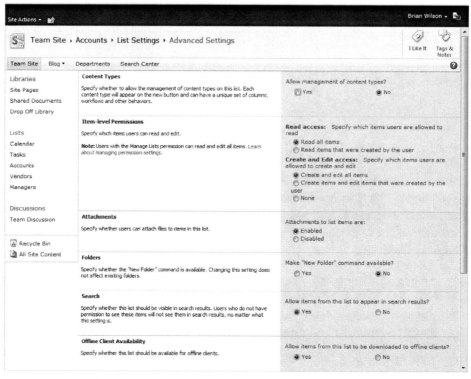

FIGURE 3-22 To remove a list or library from search results, Select the No option on the Advanced Settings page for the list or library.

Note Another method is to use the exclusion functionality provided by adding rules search scopes.

Planning User Management and Security

Properly planned user management and security is important to a well-designed SharePoint Online site. At the highest level, you will have a SharePoint Online administrator who can perform all of the user management.

User Accounts in Office 365

SharePoint Online has a set of defined administrator roles that you can assign to users. The following is a list of the roles and their purpose:

- **Billing administrator**   Makes purchases, manages subscriptions, manages support tickets, and monitors service health.

- **Global administrator**   The top-level administrator in your organization. When you sign up to purchase Office 365, you become a global administrator. Global administrators have access to all features in the Administration Center, and only global administrators can assign other administrator roles. There can be more than one global administrator at your company.

- **Password administrator**   Resets passwords, manages service requests, and monitors service health. Password administrators can reset passwords only for users and other password administrators.

- **Service administrator**   This role manages service requests and monitors service health.

- **User management administrator**   Resets passwords, monitors service health, and manages user accounts, user groups, and service requests. Some limitations apply to the permissions of a user management administrator. For example, a user management administrator cannot delete a global administrator or create other administrators. Also, user management administrators cannot reset passwords for billing, global, and service administrators.

Other user accounts are added from the Microsoft Online Services management site. When you add normal users, you do not associate them with an administrator role, but instead add them to the correct security group on your SharePoint Online site.

External Access with Share Site

SharePoint Online provides a Share Site feature so that you will be able to send an email notification to internal and external users that grants them access to your site. On your site collection, you need to activate the External User Invitations feature to be able to send emails to external users. Otherwise, when you click on Share Site, a message appears, informing you that you cannot give access to external users.

Once you enter the user's email address and send the invitation, he will receive an email that contains instructions on how to accept the invitation. It's important to note that the user's email address must be a Windows Live Hotmail address (@hotmail.com, @live.com, and @msn.com). When the user clicks the Accept link in the email, he is directed to the site you are sharing. A prompt will appear, asking him to sign in with either a Windows Live Hotmail account or a Microsoft Online Services ID. After you have sent the email to the user, you can change his permission level for the site. By default, invited users are put in the Site Visitor group.

Team Site Access

When you create a new SharePoint Online for enterprises account, a Team Site is created for you by default. Your global administrator can grant your users access to the site and modify permissions and memberships from the Site Settings page. As users need access to the site, the site owner will need to grant them access.

Single Sign-On

With SharePoint Online, you can configure single sign-on so that users can apply their corporate credentials to access sites. To configure this, you must plan to have Active Directory Federation Services 2.0 (ADFS 2.0) installed and configured in the user's on-premises data center. In addition, the following must also be installed or performed:

- Windows 2003 or higher with Active Directory with either mixed or native mode for the functional level.

- Active Directory Synchronization on Windows Server 2003 or higher. You must install the Microsoft Online Services Directory Synchronization tool.

- Windows Server 2008 or higher with ADFS 2.0 installed and ADFS 2.0 proxy if your users are connecting from outside your corporate network.

- Establish a trust with Office 365 by using the Microsoft Online Services Module for Windows PowerShell.

- Install any updates or required files to your users' computers to ensure that their operating systems, browsers, and software are at the level required to work with Office 365 and SharePoint Online.

Chapter 5 covers single sign-on in much greater detail.

Permission Levels and Group Membership

SharePoint Online provides you with a default set of security groups that you can use for assigning permissions to users. Table 3-3 presents the different groups and their associated permission levels.

TABLE 3-3 Groups and Permission Levels Available in SharePoint Online

Group	Permission level	Description
Approvers	Approve	Members of this group can edit and approve pages, list items, and documents.
Designers	Design, Limited Access	Users can view, add, update, delete, approve, and customize items or pages in the site.
Hierarchy Managers	Manage Hierarchy	Members of this group can create sites, lists, list items, and documents.
Restricted Readers	Restricted Read	Members of this group can view pages and documents, but cannot view historical versions or review user rights information.
Style Resource Readers	Limited Access	Members of this group are have Read permission to the Master Page Gallery and Restricted Read permission to the Style Library. By default, all authenticated users are a member of this group.
Members	Contribute	Users are allowed to add or change items on the site pages or in lists and document libraries.
Owners	Full Control	Users have all permissions on the site.
Visitors	Read	Users are allowed to view items on the site pages.
Viewers	View Only	Members of this group can view pages, list items, and documents. If the document has a server rendering available, they can only view the document by using the server rendering.
Quick Deploy Users	Contribute to the Quick Deploy Items library, Limited Access	Members of this group can schedule Quick Deploy jobs.

When planning for security, it is important to keep your security plan as simple as possible or run the risk that it will become a maintenance problem. Also take advantage of the default groups to keep maintenance from getting out of control (Owners, Members, Visitors, and so on).

Caution SharePoint Online subsites inherit the permissions of their parent site. Exercise care if you are planning to have sensitive information on a site.

> **Note** You can break the permission inheritance and create unique security groups and permissions if you want, but try not to do this often, because the more you break inheritance, the greater the maintenance burden you'll have.

Planning Customizations

SharePoint Online provides three methods of customization: you can use the browser, supported applications, and developer tools. Each option has advantages for customizing the various areas on SharePoint Online. You can customize areas like branding and views of lists and libraries and move page contents to different zones by using the browser. These are the easiest pieces to modify and don't require extensive training.

If you want or need to apply more advanced customizations, such as modifying master pages, page layouts, and workflows, you need to use supported applications such as Microsoft SharePoint Designer 2010, Microsoft InfoPath 2010, or other supported applications like Microsoft Access 2010, Excel 2010, Visio 2010, and Word 2010.

The last area for customization requires both a developer skillset and Microsoft Visual Studio 2010. The solutions created in Visual Studio need to be deployed as sandboxed solutions, but still provide a wide variety of possibilities for customizing SharePoint Online. Solutions created with Visual Studio will take longer to develop, but offer the highest level of customization and requirements flexibility.

Just because you can use Visual Studio 2010 doesn't mean every solution needs to be done with this method. The best option for customization is to try and use out-of-the-box functionality before engaging in solution development. This will save your organization time and money. Chapter 7 provides more information about customizations.

Supported Tools

The following tools can be used to make customizations to SharePoint Online, beyond what you can do in the browser:

- **SharePoint Designer 2010** Use this application to modify data forms, update the look and feel, modify pages, create workflows with extended functionality, and connect to data sources for content aggregation.

- **InfoPath 2010** Use this when you want to create a custom form and make it more user friendly. With InfoPath 2010, you can validate information before it is submitted to your site, which helps maintain data quality.

- **Office 2010**   When combined with SharePoint Online, the Office suite of products and their associated web services can provide rich solutions that help your users save time and work more efficiently.

- **Visual Studio 2010**   If you need to create a highly-customized solution that uses the core functionality of SharePoint Online, this is the tool to use. With SharePoint Online, you have to design your solution to be deployed as a sandboxed solution, as opposed to the more traditional approach of building full-trust solutions (more on this in Chapter 7).

Plan Branding

SharePoint Online can help your business perform the actions to get work done, but users are used to having a nice-looking site to view at most organizations. SharePoint Online is designed to give you multiple ways to customize the look and feel.

The easiest method is to use the built-in themes to change the colors of the site. You can still have the SharePoint Online look and feel, but you can alter the colors and fonts. You can also change the site icons and apply a custom style sheet through the Site Settings page if you have publishing enabled on your site.

Once your marketing or creative departments see the site, they'll likely want to change the site beyond just colors and fonts. This is where you will want a tool such as SharePoint Designer 2010 or Visual Studio 2010. For branding purposes in SharePoint Online, SharePoint Designer 2010 works for most organizations. With this tool, you can create and modify master pages, page layouts, and style sheets. With these files, you can completely remove the SharePoint Online look and apply almost any design you want. There are some elements that you must retain to provide full functionality in SharePoint Online. The ribbon contains many of the links and tools needed for your users to complete tasks in SharePoint Online, so you need to include it in your design.

Visual Studio 2010 gives you the ability to create a reusable solution and code for elements like event receivers that you can't access in SharePoint Designer 2010. You can create master pages, page layouts, and style sheets, just as you can with SharePoint Designer 2010, but now you can package them up into a solution package (.wsp files) that you can distribute to your site collection administrators so that they can upload it to the solutions gallery on their site collections as well.

With Visual Studio 2010, you can also add feature receivers for applying your branding when a feature is activated. You can also add an event receiver that applies branding automatically when a new site is provisioned.

Plan Page Customization

To customize content on a page, the easiest method is to click Site Actions, and then choose Edit Page. You can add, remove, and move Web Parts around on the page in Edit mode. There are also rich text areas in which you can type and style text using the tools provided on the ribbon.

If you need to customize, such as creating a custom view of information that is beyond the options in the browser, then SharePoint Designer 2010 can help you. With SharePoint Designer 2010, you can insert a Data View and customize the XSLT to conform to your unique look and feel.

Visual Studio 2010 is another option for customizing the page. A compelling option would be to create a Silverlight Web Part to provide a rich, graphical, and dynamic user experience. In addition, you can share Visual Studio customizations among site collections. For more information on these customizations, see Chapter 7.

Plan Workflows

SharePoint Online comes with a variety of built-in workflows. These are simple workflows with which you can perform tasks such as approval on an item when it is added to a list or library. The other workflows provided are: Collect Feedback, Collect Signatures, Disposition Approval, and the Three-State workflow.

While the out-of-the-box workflows are nice, they don't afford you the ability to perform more advanced tasks. For those tasks, you can use SharePoint Designer 2010 to create no-code, custom workflows. These workflows can send emails and use custom activities. It's likely that the majority of functionality that you'll ever need to execute a workflow can be found in SharePoint Designer 2010.

If the workflow you need to create is still too complex to develop in SharePoint Designer, and you need to create a fully customizable workflow, then you need to bring in the big guns: Visual Studio 2010. This option gives you the highest level of customization with which you can create virtually any solution for your workflow. The key is that your solution must be deployed as a sandboxed solution, so you are limited in the data sources that you can access externally, unless you take advantage of the client object model.

 Note For more in-depth information about building custom workflows, read *SharePoint 2010 Workflows in Action* by Phil Wicklund (2011, Manning Publications Co.).

Planning User Training

One of the most important elements to plan for a SharePoint Online implementation is user training. Without proper training, your users will be left to figure how to properly use the site on their own. Some users are good self-learners, but this probably won't be true of everyone in the company. The best approach is to start at the top with administrators and work your way down to the end users.

Who?

The administrators of your sites are the ones who ensure that your SharePoint Online environment is running smoothly. You need to identify the different administrators who need training. They include: Office 365 administrators, SharePoint Online administrators, site collection administrators, and site administrators/owners.

Once the administrators are trained, you can begin to focus on the site content owners and end users. The concept of *train the trainer* means that you provide the highest level of training to a select few individuals and then they can train the end users of their own respective sites and site collections.

What?

Table 3-4 shows the different administration levels and the duties associated with each.

TABLE 3-4 **The Administrative Levels and Their Duties**

Role	Duties
Office 365 administrator	Access to all features and responsible for assigning permissions and roles to other administrators. Responsible for: ■ Adding users ■ Creating security groups ■ Adding domains ■ Managing licenses ■ Purchasing additional services ■ Managing service requests

Role	Duties
SharePoint Online administrator	Manage the features of SharePoint Online, including: ■ Managing/creating site collections ■ Configuring storage and usage allocation ■ Configuring InfoPath Forms Services ■ Managing user profiles ■ Managing user profile properties ■ Personalization permissions and features ■ Managing My Sites ■ Managing social tagging and notes ■ Managing the Term Store
Site collection administrator	Manage the various site collection features, including: ■ Creating/managing security groups ■ Configuring search scopes and other search settings ■ Activating site collection–scoped features ■ Configuring site collection navigation settings ■ Creating/managing site collection policies ■ Configuring content type publishing ■ Managing sandboxed solutions ■ Monitoring audit logs
Site administrator	Manage a site for content and governance compliance. Other responsibilities are: ■ Assigning site permissions ■ Creating/managing lists and libraries ■ Setting themes and styles ■ Managing site-scoped features ■ Configuring site languages ■ Monitoring workflows

Where?

Training is provided all over the world, so you should be able to find something close to where your users are located. If it is a higher level class for someone like an administrator, he might need to travel to receive better quality training. It's helpful to formally train your site collection administrators in some sort of Power End User course. Once your site collection administrators have received training, then most of the training after that can take place at your office locations. You can hold events—perhaps a lunch—and train users without losing time at work. Another option is to create online training videos for users to watch anytime. There are several third-party training organizations that sell computer-based training for your end users, featuring helpful how-to videos of common tasks such as working with documents.

When?

The earlier you can get your administrators to training, the better. That will give them time to absorb the information and begin practicing on the SharePoint Online site. The end user training can come just before you go live with your site—this way they don't have to miss work for extended periods of time.

Planning Ongoing Maintenance and Governance

SharePoint Online is evolving all the time, which is one of the benefits of using it over an on-premises installation. You will always have access to the newest features when they are available. You need to plan for this evolution.

Ongoing Maintenance

Maintaining your SharePoint Online sites involves monitoring the amount of storage each site collection is using and performing regular evaluations of the content to see if it can be removed or archived. Audit logs can help you determine what is being used and modified on your sites. This can help you to identify content that isn't being used and can be deleted. You must enable audit logging at the site collection level for the reports to be available.

Another area about which you need to be aware is that of large lists and libraries, because they will degrade the user experience with your site if you are not prepared to throttle resources or limit the number of items returned in a view. With SharePoint Online, you can now support large lists and libraries, but you need to ensure that you understand how to use them effectively to avoid crossing the thresholds.

Governance

Governance is very important to a successful SharePoint Online implementation. Governance is best described as a set of policies, roles, responsibilities, and processes that define how your organization uses SharePoint to achieve business goals. The topic of governance covers a vast amount of information, and there are many opinions on what should be included in a governance plan. Because governance is such a large topic, this section does not intend to be exhaustive. Rather, it will help introduce you to governance by presenting some high-level considerations.

The first step toward achieving good governance is to identify the key decision makers for the governance plan. These individuals need to be at the highest level of your organization so that you have executive buy-in—and of course, because these are the people who can direct resources to get the job done. Once identified, a series of meetings needs to take place during which the policies, roles, responsibilities, and processes can be defined and agreed upon.

With the governance plan in place, your administrators and users should have a solid source of guidance when working in SharePoint Online. Users can reference the guidelines when making plans, such as which sites should be created, who should have a specific permission level, and which process must documents follow before they are submitted to the site.

Why?

So why have governance? Governance brings order and control to an area that can become chaotic and unmanageable. With well-defined leadership and a solid governance plan, your users will have better adoption. If adoption of your SharePoint Online site is good, then ROI will enjoy higher user adoption, and your SharePoint Online implementation will be a success for your organization. This is what every executive wants to see when she makes an investment for the future of her organization. The following list shows the high-level business objectives of a governance plan:

- Mitigate and reduce risk
- Establish guidelines and boundaries
- Empower business users by reducing dependency on technology experts
- Improve trust and confidence between administrators and end users

What?

Now that you know why to have governance, you need to know over what you should governance. There are many areas of your SharePoint Online environment that need to have guidelines in place, such as IA, security, roles, document compliance, standards, search, growth management, and support. These areas need to be thought through with your key decision makers and documented.

The IA of your site needs to be designed in a way that it is easy to find information and keep it from being duplicated. The trouble is that you can have good intentions and design a wonderful IA, but how do you ensure that it is enforced and kept up to date after go-live? This is where governance comes in.

Security is another consideration that needs to be carefully thought through, such as whether placing a file in one library is going to expose financial information or other secure information. Security should play a role in your IA, along with actually performing periodic audits of your content to ensure that no inappropriate content is in the wrong place. Often, auditors will use Search to find inappropriate content.

Document compliance and standards need to be well defined to handle things like Sarbanes-Oxley (SOX) compliance and the Health Insurance Portability and Accountability Act (HIPAA). Users need to know what content is required for every form of compliance your organization is required to meet. Site templates can be used to help create the shell for a compliant site, and users can reference your governance plan for the rest of their questions and concerns.

As more and more content is generated, you need to have the guidelines in place on how to handle things like retention and site cleanup. With SharePoint Online, wasted space is actually costing your organization money, particularly if you have exceeded your storage quota and had to purchase more. Users need to understand this and be aware what information is a good candidate for deletion.

Finding all of the content in your SharePoint Online site is done easily when you are utilizing all of the tools provided. You need to document which features of Search you want to take advantage of, like search scopes, keywords, Best Bets, term sets, and Search Center. The Search Center helps keep search results displayed consistently across your sites. Search scopes and term sets help you to refine your search and results to get more accurate information. Keywords and Best Bets will make sure your users are given direction to the best content related to their queries.

With all of the information and functionality provided with SharePoint Online, you can guarantee that your users will have questions. As they become more familiar with the site and your organization provides them with training, they will be able to survive on their own. It's important, though, to have support channels in place for the questions and issues that they do run into. It's good to define a structured path for escalating these questions and issues so that users understand who to go to for help. Many organizations have systems in place already, but it is important to define and document the process for your new SharePoint Online environment because many Help Desks aren't adequately prepared to answer all of the questions that SharePoint can stimulate. This also ties into making sure that your support staff has the training they need and they understand the impacts of the resolutions they are providing to end users.

How?

Governance is best done in a top-down approach, as shown in Figure 3-23. The idea is to use committees of governance team members that meet regularly to discuss the "state" of SharePoint. The following are examples of some questions that your team needs to be asking on a regular basis:

- What's our business purpose for SharePoint?
- It's been a year since we released, are we managing to our original vision or have we deviated?
- What new sites were created this month, and what are they being used for?
- What sites are going stale and need to be updated?
- How are our users utilizing Search, and are they finding the information they need?

It's helpful to create three committees that each advocate different areas of responsibility. The members of these committees are responsible for championing your environment and pushing adoption to the rest of your organization. The following are the suggested committees (which can also be seen in Figure 3-23):

- **Policy Governance Board**   This committee includes key stakeholders such as the CIO. They set the vision for SharePoint, such as what it should and shouldn't be used for, and most importantly, the 12-month roadmap. The roadmap shows where you are today, and where you need to be in 12 months. The policy committee has the authority to enforce and hold resources accountable for the execution of their roadmap.

- **IT Governance Board**   This committee takes the policy and roadmap and executes. Responsibilities could include implementing new site collections to support the vision, ongoing maintenance to keep the sites running, and promoting optimal usability (such as maintaining search and information architecture).

- **Board of Content Managers**   This committee is representative of all the site collection administrators. Administrators should regularly get together to discuss problems each are facing and brainstorm solutions and best practices. This committee serves as a platform for training, mentoring, and enforcement of best practices.

FIGURE 3-23 How to govern your SharePoint Online environment, using a top-down approach for adoption. Each level has different responsibilities to help keep compliance.

Who?

It is also important to define the various roles and the associated responsibilities. In fact, having the right people held accountable to the right tasks is probably the most important governance tenant there is. Without people actually "governing," you won't have governance.

It's important to have employees from all areas of the organization involved with the governance of your SharePoint Online environment. You need to create a governance committee that includes end-users, IT professionals, and management. The various roles that these individuals will fill are:

- **Executive champion**   An individual or individuals who are at the highest level in the company. Their buy-in and involvement will help determine the adoption throughout the organization.

- **Financial stakeholders**   This individual is going to make sure that the highest return on investment is achieved.

- **Product manager**   This is the person chiefly held responsible for the overall success and governance of your SharePoint Online deployment. The buck needs to stop somewhere, and having a dedicated product manager will greatly increase your success.

- **Technical architect**   This person is held responsible for all custom solutions deployed to your SharePoint Online sites.

- **Information specialists**   This group of individuals includes information architects and taxonomists. Their chief responsibility is to categorize content appropriately, ensure that searching produces good results, and help end users find content easier.

- **Site collection administrators**   Individuals in this group ensure that the site is functional for their respective sites.

Part II
Deploying SharePoint in the Public Cloud

Part II focuses solely on Microsoft SharePoint in the public cloud. Specifically, these chapters take a deep dive into Microsoft's public SharePoint offering, called SharePoint Online.

This part opens with Chapter 4, which introduces you to all the techniques for administering your SharePoint Online sites. This includes global administration through the Microsoft Office 365 Administration Center, including creating and managing sites, site quotas, user profiles, and managed metadata.

Chapter 5 builds on Chapter 4 by focusing on identity management and authentication. You'll learn the different identity provider options and the pros and cons of each. The chapter also focuses heavily on identity federation, the technology whereby your users can enjoy a single sign-on experience between their on-premises sites and SharePoint Online. The chapter concludes with details on managing identity with Windows Remote PowerShell.

Chapter 6 helps you understand how to migrate SharePoint on-premises to SharePoint Online. It compares the different migration approaches between SharePoint Online Standard and Dedicated editions.

Chapter 7 concludes this part of the book with an introduction to customizing SharePoint Online to meet your company's unique needs. It includes information on building your own custom sandboxed solutions and using SharePoint Designer to brand your sites, as well as a brief discussion about how to integrate SharePoint Online with Windows Azure.

Chapter 4
Administering SharePoint Online

In this chapter, you will learn to:

- Manage site collections in SharePoint Online

- Configure InfoPath Forms Services settings

- Administer the term store and apply metadata

- Manage user profiles and properties

Now that you've had an introduction to Microsoft SharePoint in the cloud as well as a thorough look at Microsoft Office 365, it's time to really dig in and start administering SharePoint Online. After you are first assigned your Office 365 site, you'll also receive a single SharePoint Online site collection. It's your job to create more site collections and assign owners to those site collections. Also, with SharePoint Online, you can host one public-facing website, so you'll need to go through the process of registering your domain and provisioning that website.

In addition to creating sites, you'll also want to pay attention to site quotas. You'll only have a certain amount of disk storage and server resources available to you, so it's important to carefully evaluate how and where to apply those resources. Disk space is somewhat predictable: "How much space will this site need?" is usually translated into *number of documents × average size × number of versions*. However, server resource allocation is a bit trickier. Resources are a point system that SharePoint assigns to you based on how many CPU cycles, database queries, and so on that your sandboxed solutions use. It's your job to provide your sites with the appropriate amount of resources, or all of your sandboxed solutions will stop working for the day when you hit your quota. Beyond monitoring quotas, there are other important administrative tasks, such as granting site collection administrator rights, assigning a default site, and managing external access to sites.

After you have a good handle on managing sites in SharePoint Online, the next step is to familiarize yourself with how to administer Microsoft InfoPath Forms Services, User Profiles, and the Managed Metadata Term Store. The Term Store is of particular significance. When Microsoft creates your first site for you, all you have is an empty shell. Without careful planning, such as how to tag and surface that content via content types and Search, your users will struggle to find their documents. By creating managed metadata, you can dramatically increase the discoverability of information; thus extracting much more value out of your site.

Managing Site Collections

Probably the most important thing you do in the Administration Center is creating and modifying the site collections for your business. There are several administrative actions that you can execute on new or existing site collections on the Site Collections tab, as shown in Figure 4-1, which include:

- Creating and deleting site collections, including public-facing websites

- Viewing properties of existing site collections

- Assigning site collection administrators

- Managing site collection quotas

- Specifying the default site collection

- Managing external sharing (Partner Access)

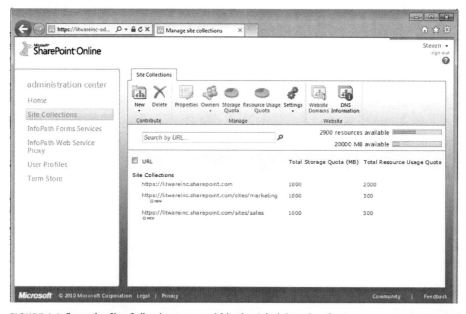

FIGURE 4-1 From the Site Collections page within the Administration Center, you can create new site collections and modify existing ones.

Creating a New Private Site Collection

Creating a new site collection is a very simple process. On the Site Collections tab (see Figure 4-1) on the ribbon, click the New button. A familiar dialog box opens, in which you can specify the site collection's properties before you provision it, as illustrated in Figure 4-2.

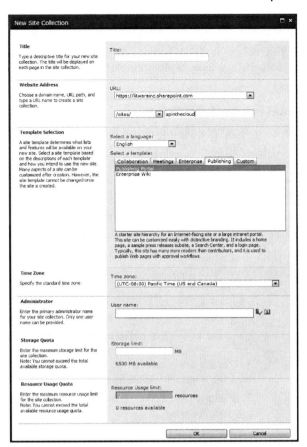

FIGURE 4-2 When you create a new site, you must specify the title, URL, and the template for the site (among other properties).

The following are the properties that you need to specify before the site collection can be provisioned:

- **Title**   The title of the site collection will appear in bold font at the top left of the site after it has been created. This value can be changed later by using Site Settings.

- **Web Site Address**   This property specifies the URL/domain where the site can be accessed. First you need to specify the root URL, which is most commonly your company name followed by ".sharepoint.com." Next, specify the path under the domain in which the site will be created. This will be either "sites" or "teams." Finally, pick a URL path that is unique to this new site, preferably with no spaces.

Note   If you registered a custom domain through the Office 365 Admin Overview dialog box, that custom domain will appear in this drop-down list.

■ **Template Selection**   You must specify the site template that you want the site to use. If you want to specify the template later, on the Custom tab, you can specify to apply no template. Table 4-1 presents the available templates, along with their descriptions.

TABLE 4-1 Available Site Templates in SharePoint Online

Template name	Template description
Team Site	This site template is the most common one that you will likely use. When provisioned, you get a host of starter content, such as an announcements list, events list, document and picture libraries, and a tasks list. Additionally, for each of those lists, there is a corresponding Web Part on the Home page to make it easy for users to retrieve their team's information.
Blank Site	This template creates a blank site with no lists, libraries, or Web Parts. If you want to build your site from scratch, use this template.
Document Workspace	This template helps your team to collaborate on a single document. Perhaps the document is a sales proposal, and the proposal has associated tasks, meetings, or other documents. The Document Workspace template is a great way to create a workspace to manage all of that associated content in a single, accessible location.
Blog	The Blog template is self explanatory; it helps you create and manage blogs in your SharePoint Online deployment. It includes some nice features such as comments, categories, and a tag cloud. Also, you can author your posts in Microsoft Word and publish them directly to the cloud, or you can author the posts from within the browser.
Group Work Site	The Group Work Site is similar to the Team Site, with the exception of a few additional lists, such as the Group Calendar, Circulations list, and the Phone Call Memo list.
Express Site	The express site is a cross between a wiki library and a Team Site. You get a document library for document sharing, a note board on the Home page for quick updates, and wiki pages for quick authoring of page content.
Visio Process Repository	This template helps you to manage your business process diagrams. You can centralize all your processes and keep standards and templates for users. It also provides browser-based rendering of diagrams as well as surfacing of validation errors in those documents.

Template name	Template description
Meeting Workspace(s)	A meeting workspace is used to track the agendas, decisions, and outcomes of a meeting or series of meetings. Often, they are used in conjunction with a calendar, in which each recurring meeting has its own workspace.
Document Center	A document center is essentially a dedicated site for a large document library.
PowerPoint Broadcast Site	You can use this template to broadcast a Microsoft PowerPoint presentation to remote user devices. All the user needs to do is click a link to begin watching your broadcast. By default, the broadcast mechanism is a public service hosted by Microsoft, but if you want a friendly URL, you can create a broadcast site and point your presentation to that site instead.
Basic Search Center	A Search Center allows you to customize the Search Web Parts, thereby altering the look and feel of the search experience.
Publishing Portal	The Publishing Portal template is the main web content management template for SharePoint. Most public-facing websites built on SharePoint use this template because of its built-in workflow and publishing capabilities.
Enterprise Wiki	A wiki is similar to a Team Site. Users can easily create new pages of content, but in addition, there's built-in rating and commenting.

Licensing and Unsupported Templates

Not all templates can be used with all licenses, or are even supported in SharePoint Online. For example, to use the enterprise features of SharePoint, you need to have either E3 or E4-level licensing for your users. Also, kiosk or partner users are not eligible for their own My Site. With this in mind, the following site templates have licensing restrictions:

- Collaboration
- Visio Process Repository (needs E3 or E4 user license)

There are also some templates that are not supported in SharePoint Online, such as the records center, FAST Search Center, Enterprise Search Center, and the My Site Host. Although these site templates are in the template picker, they should not be used because their features are not supported (or in the case of My Site Host, Microsoft creates one on your behalf).

- **Time Zone**   Select the time zone to which the site should be assigned (necessary for calendaring and other tasks).

- **Administrator**   Every site collection needs one primary site collection administrator. After the site has been provisioned, you can add more administrators.

- **Storage Quota**   To help manage your disk utilization, you can specify storage quotas for your sites. When the site collection reaches the quota, users of that site collection will no longer be able to add new content to any site in that collection. Also, after the site collection has been provisioned, you can set up email alerts to the site collection administrator to notify her when the site is reaching quota.

- **Resource Usage Quota**   Sandboxed solutions, when executing, consume what are called *resource points*. If you have a lot of solutions in a given site collection, you might find that site collection is consuming a lot of these points. The point quota is used to regulate how much load is put on the servers for these custom-coded sandboxed solutions. Each SharePoint Online customer is allotted only a certain amount of points. It is the customer's responsibility to determine how to distribute these points among its site collections.

Subsite Templates

There are other templates available only as subsites after the top-level site has been created. These include Assets Web Database, Charitable Contributions Web, Contacts Web Database, Issues Web Database, Projects Web Database, Microsoft Project Site, Personalization Site, and Search Center.

Creating a New Public-Facing Website

Creating a new public-facing website is very similar to creating a new site collection; however, there are two differences. First, you need to own a domain with a domain registrar, and that domain's DNS CNAME entry must point to SharePoint Online. After that domain has been configured with Office 365, you'll see it appear in the Website Address drop-down list, as illustrated in Figure 4-3.

For instructions on how to set up a new domain that works with SharePoint Online, see Chapter 2, "Office 365 Feature Overview."

FIGURE 4-3 After you register your domain in Office 365, it becomes available in the Website Addresses drop-down list when you create new sites.

The other big difference is the available templates from which you can choose. The only template that works in a public-facing SharePoint Online site is the publishing template. Other templates are available for subsites, but at the root, this is the only option.

Note Windows Content Management (WCM) approval workflow is not available for public-facing websites in SharePoint Online.

Deleting a Site Collection or Website

Deleting an existing site collection or website is easy—almost too easy. All you need to do is select the check box adjacent to the site on the Site Collections tab, and then on the ribbon, click the Delete button. A dialog box appears (see Figure 4-4), asking to you confirm the deletion of the site; clicking the Delete button will confirm the action.

Note When you delete a site collection, it's gone. Don't expect to be able to get it back without paying an administrative fee (if at all).

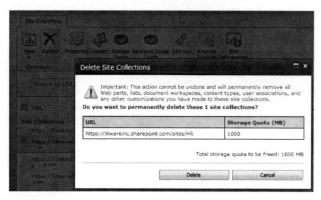

FIGURE 4-4 To delete a site collection, select it, and then on the ribbon, click the Delete button.

Viewing the Properties of a Website

After a site collection has been provisioned, you can view that site collection's properties in the Site Collection Properties window by clicking the View Properties button on the ribbon of the Manage Site Collections page. In addition to title, description, URL, and other basic information, you'll see helpful tidbits, such as the total size of the site collection as well as the number of subsites. The window also shows the administrators who are currently assigned to the site collection as well as its quota information. Figure 4-5 shows an example of the Site Collection Properties window.

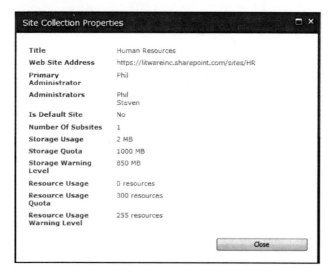

FIGURE 4-5 To view all of the main configurations for a site collection, on the ribbon, click the View Properties button.

Managing Site Collection Administrators

Site collections administrators can either be managed through the Manage Site Collections page within the Administration Center, or from within the site collection itself. However, the primary site collection administrator can only be managed through the Administration Center.

> **Note** Being a Global Office 365 Administrator does not by default grant you full control to all the site collections in SharePoint Online. You'll need to explicitly be added as a site collection administrator to each site that you need to access.

To manage administrators from within the Administration Center, click Site Collections on the left navigation pane within the Admin Center (as shown in Figure 4-1), and then on the ribbon, click Owners. A drop-down list opens that contains two options (see Figure 4-6). Select Manage Administrators to specify the site collection administrators. Choose Add Support Partner to grant access to Microsoft Support if you call the help desk with an issue that requires Help desk personnel to have access to your site.

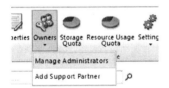

FIGURE 4-6 To grant site collection administrative permissions to a user, on the ribbon, click the Owners button, and then select Manage Administrators.

When you click Manage Administrators, a display box appears in which you can specify one primary site collection administrator and multiple secondary administrators, as demonstrated in Figure 4-7.

Manage Administrators   ☐ ✕

**Primary Site Collection
Administrator**
Specify the administrator for
this site collection. Only one
user login can be provided;
security groups are not
supported.

User name:

Phil ;

**Site Collection
Administrators**
Site Collection Administrators
are given full control over all
Web sites in the site
collection. They may also
receive site use confirmation
mail. Enter users separated
by semicolons.

Eric ; Paul ; Phil ;

OK   Cancel

FIGURE 4-7 Choose the user to whom you want to assign administrative rights to a site collection, and then click OK.

Click Add Support Partner to enable Microsoft product support staff to access your sites or your content (see Figure 4-8). By default, no one in Microsoft can access your sites or your content. If you create a ticket with product support, they may require access to one or more of your sites to rectify the issue.

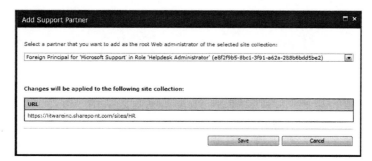

Add Support Partner   ☐ ✕

Select a partner that you want to add as the root Web administrator of the selected site collection:

Foreign Principal for 'Microsoft Support' in Role 'Helpdesk Administrator' (e8f2f9b5-8bc1-3f91-a62a-288b6bdd5be2)   ▾

Changes will be applied to the following site collection:

URL

https://litwareinc.sharepoint.com/sites/HR

Save   Cancel

FIGURE 4-8 If you need help identifying a problem, use the Add Support Partner dialog box to grant Microsoft support specialists access to your site collection.

After you click the Save button (granting product support access to the selected site collection), you'll see the support group in the administrators list of the site collection, as shown in Figure 4-9. After you've completed your work with product support, you can simply remove this group by deleting it from the site collection Administrators list, similar to how you would add a new site collection administrator.

FIGURE 4-9 The newly added support partner appears in the Administrators list in the Site Collection Properties window.

Managing Site Collection Disk and Resource Quotas

SharePoint Online provides you a limited amount of storage space and physical server resources. It's your job to then allocate this space and resources across your site collections. By default, you are allocated 10 GB of disk space. From a resources perspective, you get 5,300 points. Microsoft calculates these points based on how many physical server resources the sandboxed solutions in your site collections are consuming. For example, every 20 times you query the SharePoint database, that is one point. After your site collection reaches its resource quota, all sandboxed solutions in that site collection stop working until the next day. From a disk quota perspective, you simply cannot upload anymore documents. You can allocate storage and resources to your site collections on the Manage Site Collections page in the Administration Center. After you select one or more site collections, the Storage Quota and Resource Usage Quota buttons on the ribbon become enabled, as shown Figure 4-10.

 Note You can purchase more disk space at a rate of USD $2.50 per GB, per month.

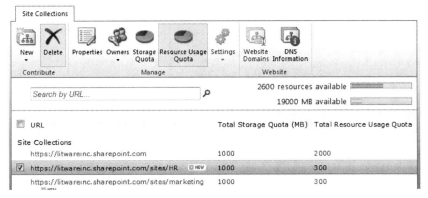

FIGURE 4-10 Storage and resource quotas can be modified by selecting the site collection, and then clicking either the Storage Quota or Resource Usage Quota ribbon buttons.

When you click the Storage Quota button, a dialog box similar to the one shown in Figure 4-11 appears, in which you can set the quota for the selected site collections. You can also set a percentage threshold at which site collection administrators will be notified that the quota limit is rapidly approaching.

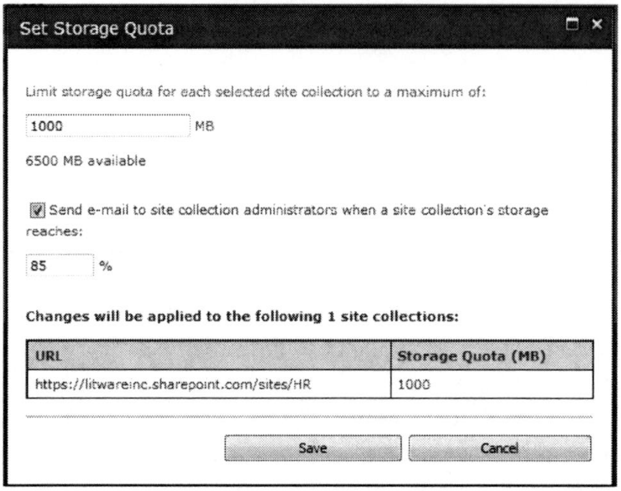

FIGURE 4-11 To set a new quota, type the number of megabytes you want to allocate, and then click Save.

The Resource Usage Quota dialog box is nearly identical to that of Storage Quota (see Figure 4-12). The most difficult aspect of this dialog box, however, is that it isn't easy to quantify in your mind what 1,000 points means. To make this more clear, Table 4-2 shows the out-of-the-box resources formula for on-premises SharePoint 2010 Server farms. SharePoint Online doesn't publish how it calculates points, but you can bet it's similar to the on-premises defaults.

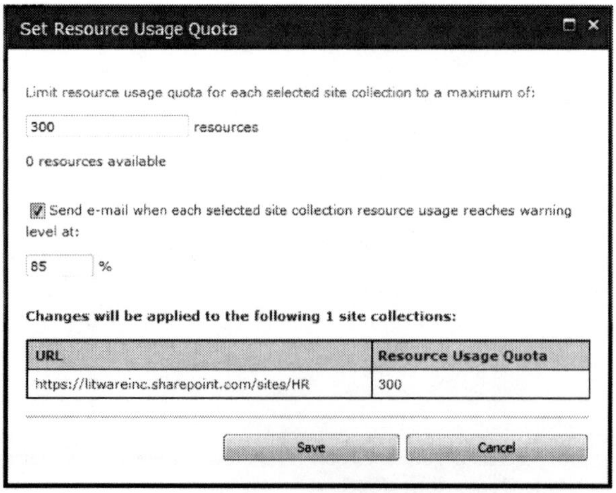

FIGURE 4-12 Similar to setting the storage quota, to enter a resource usage quota, enter the number of points in the Resources text box, and then click Save.

This calculation data is accessible by running the [`Microsoft.SharePoint.Administration`
`.SPUserCodeService]:: Local.ResourceMeasures` PowerShell command (on one line) in
an on-premises SharePoint environment. CPUExecutionTime is a notable example. Consider a
Web Part in your sandboxed solution. For each minute (3,600 milliseconds) of CPU time that
a Web Part requires, one point of your site collection's quota is used for the day. To help with
this metric, you can instruct your developers to cache as much data as possible, and therefore not utilize the CPU or SharePointDatabaseQueryCount as much. Another handy example
would be: For each 50 unhandled exceptions in your code, one point is used. The key there
would be to ensure that your developers are handling their exceptions.

**TABLE 4-2 Out-of-the-Box Resources Formula for On-Premises SharePoint 2010
Server Farms**

Server resource name	One point equivalent
AbnormalProcessTerminationCount	1
CPUExecutionTime	200
CriticalExceptionCount	10
IdlePercentProcessorTime	100
InvocationCount	100
PercentProcessorTime	85
ProcessCPUCycles:	100000000000
ProcessHandleCount	10000
ProcessIOBytes:	10000000
ProcessThreadCount:	10000
ProcessVirtualBytes	1000000000
SharePointDatabaseQueryCount	400
SharePointDatabaseQueryTime	20
UnhandledExceptionCount	50
UnresponsiveprocessCount	2

Enabling External Access to Site Collections

From the Site Actions menu in a site collection, a site collection administrator can click the
Share Site Link to send invitations to anyone in the world to come collaborate with them in
their SharePoint Online site. This is especially popular for customers or partnered users for
whom you might not want to pay the full license fee to create users in Office 365 when all
you want to do is allow them access to your SharePoint sites; for example, you don't want
to give them an email box. Plus, when you use the Partner Access feature, the accounts are
licensed similarly to kiosk users, and you're charged less per month, per user rather than the
full Office 365 license fee.

However, before your site collection administrators can start sending invitations to customers, you must explicitly allow them to do so, on a site collection-by-site collection basis. From within the Manage Site Collections page, on the ribbon, click the Manage Share By Email button. The External Users dialog box opens, in which you can allow or deny this ability for that site collection, as depicted in Figure 4-13.

For more information about licensing, see Chapter 2. Chapter 5, "Identity Management and Authentication," provides details on the process of inviting users and accepting invitations.

FIGURE 4-13 External access to a site collection must first be granted in the Administration Center. Otherwise, site collection administrators will receive an error if they try to grant a partner access.

 Note If you revert the site to Deny, all external users will be removed from the site collection. This means that your site collection administrators will need to reinvite those users if you later change your mind and want to allow them onto your site.

Configuring InfoPath Forms Services

InfoPath Forms Services is a feature within SharePoint Online that allows users to view and fill out InfoPath forms from within the browser (as opposed to downloading the form to the user's computer and editing with the InfoPath client). Filling out forms directly from the browser is significantly easier than requiring the user to download the form. Plus, the user might not even have the InfoPath client, in which case, they wouldn't be able to fill out the form.

There are two basic InfoPath configurations that can be altered in the SharePoint Online Administration Center. The first is whether or not you want to allow your users to view forms in the browser, which might not seem terribly useful, given there's not many reasons you wouldn't want them to. The second configuration enables the remote proxy so that your browser-based InfoPath forms can authenticate to web services.

InfoPath Forms Services

To enable or disable browser-based InfoPath forms, click the InfoPath Forms Services link in the navigation pane on the Administration Center page (see Figure 4-14). Within the User Browser-Enabled Form Templates heading, select the Allow Users To Browser-Enable Form Templates check box. This setting permits users to publish forms to SharePoint Online that are browser-enabled. If you'd prefer that all forms are client-only, clear this setting so that users won't be able to publish browser-enabled forms.

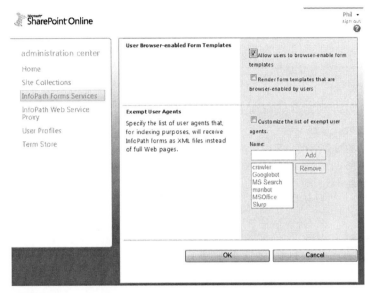

FIGURE 4-14 By default, Infopath forms render in the browser; however, you have the option to change this behavior and load them in the client instead.

To enable form rendering in the browser, select the Render Form Templates That Are Browser-Enabled By Users check box. If you have browser-enabled forms already within SharePoint Online, you can clear this check box to prevent the forms from rendering in the browser. With rendering disabled, when a user tries to render the form in the browser by clicking the New button on the ribbon, she receives an error message similar to the one displayed in Figure 4-15.

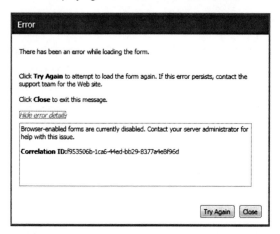

FIGURE 4-15 If a form is not permitted to render in the browser, the user will receive an error message.

To keep your users from receiving this error message, it is important to change the default behavior on all your form libraries. To do this, click Library Settings, and then click advanced settings. A section titled Opening Documents In The Browser appears (see Figure 4-16). Change the default to Open In The Client Application; the form will be downloaded to their InfoPath client, if installed.

FIGURE 4-16 To prevent the user from receiving the error message, go to Libraries Settings, and then change the default behavior to load the form in the client.

Use the Exempt User Agents setting to customize how agents and crawlers crawl browser-based InfoPath forms. Rather than render the form and put undue load on the system, it is better to simply return the XML equivalent to the crawler. It's rare to ever need to change this setting, unless you have custom-built search providers, for example.

InfoPath Web Service Proxy

InfoPath forms can connect to web services to retrieve data. The problem is when those forms are rendered in the browser; instead of calling the web service with the user's credentials, the form must use a service account because of network LAN manager's (NTLM) inherit double-hop limitation. The solution is to allow the InfoPath form to call into a proxy. The proxy then calls into the web service and can pass the user's credentials. Then, if this is your own custom web service, you could script some logic that takes that user name into consideration before it returns the result.

To enable this functionality, on the Administration Center page in the navigation pane, click the InfoPath Web Service Proxy link, and then select the Enable check box, as shown in Figure 4-17.

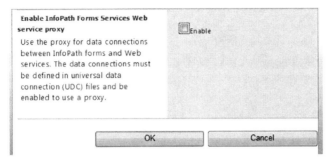

FIGURE 4-17 To allow an InfoPath form to authenticate to a web service by using the user's credentials, you must enable the service proxy, which passes the user's identity.

The proxy adds the user name to the request by adding a WS-Security *UserNameToken* into the SOAP header of the web service call. Within InfoPath, you must convert the web service data source to use a Universal Data Connection (UDC) file instead. After the conversion, you can edit the UDC file and change the *UseFormsServiceProxy* property of the service URL to *true*. Thereafter, the UDC will know to use the proxy rather than call the service directly.

Note   The account running the proxy service must be trusted by the web service to which InfoPath is connecting. The call to the web service is made under the proxy account, and the user name of the user is not directly taken into account for authentication purposes.

Configuring User Profiles

When it comes to managing profiles in SharePoint Online, there are really only four main areas with which you'll need to concern yourself. These include permissions (which social features users can or cannot use), profiles and profile properties (what metadata you want users to fill out about themselves), audiences for audience targeting of Web Parts and information, and finally, My Sites for document management.

Manage User Permissions

By default, all the social features associated with My Sites are enabled for all users. However, you can disable certain features, or enable them only for certain users or groups. To config-ure availability, click the Manage User Permissions link, specify the group the permissions apply to, and then click the permissions that you want to grant to that group, as demon-strated in Figure 4-18.

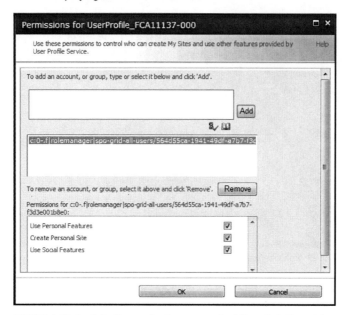

FIGURE 4-18 By default, everybody can use all of SharePoint's social capabilities, such as My Sites and tagging. However, this behavior can be customized.

The User Personal Features permission permits the user to personalize site pages; for example, by dragging his own Web Parts on to a SharePoint page or deleting the default Web Parts from a page.

Create Personal Site permission is required to allow the user to create a My Site.

User Social Features includes social tagging, the note board, and social linking functionality on public profiles.

Profiles, Profile Properties, and Profile Policies

Profiles are automatically generated when you create users in Office 365 (either manually or through synchronization). The only maintenance you'll need to do as an administrator involves properties, which is the actual individual's metadata that you want people to fill out and share with their peers.

By default, there are 68 properties for which a user can provide information. Some are optional or disabled, and many others are prepopulated, such as first and last name. You can create new properties and use property policies to mark them as viewable by everyone or just the user, and you can change the ability to edit the property to optional, required, or disabled (hidden). Policies can be used to mark properties as required, optional, or disabled. When a policy is disabled, the corresponding property does not render when the user clicks to edit their profile.

Once a user has a profile, you can delete that profile by clicking the User Profiles link, searching for that profile, and then clicking Delete.

Audiences

Audiences can be applied to Web Parts, for example, to show or hide that Web Part, based on membership within the audience. For example, if on the home page of your site you want to show a Web Part that only users in the HR department can see, you could create a new audience called Human Resources, and then add the members of the HR team into that audience. Then, when you add that audience onto a web part, it only renders for the users in that audience.

> **Note** Do not confuse audiences with security. Audiences are often called "security by obscurity" because you're not changing permissions to content, you're simply hiding it.
>
> You can audience target Web Parts with SharePoint groups, but audiences provide the benefit of being able to be reused across site collections, while also not requiring the global administrator access privileges that you'd need to create a global security group.

Managing My Sites

My Sites can be configured from within the User Profiles configuration in the Administration Center in SharePoint Online. You can use the links in the My Site Settings section to configure your My Sites experience. These links bring you to the following pages:

- Setup My Sites
- Configure Trusted Host Locations
- Configure Personalization Site
- Publish Links To Office Client Applications
- Manage Social Tags And Notes

For the most part, My Sites is automatically set up when you first subscribe to Office 365 and SharePoint Online. If you recall, one of the permissions settings deals with granting users the ability to create My Sites. By default, any user that has an E plan license has the ability to create a My Site. If you don't want to enable My Sites, disable that permission, as described in the section titled "Manage User Permissions," earlier in this chapter.

There are, however, some configurations that you might need to alter to customize your My Site experience. For instance, you can specify the default Search center that My Sites should use. You can also specify trusted My Site Host locations to redirect users to on-premises My Site locations. Additionally, you can configure links that show up in the navigation pane of

My Sites as well as within Office clients when saving documents to and from My Sites. And lastly, you can delete social tags and notes that are not appropriate.

Setting Up My Sites

There are only a few things that can be configured in this section. Namely, right at the top of the page, you can configure the default Search center that your My Site uses. When anyone performs a search from a My Site, he is redirected to a Search center with the query in the query string of the URL. The Preferred Search Center property can be set to any URL, including an on-premises Search center. The only thing to ensure is that, assuming the Search center is a SharePoint center, you'll want to set the URL to the pages library of the Search center (for example, *https://litwareinc.intranet.com/search/pages*).

Table 4-3 presents a few more settings that can be specified on this page.

TABLE 4-3 Available Options for Setting Up My Sites

Setting name	Description
Language options	(Yes | No) Allows users to toggle between languages when within My Sites.
Read Permission Level	(people or groups) When a My Site is created, these users will have read rights to the My Site. By default, all users have read rights to every My Site. Note, however, that the personal document libraries are locked down to the My Site owner.
Newsfeed	(Yes | No) Allows news feeds to appear on public views of My Sites. Newsfeeds are similar to a Facebook Wall, in that it shows users the recent actions the person has taken, such as status changes, tags, and links.
Security Trimming Options	(Check all links for permissions, Check only the following links for permissions, and Show all links regardless of permission) When users tag or link to information within My Sites, the default behavior is that SharePoint checks the links to ensure that the reader has access to the link before rendering it on the page. This can degrade performance, so this setting allows you to turn this security check off, enable it for only specific sites, or always check security before rendering the link.
My Site Email Notifications	Specify an email address that will appear in the "from" or reply to address for My Site notifications, such as when a user is approaching his 100 MB quota.
Secondary My Site owner	When a user is deleted and no longer has a profile, SharePoint attempts to reassign that user's My Site to her manager. If the user doesn't have a manager, the My Site is assigned to this secondary owner.

Configuring Trusted Host Locations

Especially in the case of hybrid clouds, your business might have more than one User Profile Service application, in which case you'd have more than one My Site Host. Perhaps you have a couple of SharePoint farms on-premises as well as the user profiles in SharePoint Online. If this is the case, when your users browse to each farm, they'll get a new My Site in each of the farms. This is problematic for self-evident reasons, including:

- There is no source of truth for profile properties.

- You can't remember which My Site holds a given document.

- User profiles must be configured multiple times.

Trusted host locations seek to fix this issue of having multiple My Sites. What you do is create a trusted host location for each farm, in each farm. When you create a trusted host location, you must specify an audience or a group (see Figure 4-19). SharePoint uses this to determine to which My Site Host the user should be redirected when she tries to browse to her site or profile. If the user falls within the audience of the first trusted host location, she will be redirected to the URL defined in that location. Otherwise, SharePoint checks the next trusted location until it finds one in which the user resides. If it doesn't find one, the default behavior is to use the current farm as a My Site Host.

FIGURE 4-19 If you have more than one My Site host location in your enterprise, you can add links to all the hosts. A user, if in the audience, will be redirected to the on-premises host instead of her cloud-based duplicate.

As far as SharePoint Online is concerned, when you also have an on-premises My Site Host, you're going to want to create a trusted My Site Host location in the Administration Center for each host. That way, if a user browses to his My Site in SharePoint Online, but he falls within an audience that points to a on-premises host, he is sent to the on-premises farm, instead.

Note The URL of the My Site host is just that: a URL. It can be a URL of an on-premises farm, but note the network limitations. Either that URL needs to be Internet accessible and published with a reverse proxy, or the user will likely need to be let into the domain by Virtual Private Network (VPN).

Personalization Sites and Linking to Office Client Applications

Personalization sites are simply links to other locations that are placed on the top navigation within My Sites, as illustrated in Figure 4-20 (LitwareInc.com). When you create a link, you can show or hide that link, based on audiences. Linking to Office Client Applications behaves in exactly the same manner except that the links are exposed in an Office client when the user opens or saves a document. The links in those cases are often used to suggest frequently used libraries.

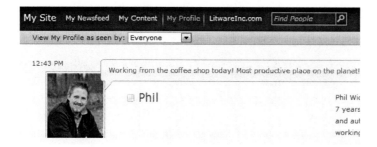

FIGURE 4-20 You can add links into the top navigation on My Sites as well as the Office client.

Managing Social Tags and Notes

When social tags and notes are enabled, users are free to tag, link to, and write anything they wish on their public profile. If a user tags or says something inappropriate, you can use this section to manage and remove those tags or notes. Simply type the user name, and then click the Find button. A list of all the tags and notes that user has ever created displays, and you can select and delete items that are not appropriate.

Configuring the Managed Metadata Term Store

The term store in SharePoint Online is a place where you can manage your managed terms as well as managed keywords. These two concepts—managed terms and managed keywords—encompass the new managed metadata in SharePoint Online. It is critical to understand the concept of managed metadata; if you don't, your SharePoint Online deployment will suffer.

Many companies simply throw SharePoint at their employees, but don't provide a thorough design or guidance on how to use it effectively. With regard to metadata, it's critical to think through your strategy so that you can increase the discoverability of documents. This includes discoverability from a search perspective, because a document tagged with metadata can appear higher in the search results. It also includes discoverability around general navigation, because users can sort, filter, and group documents together, based on the metadata applied to those documents. This is better because you're exposing documents, rather than making the user dig in and find them.

So before you jump straight into managing terms in the term store, spend some time thinking through your overall strategy. What is metadata? What are content types and site columns? What are managed terms and keywords? When do I use this or that? After you have a good handle on the answers to these questions, proceed to create your terms, and then implement your strategy.

What Is Metadata?

So what is metadata? Basically, metadata is data about data. From a SharePoint perspective, metadata is critical for the following reasons (not exhaustive):

- Without metadata, you must open and read a document to understand what the document is. Metadata allows you to qualify the document without opening it.

- Search results are improved when the document is tagged with metadata. For example, if a document includes metadata called "Document Type," and you specify that it is a Sales Proposal document, subsequent searches for "Sales Proposal" will have a higher likelihood of returning that document because it's tagged appropriately.

- When documents are tagged with metadata, you can sort, filter, and group, based on that metadata. This is especially helpful for libraries where thousands of documents exist.

- Cross-site document retrieval with content query Web Part. No matter where a document is in the entire site collection, if it is tagged with metadata, the content query Web Part can find it and present it to you.

With metadata, the paradigm is shifting away from a needle in a hay stack, to identifying documents that are relevant. Metadata is diametrically opposed to the convention of folders with which most people are familiar. In fact, most people are so familiar with folders that when you "throw" SharePoint at them, they simply replicate the old folder structure from their network file share, and thus experience little added benefit to being in SharePoint at all. Metadata is the answer to improved return on investment when it comes to finding the right document with the least amount of time and effort.

Folders *are* available in SharePoint, but consider the following issues that come with using folders:

- **Folders are inflexible**   You can't put a document in two different folders without making a copy and introducing a versioning nightmare. But with metadata, that document can be tagged as many times as imaginable to fully qualify it.

- **Folders are an abyss**   I've seen a document library with literally 16,000 folders in it, with the root folder having hundreds of child folders. It is undoubtedly impossible to find anything at the lower levels of that folder structure. It is an abyss. Sure, search can crawl those documents, but it is nearly impossible to search untagged documents and expect to find what you're looking for. Rather, with metadata, you can use refiners to assist your search as well as take advantage of the sort, filter, and group by functionality of the list view to take ten thousand documents down to fifty—a much more palatable number to browse through.

When Folders Are Actually Quite Helpful

It should be noted that with SharePoint Online 2010, there are some new improvements to folders that make them better than they were in Microsoft Business Productivity Online Suite 2007. Namely, the new feature to auto-apply metadata is quite compelling. When creating columns, you can specify location defaults for your metadata. That means if the document is uploaded into folder A, for example, different values will be assigned to it than if it were uploaded into folder B. This is helpful for users and can save time.

The other nice new feature is the Content Organizer. With the Content Organizer, users can upload a document into a drop bucket, and it will automatically route the document to the appropriate library or folder, based on the metadata the user specifies.

A third reason folders can be helpful is in managing list thresholds. SharePoint will automatically cancel a query for SharePoint data if the query spans more than 5,000 list items or documents. Folders in this case can be used to help manage below that item threshold.

Content Types and Site Columns

If you want to start tagging your documents, the most straightforward way is to go to your library settings and add a new list column. The trouble with list columns is that metadata is only available on that given list or library. What if you want that column across five libraries? You would need to re-create it five times. If you expound this further, you'll quickly find that list columns are not practical. If it is five columns, on five libraries, that's 25 columns you're creating as well as maintaining, if the column options ever need to change. This is where site columns and content types save the day.

Site columns are similar to list columns, but they are available across the entire site as well as all subsites. So, if you want a column available to all sites in a site collection, create the column at the root site of the collection.

So what if you have five columns that you want to add to each library in your site collection? Site columns help you reuse the columns, but you're still adding each column manually. This is where content types come into play. Content types can package up columns (among other things); all you have to do is apply the content type to the libraries and all the columns come with it. In addition to columns, the following can also be associated with a content type:

- **Managed Metadata**   Managed metadata is essentially columns, as well; however, the terms and options are centrally managed rather than managed on the list itself.

- **Document Template**   A document library might contain expense reports, so when you create a new document, the expense report template is used, rather than a blank document.

- **Workflows**   A document might have an associated workflow that should be started, for example, when the document is first created or uploaded.

- **Policies**   You can create policies on documents to help manage their life cycle, such as when they expire or should be archived.

Content Type Syndication

You cannot define a site as a content type hub in SharePoint Online. SharePoint Online allows for the capability to reuse content types across all your sites in SharePoint Online. You can browse to your content type hub by appending **/sites/contentTypeHub** to your domain. As an alternative, consider using Managed Metadata column types, because those terms can be shared across all your site collections in SharePoint Online.

Another important concept to understand with respect to content types is that of inheritance. You can have one content type inherit the metadata and workflows of another content type. This gives you the ability to add new columns or workflows that pertain to the "child content type," without the need to redefine all the properties of the parent. For instance, there is an out-of-the-box content type called Document. This document contains metadata inherent to all documents, such as Title, Name (file name), Created by, Created date, Modified by, and Modified date. Rather than recreate this metadata, you can create a new content type that inherits from document and only adds data that pertains specifically to Sales Proposals, for example. In the case of a Sales Proposal content type, you could add a Proposal Type column and still retain all the metadata from the parent.

You can create new content types by navigating to site settings and then clicking Site Content Types under the Gallery heading. Give it a name, a parent content type that it extends (for example, Document, Item, Contact, Link, and so on), and then add the new columns that you need. After you create the content type, you can apply it to lists or libraries by navigating to Library Settings, clicking Advanced Settings, and selecting the Allow Management Of Content Types option, as shown in Figure 4-21.

FIGURE 4-21 To add a content type to a list or library, you must first enable the use of content types on that list or library.

Thereafter, you can click the Add From Existing Content Types link to add your custom content type to the list. After you add it, users can select it from the drop-down list of the New button, as demonstrated in Figure 4-22.

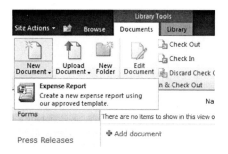

FIGURE 4-22 After you add a content type to a library, it appears in the New drop-down list.

Managed Metadata

You can use content types to package up functionality such as metadata and workflows, and make it available across the entire site collection. But what if you have more than one site collection and you want greater reusability? If so, consider managed metadata.

Another case for managed metadata is centralized control of terms. For example, if you are a manufacturer, you likely have part numbers. You probably don't want each site collection administrator managing her own list of part numbers. Rather, you can use managed terms to create a centrally managed vocabulary for your business, such as part numbers or products.

Managed Terms

With the terms in place in the term store, you can start using those terms in your site columns. When you create a new column, one of the column types is Managed Metadata, as illustrated in Figure 4-23.

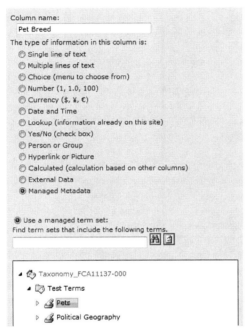

FIGURE 4-23 When you create a new managed metadata column, you must browse the term store and pick the appropriate starting place in the store from which your users can pick their terms.

When you use the Managed Metadata column type, a dialog box opens in which you can browse the term store and select the terms that accurately identify the document. Notice the hierarchy of terms in Figure 4-24. This hierarchy is not possible with site columns alone; only in the term store can you create and manage a hierarchy of vocabulary.

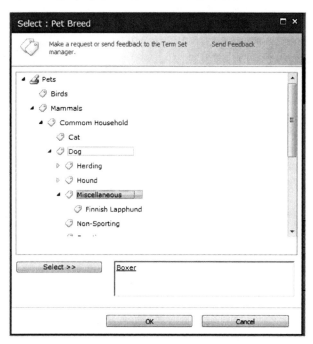

FIGURE 4-24 Term stores can create a hierarchy of vocabulary, unlike choice columns, which are a flat list of options.

> **Note** A major benefit of managed metadata is that if terms change, all you need to do is update the term store. Any documents that have been tagged with a term are updated automatically.

After the documents have been tagged, users can start sorting, filtering, and grouping on the terms. As an example, look at the action depicted in Figure 4-25. You'll notice the same hierarchy when you click the managed metadata column header. This allows you to query for all the documents that have a given term, such as showing the documents that are tagged with the breed Boxer. Moreover, you can also choose to include all descendants. So in the case of the dog breed example, you can make the view only show documents associated with breeds in the Hound family. In this case, all documents with that are tagged with terms that descend from Hound will show up in the view.

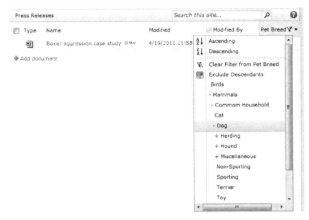

FIGURE 4-25 Another major benefit of managed terms is the ability to sort and filter the term as well as all descendent terms.

Managed Keywords

Managed keywords are similar to managed terms, but with two specific differences. First, keywords are stored in a flat structure. There is no hierarchy. Second, end users can create new keywords, whereas with managed terms, you must have administrator rights to the term store or group. With that being the case, managed keywords are much more "social" than managed terms.

> **Note** Managed keywords are akin to a *folksonomy*, in as much as the terms are defined at the grass-roots level of the organization. Conversely, a *taxonomy* is a centrally-managed set of vocabulary pushed down upon the users.

To add managed keywords to your list or library, browse to the library's settings page. On the Permissions And Management tab, click the Enterprise Metadata And Keywords Settings link (see Figure 4-26), and then select the Add The Keywords Column Onto The Library check box.

Managed keywords are still centrally managed, just not in the same manner as the Social Tagging feature. Managed in this sense means that the term store administrator can delete keywords that are inappropriate. Social tags, however, are totally decentralized. Also, managed keywords are still purely used for tagging documents and list items. Social tags are used to tag anything from sites, pages, documents, and any page where you see the I Like It and Tags & Notes buttons on the ribbon. These social tags mark content back to your My Site, whereas keywords typically stay with the document.

Figure 4-26 shows the Metadata Publishing feature, with which you can publish managed keywords back to your Profile as Social Tags. This in some sense allows you to kill two birds with one stone, because you can tag a document as well as link it back to your profile for easy reference.

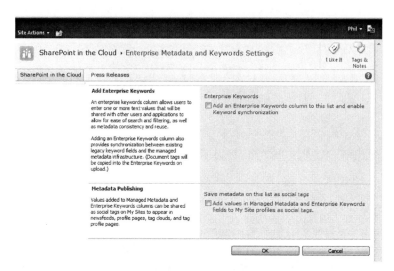

FIGURE 4-26 Managed keywords are chosen by the end users, whereas managed terms are typically centrally managed. To add managed keywords to a list, select the check box in the Enterprise Keywords section, and then click OK.

After you add the keywords column, you can start tagging documents. Figure 4-27 demonstrates how you don't need to select a term, as with managed terms. With managed keywords, you simply start typing your keywords. A suggestions box appears to provide suggestions of other terms that have been used elsewhere. This helps increase reuse of similar terms.

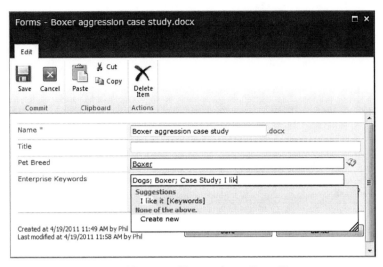

FIGURE 4-27 After you add managed keywords to a list or library, users can start tagging with whatever values seem appropriate. As the user types, a suggestion box appears, offering terms that have already been used.

Note You can filter on keywords similar to how you can filter with managed metadata (refer to Figure 4-25). The main difference is you can't sort alphabetically, and because keywords are flat, you can't show descendants.

Delete Unwanted or Inappropriate Keywords

Since managed keywords are populated by end users and are not predefined by a corporate librarian or taxonomist, you might find keywords that are less than ideal. If this happens, you can delete the term in the term store. The managed keywords are in the System term group, under the Keywords term set, as shown in Figure 4-28.

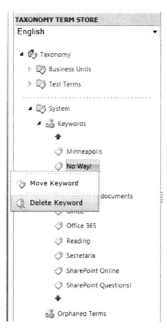

FIGURE 4-28 Because keywords aren't centrally managed, from time to time, you might need to delete those that are not entirely appropriate.

Managing the Term Store

Now that you know about list columns, site columns, content types, managed terms, and managed keywords, it's time to build out your term store. The term store itself is very simple and straightforward to use, so the hardest aspect of creating and administering your terms is undoubtedly figuring out which terms actually represent your business. This section walks you through all the basic actions that you'll likely ever need to take in the term store in SharePoint Online.

Adding Term Store Administrators

Security in the term store falls into three categories of users: term store administrators, group administrators, and term users or taggers. Term store administrators have access to the entire term store. This means that they can create new groups, delete groups, create terms and hierarchies, and more. If you want to grant someone full control to the term store, this is the role to consider. Conversely, group managers only have access to modify terms in that particular group, and end users can only tag documents with terms defined in the term store.

Note All end users can tag from any group in the term store. There is no way to say only a particular group of individuals can use terms in a particular term store group of terms.

To assign a new term store administrator, click Term Store in the navigation pane on the SharePoint Online Administration Center page. Click the root node in the hierarchy, the term store, which likely starts with "Taxonomy." Within the properties of the term store, you'll see a people picker where you can select the individuals who are to be the term store administrators, as illustrated in Figure 4-29.

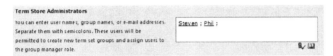

FIGURE 4-29 Term store administrators have full control across all groups and term sets in the term store.

Adding Supported Languages

Within the same properties menu as the term store administrators, you can also specify the languages that your term store supports. Figure 4-30 shows that both Swedish and English languages are supported. This means that the entire hierarchy for all groups in the term set will be replicated for each language.

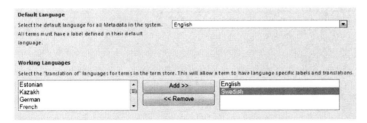

FIGURE 4-30 You can support more than one language in the term store. Essentially, each language has a copy of each term that must be translated.

It's the job of the term owners to translate each term into the other language's equivalent. Figure 4-31 shows the selected language in the upper left, which corresponds to the term Bloodhound. Within the properties of the term, you can change the language and set that language's equivalent translation, as is the case for the Swedish "Blodhund." Alternatively, you can toggle the language selector in the upper left and browse all the terms in Swedish, rather than English.

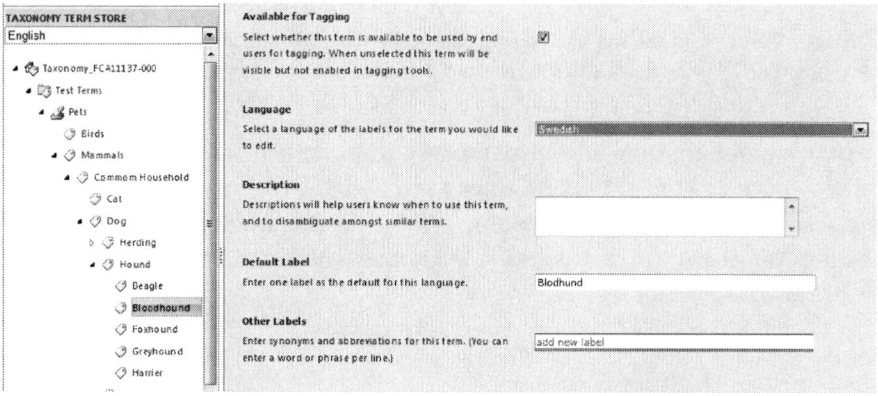

FIGURE 4-31 To translate a term, change the language from the drop-down list, and then enter the translated value.

Creating a New Group

To create a new group, right-click the term store taxonomy root. In the shortcut menu that appears, select New Group. Provide the group with a name, such as **Business Units**. When complete, you can specify an optional description in the group's properties, as shown in Figure 4-32.

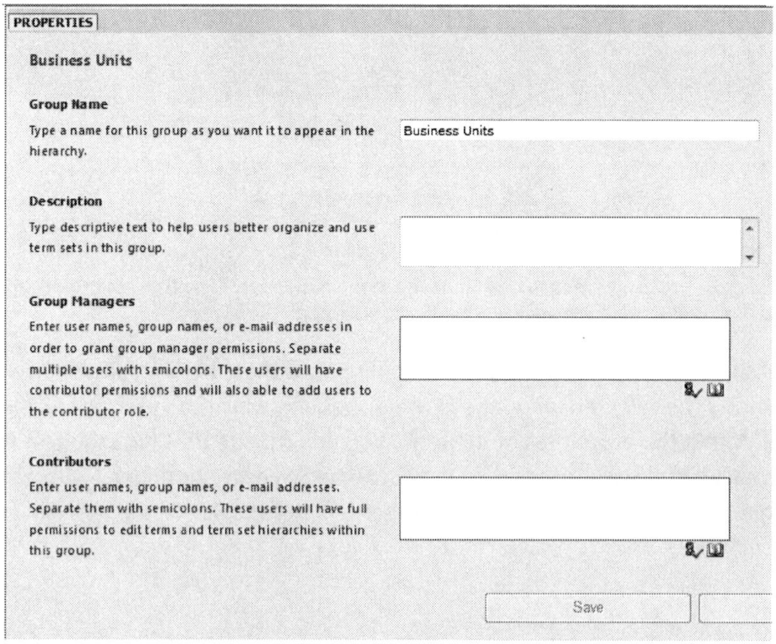

FIGURE 4-32 A term store has one or more groups. A group has one or more term sets. Create new groups when you want to assign permissions to a group of term sets.

Assigning Group Managers and Contributors

Figure 4-33 illustrates that you can specify group managers as well as group contributors. The only difference between the two is that managers have the ability to add new managers and contributors. Both have full control over the terms in the group.

Groups are handy because you might have different sets of terms for which different groups of people are owners. Often, administrators create groups that map to their business units, for example. They then assign managers in each business unit, for each group, and thereby delegate the ownership of the terms to individuals that have a closer understanding of the particular department.

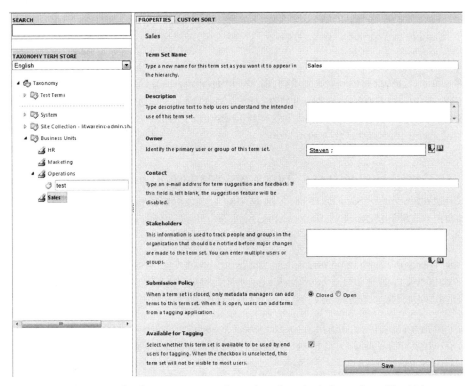

FIGURE 4-33 A term set has important properties such as the submission policy, with which you can permit or prevent end users from adding terms to the set.

Creating a New Term Set

After you've created a new group, you can create one or more term sets within that group. To do so, click the drop-down list for the group, and then choose New Term Set. After you specify the name of the term set, you can configure additional properties, such as the description, owner, and point of contact (see Figure 4-33). The Contact email address is used when a user clicks the Send Feedback link while editing a managed metadata column. The Owner and Stakeholders properties are there for enrichment purposes only; they don't provide anything beyond an FYI.

Submission policy can be used to enable end users to create terms, similar to how managed keywords works. By default, this is not enabled, since people typically prefer tighter control over managed terms. If you don't want users to be able to tag with this term set, clear the Available For Tagging check box.

On the Custom Sort tab (refer to Figure 4-32), you can change the sort order of all your terms. By default, terms are sorted alphabetically when presented to users. However, in the term store, you can sort by any order you prefer, as is the case in Figure 4-32, where Sales appears before Marketing, for example. Select the option to custom sort if you wish to maintain the order you specified in the term store.

Creating a Hierarchy of Terms and Managing Existing Terms

Creating terms within a term set is easy. Simply click the term set, click Create Term, and then enter the term. You can either continue clicking the Create Term button, or you can press the Enter key after each term; a term is created automatically each time you press Enter.

You can also create child terms, and thus start creating a hierarchy of vocabulary. You can create child terms up to seven levels deep. To create a child term, click the term, and then click Create Term from the drop-down that appears.

In addition to the Create Term button, there are several other helpful buttons that you can use when managing existing terms, as presented in Table 4-4.

TABLE 4-4 **Term Management Actions**

Button name	Description
Copy Term	Copies a term, pastes it at the same level in the hierarchy as the term from which it was copied, and appends "Copy of" in front of term.
Copy with Children	This is the same as Copy Term, but also pastes all the copied term's descendant terms.

Button name	Description
Reuse Terms	Sometimes you might need the same terms in more than one term set. Use Reuse Terms to select terms in a different term set, and bring copies of those terms into a separate term set. For example, a term with descendants called "Product Names" would be applicable to both the Sales and Marketing term sets. If Product Names is defined in the Sales term set, Marketing can simply reuse those terms. If the terms are ever updated, they will be updated in any location in which they are reused as well.
Merge Terms	Merge Terms takes all tagging instances of a given term and changes them to a different term. Thereafter, the term that was merged is deleted. This is a great way to consolidate terms that are similar.
Deprecate Terms	Deprecate Terms allows you to keep existing tagged instances of a given term, but prevent users from creating new tags with that term.
Move Terms	Using Move Terms, you can move a term and its descendants into another branch in the hierarchy. Rather than delete and re-create a term (thereby orphaning all tagged instances), you can move a term.
Delete Terms	Delete Term deletes the term from the term store and orphans any tagged instances.

Creating Term Labels

Term labels—also known as variations or synonyms—can be used to define alternate names of the same term. This can be helpful if you want to minimize the number of terms that fundamentally describe the same thing, yet that people think of differently. For example, if you use a term called Assignments, you might also want a label on that term for Tasks. This is because some people might search for "Tasks," whereas others might search for "Assignments," and yet, they are fundamentally the same term. Figure 4-34 demonstrates how when you go to tag a document, you can either type the term itself, or one of its labels. The label comes after the term name within the parentheses. After you select either the term or its label, the label is what the document is actually tagged with.

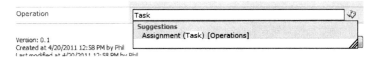

FIGURE 4-34 Some terms are not always thought of the same way for all people. You can create labels on terms to try to create synonyms that people might think of for the same thing.

On the term itself, you can add the labels by adding more text values in the Other Labels section, as shown in Figure 4-35.

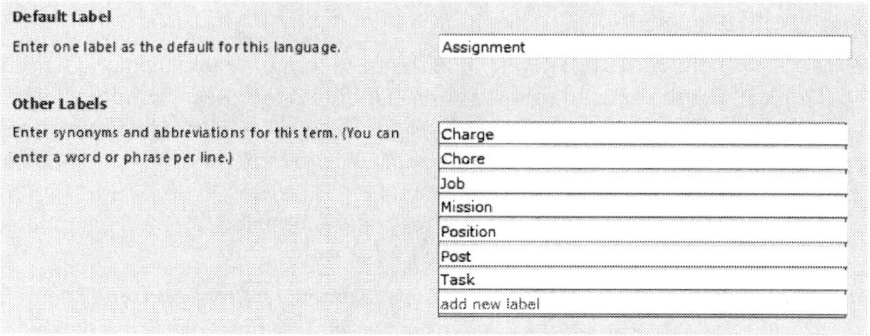

Default Label

Enter one label as the default for this language.

Assignment

Other Labels

Enter synonyms and abbreviations for this term. (You can enter a word or phrase per line.)

Charge
Chore
Job
Mission
Position
Post
Task
add new label

FIGURE 4-35 Labels, or synonyms, appear under the default label.

Importing Terms

When you first set up your term store, you might need to create thousands of terms. Creating all these terms in the browser might not be the fastest approach. An alternative is to import a .csv file that contains your terms in a very specific format. If you click a group, you'll notice an option called Import Term Set. When you click this button, you can select a .csv file to import. Thereafter, all the terms and hierarchies in the .csv will be created in the term store.

The best way to understand how to create this .csv file is to look at an example. If you click the term store taxonomy root, you'll see a link in the properties tab called View A Sample Import File. Open this file and add your terms in the same way. When you're done, import them into the term store in one action. Figure 4-36 shows an example term set in .csv format.

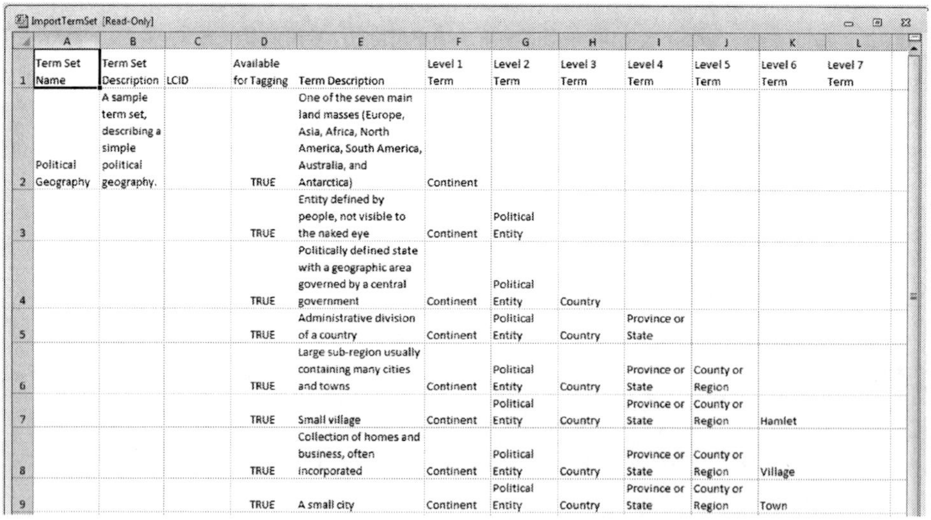

	A	B	C	D	E	F	G	H	I	J	K	L
1	Term Set Name	Term Set Description	LCID	Available for Tagging	Term Description	Level 1 Term	Level 2 Term	Level 3 Term	Level 4 Term	Level 5 Term	Level 6 Term	Level 7 Term
2	Political Geography	A sample term set, describing a simple political geography.		TRUE	One of the seven main land masses (Europe, Asia, Africa, North America, South America, Australia, and Antarctica)	Continent						
3				TRUE	Entity defined by people, not visible to the naked eye	Continent	Political Entity					
4				TRUE	Politically defined state with a geographic area governed by a central government	Continent	Political Entity	Country				
5				TRUE	Administrative division of a country	Continent	Political Entity	Country	Province or State			
6				TRUE	Large sub-region usually containing many cities and towns	Continent	Political Entity	Country	Province or State	County or Region		
7				TRUE	Small village	Continent	Political Entity	Country	Province or State	County or Region	Hamlet	
8				TRUE	Collection of homes and business, often incorporated	Continent	Political Entity	Country	Province or State	County or Region	Village	
9				TRUE	A small city	Continent	Political Entity	Country	Province or State	County or Region	Town	

FIGURE 4-36 If you need to add a large number of terms into the term store, it might make more sense to import them instead, because Microsoft Excel is probably faster than entering the terms by using a browser.

Changing Keywords into Managed Terms

Sometimes, certain keywords become very popular. This might be because new vocabulary has been defined in your organization but hasn't since made it into the term store. Or, the term might simply have been missed during the design process. In either case, if keywords are heavily used, you might want to move them into managed terms so that more users are aware of the term and can start using the term. To move a keyword into a managed term, click the keyword, and then click the Move button. Next, specify the term set and the location within the set's hierarchy where you want the term to appear. After you move the keyword, you don't need to worry about orphaning tagged instances. The tags in the enterprise keywords columns will continue to point to the term in its new location in the new term set.

Chapter 5
Identity Management and Authentication

In this chapter, you will learn about:

- Comparing all the identity management options for Office 365

- Understanding what it takes to support single sign-on

- A step-by-step guide to setting up a federation trust with Office 365

- Managing your identities with Windows Remote PowerShell

Determining how your users log on and access their SharePoint Online information is critical. There are many ways to authenticate to SharePoint Online. There are also many different ways to manage identities and credentials that individuals use to log on to SharePoint Online. Each of these approaches has its own unique set of pros and cons.

For example, it's easy enough to simply create Microsoft Online Services accounts within Microsoft Office 365. The Office 365 administration page has an intuitive browser-based interface with which you can create users and assign licenses. The trouble with this approach is two-fold. First, if you have hundreds or thousands of users, it would take a considerable amount of time to create each user, one by one. Second, if you have an existing on-premises domain, your users are relegated to remembering multiple sets of user names and passwords—something that almost all users loathe.

If you still want Microsoft Online users, there are a few ways to load them in bulk load. For example, you can upload a .csv file (comma separated values file) with all the users. This doesn't help, however, when you need to keep on-premises users synchronized. In this case, you can use Active Directory synchronization (DirSync) to propagate your on-premises users into Office 365. It should be noted, however, that it is a copy, so users will still need to remember two passwords, even if the logon is the same. The plus side, however, is that subsequent changes to on-premises accounts will also be reflected in Office 365 the next time DirSync runs (the exception being password changes).

So how do you accommodate your users who only need to use a single set of credentials between their on-premises domain and Office 365? It's an obvious requirement that most companies will need to adopt. The solution is to use Active Directory Federation Services 2.0 (ADFS 2.0), with which you can federate users between your on-premises domain and Office 365. Basically, you configure Office 365 to trust your on-premises ADFS 2.0 identity provider. With this trust in place, when a user submits a secure token issued by your trusted provider to Office 365, Office 365 simply lets them in. This, of course, is called *single sign-on*.

The trust relationship between Office 365 and your ADFS 2.0 deployment is set up through Remote PowerShell. You can also do other neat things with Remote PowerShell, such as creating and editing users, resetting passwords, disabling password expiry, and many others.

This chapter is intended to help you to understand the ins and outs of identity management in Office 365. Specifically, it's designed to help you to compare identity options and weigh the impact of choosing one over the other.

Identity Management Technologies and Techniques

Before jumping and discussing step-by-step procedures around configuring identity synchronization, federation, and authorization, it's important that you take a holistic view of identity management in Office 365. There are two places from which users authenticate: the browser and the client. Also, there are typically two mechanisms through which they authenticate: Microsoft Online (Office 365) accounts, or accounts that are federated from their on-premises Active Directory (AD). Another option is external access through the Partner Access feature, whereby you can invite external users into your SharePoint Online accounts. This relieves you from the need to manage identity at all.

Other things that are important to consider at a high level are your users' desktop setups and the sign-in assistant, which enables single sign-on for client applications. Also, two-factor authentication for those companies that are especially security conscious, as well as how you manage passwords, are yet more areas to consider as you plan your identity strategy.

Authentication Sources

There are two ways by which your users can authenticate to Office 365 and SharePoint Online. The first is through the browser, and the second, you can authenticate from within a rich client application.

Authentication from a Web Browser

There are several places within Office 365 where you use a browser. Some examples are the Office 365 Administration portal, Office Web Apps, and obviously, SharePoint Online. When using the browser, you can authenticate with cloud-based identities, such as Microsoft Online accounts, or you can authenticate with Federated Identities. Federated Identities are stored in the company's on-premises AD domain, but are federated with Microsoft Online's domain through the use of ADFS 2.0. The Cloud Identity and Federated Identity work as follows:

- **Cloud Identity** The web browser is redirected to the Office 365 sign-in service, where you type your Microsoft Online Services ID and password. The sign-in service authenticates your credentials and generates a service token, which the web browser posts to the requested service, and then logs you on.

- **Federated Identity**   The web browser is redirected to the Office 365 sign-in service, where you type your corporate ID. The sign-in service determines that you are part of a federated domain and offers to redirect you to the on-premises ADFS 2.0 for authentication. If you are logged on to the desktop (domain joined), you are authenticated, and ADFS 2.0 generates a Secure Assertion Markup Language (SAML) logon token, which the web browser posts to the Office 365 sign-in service. Using the logon token, the sign-in service generates a service token that the web browser posts to the requested service, and then logs you in.

Authenticating from Rich Client Applications

Rich clients can also connect to SharePoint Online. For example, you can publish a Microsoft Word document directly to SharePoint Online from within Word, without the need to manually upload it. When you publish the document, Word uses basic authentication over Secure Sockets Layer (SSL) to safely connect to SharePoint Online and publish the document. Rich clients, just like the browser, can also use Microsoft Online accounts or Federated Identity. However, clients can use the Sign-In Assistant to save credentials for future use; this means that they're prompted for credentials only once, even if they're jumping between more than one client product.

- **Basic authentication over SSL**   Office clients pass basic authentication credentials over SSL to the Office 365 identity platform. If it is detected that the user is a Federated Identity, the request is forwarded to your company's on-premises ADFS 2.0 (for single sign-on).

> **Note** If you have configured single sign-on, then this authentication requires deployment of a proxy server or an ADFS 2.0 proxy server in your perimeter network, also known as the demilitarized zone (DMZ).

- **Microsoft Online Services Sign-In Assistant**   The Microsoft Online Services Sign-In Assistant, which is installed by the Office 365 desktop setup, contains a client service that obtains a service token from the Office 365 sign-in service and returns it to the rich client. If you have a Cloud Identity, you'll be prompted to provide your credentials, which the client service sends to the Office 365 sign-in service for authentication (using WS-Trust). If you have a Federated Identity, the client service first contacts the ADFS 2.0 server to authenticate the credentials and obtain a logon token that is sent to the Office 365 sign-in service (using WS-Federation and WS-Trust).

Creating Cloud Identity User Accounts for Office 365

There are quite a few ways to create new users for Office 365 and SharePoint Online. Figure 5-1 shows the most obvious of them, the Office 365 browser-based administration console. After you create a new user, you can assign him properties, such as name and email address. You also can assign licenses to a user to enable varying Office 365 functionality on a user-by-user basis. Chapter 2, "Office 365 Feature Overview," contains step-by-step procedures for creating users through the Office 365 administration page, such as:

- Creating users
- Editing users
- Deleting users

FIGURE 5-1 To create a new user, navigate to Users within the Administration Center, and then click the New drop-down list to either select to add one at a time, or to bulk upload with a .csv file.

Other options for creating users in Office 365 include a bulk import with a .csv file, DirSync, simple migration for exchange, as well as through Remote PowerShell.

- **Bulk user creation via .csv upload**   If you have hundreds of users who you want to add into Office 365, doing so by using the browser would be time consuming and tedious. As an alternative, you can use a .csv file import. To do this, on the Admin page, under Management in the navigation pane, click Users. In the Users section, click the down arrow next to the New button, and then in the drop-down list, click the Bulk Add Users command (see Figure 5-1). You can download a sample .csv file to use as your template (see Figure 5-2). Simply add all of your users into the spreadsheet and then upload it. Office 365 will send an email that contains a temporary password (that must be changed upon first log on) to each user.

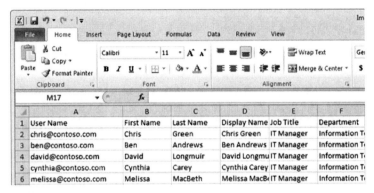

FIGURE 5-2 You can add users to Office 365 via the browser, or you can bulk upload by using a .csv file.

- **The DirSync Tool**   Similar to a bulk import, with DirSync, you can save a lot of time if you need to import hundreds or thousands of users. This tool can completely replicate the AD onto Office 365. DirSync also populates all of the user attributes on your behalf directly from their AD profile. Profiles that are synchronized cannot be edited in Office 365; this can only be done in the AD domain from which they originated. The synchronization is one-way, and can be configured to run nightly, for example, to pick up new users or metadata changes. By default, it runs every 3 hours.

- **Simple Migration for Exchange**   Users' accounts and mailboxes will be created automatically if an organization wishes to migrate the entire email setup from on-premises Microsoft Exchange to the cloud. This particular method is called the simple migration or the cutover migration for Exchange.

- **Remote PowerShell**   Office 365 can be administered via Remote PowerShell, as was discussed in Chapter 2, and from an identity perspective, as is discussed at the end of this chapter. This includes creating new users, for example, through the *Add-MsolUsers* cmdlet.

Assigning a Custom Domain to Users

Office 365 accounts use the *<username>*@*<company name>*.onmicrosoft.com domain format by default. This domain can be changed to a custom domain by registering that domain with Office 365. All custom domains go through the domain ownership verification process to verify that you own the domain through your favorite domain registrar.

When you create a new account, you select your custom domain (for example, litwareinc.onmicrosoft.com or simply litwareinc.com). This domain must be unique and not claimed by any other Office 365 customer.

Once the custom domain name is verified, you can set the custom domain as the default domain for new users. When set, new users created in Office 365 are assigned to the new default domain (that is, the custom domain) instead of the onmicrosoft.com domain. Users that already exist when you validate the custom domain will not be automatically changed to use the new domain; you will need to do that manually.

Office 365 Desktop Setup and the Sign-In Assistant

The Microsoft Online Services Sign-In Assistant connects to the Office 365 identity sign-in service and obtains a secure token that is passed to any client applications that need to connect to Office 365. This saves your users from logging on more than once when they connect with Office products, such as Microsoft Outlook and Word. You must run the Office 365 desktop setup to install the Sign-In Assistant. Alternatively, you can push the tool down to your users through a domain policy.

The desktop setup also installs other updates beyond just the Sign-In Assistant. It checks any Office Professional installation for needed security updates and downloads and installs them if they are not present. The desktop setup also regularly checks for Office 365–specific Office updates and automatically installs them to continually keep your user's clients up to date. Lastly, the desktop setup also alters your user's registry to mark your SharePoint Online and Office 365 Admin sites as trusted sites so that you can pass credentials seamlessly, as well as allow SharePoint features such as Windows Explorer. These registry settings can also be configured through domain policy if you'd prefer to do it manually.

Setting Trusted Sites Manually

You can set the Trusted Sites Registry settings manually for your end users through a domain policy. You can do this by modifying the following SharePoint Online registry settings for each provisioned user under HKEY_CURRENT_USER\Software\Microsoft\ Windows\CurrentVersion\Internet Settings\ZoneMap\Domains. First, add a key for the SharePoint Online domain. Next, add a subkey to the newly added domain key for your company's SharePoint Online home site. Finally, add a *dword* named https and set it to a value of 2. The SharePoint Online Host Name is added to the Trusted Sites zone in Internet Explorer after you have modified the registry settings.

To launch the Desktop Setup wizard, browse to the Office 365 Home page. Under Resources on the right side of the page, click Downloads. Underneath Set Up And Configure Your Office Desktop Apps, click Set Up, as shown in Figure 5-3.

FIGURE 5-3 Use the Desktop Setup wizard to install all the pertinent hotfixes and the Sign-In Assistant.

A window opens, prompting you to sign into Office 365, and thereafter the download will commence. Once you click Run, the Desktop Setup Wizard will start. Select the check box adjacent to Microsoft SharePoint to setup the trusted sites, as illustrated in Figure 5-4. Click Continue to finish the installation.

Note If you use Outlook or Microsoft Lync to access more than one account, you might not want to configure them with the desktop setup tool. Office 365 will become the default account and you will need to reinstall those products to revert to their default configurations.

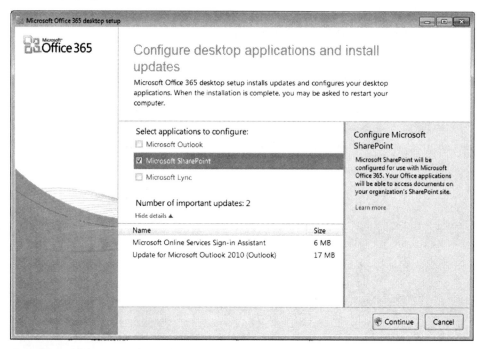

FIGURE 5-4 When you run the Desktop Setup Wizard, you can specify for which Office 365 services you want to configure your desktop.

Two-Factor Authentication

Two-factor authentication (also called *strong authentication*) provides improved security by requiring users to meet two authentication criteria such as a user name/password combination and a token, certificate, or other data such as a PIN. Instead of just one factor, which is typically the combinations of a user name and password, a second factor is introduced to decrease the odds of someone hacking an account. Identity federation with ADFS 2.0 is the only way in Office 365 to incorporate two-factor authentication scenario. When a user tries to gain access to Office 365 without a signed security token, he is redirected to his ADFS 2.0 identity provider. The logon page of ADFS 2.0 can be modified to include extra fields that would enable the organization to collect the two-factor credentials, thus enabling the two-factor server/system to authenticate the user. Then, after the user authenticates and receives the token Office 365 needs, he is redirected back to Office 365 and is let in.

Planning for Two-Factor Authentication with Single Sign-On

To use two-factor authentication, you must implement a single sign-on strategy by using ADFS 2.0 with Office 365. When planning your implementation, consider whether users have a supported operating system, are inside or outside the corporate network, and are using rich clients or web browsers. Also consider the ability of your authentication provider to interoperate with other services.

Deploying Two-Factor Authentication for SharePoint Online

Two options exist for enforcing two-factor authentication with single sign-on for users accessing SharePoint Online outside the corporate network (such as a home computer):

- **Integrate the ADFS 2.0 proxy logon page with your strong authentication provider**   Customize the ADFS 2.0 proxy logon webpage to introduce the extra fields needed to gather information for the two-factor authentication. Further customize the page to interact with two-factor authentication servers or services to authenticate users.

- **Use the Microsoft Forefront Unified Access Gateway (UAG) server**   Use a UAG SP1 server to support a wide range of two-factor authentication providers as well as direct access to an expanded set of scenarios that involve two-factor authentication.

DirSync

DirSync is helpful for larger companies that perhaps have hundreds or thousands of users, along with large on-premises AD deployments. A company like this can use DirSync to replicate all their on-premises AD accounts into Office 365. This can save a lot of time when compared with manually creating each user account through the browser, or even formatting those accounts into a .csv file for bulk upload purposes.

The DirSync client is installed into a server on your data center, and it connects to your domain to read all the user identities that you want to push to Office 365. As it reads the accounts, it communicates to the identity provisioning service of Office 365 and passes the accounts to the service, whereby those accounts are then duplicated in Office 365. The DirSync service runs every three hours by default, so new accounts or account metadata changes are continually updated in Office 365. Figure 5-5 presents a graphic representation of this architecture.

> **Note** Account passwords are not migrated, so even though the accounts are duplicated, your end users will need to remember two passwords. To get around this, consider federating identities with ADFS 2.0, which also gives you single sign-on capabilities.

FIGURE 5-5 DirSync requires that you install a client application on your server that propagates user information to Office 365 every three hours.

The advantages of this solution are that the users and groups can be managed in the local AD, users have a consistent user name—both on-premises and in the cloud—and that coexistence can be created between the local email system and Exchange Online. The disadvantage of this solution is that an end user needs to remember two sets of credentials, one for the local AD and one for their Office 365 account.

The synchronization tool offers different options. Using the One-Way push method of synchronization, you can replicate AD objects to Office 365. Any changes made in the AD will reflect the next time the tool is executed. But, if changes are made to Office 365, those changes do not reflect in AD. If an organization wants a two-way mechanism wherein changes made on one side should reflect on the other, then it should consider the write-back capabilities offered by the synchronization tool. There are limitations, however, on which data can be written back to your on-premises domain. Most of the write back capabilities are around Exchange Online, such as sent and deleted items.

ADFS 2.0 and Single Sign-on

If you want single sign-on between your on-premises domain and Office 365, you'll need to incorporate ADFS 2.0 (ADFS) into your infrastructure strategy. ADFS allows you to federate your on-premises identities with Office 365, such that when a user browses Office 365 with their Windows token, she is let into Office 365 without the need to reenter her user name and password. If a user browses Office 365 without a token, she is redirected back to her identity provider on-premises to authenticate, be issued a token, and thereafter to be redirected back to Office 365 with that token, and thereby be allowed in.

If you use DirSync to replicate your on-premises accounts into Office 365, you can create a coexistence scenario in which your users can connect to Exchange either on-premises or in the cloud. ADFS 2.0 can extend this foundation by also enabling single sign-on so that users won't need to remember two different passwords. Note that DirSync is a requirement for single sign-on. Figure 5-6 shows how ADFS is layered into the previous DirSync architecture illustrated in Figure 5-5.

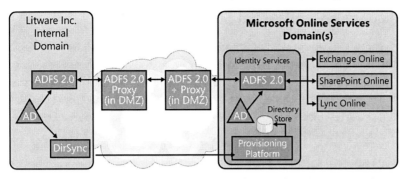

FIGURE 5-6 ADFS builds on DirSync by supporting identity federation and single sign-on.

A relying party federation trust is established between the federation servers of Office 365 and your on-premises ADFS 2.0 servers. When a user browses SharePoint Online, for example, without an ADFS token, they are sent to Microsoft Online's federation service to get a token (steps 1–3, as presented in Figure 5-7). Microsoft Online determines that this is a Federated Identity, and then forwards the authentication request to the user's on-premises ADFS 2.0 server to have the user log on and get a token (steps 4–5). Often, a company will use an ADFS proxy server in the DMZ to forward the request to the actual ADFS server internally. ADFS 2.0 then presents a challenge screen to the user to log on, validates the credentials with your AD (step 6), and then afterward issues a signed token and forwards the user back to SharePoint Online (step 7). SharePoint Online then recognizes that it trusts the issuer of the token (because of the federation trust) and lets the user access SharePoint Online resources.

Figure 5-7 depicts this logon process. Later in this chapter, you'll find the step-by-step instructions to set up a federation server, along with the system requirements and dependencies.

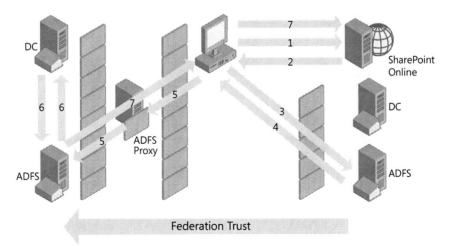

FIGURE 5-7 When a user makes a request to SharePoint Online, he runs into a series of redirects until he has the necessary security token that SharePoint Online is expecting.

Partner Access and External Sharing

Another interesting mechanism with which users can gain access to SharePoint Online resources is through the partner access feature. When enabled, site owners can send invitations to users who are not Office 365 accounts. For example, you might have partners or customers with whom you want to collaborate, but you don't want to pay top-tier user license fees for each user. Partner access is also beneficial if you don't want to carry the burden of managing their accounts, such as password resets, and so on.

To send an invitation to a partner or customer, click the Site Actions menu from within your SharePoint Online site collection, and then click the Share Site button (Figure 5-8). A form opens, into which you can start entering the email addresses of the individuals you want to invite into your site. After you invite the users, each of them will receive an email with instructions on how to log on to SharePoint Online.

FIGURE 5-8 A site owner can share their SharePoint Online content with external users by clicking the Share Site button on the Site Actions tab.

Currently, the partner access feature only works for Hotmail users who have hotmail.com, live.com, or msn.com email domains. When you invite a Hotmail account into SharePoint Online, the account owner is presented with a logon form. The user name is her Hotmail email address, and the password is the same as her Hotmail password.

> **Note** The external user must click the Use A Hotmail Account To Sign In link (Figure 5-9) on the sign-in page. Her Hotmail account will not work if she types it in the Microsoft Online Services ID text box.

sign in

Microsoft Online Services ID:

Password:

Forgot your password?

☐ Remember me
☐ Keep me signed in

[Sign in]

Don't have a Microsoft Online Services ID?
Use a Hotmail account to sign in

FIGURE 5-9 An external user will need to click the Use A Hotmail Account To Sign In link because she doesn't have a Microsoft Online Services user name.

Partner access present security vulnerability since any site owner has the ability to grant access to potentially any person in the world. It should only be used under intentional situations, and in a controlled manner. Because of this risk, partner access is disabled by default. To enable it, you must click the Manage External Users button while administering site collections within the Office 365 Administration Center, and then in the External Users dialog box, click Allow (see Figure 5-10). After you allow external access, site owners can start inviting external Hotmail accounts into their sites through the Site Actions menu (refer to Figure 5-8).

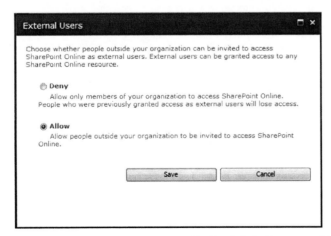

FIGURE 5-10 Partner Access is not enabled by default. You can enable it through the Office 365 Administration Center, under Site Collection Management.

Once the external user authenticates with her Hotmail credentials, she is allowed into SharePoint Online. Note that external users can be assigned up to contributor permissions in SharePoint Online. External users will have functionality similar to a kiosk user and can pretty much do anything a normal Office 365 user can do, with the following exceptions:

- They can't interact with SharePoint web services, such as Access, Excel, and Visio Services.

- External users can't be an Office 365 administrator (global or other).

- They can't use Office Web Apps (browser-based Office suite) to author Office documents (Word, Excel, and so on).

Password Management

Users must change their passwords when they first access the Office 365 services such as SharePoint Online. When you first browse SharePoint Online with a system-generated password, a prompt appears, asking you to change that password to something that is easier to remember. If you do not change the password at this time, SharePoint Online displays an Access Denied message.

If you lose or forget your password, administrators with the global administrator, password administrator, or user management administrator role can reset it in the Office 365 administration site or through Windows PowerShell. You cannot change your own password without providing your existing passwords.

Note In general, subsequent access to SharePoint Online doesn't require reauthentication after a password change. However, some factors such as the browser or client in use, or the time since last access might require reauthentication.

If an administrator loses or forgets his password, a different administrator with the global administrator role can reset another administrator's password in the Office 365 administration site or through Windows PowerShell. If no administrators are available to reset passwords, users must contact Office 365 support to request a reset password.

Note When using ADFS 2.0 for identity federation, users don't have Office 365 passwords; therefore, the Office 365 password policy does not apply.

Figure 5-11 shows the User Management dialog box, in which a global administrator can select users and reset their passwords. After the user(s) are selected, click the Reset Password button to reset their password to a system-generated password. The user will receive her password via email. Again, after the user logs on to Office 365, she will immediately see the prompt to change the password to something more meaningful. It's important for you to understand the password policies and restrictions by which you are governed. Table 5-1 presents these policies.

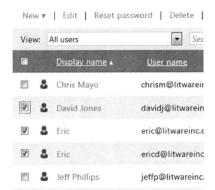

FIGURE 5-11 A global administrator can reset a user's password by selecting the user, and then clicking the Reset Password button.

TABLE 5-1 The Password Policies and Options for Cloud Identities

Property	Description
Password restrictions	8 characters minimum; 16 characters maximum.
	Allowed values:
	A–Z
	a–z
	0–9
	! @ # $ % ^ & * - _ + = [ ] { } | \ : ' , . ? / ` ~ " < > ( ) ;
	Prohibited values:
	UNICODE
	Username alias (part before @ symbol)
Password expiry duration	90 days (non-configurable)
Password expiry	Password expiry is enabled by default. Passwords will expire after 90 days when enabled, and it is important to note that you will not receive an expiry warning or notification. When you browse to SharePoint Online after expiry, you are prompted to change your password.
	Note: Administrators can enable and disable the password expiry on a user-by-user basis with PowerShell.

Property	Description
Password strength	Strong passwords require 3 out of 4 of the following: Lowercase characters Uppercase characters Numbers (0–9) Symbols (see password restrictions above) **Note:** Administrators can disable strong password requirements through PowerShell.
Password history	Last password cannot be used again.
Password history duration	None
Account lockout	After 10 unsuccessful sign-in attempts with the wrong password, the user must solve a CAPTCHA dialog as part of the sign-in process. After 10 unsuccessful additional sign-in attempts with the wrong password and correct solving of the CAPTCHA dialog, the user is locked out of their account for a time period.

Configuring Identity Federation and Synchronization

With the high-level identity concepts out of the way, it's time to get down to business and configure identity federation and synchronization. Any serious Office 365 customer will most likely be implementing federation. The only exceptions would be companies with no existing on-premises domains, or perhaps very small companies.

This section covers the high-level roadmap to accommodate single sign-on. It also gives you advice about what to plan for from a federation perspective. You'll be introduced to some network diagrams and server configurations that can help you to prepare for your eventual configuration. Finally, you'll see the high-level steps that you can use to build and configure your own ADFS 2.0 farm as well as create a federation trust with Office 365.

Federation Roadmap

Configuring identity federation and single sign-on is a process comprising a few rather technical steps. The following can be used to help you to understand all that is involved in configuring single sign-on.

> **Note** Configuring single sign-on isn't a trivial process. It is highly recommended that you have an IT professional configure these systems. This person should be highly experienced with directory services, infrastructure, and networking.

Phase 1: Plan for Identity Federation

Planning is a critical first step in configuring single sign-on with Office 365. You need to carefully consider capacity and how many federation servers and proxy servers you'll need to handle your authentication load. You should survey your internal and perimeter networks to ensure that they're available, stable, and scalable to support new services. These services include one or more federation servers, federation proxy servers, dedicated network load balancers (NLB), domain name systems (DNS), as well as AD domains. Also, you'll want to consider networking implications such as firewall rules (HTTPS) as well as certificate and domain requirements.

Phase 2: Create Internal and Perimeter Federation Farms

This phase is likely one of the more technical phases. During Phase 2, you create a federation farm in your internal network and one or more federation proxy servers to redirect requests coming from the Internet through your DMZ back into your internal networks. These requests must be encrypted over HTTPS/SSL, and you need to purchase and import certificates to ensure that requests are handled securely. Additionally, it is highly recommended that you have more than one federation server and proxy for high availability/redundancy purposes. With this being the case, you'll be building two NLB clusters in this phase to split requests across all federation nodes in each cluster. DNS also needs to be configured to route traffic through the fully-qualified domain name (FQDN) to the NLB host.

Phase 3: Verify domains and Use PowerShell to configure a federation trust

With your federation farm and DMZ configured properly, it's time to set up the federation trust between Office 365 and your federation service. Any requests coming into Office 365 are handled by your federation service because Office 365 will be configured to trust your identity provider's secure token. This is all configured through PowerShell. However, it should be noted that you need to register and verify your domains with Office 365. When the trust is set up, you need to change your domains through your registrar to point to Office 365's DNS servers.

Phase 4: Configure Active Directory Synchronization

The final phase is to configure DirSync to replicate AD accounts in your on-premises AD onto Office 365. This will help you achieve co-existence with Exchange on-premises and Exchange Online. This is also a prerequisite to configuring single sign-on. DirSync is a client application that runs on a server in your internal domain. It runs every three hours, propagating new accounts and account changes up to Office 365.

Planning Your ADFS 2.0 Deployment

ADFS 2.0 is a Windows service that can be installed on any Windows 2008 or 2008 R2 server. The service is configured as a server role on any server on which it runs. When you install ADFS 2.0, the installation wizard automatically checks for any hotfixes that need to be applied and installs them on your behalf. It's important to note that when you go to configure the ADFS 2.0 service, you should have domain administrator privileges.

> **Note** Microsoft .NET 3.5 SP1 is a prerequisite for ADFS 2.0 installation. The installer will not automatically install SP1 on the server, so be sure to plan on downloading and installing SP1 prior to installing ADFS 2.0.

When ADFS 2.0 is configured and maintained, it stores configuration data in a proprietary database. You have two choices when selecting the type of database mode to use: Windows Internal Database (WID) or Microsoft SQL Server. There are specific pros and cons to each approach.

WID is a simpler architecture and is configured on your behalf. SQL Server on the other hand is installed and configured separately. The WID database is replicated onto each federation server in the farm. However, when using WID, only one service in the farm (the primary server) has both read and write permissions to the database. The rest of the farm has only read permissions (secondary servers). This requires you to use the primary server when making configuration changes. On the other hand, because SQL is centralized for all federation servers in the farm, it doesn't matter which federation server you use to make configuration changes. Because they share the same database, all servers immediately reflect those changes. With WID, other servers must wait until the changes are propagated in their local copy before getting the update.

This centralized database isn't, however, the main reason people choose SQL. SQL has the benefit of scalability and high availability. You can use SQL's clustering and mirroring capabilities to achieve high availability, and you can always add more SQL servers to the cluster to increase throughput. What's more, with WID you have a maximum of five servers in the federation farm. Five servers can support up to approximately 60,000 users. If you're working in a large enterprise with more than 60,000 users, you'll need to use SQL so that you can add more than five servers in your federation farm.

> **Note** Even though SQL has many benefits that are not available with WID, most ADFS 2.0 installations still use WID because it's so easy to configure (the wizard does the work for you).

No matter how many users you have in your company, it is always recommended to have at least two federation servers for redundancy. Also, if you virtualize those servers, ensure that they are split across at least two physical servers; otherwise, you'll still have a single point of failure. Table 5-2 lays out the rule of thumb for scaling your federation farm.

TABLE 5-2 Guidelines for Scaling Your Federation Farm, Based on Number of Users

Number of users	Suggested configuration
<1,000	0 dedicated federation servers. Use existing domain controllers, DNS servers, and so on, if available.
	0 dedicated federation proxy servers. Use existing domain controllers, DNS servers, and so on, if available.
	1 dedicated network load balancer. Perhaps more than one so that the NLB won't be a single point of failure.
1,000–14,999	2 dedicated federation servers.
	2 dedicated federation proxy servers.
15,000–59,000	3–5 dedicated federation servers.
	2+ dedicated federation proxy servers.
>60,000	Use SQL Server database, not WID.
	Start with 5 federation servers, and then add a new federation server for each 15,000 users above 60,000.
	2+ dedicated federation proxy servers, scale as necessary.

Planning Your Internal Federation Farm

Setting up the base federation farm is the first step of the deployment. You should place all federation servers in your internal domain/network behind a firewall. Use an NLB host to create a cluster with a dedicated cluster DNS name and cluster IP address. When you create your federation service, use the same FQDN as your NLB cluster's DNS name.

> **Note** Single sign-on with Office 365 does not support multiple forests.
>
> The cluster DNS name and the federation service name must be the same; for example, fs.litwareinc.com. The FQDN must also be Internet routable through your preferred third-party domain registrar.

The NLB host forwards requests to the individual federation servers. Figure 5-12 shows how Litware Inc. might set up the first phase of its deployment by using a two-computer federation server farm (fs1 and fs2). This configuration uses the simple WID approach for its configuration database. Figure 5-12 also shows the positioning of a DNS server and a single NLB host on the internal network.

> **Note** There are many places that could be a single point of failure in this farm. If high availability is a concern for you, consider redundant NLB and DNS servers, along with your federation servers (not to mention redundant switches, firewall, network interface cards [NIC], and so on). If you're using virtualization, ensure that each pair is represented across more than one physical host.

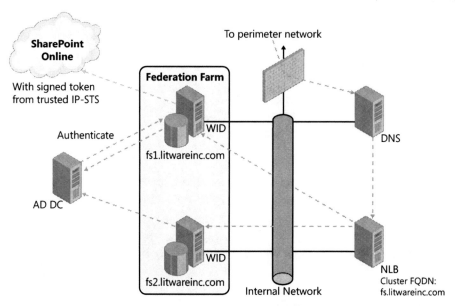

FIGURE 5-12 The dotted arrows show the path of an authentication request coming in from the perimeter network. The domain is resolved to the NLB cluster, which forwards it on to a node in the federation farm.

Planning Your Perimeter Network

Federation proxy servers redirect client authentication requests coming from the Internet into your internal domain. These servers are most commonly placed in a DMZ that is segregated from your internal network. In addition to the ADFS 2.0 servers in your internal network, you'll need at least two more ADFS 2.0 servers (proxies) for redundancy, DNS, as well as another dedicated NLB. Another AD domain is optional, but it is common to join the proxies to an external domain.

This second NLB in the DMZ must be configured with an Internet-accessible IP address that the domain is registered to use. For example, you would want to register a domain similar to fs.litwareinc.com with your registrar and point it to the NLB cluster in your DMZ. The NLB cluster FQDN also must use the same cluster domain name as the internal NLB cluster domain name. For example, both clusters as well as the federation service will use the same FQDN (for instance, fs.litwareinc.com). Also, the federation proxy servers themselves must be configured with Internet-accessible IP addresses. You can see this configuration represented in Figure 5-13.

> **Note** You can use UAG or TMG to publish ADFS 2.0 to the extranet. You can also use other third-party reverse proxies to do this as well.
>
> All ADFS 2.0 traffic that communicates through the firewall uses HTTPS on port 443 by default. You'll need to purchase a certificate to secure the traffic. Most people use the same certificate that they use for their internal network.

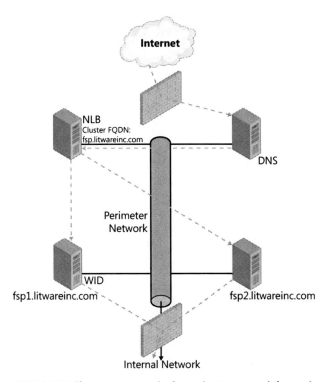

FIGURE 5-13 The proxy servers in the perimeter network forward requests back into the internal network.

Configuring Single Sign-On in 12 Easy Steps

The following high-level steps will help you configure single sign-on, identity federation, and AD synchronization with Office 365. Some of these techniques can be quite technical and are best suited for IT professionals with strong infrastructure, directory services, and networking backgrounds.

1. Join federation servers to the internal domain.

   All federation servers in the farm must be joined to your domain. You'll want to keep your federation farm in your internal domain and place your federation proxy servers in a DMZ. The proxy servers can be joined to a perimeter domain, but it is not a requirement.

2. Create new NLB cluster and DNS names.

   It is highly recommended that you have more than one federation server and that you load balance the federation servers. This is needed if you want a highly available farm. Again, note that if you virtualize your federation roles, ensure that you keep the virtual servers split across more than one physical host.

   It is very common to simply use the NLB role within Windows 2008 to facilitate the load balancing and create the cluster. A key point to note here is that the cluster must use the same FQDN that the federation service itself is using (for example, fs.litwareinc.com). Also, the DMZ's proxy NLB cluster must also use this same FQDN as well (more on the proxy NLB later). Start by creating a new NLB cluster, preferably on a dedicated server. Assign the cluster its own IP address. In DNS, create an (A) record that resolves to the internal NLB cluster's dedicated IP Address.

   For more information, read the Technet article on creating an NLB cluster (Windows 2008: http://bit.ly/nm1dtW. *Windows 2008 R2:* http://bit.ly/nP2pES*).*

3. Import SSL Certificate into each server in the federation farm.

   Client authentication requests and inter-server farm communication all must be secured via HTTPS/SSL. Since traffic comes from the Internet in an Office 365 scenario, you need to purchase a certificate from a third-party Certificate Authority (CA) such as VeriSign, Thawte, or GoDaddy. After you receive your certificate from your favorite CA, the next step is to install the certificate on the default site in Internet Information Services (IIS) on all the federation servers in the farm. The following are the high-level steps to import the certificate:

   3.1. Open IIS, and then in the console, click Computer Name.

   3.2. In the center page, click Server Certificates, and then click Actions | Import.

   3.3. Browse to your certificate. Click Open, type the password, and then click OK.

 Note The subject name of the certificate must match the FQDN of the cluster DNS name (for example, Fs.litwareinc.com) that you created on the NLB host.

4. Create the federation service account.

   The step where you configure the ADFS role on your federation servers requires you to specify a service account under which the service will run. All federation servers must use the same service account. Create a new service account in your AD and set the password to never expire.

5. Install the ADFS 2.0 software on the federation servers.

You must install and configure the ADFS 2.0 role on every server in the federation farm. The first step is to download the installer from *http://bit.ly/ojSsvc*. Next, run the AdfsSetup.exe executable. The install wizard is very basic. On the Server Role page, select Federation Server. Click Next through the ensuing wizard pages, and then click Finish.

> **Note** The installer automatically installs the necessary hotfixes required to connect your federation farm with Office 365. However, since hotfixes can be released unexpectedly and the installer usually takes longer to be updated, it is important to compare the required hotfixes (*http://bit.ly/LLPSzu*) with the hotfixes included in the installer (*http://bit.ly/mbCNNu*).

6. Configure the primary server federation role on first server.

When configuring your ADFS 2.0 federation servers, it is recommended that you are logged on as a domain administrator. Run the ADFS 2.0 Federation Server Configuration Wizard by opening ADFS 2.0 Management from Administrative Tools. Use the following steps to configure your primary server:

6.1. On the Welcome page, choose Create A New Federation Service, click Next, choose New Federation Server Farm, and then click Next again.

6.2. On the Specify The Federation Service Name page, verify that the SSL certificate name matches the certificate you just imported previously, and then click Next.

> **Note** If you previously installed ADFS 2.0 on this server, the next page shows that the wizard detected an existing database. Delete the database, and then click Next.

6.3. On the Specify Service Account page, select the ADFS service account that you created in step 4. Click Next, and then click Close to end the wizard and complete the configuration.

> **Note** When you finish the wizard, the management snap-in loads, indicating that the installation is incomplete because you need to add a trusted relying party. Disregard this message because the relying party (Office 365, in your case) will be configured in the following steps.

7. Configure the secondary servers in the federation farm, and then verify the federation farm.

   After you configure the primary federation server, the next step is to add one or more secondary servers for redundancy. Ensure that the certificate is set up in the default IIS site before continuing (as described in step 3).

   As with step 6, load the ADFS 2.0 Federation Server Configuration Wizard. However, on the Welcome page, choose Add A Federation Server To An Existing Federation Service instead of Create A New Federation Service. A prompt appears, asking you to type the server name of the primary server as well as the service account. Be sure to use the same service account that you used when you configured the primary server.

   With the secondary servers in place, it's time to verify that the federation cluster is working properly. Browse to the endpoint of each federation server, such as:

   ```
   http://<servername>.litwareinc.com/adfs/fs/federationserverservice.asmx
   ```

   If you browse to the service and get the service description XML, the service is configured properly.

    Note Another way to verify is to look for an event in the event viewer with 198 as its event ID. If present, you'll know that the server has been configured correctly.

8. Deploy the federation proxy servers.

   The federation proxy services reside in the DMZ and redirect requests to the federation farm inside the internal network. The configuration of the proxy servers is very similar to that of the internal federation servers. Again, you use NLB to load balance requests between the two or more proxy servers. You use host entries to point to the internal NLB cluster because the DNS name is the same between internal and perimeter DNS (for example, fs.litwareinc.com). And again, you configure a DNS record, but this time in the perimeter network pointing to the perimeter NLB cluster. This will allow requests inside the perimeter, or coming in from the Internet, to be directed to the perimeter NLB cluster, followed by one of the federation proxies, which then reverse the request through the firewall into the internal network's NLB cluster to be handled by the internal federation server. Use the following steps to guide you through this process:

   8.1. The first step is to add the host entry on each proxy server. Under c:\System32\ Drivers\etc, open the Hosts files with Notepad. Enter the dedicated IP address of the NLB cluster in the internal network, along with the FQDN name, such as: 10.0.10.1 fs.litwareinc.com

   8.2. Create a new NLB cluster in the perimeter network with a dedicated IP address. Add the proxy servers into the cluster.

8.3. Next, add a DNS (A) record on the perimeter DNS server pointing to the NLB cluster IP in the perimeter network. Use the same FQDN that you've been using throughout this procedure (fs.litwareinc.com).

8.4. Similar to step 3 (internal config), import the same certificate into each default website in IIS on each proxy server.

8.5. Similar to step 5 (internal config), install the ADFS 2.0 server role on each proxy server in the perimeter proxy farm. The only difference is you want to specify Federation Server Proxy On The Server Role within the wizard (instead of Federation Server as was specified in step 5).

8.6. After the ADFS role is installed on each proxy server, the ADFS 2.0 Federation Server Proxy Configuration Wizard will load by default. Click Next on the Welcome page, type the federation service name (**fs.litwareinc.com**), and then click Next.

8.7. If you're using a reverse proxy, such as UAG, TMG, or Big IP, you can select the check box for Use An HTTP Proxy Server When Sending Requests To This Federation Service, and then type the name of the proxy server in the HTTP proxy server address box. Click Test Connection to verify the connection to the proxy server, and then click Next. Otherwise, Click Next (use the Hosts entry created in step 1).

8.8. A prompt appears asking for credentials. Enter the credentials of the ADFS 2.0 service account you specified in step 4 of the internal configuration. Click Next, and then click Close to complete the configuration. Repeat these steps on each proxy server in the perimeter network.

With the proxy servers set up, it is helpful to verify that the installation and configuration was successful. An easy way to do this is to look for an event with 198 as its event ID on each proxy server's event log (Event Viewer). If present, you'll know the proxy server has been configured correctly.

9. Download and install the Microsoft Online Services PowerShell module.

You must use PowerShell to set up the federation trust between Office 365 and your federation farm. You can run the commands from your personal computer or from a server, if you prefer. To download the module, use the following links:

X64: http://bit.ly/L8LS9z

X86: http://bit.ly/jTqbJW

To begin, open PowerShell on your computer and run the *Import-Module MSOnline* cmdlet to load the module that you just downloaded and installed. Next, you'll need to connect to Office 365 by using a set of credentials. Use the *Get-Credential* cmdlet to set your credentials to a variable that you can pass into the *Connect-MsolService* cmdlet. The *Connect-MsolService* cmdlet passes your credentials to Microsoft Online and sets up the secure connection. Once you're connected to Microsoft Online, you can start scripting your administrative actions. Figure 5-14 shows an example of how to connect to Microsoft Online with PowerShell after you've installed the module.

10. Configure Office 365 to trust your federation service domain.

    To add a new federated domain, you use the *New-MsolFederatedDomain* cmdlet. If you have an existing domain that you want to convert, you'll use the cmdlet *Convert-MsolDomainToFederated*. Converting is common if you previously configured DirSync, but now you want it to be fully federated.

    Before you begin, you must add the domains to Office 365 and go through the domain verification process. From the Office 365 Administration Center, click Domains, and then click Add A Domain. Follow the process to verify that you own the domain. If you need to register a subdomain, first verify the root domain (for example, litwareinc.com), and then verify the subdomain (for example, corp.litwareinc.com).

    The following shows an example of the *New-MsolFederatedDomain* cmdlet:

    ```
    New-MsolFederatedDomain –DomainName litwareinc.com
    ```

> **Note** Set the *SupportMultipleDomain* switch to true if your users have more than one UPN suffix.
>
> If you're not running the *New-MsolFederatedDomain* cmdlet from the primary federation server, you'll first need to set the content by running the following cmdlet:
>
> *Set-MsolAdfscontext –Computer <primary ADFS FQDN>*

    After the *New-MsolFederatedDomain* cmdlet finishes executing, it outputs DNS information. You need to change your domains at your domain registrar to point to this address before federation will start working. It's important to note that propagation can take up to 48 hours when making these DNS changes.

11. Install and configure DirSync.

    Directory synchronization is required for single sign-on and federated identity. DirSync is a client application that you install on one of your servers in your internal domain. The application synchronizes accounts each night with Office 365. To install the application, browse to the Office 365 Administration Center from a server in your internal domain. From the Administration Center, click Users, and then click Active Directory Synchronization. Under step 4, you'll notice a link to download the client application. Download it and run the installation executable. After the installation process finishes, select Start Configuration Wizard Now, and then click Finish.

When the wizard starts, you are prompted to enter your Office 365 global administrator credentials. These credentials are not saved; they are just used to connect the wizard to Office 365. After the wizard completes, it will be set up to synchronize every three hours. Note at the end of the wizard, you can select Synchronize Directories Now to initiate an immediate synchronization.

> **Note** By default, DirSync runs every three hours. If you want to force a synchronization rather than waiting, you can use PowerShell. Open the DirSync install directory (program files\Microsoft Online Directory Sync), and then run the *DirSyncConfigShell.psc1 PowerShell* cmdlet. At the PowerShell window, type **Start-OnlineCoexistenceSync**, and then press Enter.

12. Verify DirSync, activate users, and verify single sign-on.

    After you finish the DirSync wizard and the first synchronization runs, you'll start to see your AD user objects being populated in Office 365. As a test, you can make a small edit to an existing user, such as their first name, and after DirSync executes again, you'll notice that user's first name is updated in Office 365.

    It's important to note that the synced users in Office 365 will not be operable until you both activate each user as well as assign a license to each user. To do this through the browser, click Users from the Administration Center, select each user and click the Activate Synced Users button, and then thereafter assign them a license. You can also use PowerShell if you have many hundreds of users. See the next section on managing identity with PowerShell for more information.

    To validate that single sign-on is working, try logging into Office 365 from a domain joined computer. When you browse to Office 365, the password box is disabled and you see a link to log on at your company's on-premises ADFS 2.0 service. When you click the link, you log on through ADFS and are redirected back to Office 365, where you are granted access.

Managing Identities with Remote PowerShell

With Remote PowerShell, you can connect to Office 365 to perform management tasks that are not available or practical in the web management interface. For example, you can use Remote PowerShell to automate repetitive tasks, extract data for custom reports, customize policies, and connect Exchange Online to existing infrastructure and processes. This is especially useful when you need to perform the same task thousands of times. What would take days through the browser takes minutes with a script. The following is a list of common settings configured with Remote PowerShell:

- User management
- License assignment
- Security group management
- Domain management
- Admin role assignments

To use Remote PowerShell, your computer must be running the Windows Management Framework, which contains Windows PowerShell v2 and WinRM 2.0. These components are already installed in computers running Windows 7 or Windows Server 2008 R2. You can manually download these components for computers that are running other operating systems. You do not need to install any Exchange Server management or migration tools in order to use Remote PowerShell, however, you do need to download and install the Microsoft Online PowerShell Module.

The Microsoft Online PowerShell Module contains the core cmdlets for Office 365, such as those for managing users, groups, and so on. To download the module, use the following links:

X64: http://bit.ly/L8LS9z

X86: http://bit.ly/jTqbJW

To get started, open PowerShell on your computer, and then run the *Import-Module MSOnline* cmdlet to load the module that you just downloaded and installed. Next, connect to Office 365 by using a set of credentials. Use the *Get-Credential* cmdlet to set your credentials to a variable that you can pass into the *Connect-MsolService* cmdlet. The *Connect-MsolService* cmdlet passes your credentials to Microsoft Online and sets up the secure connection. Once you're connected to Microsoft Online, you can begin scripting your administrative actions. Figure 5-14 shows an example of how to connect to Microsoft Online with PowerShell after you've installed the module:

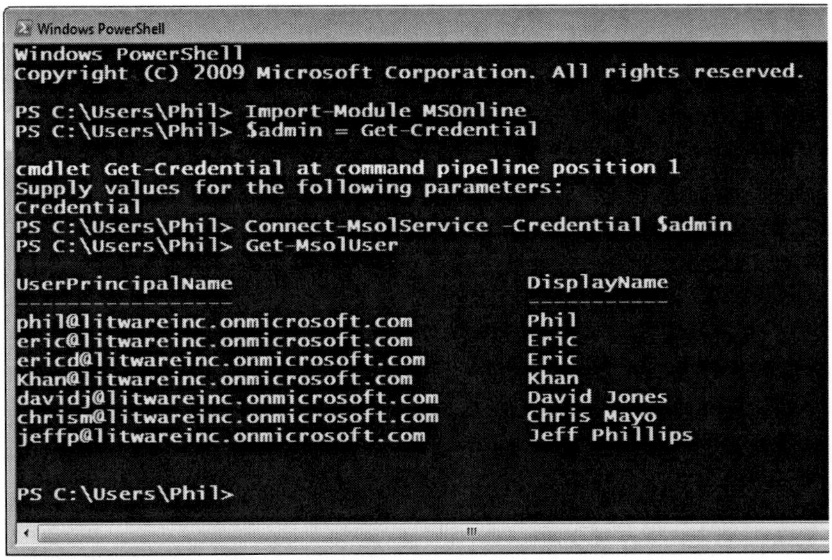

FIGURE 5-14 You can connect to Microsoft Online by passing your credentials into the *Connect-MsolService* cmdlet.

Notice in Figure 5-14 that the *Get-MsolUser* cmdlet was executed to fetch all the users in Microsoft Online. From a user management perspective, there are many cmdlets that you can use. The following scenarios will help you add/remove users, reset passwords, add/remove security groups, enable/disable password expiry, and enable/disable password strength requirements.

Creating a New User

To create a new user, use the *New-MsolUser* cmdlet. The following is an example of the cmdlet in use:

```
New-MsolUser -UserPrincipalName john@litwareinc.com -DisplayName "John Doe" -FirstName
"John" -LastName "Doe"
```

Assigning a License to a User

When you first create a user, that user doesn't have a license assigned to him and therefore cannot access SharePoint Online. To assign the user a license, you must use the *Set-MsolUserLicense* cmdlet. However, first you must retrieve the license key that you want to assign him by using the *Get-MsolAccountSku* cmdlet. Figure 5-15 demonstrates that the Get-*MsolAccountSku* cmdlet returns all the licenses you have purchased (ActiveUnits) along with a count of how many of those licenses have already been allocated to users (ConsumedUnits).

```
PS C:\Windows\system32> get-msolaccountsku

AccountSkuId                       ActiveUnits    WarningUnits    ConsumedUnits
litwareinc:ENTERPRISEPACK          25             0               7
litwareinc:DESKLESSWOFFPACK        25             0               0
litwareinc:SHAREPOINTSTANDARD      1              0               1

PS C:\Windows\system32>
```

FIGURE 5-15 Before you can assign a license, you must find a license that hasn't been fully allocated.

With this information available, you can run the *Set-MsolUserLicense* cmdlet. Use the *AddLicenses* parameter to assign a license, and use the *RemoveLicenses* parameter to remove a license. This can be seen in the following example:

```
Set-MsolUserLicense -UserPrincipalName user@litwareinc.onmicrosoft.com -AddLicenses
"litwareinc: ENTERPRISEPACK" -RemoveLicenses "litwareinc:SHAREPOINTSTANDARD"
```

> **Note** You can only assign one license to any given user. If you want to upgrade a user's license, first remove the one that he currently has, and then add the new license that you want to give him.

Removing a User

You can remove a user by using the *Remove-MsolUser* cmdlet, as illustrated in the following:

```
Remove-MsolUser -UserPrincipalName john@litwareinc.onmicrosoft.com
```

Resetting a User's Password

Quite commonly, users forget their passwords and they need an administrator to reset it for them. Resetting passwords with PowerShell is quite easy. Use the *Set-MsolUserPassword* cmdlet. Set the *NewPassword* property if you want to specify a specific password. You have the option to use the *ForceChangePassword* property if you don't want to require the user to change the password when she first logs on. If you don't use the *NewPassword* property, the user will be assigned a system-generated password. In either case, the user receives an email with her password after you run the cmdlet.

```
Set-MsolUserPassword -userPrincipalName john@litwareind.onmicrosoft.com
    -NewPassword "password" -ForceChangePassword $false
```

Blocking a User

To block a user from accessing Office 365 or SharePoint Online without permanently deleting the user, utilize the *Set-MsolUser* cmdlet and set the *BlockCredential* property to *true*:

```
Set-MsolUser -UserPrincipalName user@ litwareinc.onmicrosoft.com -blockcredential $true
```

Disabling Password Expiration for a User

By default, all passwords expire after 90 days. To disable this for a given user, utilize the *Set-MsolUser* cmdlet, and then set the *PasswordNeverExpires* property to *true*:

```
Set-MsolUser -UserPrincipalName user@ litwareinc.onmicrosoft.com
    -PasswordNeverExpires $true
```

Disabling Strong Password Strength Requirements

By default, all passwords must meet a certain level of complexity. You can disable these complexity requirements on a case-by-case basis by using the *Set-MsolUser* cmdlet. Set the *StrongPasswordRequired* property to *true*:

```
Set-MsolUser -UserPrincipalName user@litwareinc.onmicrosoft.com
    -StrongPasswordRequired $true
```

Adding a New Security Group

Security groups in Office 365 are helpful for SharePoint Online users because they can be used across multiple site collections. SharePoint groups can only be used in a single site collection, so if you want to manage authentication across more than one site collection, an Office 365 security group can be beneficial. To create a new group, use the *New-MsolGroup* cmdlet, as follows:

```
New-MsolGroup -DisplayName "Sales Executives" -Description "All sales staff"
```

Adding Users to a Security Group

To add a user to a group, you can use the *Add-MsolGroupMember* cmdlet. The problem, however, is this cmdlet requires a handle to the group to which you want to add the user, and to get a handle to that group, you first must use the *Get-MsolGroup* cmdlet and search on the group's display name, as shown in the following:

```
$salesGroup = Get-MsolGroup | where-object { $_.DisplayName -eq "Sales Executives"}
```

> **Note** You can use the *SearchString* parameter rather than the *where-object* option to make searching for a group or user easier; however, it might return more than one result, which you wouldn't want.

After you have your group assigned to a variable, you'll also want a handle on the user you want to add to that group, as demonstrated in the following example:

```
$user = Get-MsolUser | where-object { $_.DisplayName -eq "Phil" }
```

Hereafter, you can use the *Add-MsolGroupMember* cmdlet and add a user to that group, as shown in the following example:

```
Add-MsolGroupMember -GroupObjectId $salesGroup.ObjectId -GroupMemberType "User"
    -GroupMemberObjectId $user.ObjectId
```

Deleting a Security Group

To delete a security group, use the *Remove-MsolGroup* cmdlet, as shown here:

```
Remove-MsolGroup -objectid $salesGroup.ObjectId
```

Chapter 6
Migrating to SharePoint Online

In this chapter, you will learn about:

- Migrating to SharePoint Online through the browser
- What migration-related differences exist between Standard and Dedicated hosting models
- Planning migration downtime
- Which features can break when migrating

With the release of Microsoft Office 365, and with it, the ability to bring Microsoft SharePoint to the cloud, SharePoint is destined to fully enter the computing mainstream. As discussed in Chapter 1, "Introducing SharePoint Online," the return on investment (ROI) from using SharePoint in the cloud is staggering. Notably, there are no more availability concerns or expensive data centers to maintain. With SharePoint in the cloud, you can focus on adding business value rather than maintaining infrastructure. This situation is analogous to the introduction of electrical power, back in the early 1900s. Why should every company have to generate its own electricity? Doesn't it make more sense to buy this service from a company whose core business is generating electricity? Information technology works the same way: customers should focus on their core business rather than on re-creating the wheel.

Of course, that's all fine and good, but there is one problem with this model: an estimated 98 percent of SharePoint deployments are still on-premises operations. Why aren't people clamoring to move to the cloud? A big reason is that Office 365 was just released in July 2011, so it has only been available for a short while. Its predecessor, the Business Productivity Online Suite (BPOS), was deficient in feature parity relative to its on-premises companion. Fortunately, Office 365 has largely remedied this imbalance. With this release of Office 365 and the near feature parity that comes with it, SharePoint Online is sure to turn the tables. In turn, over the coming decade, 98 percent of SharePoint deployments will likely be in the cloud rather than on premises.

That point leads to the second reason why businesses have been slow to move online—namely, the widespread myth that Microsoft doesn't have a migration path to get you online. This rumor is both rampant and woefully untrue. In fact, there are a half-dozen or so different migration options that you can consider. For example, the obvious scenario would be a manual migration whereby you simply move your documents to the new site via Windows Explorer. Just drag from your on-premises site to your online site!

Unfortunately, the example of Windows Explorer doesn't scale well past small customers. To satisfy larger customers, many third-party tooling providers offer a convenient path toward SharePoint in the cloud. These third parties charge only a sliver of a fee in comparison to your annual infrastructure investment.

If you don't want to buy third-party software, you can still ship your content databases to Microsoft and it will restore them on your behalf. This is a practical approach for larger companies that purchase SharePoint Online dedicated hosting. All of these scenarios and more are the focus of this chapter. Migrating to SharePoint Online isn't necessarily brainless, but it might be easier than you would think.

Migration Scenarios

Not everyone will migrate 100 percent of content from on-premises SharePoint to SharePoint Online. Some content might be stored in a file sharing system, or perhaps in an exchange public folder. Or perhaps you're migrating from Lotus Notes to SharePoint Online. Following are some sample migration scenarios and some ideas for how to accomplish each:

- **Migrating on-premises SharePoint to SharePoint Online**   This is the most common scenario, and many techniques can be used to move an on-premises SharePoint setup to the cloud. The next section on techniques focuses on different ways to accomplish this task, including migration differences between Standard and Dedicated editions of SharePoint Online.

- **Migrating a file share to SharePoint Online**   If you have file share content that you want to bring into SharePoint Online, you have a few options. You can add the content to SharePoint before you migrate the system, or you can do so after you migrate the system. One way to bring file share content into SharePoint is simply through the browser or Windows Explorer. If you have many thousands of documents to move, you might want to purchase a third-party product to assist with this task. A variety of third-party providers offer tools that fit this niche.

- **Migrating a Microsoft Exchange public folder to SharePoint Online**   Similar to file share documents, documents in Exchange public folders might need to be moved into SharePoint Online. Third-party vendors also offer tools that fit this need.

- **Migrating Lotus Notes to SharePoint Online**   Some Office 365 customers might be migrating from Lotus Notes. Quest Software provides a great tool called Notes Migrator for SharePoint 6.0 that supports migration of Notes databases to SharePoint Online. For more information, visit the company's website at *http://www.quest.com/ notes-migrator-for-sharepoint/*.

All of the preceding scenarios focus on moving content from an on-premises system to the cloud, with the obvious intention of the sun setting on your on-premises SharePoint installation at some point. However, there are many scenarios in which you would want to maintain a hybrid cloud—that is, keep some content on premises and some online. A few example hybrid migration scenarios are presented here:

- **Gradual migration to SharePoint Online**   Not all companies necessarily want to migrate all of their content at once. Migrations to SharePoint Online Dedicated are relegated to an all-or-nothing approach, meaning that all sites in a given content database are migrated. Because this might not be the desired outcome, you might want to use a third-party product to target content in a database and move it in a piecemeal fashion. For example, if you have a database with 50 site collections in it, you could migrate one site collection at a time, rather than all 50 at once.

- **One-way or two-way synchronous content**   Some companies might want to take a hybrid approach and keep both on-premises and cloud content synchronized. Often, this strategy is used for extranet scenarios in which a company wants to publish content to the extranet and not expose its internal networks to any security vulnerabilities.

- **Hybrid SharePoint and geo-replication**   Another option along the lines of two-way synchronization is geo-replication. If your company has an office in the United States and, say, another office in Singapore, it could host its on-premises SharePoint in the United States data center and use Microsoft's data center in Singapore for its SharePoint Online content. You could then use a third-party product such as Metalogix to accommodate two-way synchronization between the two data centers.

> **Note**   You can have only one primary data center identified for all your Microsoft Online Services content.

- **Backup and failover**   Rather than implementing geo-replication, you could take a simpler replication approach for the sole purpose of creating a failover farm. With this arrangement, should an outage occur on your on-premises SharePoint deployment, you can still direct users to the SharePoint Online copy.

- **Security**   As mentioned in the two-way synchronous content scenario, extranets are a commonly used hybrid approach between SharePoint Online and on premises. Putting SharePoint in a demilitarized zone (DMZ), for example, is no feeble endeavor, and with Microsoft's security guarantees, using SharePoint Online is a pretty compelling option.

- **Cloud bursting**   Another benefit of two-way synchronization is the ability to divert traffic from an on-premises system to the cloud as on-premises demand increases. With this approach, you could split your domain name systems (DNS) to point some requests to the normal servers, while sending a percentage to cloud-based IPs to distribute the load.

Third-Party SharePoint Migration Products

Microsoft doesn't have an out-of-the-box approach for each migration scenario, so many of the following scenarios involve purchasing third-party software to make the migration easier. There are a half-dozen or so third-party migration products on the market that you should compare before making a purchase. Some third-party tools accommodate one scenario particularly well, but do not handle other scenarios quite so adroitly.

The following list organizes third-party software vendors in alphabetical order. Many of the vendors are currently transitioning to support Office 365:

AvePoint
(*http://www.avepoint.com*)

Binary Tree
(*http://www.binarytree.com*)

Idera
(*http://www.idera.com*)

Metalogix
(*http://www.metalogix.com*)

MetaVis
(*http://www.metavistech.com/*)

Quest Software
(*http://www.quest.com*)

Thinkscape
(*http://www.thinkscape.com*)

Note This list is not meant to be exhaustive, but rather focuses on companies that had a production or beta release of a SharePoint Online migration tool available at the general release of Office 365 (July 2011). If you don't see your product in this list, please contact the author to have it included in an updated version of the list.

Migration Techniques

Now that you have an idea about *what* you want to migrate into SharePoint Online, it's time to start considering the many options for *how* you will actually move this content. There are four basic techniques that you can use.

The first approach is to simply manually migrate the content through the browser user interface. This implies re-creating site hierarchies, lists, libraries, and content types. This approach is time consuming if you have a lot of content.

If you're using SharePoint Online Dedicated, you have a second option: you can ship the external hard drives that hold your content databases to Microsoft, and it will restore them on your behalf. As a third option, you can use a third-party migrator to implement your migration approach gradually, or if you need to restructure your content en route. The fourth option is to use a product that uses SharePoint's web services to migrate content. This approach is an excellent choice for customers that are too big to use the browser strategy, but too small to justify the cost of dedicated hosting.

Manual Migration Through the User Interface

Manually migrating your content through the user interface is undoubtedly the most straight-forward approach. This is especially true for customers that don't currently have a lot of on-premises content. When you use the user interface, you're actually re-creating the content sites, lists, and libraries, and then uploading or moving the documents by hand. The following are some pros and cons of manual migration:

Pros	Cons
Free	Can be time consuming (site-by-site, library-by-library basis)
Easy, intuitive	Site templates have a cap of 50 MB
	Must re-create all SharePoint containers, such as sites, lists, and libraries if moving content via Windows Explorer
	Windows Explorer won't migrate metadata or permissions

Migrating a Site, List, or Library by Saving Them as Templates

If you have a lot of documents, libraries, and lists within a single site, migrating a template of the site is probably the fastest, easiest approach. When you save a site as a template, you can specify that all content of the site be packaged into a template solution file and saved into the site collection's solution gallery.

 Note You cannot save a site as a site template if the Publishing feature has been activated.

The solution will contain all the pages, libraries, lists, documents, list items, web parts, and workflows in the site. You can download the solution template onto your computer and then upload the solution template into your SharePoint Online site collection's solution gallery. Once in the solution gallery, you'll be able to provision sites off the template because they will appear in the site template selection dialog, as shown in Figure 6-1.

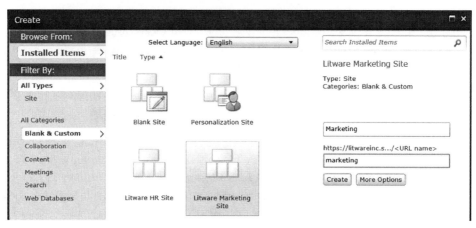

FIGURE 6-1 You can save your on-premises sites as templates and then import them into your SharePoint Online site collections, thereby provisioning sites off those templates and migrating the content.

The size of the site is probably the major limitation that would cause you to seek another approach. By default, the maximum size of a site template is 10 MB—not very big. You can change the maximum template size to a bit more than 500 MB if you have farm administrator access, but increasing it to more than 250 MB is really the largest size that makes sense: SharePoint Online has a maximum file upload size of 250 MB. This file upload size restriction also applies to solutions and site templates. To change the maximum template size on your on-premises farm, run the following PowerShell command against your SharePoint administration content service:

```
$sizeInB = 250000000
$contentService = [Microsoft.SharePoint.Administration.SPWebService]::ContentService
$contentService.MaxTemplateDocumentSize = $sizeInB
$contentService.Update()
```

Note This PowerShell script should be run from the SharePoint 2010 PowerShell management console. Otherwise, you must load the SharePoint 2010 PowerShell modules by giving the following commands:

```
[void][System.Reflection.Assembly]::LoadWithPartialName("Microsoft.SharePoint")
[void][System.Reflection.Assembly]::LoadWithPartialName(
  "Microsoft.SharePoint.Administration")
```

After you update the content service with your increased maximum template size, you'll be able to start saving sites as templates at a much larger capacity. To save a site as a template, click Site Actions | Site Settings, and then under Site Administration, click Save Site As Template. You'll need to give the template a file name and a display name. The display name is what appears in the Template Selection dialog box (see Figure 6-1). Ensure that you select the Include Content check box. If you don't include the content, only the framework of the site will be saved, and none of the documents, pages, and list items will be migrated to the new SharePoint site.

After you click the OK button to save the site as a template, the template will be saved to the solution gallery of the site collection. The next step is to download the template and upload it into the solution gallery of your SharePoint Online site collection. To do so, click Site Actions | Site Settings, and then under the Galleries heading, click Solutions. You'll see your template in the list of solutions; if you click the template name, you'll be prompted to download it. On the ribbon, save the file to your computer and upload it into your SharePoint Online solution gallery by clicking the Upload Solution button from the equivalent location. After you uploaded your solution, ensure that you click the Activate button on the ribbon from within the Solution Gallery to activate the template (see Figure 6-2). If the solution is not active, users will not see it in the site template selection dialog.

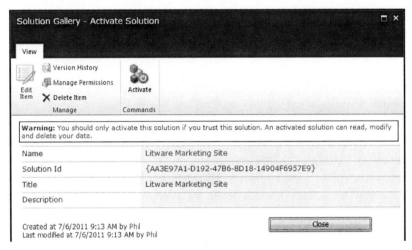

FIGURE 6-2 Ensure that you activate your solution site template; otherwise, users will not be able to provision sites using the template.

It's important to consider a few limitations that are inherent with this approach before wholeheartedly embracing it as the right track to take. The key takeaway message is that this migration approach works best for vanilla, out-of-the-box sites with little or no customizations. The following list describes some other potential limitations that you should consider when using this approach:

- The maximum template size is 10 MB (adjustable to 250 MB).

- Saving a site as a template does not save subsites. Thus, if you have subsites, you'll need to save them individually as templates and reprovision the hierarchy when in the cloud. This step can take a lot of time.

- If a template was saved that uses a feature that is not active on the destination site collection, that site will fail during provisioning. This is a trial-and-error situation; it is difficult to tell which features are active in the source and destination sites (some features are hidden, which can be a pain).

- Custom Web Parts might not work after the site is migrated. For full-trust Web Parts, ensure that your solutions were deployed to SharePoint Online Dedicated. For sandboxed Web Parts, ensure that the Web Part's solution is uploaded and active in the site collection's solutions gallery.

- Custom workflows might not work, much like the case for custom Web Parts. The exception is SharePoint Designer workflows, which should migrate seamlessly if they're found at the list, library, or site level. Globally reusable SharePoint Designer workflows need to be republished and reassociated.

- Metadata stored on documents using custom content types will not migrate.

- The Modified (date), Modified by (person), Created (date), and Created by (person) metadata columns will be reset with the date and the user who created the site off the template.

Migrating List Data and Documents by Saving as List/Library Templates

When you want to migrate lists or documents from on premises to SharePoint Online, you have the option to save the list or library as a list template. You can then move that template to your SharePoint Online site collection's Solution Gallery, in much the same fashion as you'd migrate a site template. This process of how to move the template from one gallery to another was discussed in the previous section. The exception to this is that list and library templates are uploaded to the List Template gallery rather than the solutions gallery.

Note Unfortunately, you cannot use Windows Explorer to move list data, only documents.

Just as site templates have a maximum size of 10 MB, list and library templates also use that same configuration to dictate their maximum size. If you need to increase the size of your list templates, set the maximum size on the content web service with the same PowerShell script that was used in the previous section. Additionally, saving lists and libraries as templates come with the same limitations as site templates, such as loss of original metadata, content types, and workflow dependencies.

Migrating Documents Through Windows Explorer

If you have hundreds of documents (perhaps thousands) that you need to move to SharePoint Online, the first step is to create the sites, libraries, and metadata in SharePoint online that will hold all your documents. After you have your libraries and content types in place, a fast way to start moving documents into SharePoint Online is by using Windows

Explorer (see Figure 6-3) to copy and paste or drag those documents into SharePoint Online. It would be very easy to open your on-premises SharePoint library as well as your SharePoint Online library in Windows Explorer, and then simply drag your documents from one folder to the other. To navigate to Windows Explorer from within a document library, on the ribbon, click the Library tab, and then click the Open With Explorer button as shown in Figure 6-4.

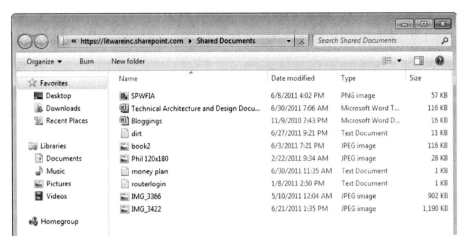

FIGURE 6-3 The Shared Documents library in the site at https://litwareinc.sharepoint.com is shown open in Windows Explorer. It's easy to drag documents into SharePoint Online from other Windows Explorer locations.

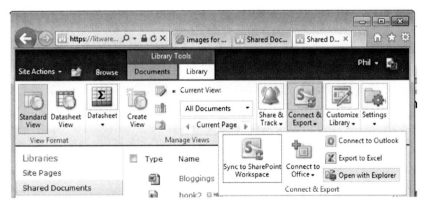

FIGURE 6-4 Opening a library by using Windows Explorer is done on the ribbon in the Connect & Export group.

There are two downsides to using Windows Explorer to migrate documents. The first is that if you have many libraries or folders, it can take quite a long time to move all of your documents because you can't just drag all documents across all libraries in one action. The second major issue is that metadata won't be applied when you migrate. So, if you have a content type that contains ten pieces of metadata, and you copy and paste 100 documents, it will take you several hours to edit each document and reapply the appropriate metadata.

Additionally, all created date and user metadata elements will be reset to the date on which you migrated the documents, and the user information will change to that of the person who copied the documents.

> **Note** If your columns are configured to assign default values, those defaults will be applied when you use Explorer view to migrate documents. So in this case, some metadata in fact will be applied.

Your Client Does Not Support Opening This List with Windows Explorer

If you get an error that says "Your client does not support opening this list with Windows Explorer," you need to add your SharePoint Online site as a local intranet site in Internet Explorer options so that your credentials will automatically be passed through. This will grant Windows Explorer access to connect to your site. From within Internet Explorer, click Tools | Internet Options. On the Security tab, click the Local Intranet icon. Next, click the Sites button and enter the URL of your SharePoint Online site, and then click OK (see Figure 6-5). Thereafter, you will be able to open your libraries from that URL with Windows Explorer.

FIGURE 6-5 Be sure to add your SharePoint Online site as a trusted site so that you can connect to it with Windows Explorer.

Mail and Restore Content Database

Another option for performing your SharePoint Online migration is to literally mail your on-premises content databases to Microsoft (or use your favorite parcel delivery service). That's right; you read this correctly. Place your on-premises content in a package, bring it to the local Post Office, purchase the correct postage, and then send it on its way. Microsoft will then take your databases and restore them into your SharePoint Online farm. This approach only works for the SharePoint Online Dedicated hosting model, and is not supported for SharePoint Online Standard.

If your databases are small enough, you might be able to send them to Microsoft over a secure WAN link. If your databases are too large, you'll need to ship them, as just mentioned. Because it can take several days to ship a hard disk with your databases, another option is to ship a full back up, and then send a differential backup over the WAN. Microsoft can then restore the full database backup when it receives the external hard disks in the mail, and thereafter restore the latest differential backup. This affords you minimal on-premises downtime when migrating to SharePoint Online Dedicated. For more information on minimizing downtime, see the section "Planning for Migration Downtime," later in this chapter. The following are some pros and cons of mail-and-restore migration:

Pros	Cons
Free (except shipping costs).	Only works for SharePoint Online Dedicated hosting model.
Microsoft handles the restoration of the content.	You need a well thought through strategy to minimize downtime while the databases are en route.
	Doesn't support a gradual migration within a single content database.
	Can't change up your information architecture when en-route. Optimizations must be done beforehand.
	Again, assumes a fairly vanilla, out-of-the-box SharePoint on-premises site. Customizations are subject to approval by the SharePoint Online Dedicated team at Microsoft.

Note Be aware that Microsoft will insist that you manage the migration to their supported capacities, such as keeping your site collections under 200 GB. See the section "Supported Items and Migration Gotchas," later in this chapter, for more information on which capacities Microsoft will require compliance.

Central Administration SharePoint Backup

SharePoint backups can be performed from Central Administration. However, the SharePoint Online Dedicated team will not take a SharePoint backup and restore it. The problem is that SharePoint backups rely heavily on server names matching because of the values stored in the configuration database. With this limitation, it is nearly impossible to restore a SharePoint backup to SharePoint Online, and conventional SQL backups remain the best restore and migration strategy.

Migrating Miscellaneous Configurations and Content

Not all SharePoint content is stored in the content database. For example, user profiles, audiences, and search settings such as managed properties are all stored in their respective service application databases. When you migrate to SharePoint Online Dedicated, you're going to want to communicate these configurations to Microsoft as well as send it your user profile service application databases and search service application databases so that they can restore them as well.

Also, consider any central administration settings that you might need to migrate to SharePoint Online. For instance, suppose that you have web application policies that grant or deny access to certain users or groups. Microsoft will need to manually set those up on your behalf. Also, you might have customized the permission levels, such as disabling themes or SharePoint Designer access. Whatever the concern, be sure to document for Microsoft all your miscellaneous configurations so that they are migrated along with the content.

Migration Agents Used with SharePoint Online Dedicated

If you're using SharePoint Online Dedicated edition, you'll have the advantage of using third-party tooling options. That's because SharePoint migration products that involve installing "agent" software on the SharePoint web front-ends tend to support much more compelling features than those third parties that simply rely on the out-of-the-box web services. This affords these products neat features that aren't otherwise available.

One of the biggest players in the agent space is Metalogix (*http://metalogix.com*). Metalogix has frequently been approved for use when migrating from on-premises SharePoint to SharePoint Online Dedicated.

The key benefit to using Metalogix over shipping Microsoft your databases is the ability to implement a gradual migration. With Metalogix, you can migrate your on-premises content in bite-sized pieces and even restructure that content as it moves to the cloud. So, if you have a content database with 1,000 site collections, you might want to consolidate 250 of them, keep 250 on premises, and migrate the remaining 500 into SharePoint Online. To learn more about the benefits of using a third-party migrator for SharePoint Online Dedicated, see *http://metalogix.com*. The following are some pros and cons of migration agents:

Pros	Cons
Supports gradual migration.	Not free.
Supports other hybrid scenarios such as geo-replication, failover farms, and two-way synchronization.	Not many third-party products are supported— your hands might be tied due to a limited number of vendors.
Allows you to reorganize content as you move it.	
Allows you to also migrate from many different sources, such as file shares, Exchange public folders, and so on.	

SharePoint Web Services

Using the SharePoint Online web services to migrate content is sort of the "middle ground" between the browser and content database restore approaches. Consider a scenario in which using the browser causes data loss (metadata) and is too time consuming. Also, in this same scenario, the customer is too small to justify the extra cost of SharePoint Online Dedicated. Obviously with the Dedicated edition, the customer could just ship their databases and let Microsoft handle it; but again, Dedicated isn't for a feeble pocket book. What hope then is there for this medium-sized customer?

Well unfortunately, there's no "official" Microsoft response to this problem. However, there are several third-party software vendors that focus on filling this niche gap. With a few thousand dollars, you can buy software that connects to SharePoint Online's out-of-the-box web services and uses those services to migrate content. The services can provision sites, pages, libraries, lists, and so on. Many of the third-parties offer the ability to have your on-premises SharePoint site on the left, and your SharePoint Online site on the right, and you can simply drag entire site hierarchies from one to the other. If you need to move 100 sites, with deep hierarchies of child subsites, a third-party tool will be far more cost effective than manually re-creating those hierarchies through the browser. The following table lists some pros and cons of third-party software migration tools.

Pros	Cons
Works with both SharePoint Online Standard and Dedicated hosting models.	Not free.
Easy and intuitive interface to move content.	Less feature functionality than its agent version counterpart (as described in the previous section).
You can reorganize content as you migrate.	
You can also migrate from many different sources, such as file shares, Exchange public folders, and so on.	

The following are examples of common sources third-parties can migrate into SharePoint Online:

- From on-premises SharePoint 2010, 2007, or even 2003

- From Business Productivity Online Suite Standard and Business Productivity Online Suite Dedicated

- From file shares

- From Microsoft Exchange Public Folders

- From Microsoft Outlook

- From cloud to cloud (for example, SharePoint Online to SharePoint Online)

The following are some key benefits to using a third-party tool:

- Copy entire sites, lists, and libraries along with their content types and columns while retaining version history

- Copy selected items between folders, lists, sites, or servers, and simultaneously change or preserve content types and column values

- Change content types and assign column values in bulk

- Save rules for column mapping as templates for reuse in the future

Metavis agentless migrator is one of the premiere third-party tools in this space. For more information, go to *http://www.metavistech.com*.

Supported Items and Migration Gotchas

There are some "gotchas" when migrating from on-premises SharePoint to SharePoint in the cloud. Some of them are subtle, such as one of 50 of your custom Web Parts no longer work and you can't figure out why. Others stare you right in the face, such as Microsoft telling you it won't restore your content because you have a site collection that's 500 GB in size. The following sections walk you through some of these unique areas to which you need to pay attention when planning your migration.

Managed Paths

Unfortunately, custom managed paths are not supported in SharePoint Online. If you have site collections within custom managed paths, those site collections will not be accessible via the same URL after you migrate to SharePoint Online. All sites in SharePoint Online (besides My Sites and the root) reside within the "sites" managed path. Plan on updating your information architecture before Microsoft lets you migrate. Also, develop a communication plan to help your users with the transition.

Capacity and Threshold Constraints

The team at Microsoft won't restore your content if that content doesn't manage to their supported capacity guidelines. For example, if you ship a database that contains 3,000 site collections, the company is going to give you the bad news that you need to split that database apart before you ship it back to them again. Table 6-1 describes some of these constraints that you ought to consider when planning your migration.

TABLE 6-1 Limitations to Consider When Shipping a Database to Microsoft

Name	Limit	Notes
Site collections/content database	Less than 2,000/database is recommended; 5,000 maximum.	
Sites/site collection	Less than 250,000	
Site collection maximum size	Less than 100 GB	Unless it is the only site collection in the content database, then it may be 200 GB.
Content database maximum size	Less than 200 GB	Unless it is a read-only database (records/document center), then this can be 5 TB.
Maximum number of documents or list items in a given library or list	Less than 60 million	Note that 60 m documents totaling less than 100 GB means they are very small on average. Thus, 30 m is effectively lower for SharePoint Online.
Versions per document	Less than 400,000	

In addition to the limits presented in the Table 6-1, there are also thresholds with which you'll want to acquaint yourself. In SharePoint 2010, when a threshold is achieved, the underlying SQL query terminates the query and the user interface throws an error. This phenomenon is especially important if you're migrating from SharePoint 2007 on-premises or BPOS into SharePoint Online (2010). The reason for this is that these thresholds are a new "feature" of SharePoint 2010. Alternatively, you might have these default thresholds customized to higher values in your on-premises farm, and if so, your users might have issues because of Microsoft's lower settings.

A common example would be a large list that you have in your SharePoint 2007 site. Suppose that you have 20,000 items. If you have a view that queries against 8,000 items, for example, that view will reach the 5,000-item threshold (default setting) and will be inoperable in SharePoint Online. Thus, it is important to survey your large lists and libraries and ensure that you have no views that will attain this threshold. Table 6-2 shows a few more thresholds that you will want to consider in your planning.

TABLE 6-2 Additional Limitations to Consider When Shipping a Database to Microsoft

Name	Threshold (default settings)	Notes
List view threshold	5,000 items	Any view that queries against more than 5,000 items in the database will fail.
List view threshold for admins	20,000	
List view lookup columns	8 columns/query	If you have a list with lookup columns (including managed metadata), those columns require a separate query. SharePoint Online won't support more than eight queries.
Sub sites	Less than 2,000/parent site	
Security scopes	Less than 1,000/list or libraries	Each time you break inheritance in a list or library, you're creating a new Access Control List (ACL). SharePoint Online now has a threshold where a list or library will become inoperable after 1,000 ACLs.

Note Another way to help with the 5,000 view threshold is to index columns on your lists. For example, with the same 20,000 item list, if you have a filter in the view, be sure to index the column that is being filtered. This acts as a "where" clause, and if that column is indexed, you can push beyond the 5,000 threshold. Otherwise, the query will need to scan all 20,000 items to see if the columns are equal to your filter. With that example, it would fail because the scan is greater than the 5,000 threshold.

Authentication Providers

When migrating to SharePoint Online, you're going to need to spend a lot of time considering how you handle identity and authentication. Chapter 5, "Identity Management and Authentication," covers this topic in detail, but from a migration perspective, it's important to note a few sticky points here. The first, most obvious one is that if you migrate through the browser, no security permissions will migrate along with the content. You're going to need to reapply all instances of SharePoint groups, custom permission levels, and broken inheritance. This is even true for most third-party migrators that use the out-of-the-box web services. If you migrate from on-premises Active Directory (AD) accounts on to Microsoft Online accounts, those third-party tools have no way to translate and map one identity to another; thus, you're stuck reconfiguring all your permissions.

The silver lining is if you plan on using Active Directory Federation Services 2.0 (ADFS 2.0) to accommodate single sign-on between your on-premises identities and your SharePoint Online content. Any claims in your SharePoint on-premises content are migrated over with the help of third-party products. Because the claim on premises is the same claim when in the cloud, those on-premises identities will have the exact same access that they enjoyed pre-migration. Therefore, if avoiding the need to redo security is a priority for you, you must get on to claims-based authentication in your on-premises SharePoint farm as well as configure ADFS 2.0 to federate your on-premises identities with SharePoint Online.

Note SharePoint Online Dedicated edition requires that you move from classic mode authentication and implement Windows claims-based authentications. It's a line in the sand, so you might as well plan on getting there soon.

It's important to note that Windows claims is the requirement. If you're using Security Assertion Markup Language (SAML) claims and you think you're all set, think again. SharePoint Online will not recognize a claim from an unreachable on-premises identity provider (in fact, ADFS 2.0 is the only supported Identity Provider STS [IP-STS]). Obviously, pluggable authentication is not supported in SharePoint Online.

Unsupported Customizations

Chapter 7, "Introduction to Customizing and Developing in SharePoint Online," covers customizations in greater detail than is covered here, but it is important to note a few migration trouble spots that can arise with your customizations. The foremost gotcha is a failure to migrate your full-trust coded Web Parts into sandboxed solutions.

Recall from Chapter 1 that sandboxed solutions are favored by Microsoft over full-trust code, because code that runs in the sandbox is isolated from one site collection to another. A particular Web Part in a given site collection can never negatively impact the performance and availability of a different site collection. This is because sandboxed code is governed by resource quotas (CPU, Memory, IOPs, and so on), and it cannot access beyond the bounds of the site collection in which the code is active.

This is all fine and good, but the trouble is that SharePoint Online Standard edition only supports sandboxed solutions. If you migrate pages that have full-trust Web Parts on them, those Web Parts will not be functioning. You'll need to deploy them in the solution's gallery and hope that they still work as they did before.

Beyond Web Parts, the following is a sampling of other customizations that might break when you migrate from on-premises SharePoint to the cloud:

- Microsoft Visual Studio .NET workflows. Any workflow functionality needs to be reworked as sandboxed actions and deployed via SharePoint Designer workflows.

- Visual Web Parts. Visual Web Parts utilize a user control that is deployed to the _CONTROLTEMPLATES virtual directory. Because SharePoint Online Standard doesn't support customizations on the server, visual Web Parts will be inoperable.

 Note An exception to visual Web Parts are sandboxed visual Web Parts deployed via the SharePoint Power Pack. See Chapter 7 for more information.

- Office InfoPath forms with custom coded business logic that leaves the bounds of the sandbox.

- Pluggable authentication providers.

- Site definitions.

- Web.config custom additions.

- Custom code access security policies.

- Customizations that leverage external systems such as proprietary databases.

With all these limitations, you might find yourself hamstrung with very limited options. If this is you, you need SharePoint Online Dedicated edition. The Dedicated version of SharePoint Online affords you much more flexibility from a customizations perspective because the physical hardware is dedicated to you, and thus won't affect another one of Microsoft Online's customers. The only downside is a formidable approval and code promotion process. See Chapter 7 for more details about how this process works.

Unsupported SharePoint 2010 Features

Not all features of SharePoint 2010 work for both SharePoint on premises and SharePoint Online. Such features include the majority of the Business Intelligence (BI) stack, such as SQL Server Reporting Services (SSRS) integration, PerformancePoint, and PowerPivot. Also, FAST for SharePoint is not available in SharePoint Online. Business Connectivity Services would be another example of a popular feature that is not available either. These are just the main features. For a full list of SharePoint's 100-plus features and their availability in SharePoint Online, see the Appendix, "Server, Online SharePoint, and Online Dedicated Compared."

Planning for Migration Downtime

When you migrate to SharePoint Online, you're going to experience some transition time. This is true no matter which migration approach you take—manually through the browser, shipping databases to Microsoft, or via third-party products.

A key tip to minimize downtime is to change your on-premises databases to be read-only during the migration. By doing this, even if it takes 24 hours to migrate, you'll guarantee that no new content is added to the farm and mistakenly not migrated. And the other main benefit, over simply turning the farm off, is that when the farm is in read-only mode, users can still access their content (although, they cannot modify it). Figure 6-6 shows a sample of this process.

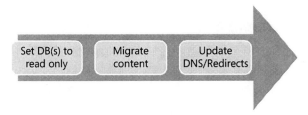

FIGURE 6-6 Set your content databases to read-only mode to prevent data loss during migration.

Figure 6-6 illustrates that the on-premises content databases are first set to read-only. Next, the migration of the content begins, and then after that has finished, user traffic is sent to the new location in SharePoint Online. You could use a DNS change on premises or set up redirects in IIS to handle the redirection of traffic to SharePoint Online.

Setting a Content Database to Read-Only

To set a content database as read-only, you must have access to the SQL databases through SQL Management Studio. Right-click the database, and then from the context menu that appears, click Properties. The Database Properties window opens. On the Options tab, scroll down until you see Database Read-Only (see Figure 6-7). Set the value to True, and then click OK. Thereafter, your database will look similar to what's seen in Figure 6-8 below.

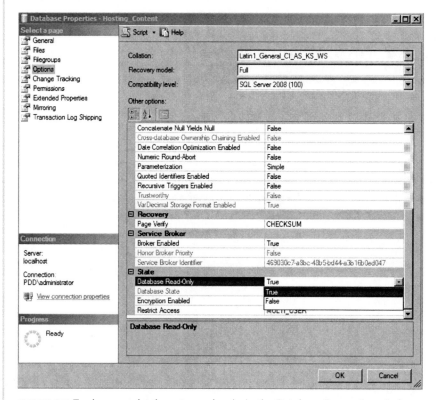

FIGURE 6-7 To change a database to read-only, in the Database Properties window, set the Database Read-Only property to True.

FIGURE 6-8 After the database is set to read-only, it is grayed-out and flagged "(Read-Only)."

SharePoint promotes this read-only setting all the way up through the stack, and all administrative and contributor functions within the sites in that database will no longer be available. In fact, those settings are trimmed out of the user interface. Users can simply view, read, and download content from SharePoint.

If you're migrating to SharePoint Online Dedicated edition, you'll have a few more scenarios to consider. Beyond simply setting your databases to read-only and performing the migration, you're going to incur shipping time. If you have one terabyte of databases, you will need to ship those databases to Microsoft on an external hard disk. This can take a several days—possibly up to a week if you include the time that Microsoft needs to turn it around and restore the databases. So in this scenario, what are your options? Figure 6-9 shows a possible approach.

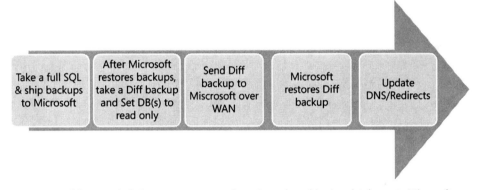

FIGURE 6-9 This scenario helps you to manage downtime when shipping databases to Microsoft.

In this second approach, the first step is to take a Full SQL backup of all your content databases and ship those backups to Microsoft. After a few days, Microsoft will receive the backups and restore them to your SharePoint Online Dedicated farm. At this point, you take a differential backup of all your content databases and send them to Microsoft. because differentials should be considerably smaller than your full backups, you should be able to send them over the WAN rather than delivering them physically.

Note Do some research and see how big your differentials are, along with your bandwidth and latency between your data center and Microsoft. It would be prudent to send Microsoft a sample differential backup to test transfer times. If you know precisely how long it will take to transfer, you can better set expectations with your users regarding how long their content will be in read-only mode.

A key point at this juncture is to set the databases to read-only so no content is lost. The differential backup is now the source of truth. After Microsoft receives your differential backups, it will restore them on to your fulls. Now, you just need to update DNS and/or install redirects on your on-premises SharePoint farm to send your users to their new destination!

> **Note** Consider sending Microsoft compressed backups. SharePoint databases compress 30–50 percent on average, and if you're sending your backups over the WAN, this can save a considerable amount of transfer time. This feature is only available with SQL Server Enterprise edition, however.
>
> This second scenario does not accommodate a gradual migration approach. All sites in the backup will be migrated at once. Research a third-party migrator to achieve gradual migrations. Currently, Metalogix is the only agent version supported for SharePoint Online Dedicated.

Chapter 7
Introduction to Customizing and Developing in SharePoint Online

In this chapter, you will learn about:

- Customizing SharePoint Online with SharePoint Designer and InfoPath
- Building custom .NET solutions for the sandbox
- Leveraging the client object model to access SharePoint Online data
- Integrating SharePoint Online with Azure applications

Microsoft SharePoint Online is nearly identical to SharePoint on-premises with the clear exception that it is hosted by Microsoft in the cloud. The great news is that SharePoint Online is nearing feature parity with the on-premises version; thus, organizations can take advantage of nearly all the features to which they are accustomed. Developers can build cloud-based SharePoint solutions in a similar fashion as they would for an on-premises deployment. The different ways to develop solutions for SharePoint Online, along with the main differences between on-premises customizations and cloud customizations, are the highlight of this chapter.

Multiple tools are available for customizing your SharePoint deployment, such as the browser, SharePoint Designer 2010, Microsoft InfoPath Designer 2010, and Microsoft Visual Studio 2010. This chapter will discuss these tools and how you can use them to customize and build solutions for SharePoint Online. Additionally, there are two different approaches to building solutions for SharePoint Online: via sandboxed solutions and via full-trust code. *Sandboxed solutions* often contain custom-coded .NET assemblies that are limited to the scope of a given site collection. *Full trust solutions* are usually deployed to the global assembly cache (GAC), and thus are only permissible for the SharePoint Online dedicated model. The Standard and Dedicated models follow very different deployment processes. Later sections of this chapter explain these two development approaches and their capabilities in detail.

Beyond tools, cloud-based SharePoint solutions will also frequently take advantage of a few development techniques. With the client object model, developers can build applications on SharePoint 2010 that run client side as opposed to server side. This gives you more flexibility than the sandboxed model. Three different but similar client-side application programming interfaces (APIs) are available: the Microsoft Silverlight client-side object model, the JavaScript/ECMAScript client-side object model, and the managed code client-side object model.

Another common cloud technique is to leverage Microsoft Windows Azure to host the major components of your application. Azure and SQL Azure are two cloud-based services offered by Microsoft that let you build, scale, and host applications in Microsoft data centers, essentially letting you host your application and SQL data in the cloud. Fortunately, there are ways to integrate your applications and data stored in Azure with SharePoint Online, and we will discuss them in the last section of this chapter.

Developing Against the Cloud vs. On-Premises

Developing solutions for an on-premises SharePoint application is the most flexible approach. It gives you unfettered access to the SharePoint environment. You can deploy farm solutions, change web.config settings, read/write to the file system, and so on. The SharePoint Online Standard edition places many restrictions on the types of solutions you can deploy because these solutions are deployed to the multitenant environment in the cloud. The SharePoint Online Dedicated edition is similar to an on-premises deployment, but you must follow a detailed deployment process to get your code deployed in the Microsoft data center. The following subsections explain the different development approaches in more detail.

Development for On-Premises

In this scenario, there are no restrictions on what kinds of solutions you must build as a developer. You can use the standard customization tools, such as the browser, SharePoint Designer, and InfoPath, but you can also build and deploy farm (full-trust) solutions into your SharePoint deployment. Often, a developer doesn't have box administrative rights to production, so full-trust solutions usually must go through an IT administrative approval process.

With full-trust solutions, your code can write to the file system, reference assemblies in the GAC, call external web services, surface your Line-of-Business (LoB) external data, use Performance Point services, and so on. In short, you can use the complete (licensed) feature set of SharePoint 2010 with no programmatic limitations.

Development for SharePoint Online Standard

In this scenario, your SharePoint site and your solutions are hosted in a multitenant environment. Therefore, Microsoft implements safeguards to prevent organizations from running code that would interfere with other tenants on the same hardware. Tools such as the browser, SharePoint Designer, and InfoPath are fully functional in a multitenant environment, which makes it easy to transition from one environment to another if a power user is used to building on-premises, no-code solutions.

From a Microsoft .NET perspective, organizations can only upload sandboxed solutions that run in a separate, monitored user process and that do not affect the performance of the rest of the SharePoint Online site. Sandboxed solutions are a new feature of SharePoint 2010 that lets site collection administrators upload their own custom solutions without help from an IT resource that has server access.

These solutions are uploaded to the solutions gallery and run in their own isolated process, so they do not interfere with the normal functioning of the rest of the site. Site administrators can also monitor solutions that have been uploaded to the site collection. This is advantageous because they have a minimal impact on the rest of the site/farm, thereby making them good candidates for a SharePoint Online Standard deployment scenario.

Here are a few examples of restricted actions in sandboxed solutions:

- Making references to the file system
- Deploying assemblies to the GAC (full-trust)
- Using server-side code to call external web services
- Surfacing line-of-business data using Business Connectivity Services (BCS), except via external lists
- Exposing data through Performance Point services

Here are a few examples of functionality that is allowed in sandboxed solutions. A detailed list of allowed and restricted items is provided in later sections.

- Feature receivers
- Event receivers
- Navigation
- Web Parts (excluding Visual Web Parts)

Development for SharePoint Online Dedicated

In this scenario, your SharePoint site and your solutions are hosted in a dedicated environment for your organization within Microsoft Online Services/Office 365. This is similar to hosting an on-premises SharePoint environment in your farm, except that Microsoft takes on the operational burden. You can use pretty much all the features available to your on-premises deployment in this option. Full-trust solutions are available in this scenario. Microsoft also offers a pre-production environment that you can use to view and validate your custom solutions before they are deployed to your production farm. The process for uploading customizations into the SharePoint Online Dedicated environment is also outlined in a later section.

Customization Tools

Organizations have several options when it comes to customizing and developing solutions for SharePoint Online. The different options are to use the browser, SharePoint Designer 2010, InfoPath 2010, or Visual Studio 2010. The process for customizing SharePoint Online using the browser is the same as that for an on-premises deployment: you can make changes that are available through the user interface. Customizations using SharePoint Designer 2010 are also similar to an on-premises deployment: You can simply connect Designer to a SharePoint Online site as you would with an on-premises site and start customizing. InfoPath 2010 with SharePoint Online is again similar to an on-premises development: you can build the form in SharePoint Online and connect to lists and libraries as data sources.

Visual Studio 2010 provides a different approach to SharePoint development. The development process for solutions tailored to SharePoint Online Standard differs from an on-premises deployment or SharePoint Online Dedicated. The customization/development tools are outlined in greater detail in the following subsections.

Customization Tools: The Browser

Customizing using the browser for a SharePoint Online site is largely the same as an on-premises deployment. Your SharePoint Online administrator gives users permissions to the different sections of the site. Using the browser, you can switch pages into edit mode and add or remove Web Parts from the page, change Web Part properties, and add/remove content and images from the page. You can also create pages, lists, libraries, site columns, and content types, as well as change site and list properties, and start workflows. It is also possible to change the theme of the entire site by changing the site configuration by using the browser. You can upload the jQuery API into a document library in SharePoint Online and add a Content Editor Web Part that references and uses that API in your SharePoint Online sites. Because browser-based customizations in SharePoint Online are similar to on-premises deployments, they are not discussed in detail in this chapter.

For more information about how to perform some of the browser-based customizations just described, read Microsoft SharePoint 2010 Foundation Step by Step, *by Olga Londer and Penelope Coventry (2011, Microsoft Press).*

Customization Tools: SharePoint Designer

SharePoint Designer 2010 is a great tool to use for customizations and quick development of no-code SharePoint applications. Advanced business users and developers can build out quick applications that meet their business needs, all without writing a single line of code. You can use SharePoint Designer 2010 for a variety of purposes, as we will discuss in the following subsections.

Where to Download SharePoint Designer?

SharePoint Designer is available as a free download from Microsoft. For more information or to download the 32-bit version, go to *http://bit.ly/jWpLOw*. To download the 64-bit version, go to *http://bit.ly/mNfx17*.

It is worth noting that SharePoint customizations using SharePoint Designer 2010 are the same whether you are customizing an on-premises installation or a SharePoint installation in the cloud. Here are some of the key tasks that you can perform by using SharePoint Designer 2010:

- Create a SharePoint site.

- Customize components that compose that site, such as enabling features, as well as creating lists and libraries and the relationships between them.

- Design business processes that let the components of the site work together by using Designer's workflow capabilities.

- Package the site into a solution package (.wsp files) to deploy directly to SharePoint Online or include as part of a larger solution in Visual Studio 2010.

For more information about how to perform some of the browser-based customizations just described, read Microsoft SharePoint Designer 2010 Step by Step, *by Penelope Coventry (2010, Microsoft Press).*

Customization vs. Development

The tasks you perform using SharePoint Designer 2010 are referred to as "customizations" rather than "development." This is because SharePoint Designer revolves around no-code customizations of the existing SharePoint site. This is opposed to custom-coded development done with Visual Studio. SharePoint development for SharePoint Online using Visual Studio 2010 is discussed later in this chapter.

> **Note** SharePoint Designer customizations are not very portable, meaning that if you need to make the same customization to 100 sites, you should consider using Visual Studio.

This also means any changes you make against that site are immediately available on the live site. There is no "deployment" process that will formally enable these changes. Therefore, grant SharePoint Designer access to key people in the organization that you trust, because they can make live (sometimes breaking) changes to your site.

Designing and Branding Sites with SharePoint Designer

SharePoint Designer 2010 is the primary tool for customizing SharePoint branding and creating master pages, page layouts, and Cascading Style Sheets (CSS). These artifacts provide a consistent look and feel on the entire site, thus meeting the business goals of unified branding. You can use Designer to brand your sites by applying a corporate logo, color schemes and images, navigation and supporting graphics, and so on. Figure 7-1 shows the default Designer view for the site. Note that properties and quick actions are readily available in this default view of the site.

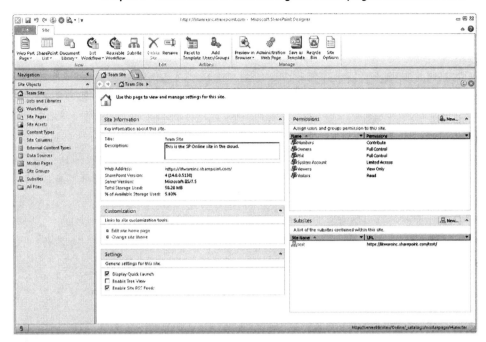

FIGURE 7-1 The Home view when you first load SharePoint Designer.

Figure 7-2 shows the navigation down to the master page gallery. All SharePoint sites are associated with a master page that, when edited, controls the look and feel of all the sites using that master page. The master page has all the main navigational components defined within it, such as the top and left navigations. Also, you can add references to custom CSS and JavaScript in the master page so that all sites will incorporate those elements. From the master page gallery, you can locate the v4.master. This master page is the main master that SharePoint Online sites use.

FIGURE 7-2 You can edit the v4.master master page to customize the look and feel of the sites in SharePoint Online.

After you edit the master page, you can start making your desired changes. A common thing that many folks want to do is to customize the master page to show their company's logo at the top. You can also do this by clicking Site Actions | Look And Feel; however, to get it to look just right, you might need to edit the HTML in the master page. Figure 7-3 shows how easy it is to use SharePoint Designer to change the site logo.

> **Note** Rather than edit the V4.master master page, it is preferable to first copy V4.master, and rename the copy. Then, make your changes to the copy rather than the original. Afterward, you can instruct SharePoint to use your custom master page rather than the out-of-the-box V4.master. This provides the benefit of always having a reliable fallback point if you ever break your customized copy.

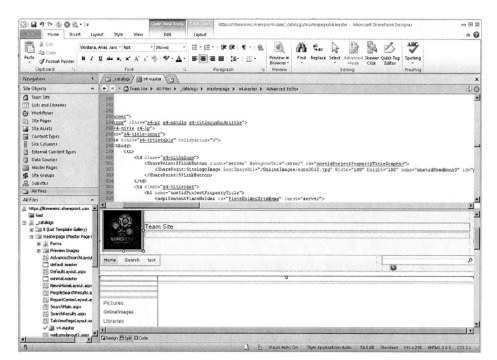

FIGURE 7-3 When you edit the v4.master master page, you can change the HTML to meet your unique branding requirements, such as positioning a custom logo.

Connections to Data

You can connect to various data sources within and outside SharePoint by using the capabilities in SharePoint Designer 2010. This lets developers build composite applications that can gather data from multiple sources. For example, you might build a page where your customer details are highlighted. This page can include components from a customer list in SharePoint as well as additional data from a LoB application such as CRM or SAP. Using

SharePoint Designer 2010, it is straightforward to connect to an external database, SOAP service, and REST service as some of the available options. Figure 7-4 shows how to view the available data sources within SharePoint Designer.

FIGURE 7-4 It is very easy to use SharePoint Designer to configure connections to external systems to build dashboards of external data.

Perhaps you want to render the data from a Real Simple Syndication (RSS) feed. For example, you might want to render weather information for one of your office sites. To connect to an RSS feed, on the Data Sources tab, click the REST Service Connection (see Figure 7-4). In the Data Source Properties dialog box that opens, fill in the appropriate information, as shown in Figure 7-5.

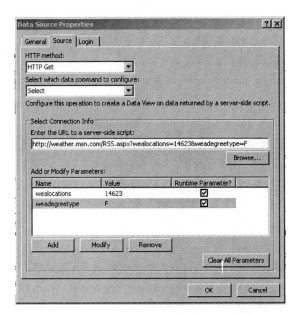

FIGURE 7-5 To pull data in from an RSS feed, enter the URL to the feed, and then click OK.

Note In SharePoint Online, it is not currently possible to connect to external business systems by using the BCS feature. This might be available in a future release of SharePoint Online.

Interactive, Data-Rich User Interface Elements

With SharePoint Designer 2010, you can build powerful and dynamic user interfaces for your SharePoint data and surface that data to different sets of users. Some examples of custom interfaces you can create include custom views, forms, Web Parts, and navigation, as well as custom Office client and task panes. With this flexibility, you can create completely custom and easy-to-use experiences tailored to your organization's business process.

Using the RSS weather feed example again, you can create a Data Form Web Part to render that feed on the page (see Figure 7-6). To configure a Data View Web Part using the weather RSS feed, follow these steps:

1. Open your SharePoint page, and then in Site Actions, select Edit In SharePoint Designer.

2. To set up your RSS data connection, click REST Service Connection, and then enter the feed's URL, such as the RSS feed for MSN's weather info.

3. Select a zone on the page where you want to add the Data View Web Part.

4. On the Insert tab, select Data View.

5. In the drop-down list of the Data View menu, in the RSS, REST And Scripts section, select MSN Weather Info.

6. Drag the columns into the Data View Web Part from the Current Data Source pane.

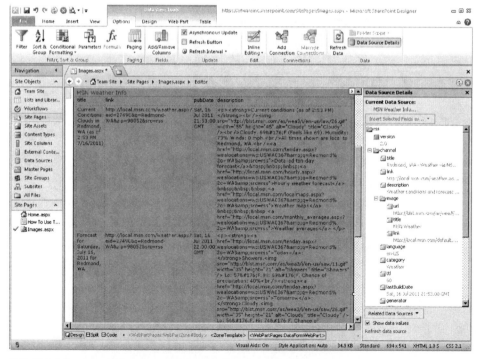

FIGURE 7-6 You can render external data with SharePoint Designer by connecting a Data Form Web Part to an external data source, such as an RSS feed.

SharePoint Designer Access

The SharePoint Online administrator can lock down customization ability with SharePoint Designer. Changes made using SharePoint Designer are live on the site immediately; therefore, to prevent the entire company user base from making unauthorized (and sometimes breaking) changes to the site, administrators can do some security planning in advance and only grant trained and trusted users the ability to use SharePoint Designer to make customizations.

Giving the right user base sufficient permissions to make changes using SharePoint Designer, as per their business needs, results in a SharePoint deployment that is flexible and can meet business needs quickly and effectively.

Here are some of the permission levels available to the administrator:

- Restrict who can detach pages from the site definition.
- Restrict who can edit the master page and page layouts.
- Restrict who can view and manage the URL site hierarchy.
- Prevent the use of SharePoint Designer 2010 to edit sites.

Deployment with SharePoint Designer

There's a nifty new feature available in SharePoint Designer 2010, which—in addition to building your customizations as you see fit—gives you the ability to also package those customizations into a .wsp file that can be either deployed to any SharePoint Online site or imported and opened in Visual Studio 2010 for additional development. To package your customized solution as a .wsp file, simply use the Save As Template feature in SharePoint Designer 2010. The file can contain the entire contents of your site, including data sources and structure, views and forms, workflows, and Web Parts, or you can save individual components, such as a list, a view, or a workflow.

Two key scenarios arise from the ability to package up your SharePoint Designer 2010 solution:

- A designer can make customizations to SharePoint using the friendly SharePoint Designer 2010 interface and then hand over those changes to the development team for further development in Visual Studio 2010.
- A SharePoint developer can use SharePoint Designer 2010 to get a quick start on common development activities, such as building out lists and libraries, creating site columns and content types, and performing lookups. The developer can then package up the site, and import it into Visual Studio 2010 and get a head start on the development pieces needed to create the site columns, content types, lists and libraries, and lookups between them. This can be a real time saver when compared to figuring out the XML necessary to build the aforementioned components from scratch in Visual Studio 2010.

For a deep dive into SharePoint Designer 2010 capabilities, refer to Microsoft SharePoint Designer 2010 Step by Step.

Customization Tools: Office InfoPath

InfoPath 2010 is a Microsoft application with which you can quickly design forms with easy-to-use tools, build advanced forms and connect forms to LoB systems, or create collaborative workflow solutions in SharePoint 2010. InfoPath 2010 is designed for both advanced business users and developers, depending on the type of the solution.

Advanced business users can use InfoPath 2010 to design electronic forms to gather information without the need to write any code. Developers can use InfoPath 2010 to create more advanced forms that surface data from, or save data back to, different LoB systems. You can edit the out-of-the-box list forms with InfoPath, or you can publish a custom form template to a form library. InfoPath forms are also often used as initiation and task forms in workflows. These areas are explained in more detail in the following sections.

Which Publishing Approach to Use and When

Before you analyze which method to use for publishing your InfoPath form, there are some considerations to keep in mind. When you publish an InfoPath form to a form library, the form stores all its data as XML. Customizing an out-of-the-box form still requires that data be mapped to columns in the list item. If you have a lot of data on the InfoPath form, it is advisable to go the form library route since you do not want to have a large number of columns in your list. However, if you are making small changes or tweaking some controls or branding the form, customizing an out-of-the-box list form will be the right approach.

It is also important to remember that you'll need the Enterprise edition of SharePoint Server if you're editing the out-of-the-box forms with InfoPath on-premise.

Customizing the Out-of-the-Box Edit Forms by Using InfoPath

Form creation is relatively simple with easy-to-use drag-and-drop controls, prebuilt layout sections, validation, formatting, and styling. Forms can also be published to SharePoint 2010 simply by using the commands on the ribbon, such as the Quick Publish button in InfoPath. You can also build InfoPath forms based on SharePoint lists. You can then use these generated fields as the starting point and add/remove fields to customize the form.

Note With Microsoft SharePoint Workspace, you can also fill out forms offline.

To help solidify this concept for you, take the following as an example of how to customize an out-of-the-box edit form with InfoPath 2010. Suppose that your corporation leases cars and must track the make, model, year, and status of each car. You create a SharePoint list with those columns, as shown in Figure 7-7 (Make, Model, Year, and Status). To edit the out-of-the-box forms with InfoPath Designer, click the Customize Form. This opens the form in InfoPath 2010.

FIGURE 7-7 Example list with custom columns. Use the Customize Form ribbon button to edit the out-of-the-box form in InfoPath.

Once you have the form open in InfoPath, you can add a heading to it, or add your own logo and add, remove, or customize the fields themselves. Figure 7-8 shows the Title field removed and a heading added to the form.

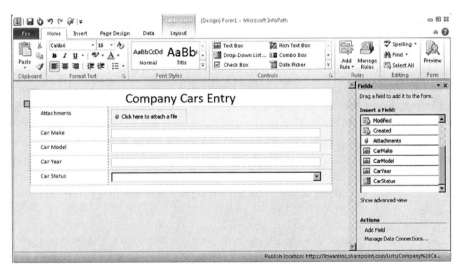

FIGURE 7-8 With the form in InfoPath, you can easily customize its behavior. Simply click File | Quick Publish to save your changes back to SharePoint.

After you are satisfied with these changes, all that's left to do is to publish the form back into the Company Cars list. Under the File menu in the Info tab, click Quick Publish. Now, when you go and create a new task in your Company Cars list, the form you designed and published from InfoPath opens as shown in Figure 7-9.

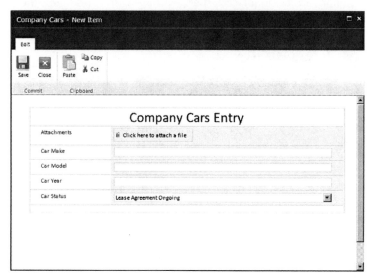

FIGURE 7-9 After you edit the out-of-the-box form in InfoPath, that customized form will render in the browser instead.

Publishing an InfoPath Form to a Form Library

Publishing an InfoPath form to a form library is a good approach to use when you are designing an InfoPath form from scratch instead of modifying an out-of-the-box list form. This approach makes it easy to use InfoPath to build complicated forms and publish them to a forms library. The data the user enters on the form is saved in XML format in the form library; you can also promote the data to columns in the form library, as well. InfoPath forms in form libraries let you store hundreds of pieces of data in the form. If you're simply editing the form of a list, you're limited by how many columns you can add to the list. But because the data is stored as an XML document when it's in a form library, you can support much more data in the forms.

You also have the benefit of supporting code behind in the forms, too. You can add .NET code behind an InfoPath form if the form is stored in a form library. This doesn't work for list forms.

The following walkthrough shows a simple form similar to the out-of-the-box form that you saw in the previous section. However, this form example publishes to a form library rather than simply editing the out-of-the-box list form.

In this scenario, you build a new form based on the Blank template by first opening InfoPath. Click File | New, and then under Popular Form Templates, choose Blank. Next, click Design Form on the right. This will open a sample form template (see Figure 7-10) in which you can start inserting text, controls, or data elements.

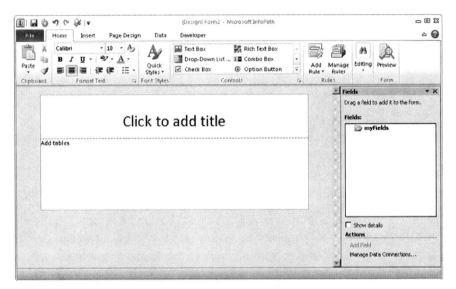

FIGURE 7-10 This is what a "blank" InfoPath form looks like when you first create it.

Figure 7-11 shows how to build a form to capture feedback about the SharePoint site. Start by inserting a table, changing text, inserting a few text controls, and inserting a drop-down list in the form. Use the Insert tab on the ribbon to insert a new table, and use the Controls selector on the Home tab to insert controls such as text boxes and buttons. By right-clicking the drop-down control and selecting Properties, you can populate some choices in the drop-down list. The form is now ready for publishing to SharePoint.

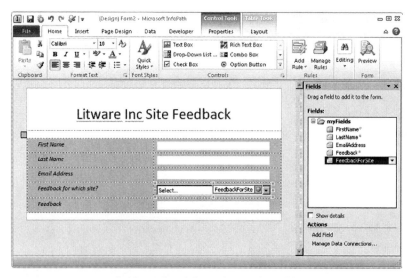

FIGURE 7-11 An example of an InfoPath form that can be published to a form library.

Next, you need to set submit options on the form. To do this, click Data | Submit Form, and then click Submit Options. The Submit Options dialog box opens, as shown in Figure 7-12. If you want to submit the form to a SharePoint document library, select the Allow Users To Submit This Form check box. Another option is Show The Submit Button In Both The Ribbon And The Info Tab In The InfoPath Filler. If you don't select to show the Submit button on the ribbon, you'll need to drop a button control on the form and configure it to submit to the library.

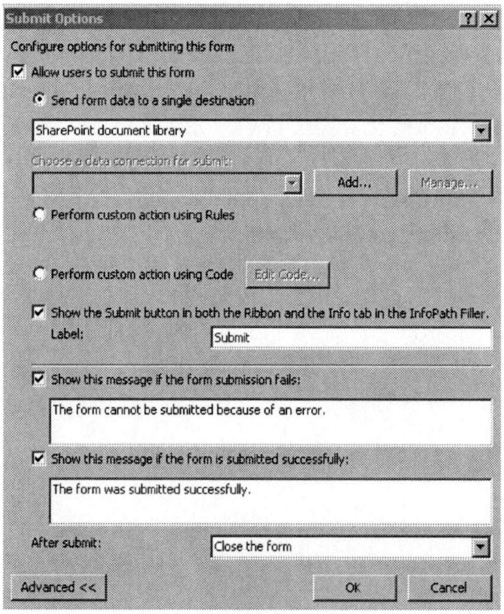

FIGURE 7-12 You must configure the submit options so that users can submit the custom InfoPath form as well as specify to which library the form should be uploaded.

When you click OK on this form, you see a message stating that you must select a data connection for submitting data to a SharePoint document library. To create a new connection, click Add. Next, you need to type the URL to the form library to which you want the forms to be sent when the user clicks the Submit button (see Figure 7-13).

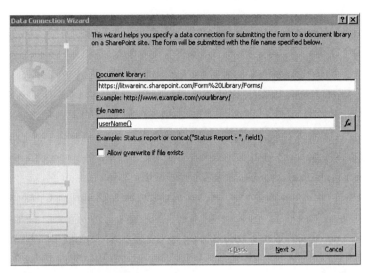

FIGURE 7-13 You must specify the URL of the form library where the form will be sent to when the user clicks the Submit button.

Now the data connection to the SharePoint library is complete and you can publish the form to SharePoint Online. To publish the form, go to File | Publish | SharePoint Server. The Publishing Wizard opens, in which you can publish the form to the SharePoint form library you specified. The wizard wants you to enter the location of your SharePoint or InfoPath Form Services site. Enter the name of the site where you want to publish the form, and then click Next.

On the next screen, select the check box to Enable This Form To Be Filled Out By Using The Browser (see Figure 7-14). If you do not select this, users will need to have the InfoPath Filler client installed on their computers. Also, select the Form Library option to publish this form to a form library.

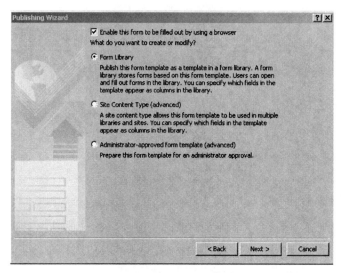

FIGURE 7-14 Be sure to select to enable the form to be filled out in the browser; otherwise, your users will need to have the InfoPath client installed on their computers.

On the next page, you can create a new form library or upload the form template to an existing form library. Since a form library already exists on the site in most templates, you most likely can just update the form template in an existing library. This is shown in Figure 7-15.

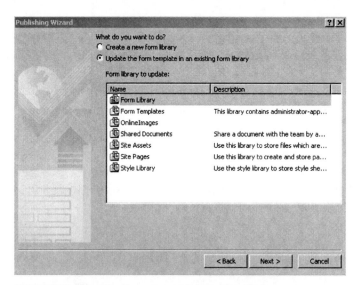

FIGURE 7-15 Select the library to which to publish the form.

On the next page, you can pick fields that will be available as columns in the SharePoint site and Outlook folder. Here you can select fields to be "promoted" to columns on the form's list item. Thereafter, click Next and then click Publish to publish the form to the SharePoint Online library.

Using InfoPath Forms in Workflow Solutions

When using SharePoint Designer or Visual Studio to build workflow solutions, you can use InfoPath 2010 to build the forms that will be used in the workflows, such as association forms, initiation forms, and task forms. These forms are wired into the workflow and let the workflow collect information submitted by the user on the form. These forms can be built using no code, or capabilities can be enhanced with code.

Customization Tools: Visual Studio

The process for developing solutions for SharePoint Online using Visual Studio 2010 as the development platform is different from the approaches outlined in the preceding sections. For SharePoint Online Standard customers, Microsoft provisions site collections for organizations in a multitenant farm. Because all the hardware is shared, Microsoft requires you to deploy your Visual Studio .NET solutions into a sandboxed solution. Each site collection has its own sandboxed solution gallery, in which these solutions can be managed. With this being the case, sandboxed solutions are scoped to the site collection (or lower) instead of the web application or the farm. This means your code will only be available in each site collection that the solution is deployed. For SharePoint Online Dedicated users, you'll have more flexibility because you can still write full-trust farm solutions. When you create a new project in Visual Studio, you must select which type of project to create: a sandboxed solution, or a farm solution (see Figure 7-16).

- **Sandboxed solutions**   These are a special feature of the SharePoint solutions framework. With this feature, developers can create SharePoint solutions that can be hosted in a multitenant environment without affecting other Microsoft customers. The solutions are uploaded directly to the site collection and activated by the SharePoint Online administrator. Sandboxed solutions have access to a limited subset of the server object model (objects at or below the site collection level).

   See the "Building and Deploying a Sandboxed Web Part," later in this chapter, for a walkthrough on how to create a sandboxed Web Part.

- **Farm solutions**   Farm-level solutions can be scoped at the SharePoint farm level or lower. They have full access to all resources and functionality in SharePoint. Farm solutions also run using full-trust code. *Full-trust code* is code that is installed in the GAC of the computer on which it is running (or via custom code access security policy). Full-trust code is available for use by all web applications in the farm. Full-trust code has no restrictions or security checks performed on it. For example, full-trust code can make calls out to other site collections via the object model, read/write to the local file system, or make calls to external applications/databases.

   See the section "Deploying Full Trust Code in SharePoint Online Dedicated," later in this chapter, for a description of what it takes to pass Microsoft's standards for full trust code deployment.

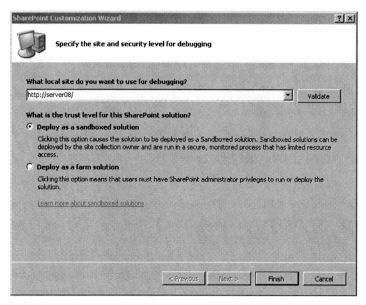

FIGURE 7-16 Sandboxed solutions are the only .NET solutions that are compatible with SharePoint Online Standard edition. The SharePoint Online Dedicated edition allows farm solutions, but only through a rigorous approval process.

Getting a Head Start with SharePoint Designer 2010

Developers can get a head start on Visual Studio development projects when they first prototype the solution in SharePoint Designer. SharePoint Designer lets you export the feature, such as a workflow, as a .wsp file. You can then import that .wsp file into Visual Studio 2010. When you import the .wsp file into Visual Studio you'll notice that all the dependencies and code files have been created for you and all you need to do is simply extend the solution to meet your advanced need.

Accessing SharePoint Data with the Client Object Model

The SharePoint 2010 client object model provides three similar representations of core objects in the server-side object model. The three different application programming interface (APIs) are the ECMAScript (JavaScript, JScript) model, the Silverlight model, and the .NET Framework managed model. Using these object models, you can write code using SharePoint objects that executes remotely on the client. The client object model also lets you access web services outside of SharePoint Online.

Visual Studio 2010 provides great support for sandboxed solutions as well as the client object model. It provides project template and project item template support, a SharePoint customization wizard for creating new projects as .NET, Silverlight, or sandboxed solutions; IntelliSense support for the site collections' scoped server and client-side APIs; as well as enhanced debugging and packaging support. A sandboxed solution developed by using Visual Studio 2010 is highlighted later in this chapter.

Introduction to Sandboxed Solutions

Sandboxed solutions for SharePoint Online are developed by using the same solutions framework that you would use to build an on-premises deployment of SharePoint. When creating a new solution, you can choose whether the solution is a sandboxed solution or a farm (full-trust) solution (refer to Figure 7-16).

A sandboxed solution is a deployable, reusable package that you can enable at the site collection level. It is packaged as SharePoint .wsp files that may contain assemblies and other noncompiled components. A site collection administrator uploads the solution package to a specialized library called the solution gallery in the root site of the site collection. Every sandboxed solution is executed in a unique application domain. An application domain is used to isolate applications from one another. Because the application domain is unique to your solution, SharePoint can monitor your solution for performance issues and resource use, and it can terminate your code if it exceeds the boundaries set by the IT team.

SharePoint 2010 monitors the performance and resource usage of sandboxed solutions by means of a system of resource points. A site collection administrator can set limits on the number of resource points that sandboxed solutions in a particular site collection can use daily. These are shared among all the sandboxed solutions in that site collection. Administrators can monitor the resource points used by individual solutions from the site's solution gallery. If all the sandboxed solutions in the site collection exceed the daily resource allocation, SharePoint will take all the sandboxed solutions in that site collection offline for the remainder of the day. Figure 7-17 shows a screenshot of resource quotas.

FIGURE 7-17 Your sandboxed solutions will run until they hit their quota.

The application domain runs within an isolated process, using an account with a lower set of permissions than the web application service account. The account is also subject to various restrictions on functionality and scope.

Sandboxed Solutions: What Works and What Doesn't

Table 7-1 shows the components that work with SharePoint Online solutions:

TABLE 7-1 Code Components That Work with SharePoint

Code components	Impact
Feature receivers	Can be used when features are being activated, deactivated, installed, uninstalled, and upgraded.
Event receivers	Can be used to respond to create/update/delete events
SPItemEventReceiver	Event receiver for events on list items
SPListEventReceiver	Event receiver for events on lists
SPWebEventReceiver	Event receiver for events on the web
Navigation	Site or web navigation
Web Parts (if derived from the *WebPart* class)	Build Web Parts for activation within the site collection
Microsoft InfoPath forms logic	Can be used in InfoPath forms
Sandboxed SharePoint Designer workflow activities	Can be used to build sandboxed workflow activities that can be used in SharePoint Designer

Table 7-2 shows the declarative components that work with SharePoint Online solutions:

TABLE 7-2 Declarative Components That Work with SharePoint Online

Declarative components	Impact
Declarative workflows	Can be easily built using SharePoint Designer
Content types, site columns	Defines the structure of your solution
Lists and list definitions	Defines the storage of your solution
Data Form Web Parts	Allows for custom UI with no code
Custom actions, ribbon extensions	Lets you extend SharePoint functionality using JavaScript
Client-side technologies such as Silverlight, JavaScript, and jQuery	Allows for client-side code (these are explained in a later section)
Web templates, site pages, page layouts, and master pages	Defines brand, layouts, pages, and so on

Visual Web Parts Require SharePoint Power Tools

By default, Visual Web Parts are not supported in sandboxed solutions because they contain a user control (.ascx file) that deploys to the file system (*under _controltemplates*). SharePoint Power Tools contain an item template with which you can package up and deploy sandboxed solutions containing Visual Web Parts. In addition, with SharePoint Power Tools, you get compile-time checks on what code will not work in SharePoint Online as part of a sandboxed solution. To read more about SharePoint Power Tools, see Visual Studio 2010 Power Tools at *http://bit.ly/hmx9hS*.

Table 7-3 presents non-supported functions in sandboxed solutions:

TABLE 7-3 Components That Are Not Supported with SharePoint Online

Function not supported	Impact
Access to the Internet to make web service calls	Cannot access external web services such as weather information or stock quotes
Access to a hard disk to read or write files outside of SharePoint Online	Cannot read configuration values from web.config or any other hard disk resource in sandboxed solutions
Web application-scoped or farm-scoped features	Cannot activate feature at a higher level than site collection
Adding assemblies to the GAC	Cannot deploy full-trust code that other applications can use

Function not supported	Impact
Running security-related functionality; for example, *RunWithElevatedPrivileges* or other *SPSecurity* methods	Cannot elevate privileges to complete task that currently logged on user might not have sufficient access to complete, such as update a higher permission list based on some event that the current user caused
Custom Action groups	Cannot add custom groups in site settings and other pages
HideCustomAction element	Cannot hide an existing action within Windows SharePoint Services (WSS) or within another custom action
Content type binding	Cannot bind content types on site
Web Part connections	Cannot create Web Parts that connect to other Web Parts on page

Additional Restrictions of Sandboxed Solutions

Because it is a multitenant environment, when you upload a sandboxed solution to the solution gallery, SharePoint Online performs a further round of validation checks, in addition to those performed by on-premises SharePoint installations. It is important to know the namespaces that are not allowed so that you can design around them. For example, as you can observe by looking at the disallowed namespaces in the following list, you cannot make direct calls to SQL Server or to the file system. A sandboxed solution cannot be activated if it contains code calling any of the following namespaces:

- *Microsoft.SqlServer*
- *Microsoft.Win32*
- *System.Data.Sql*
- *System.Data.SqlClient*
- *System.Data.SqlTypes*
- *System.IO.Pipes*
- *System.IO.Ports*
- *System.Reflection*

> **Note** Some members within the *System.Reflection* namespace are allowed within sandboxed solutions. You can use the following members from this namespace in your sandboxed solution code: *Name*, *GetCustomAttributes*, *PropertyType*, *GetValue*, and *SetValue*.
>
> System.Runtime.InteropServices
>
> You can use the *LayoutKind* enumeration in your sandboxed solution code, with which you can control the layout of an object when exported to unmanaged code.
>
> *System.Runtime.Remoting*
>
> *System.Threading*
>
> You can use the following members from the *System.Threading* namespace in your sandboxed solution code, which lets you get exclusive locks on an object, give up exclusive locks, get the current thread ID, and manage the current thread: *System.Threading.Monitor.Enter*, *System.Threading.Monitor.Exit(System.Object)*, *System.Threading.Thread.ManagedThreadId*, and *System.Threading.Thread.CurrentThread*.

In addition, the following types and members cannot be called from code in a sandboxed solution in SharePoint Online. These types are used to initialize a new instance of the array class, create types that invoke methods, get a *Type* object for a type in another assembly, or invoke a specific member of the current type:

System.Array.CreateInstance

System.Delegate

System.Type.GetType(System.String)

System.Type.InvokeMember

Sandboxed Solution Additional Resources

For additional information on sandboxed solutions, see Sandboxed Solutions at MSDN at *http://bit.ly/fyX1RX*.

Tips and Tricks for Using Sandboxed Solutions

Because sandboxed solutions are more restrictive than regular farm-scoped solutions, certain tips and tricks are available to developers to ease the development and debugging of sandboxed solutions. The following subsections describe a few of them.

Create Site Collections in SharePoint Online to Validate Deployment

As a best practice with SharePoint development, your local environment should mirror your production environment as much as possible. This is also true for SharePoint Online, so set up your local development environment to mirror the SharePoint Online environment as much as possible. Another trick is to create site collections in SharePoint Online that mirror your production site collections but are not used by people in the organization. This lets you perform final testing and verification in the SharePoint Online environment, as well as output debugging information in a debug configuration.

Use Visual Studio 2010 Power Tools

Visual Studio 2010 Power Tools include features that ease the development of the sandbox. There are two major advantages of using Visual Studio 2010 Power Tools. The first is that they let you build and deploy artifacts in sandboxed solutions that would otherwise be disallowed. A good example of such an artifact is Visual Web Parts, which you can deploy to the sandbox by using Visual Studio 2010 Power Tools. The second advantage is that Visual Studio 2010 Power Tools are sandbox-aware, so they provide you with compile-time checking on classes and namespaces so that you can be sure the solution you build will be supported in the sandbox on the server.

Debug Sandboxed Solutions Locally

Once your code is deployed to SharePoint Online, you cannot attach the Visual Studio 2010 debugger to the SharePoint Online server-side processes. Therefore, you must do your debugging locally to ensure that your code works correctly. Because the development will be done on your local development computer, you need to ensure that the User Code service is running locally after you install SharePoint 2010. Also, you need to attach the debugger to the SPUCWorkerProcess.exe process in order to debug the code.

To enable the User Code service locally, go to Central Administration, click Application Management | Services On Server, and then ensure that the Microsoft SharePoint Foundation Sandboxed Code Service service is started, as shown in Figure 7-18.

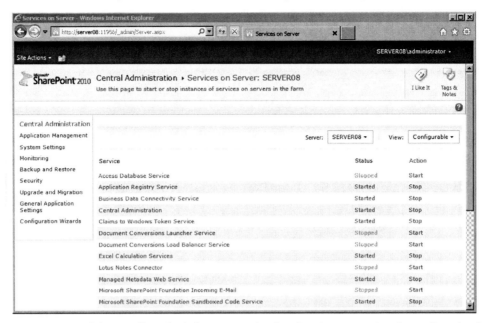

FIGURE 7-18 To debug sandboxed solutions on your local workstation, ensure that the sandboxed code service is running and then attach to the SPUCWorkerProcess.exe process.

Output Debug Information in SharePoint Online

Once your code is deployed as a sandboxed solution into SharePoint Online, you will no longer have access to the file system or the event viewer to log information regarding the functioning of your code. A trick is to use the SharePoint Online list as a repository of your log information and output debug/exception information to a SharePoint Online list. This lets you view your log/exception messages being generated by your code in SharePoint Online. This is often called "poor man's debugging," but nevertheless it remains an effective approach given the inherent limitation to proper logging mechanisms.

Use FXCop to Test Your Code

Use the static code analysis rules to ensure that your code executes properly in SharePoint Online. To learn more, go to http://o365fxcoprules.codeplex.com/.

Building and Deploying a Sandboxed Web Part

Let's do a walkthrough of building a sandboxed Web Part and deploying it to your SharePoint Online site. To get started, open Visual Studio 2010, and then select File | New | Project. In the New Project dialog box, in the Installed Templates section, click SharePoint | 2010. Select Empty SharePoint Project from the middle pane (see Figure 7-19). Give the project a suitable name, such as **SiteInformation**. The example in this section features a Web Part that shows you the title and the URL for every site in your site collection. Finally, click OK to create the project.

FIGURE 7-19 Visual Studio Template Items.

After you click OK, a dialog box appears prompting you to specify the site and security level for debugging. On this screen, select Deploy As A Sandboxed Solution, as shown in Figure 7-16. Click Finish to create the solution.

> **Note** Do not type the URL of your SharePoint Online site. This site should be a local, development installation of SharePoint, where SharePoint and Visual Studio are running on the same computer. If you don't have such an environment, you won't be able to debug your code.

Next, in Solution Explorer, right-click the newly created project, and then in the context menu that appears, click Add | New Item. In the Add New Item dialog box, in the Installed Templates node, select SharePoint 2010 to show the supported SharePoint item templates. It's important to note that not all of these project templates are supported within sandboxed solutions. It would be easy to select a template that doesn't work, only to find this out when you go to deploy to SharePoint Online. Table 7-4 shows all the templates supported in sandboxed solutions and, thus, SharePoint Online.

TABLE 7-4 **Project Templates Supported with SharePoint Online**

Item template	Sandbox-compatible?	Notes
Visual Web Part	No	Doesn't work because it requires .ascx file be installed on SharePoint servers
Visual Web Part (Sandboxed)	Yes	Made possible by installing the Visual Studio 2010 SharePoint Power Tools
Web Part	Yes	
Sequential Workflow	No	Doesn't work because it requires workflow solution to be deployed as farm solution
State Machine Workflow	No	Doesn't work because it requires workflow solution to be deployed as farm solution
Business Data Connectivity Model	No	Doesn't work because it requires BCS solution to be deployed as a full trust solution; feature not supported in SharePoint Online
Application Page	No	Doesn't work because it requires .aspx page to be deployed to SharePoint server
Event Receiver	Yes	
Module	Yes	
Content Type	Yes	
List Definition from Content Type	Yes	
List Definition	Yes	
List Instance	Yes	
Empty Element	Yes	
User Control	No	Doesn't work because it requires .ascx file to be installed on SharePoint server

To create a sandboxed Web Part, select Web Part from the template items (see Figure 7-20). Give the Web Part a name, such as **SiteInfo**, and then click Add.

Note The Visual Web Part (sandboxed) template is made available through the installation of the Visual Studio 2010 Power Tools.

FIGURE 7-20 When creating a new project item, many items are designed specifically for SharePoint, such as Web Parts.

Once the Web Part has been added to the project, replace the *CreateChildControls* method in the *SiteInfo.cs* class with the following code:

```
protected override void CreateChildControls()
{
base.CreateChildControls();

StringBuilder sb = new StringBuilder();
sb.Append("<b>Hello " + SPContext.Current.Web.CurrentUser.Name + "</b>");
sb.Append( "<br/><br/>");
sb.Append("Here are the sites available in this site collection<br/>");

Label siteTitle = new Label();
siteTitle.Text = sb.ToString();
this.Controls.Add(siteTitle);

foreach (SPWeb web in SPContext.Current.Site.AllWebs)
{
Label lblWebInfo = new Label();
lblWebInfo.Text = web.Title + " - " + web.Url + "<br/>";
this.Controls.Add(lblWebInfo);
web.Dispose();
}
}
```

The preceding code adds a label that displays the current user's name. It then iterates through every site in the site collection and renders the title and URL properties of each site. Make sure the feature is scoped to the site collection level, as shown in Figure 7-21. Right-click the project, and then select Deploy. Visual Studio 2010 will generate a solution file (.wsp file) as well as deploy it to your development site collection.

Note If you use restricted namespaces and object types, the Visual Studio 2010 build process will still succeed if you don't have Visual Studio Service Pack 1 (SP1) installed. This is because compilation is performed by Visual Studio against the full object model, regardless of whether the solution is sandboxed. However, when you try to deploy a sandboxed solution to SharePoint Online by uploading and activating it in the Solution Gallery, SharePoint Online validates the contents of the solution package (.wsp file) and does not deploy it if it contains prohibited artifacts.

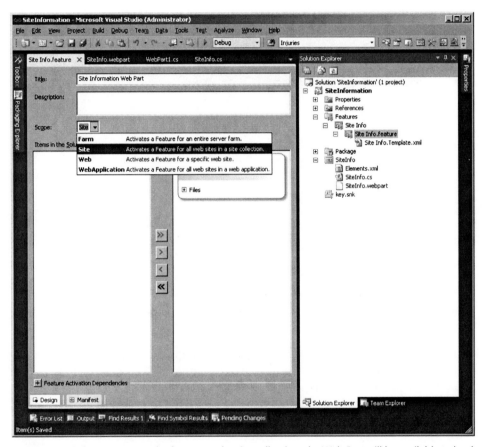

FIGURE 7-21 When you scope the feature to the site collection, the Web Part will be available to be dropped on every subsite in the site collection.

Once you verify that your code works in your local development environment, you can upload the solution to your SharePoint Online site collection.

Figure 7-22 shows the Solution Gallery page. You can get to this page by clicking Site Actions | Site Settings, and then under Galleries, selecting Solutions. Use the Upload button to upload a sandboxed solution (.wsp file). After you click the Upload button, browse out to the .wsp file generated when you built the Visual Studio project. You can find this by default in the Project directory, under Bin/Debug. After you select your .wsp, click OK to upload it. Thereafter, you'll be presented with a confirmation screen that shows Activate and Close buttons. Your Web Part won't be functional until you click the Activate button, so click Activate, and then click Close to close the dialog box. Now that the solution is activated, the Web Part can be used in any site in the site collection.

 Note A site collection–scoped feature can be activated in the Solution Gallery. A web-scoped feature will need to be activated in each individual Web Part in which it is required.

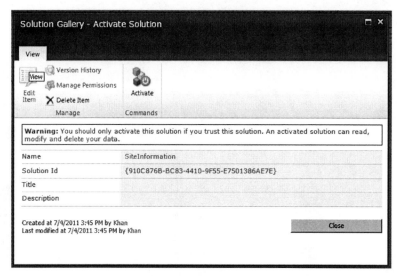

FIGURE 7-22 When you upload a solution, ensure that you click the Activate button, or the solution will be inoperable.

The next step is to drop the Web Part onto a site in the site collection. To do this, edit a page, and then on the ribbon, click Insert | Web Part. Select the Custom Web Part group and you'll see the SiteInfo Web Part in the list of custom Web Parts. Figure 7-23 shows the result of the SiteInfo Web Part in action.

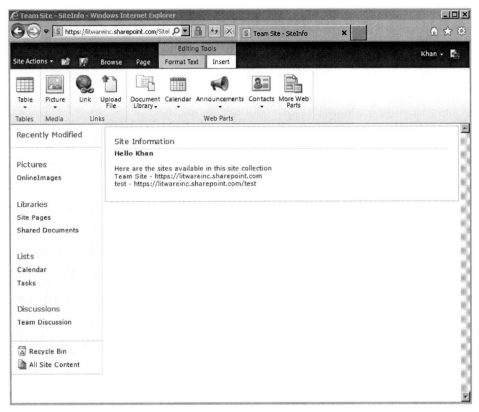

FIGURE 7-23 On the ribbon, select Insert | Web Part to insert your custom Web Part. You'll see all your custom Web Parts in the Custom group in the Web Part Picker.

Deploying Full-Trust Code in SharePoint Online Dedicated

Microsoft is strict about the process for deploying full-trust code in SharePoint Online Dedicated. The process is outlined in the following subsections. Since procedures can change without notice, it is also recommended to review the Custom Solution Developer Guide for SharePoint Online Dedicated edition, found at *bit.ly/lgEpwg*.

Microsoft SharePoint Online Code Analysis Framework

Microsoft SharePoint Online Code Analysis Framework (MSOCAF) is a new application introduced in SharePoint Online to streamline the custom solution review process. Organizations can use this application to test their solutions and fix code issues before submitting them to Microsoft.

MSOCAF communicates with a web service hosted on the customer's SharePoint environment to submit the deployment package, thereby automating the solution upload process. You can also use MSOCAF to roll back or remove components of a deployed solution.

MSOCAF is built using an extensible framework to run a set of executable rules against custom solution(s), before submitting the custom solution(s) for approval and deployment. MSOCAF incorporates existing Visual Studio components such as FxCop, CAT.NET, and SPDisposeCheck to perform the code analysis and generate the report. The report that MSOCAF generates as a result of running these components informs developers about the parts of the solution that must be changed to successfully meet the validation criteria.

> **Note** To read more about MSOCAF, go to *https://caf.sharepoint.microsoftOnline.com*.

Dedicated Code Review and Deployment Process

To deploy full-trust code in SharePoint Online Dedicated, you must follow a six-step process as outlined by Microsoft. This due diligence and documentation on your part helps Microsoft to understand the purpose of the solution and what business needs it is trying to solve, as well as to offer any best practice tips/tricks or alternate ways to meet the business needs that might fit your business model better. It also helps to uncover any unsupported scenarios so that you can be sure that your solution will be accepted for deployment for your target deployment date. Figure 7-24 shows the six-step process, which is explained in more detail in the following subsections.

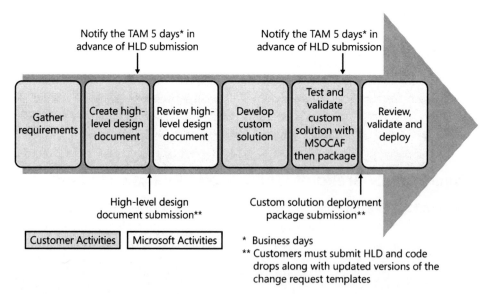

FIGURE 7-24 Microsoft has a fairly regulated, six-step process to get approval to deploy custom code to SharePoint Online Dedicated.

Steps 1 and 2: Create the High-Level Design Document

Before implementing any custom solution, the organization's development team must describe all the details of the proposed custom solution using the most current High-Level Design (HLD) document template (available to current customers only, on the Customer Handbook Knowledge Base site).

The development team must document both the logical and the physical architecture of the proposed custom solution. The HLD document must also contain information about how the custom solution is implemented, how any configurations are managed, and whether there are dependencies on other custom solutions, third-party components, or external systems.

Five days prior to when the customer submits the HLD document, he must inform his Microsoft Technical Account Manager (TAM) of his intentions. The TAM will open a Change Request (CR) and give the customer a CR number that must accompany the HLD document when it's submitted to Microsoft.

> **Note** The development team should not proceed with any development work until after the HLD document has been approved by Microsoft; otherwise, this will lead to lost time and delayed productivity. There are several instances in which the HLD document might be rejected by Microsoft for reasons that will be described shortly. In that case, the customer will have to redesign the proposed solution. Also, do not buy any third-party components until after the HLD document is approved.

Step 3: Review the HLD

The HLD review process lets Microsoft verify that the solution is supported by SharePoint Online and can be deployed using the existing deployment process. It also lets Microsoft review the design and propose any alternatives to the solution.

Step 4: Develop the Custom Solution

Once Microsoft has approved the HLD document, the development team can begin to implement the design. The customer is responsible for developing the custom solution. The customer is also responsible for hosting a development/testing environment, which should match the SharePoint Online production environment. To provide guidance on how to build a development/testing environment that mimics the production environment, Microsoft offers the SharePoint Online Build Guide (available to current customers only, on the Customer Handbook Knowledge Base site).

The development team should also check with Microsoft to determine if they are on the same patch level as the production environment and whether any patches are scheduled to be installed prior to deployment of the custom solution.

Note Development and testing must be done with the same SharePoint version, including the patch levels, that is installed in the customer's production environment. Other environmental factors that impact functional behavior should also be duplicated as closely as possible. The environmental factors include LoB applications and services that the custom solutions integrate with, such as interfacing applications and services, and domain trusts. Additionally, the test environment should have the same monitoring environment (Microsoft System Center Operations Manager) as the SharePoint Online environment.

Step 5: Test and Validate the Solution

After the development is completed, it is the customer's responsibility to test the solution. In addition to manual testing, MSOCAF needs to be used to validate the custom solution code.

Note The customer is fully responsible for testing the solution (including third-party solutions). If the Microsoft engineering team is concerned that the solution has not been well tested, the code is rejected during the review process.

The customer must document all the testing activity undertaken by their development and testing teams as part of the Custom Solution Deployment Checklist, described later in this chapter. The testing should include functionality, performance, scale, and full unit testing.

Note Microsoft provides customers with a preproduction environment to perform functional validation of custom solutions. This is not a substitute for a test environment and should not be used as such.

Step 6: Build and Analyze the Deployment Package

After the development and testing are completed, the development team can build the development package and analyze it by using MSOCAF. The package must contain all the solution files, the deployment guide, the MSOCAF report, and all other package components. The customer can then submit the package directly from MSOCAF to Microsoft. Microsoft does not begin testing until the final code and documentation have been received. After approval, Microsoft deploys the custom solution packages to the pre-production environment and then both to a primary and secondary data center (maintained for disaster recovery).

Deployment Guidelines

In the deployment guide, Microsoft requires that you provide details on how to install all the custom solution components, any architectural diagrams that are related to the installation of the custom code, and procedures for validating that the solution has been properly deployed. Microsoft provides a deployment guide template to start (available to current customers only, on the Customer Handbook Knowledge Base site). The deployment guide must be completely self-contained; otherwise, Microsoft will reject the custom solution package.

Microsoft requires that customer-developed solutions use solution files with a .wsp extension to deploy custom solutions. These are easy to build with Visual Studio 2010 when doing SharePoint development. They should also be available from any third-party vendors from which you buy solutions. Microsoft will not manually deploy other files that are not otherwise deployed via a solution package using *Add-SPSolution* or *Update-SPSolution* PowerShell cmdlets.

There are only five supported deployment actions in the SharePoint Online dedicated environment. The five supported actions are as follows:

1. **Install**   Deploy a custom solution.

2. **Update**   Change an existing custom solution to the next version. Certain elements of the custom solution are altered or replaced, but the existing custom solution is not uninstalled.

3. **Rollback**   Restore an existing custom solution to a previous version. Certain elements of the custom solution are altered or replaced, but it is not completely uninstalled.

4. **Reinstall**   Uninstall (remove) a custom solution completely, and then reinstall (redeploy) it. This new deployment could be the same version, or a newer version.

5. **Remove**   Completely uninstall a custom solution.

Physical Directory Structure and Components in the Deployment Package

The submitted custom solution package must be organized into a specific directory structure as shown in Table 7-5. If these components are not listed in the correct directory, MSOCAF does not allow the package to be submitted. Tables 7-5 and 7-6 show these required directory structures. To read more about Microsoft's guidelines for packaging code, review the Custom Solution Developers Guide white paper found at *bit.ly/LgEpwg*.

TABLE 7-5 Directory Structure Needed for Deployment Package

Directory	Purpose
Root Directory	Named for the solution being submitted.
Solutions Artifacts	Contains the solution packages, including final tested code. This folder must contain at least one .wsp file. MSOCAF uses this directory to create a .cab file, which will be placed in the root directory.
Release Documents	Contains all the relevant documents related to the release. This folder must contain at least one .doc or .docx file.
Source Code	Contains the source code.
Installation Scripts	Contains any installation or uninstallation scripts that must be run as part of the deployment.
Test Documents	Contains all the test documentation.

Table 7-6 expounds upon the previous table. It shows all the documentation and artifacts that must reside in all the directories shown in the previous table (Root, Solution Artifacts, Release Documents, Source Code, Installation Scripts, and Test Documents). The bottom line to understand here is you need to have your I's dotted and T's crossed before you throw your code "over the wall".

TABLE 7-6 Documentation Needed for Artifact Deployment

Package component	Directory	Description
Solution packages	Solutions Artifacts	Include the final versions of all the solution packages, including final tested code. The MSOCAF report will automatically be added to this folder by MSOCAF.
Deployment manifest	Solutions Artifacts	The XML manifest file that the customer must create to utilize the Test Deployment and Rollback features within MSOCAF for deployment to the customer's test environment. Must have the filename DeploymentManifest.xml.
Scheduling information	Release Documents	State the expected date for code-drop submission and deployment. Also include the expected duration of downtime for deployment configuration and post-deployment configuration.
MSOCAF report	Release Documents	Include the MSOCAF report about the final code drop. Also include all the exception comments from the exceptions found by MSOCAF as part of the report.
Deployment guide	Release Documents	A comprehensive set of instructions for deploying the custom solution, following the most current deployment guide template provided by Microsoft.

Package component	Directory	Description
Dependencies list	Release Documents	Submit a list of all dependencies for the code. This can include accounts and passwords, web services, databases, other solutions, features, patches, tool sets, and libraries.
Rollback plan	Release Documents	Provide a rollback plan, in case the custom solution must be removed. A rollback must remove all customized functionality in its deployed scope. Include screenshots of how the environment must look after a successful rollback.
Client troubleshooting documentation	Release Documents	Submit end-user troubleshooting guidance to Microsoft with one or two test accounts, if appropriate, to diagnose problems that are related to the customer's dependencies. If a user account is provided, it should be set up with low privilege and be used for no other purpose.
Event/ULS log	Release Documents	Provide a list of all event entries generated by the custom solution, and the troubleshooting actions to take for them. The list commonly takes the form of a table of error codes, the corresponding severity, and root cause.
Monitoring document	Release Documents	Provide all details related to monitoring the custom solution, including logging details and documentation about all instrumentation.
Third-party licensing document	Release Documents	If using a third-party component or solution, provide the licensing details and any necessary keys or certificates for installation. Also include all details about the testing that has been done against it.
Open/shared source code waiver	Release Documents	If any open source or shared source code or components are used in the solution, the customer is required to provide a waiver in writing stating that the customer will be responsible for supporting any issues that arise from the use of open source software.
Customer's security and compliance review document	Release Documents	Customers should have their own security and compliance team review and approve all custom solutions that are being presented to Microsoft for deployment. Include your organization's Security and Compliance Review approval of the design, and all test details from this review process.

Package component	Directory	Description
Source code	Source Code	Include the project files and entire source code (validated through MSOCAF and manual test cases), if developed in-house. Microsoft treats all source code with utmost confidentiality. **Note:** If the solution is a third-party off-the-shelf application, no source code is required for submission.
Public debug symbols	Source Code	To aid in the possible troubleshooting scenarios, include the public debug symbols for all custom code. This symbol file is automatically created by Visual Studio as long as either "pdb only" or "full" is selected from the Debug Info setting, which you can access via the Advanced settings on the Build page in Visual Studio.
Scheduling information	Installation Scripts	State the expected date for code-drop submission and deployment. Also include the expected duration of downtime for deployment configuration and post-deployment configuration.
Test documents and results	Test Documents	For testing and validation purposes, it's extremely important to supply a copy of the manual test cases, test plan, test scenarios, unit test results, and all performance and scale testing that has been performed related to the code (and that is not covered by MSOCAF). This is even more important for all code that has a dependency (web service, data, or system) that cannot be tested during validation by Microsoft. Include details about all elements of the custom solution that your organization wants deployed, including any third-party components and other solutions that the organization has purchased.

Validating and Submitting the Deployment Package

After you have all your documentation and artifacts made ready in the prescribed fashion, you must use MSOCAF to submit the completed package. This requires a CR, which you should obtain five days prior to the planned submission date by opening a CR with the TAM. You should deliver the custom solution package at least 16 business days before a scheduled outage change window to ensure that Microsoft can implement the deployment in a timely manner.

To validate and submit the custom solution deployment package, follow these steps:

1. Ensure that the root directory for the custom solution deployment package contains all required directories and components (listed in Tables 7-5 and 7-6, earlier in this chapter).

2. Use MSOCAF to analyze the deployment package.

3. If any errors are reported, fix the errors and then rerun the analysis.

4. Provide the required justifications for any remaining errors that will not be fixed.

5. Use MSOCAF to test the deployment of the custom solution in your test environment, and then to test the rollback.

> **Note** Any changes made after this testing will require that you repeat steps 2, 3, and 4 before you can proceed to step 6.

6. Use MSOCAF to submit the custom solution deployment package to Microsoft.

> **Note** A CR ticket number is necessary for submitting the custom solution deployment package.

7. MSOCAF communicates with a web service hosted by SharePoint Online to facilitate submission of the deployment package by browsing to *bit.ly/fNuho6* and submitting your package.

Introduction to the Client Object Model

SharePoint 2010 has a host of new and enhanced client-side functionality. This is a significant addition to the platform, as this lets developers use Rich Internet Application (RIA) technologies that run in the browser and deliver an enriched user experience, unlike the server-side model. SharePoint 2010 introduces native support for RIA technologies and mechanisms for client-side or remote data access.

SharePoint 2010 provides a client object model that is similar to the server-side model and is easy to use. It also supports many more operations than traditional web services. The client-side object model provides a subset of a server-side object model that is defined in Microsoft.SharePoint.dll. It consists of three separate APIs that are similar to one another in functionality. The three client-side object models are the ECMAScript (JavaScript, JScript) object model, Silverlight-managed model, and .NET-managed model. Each model includes objects that correspond to major objects at the site collection or lower in the SharePoint hierarchy.

Client Object Model Architecture

The SharePoint 2010 client object model presents you with familiar concepts similar to the server-side concepts that you can use to develop SharePoint solutions. For example, the SharePoint 2010 client object model provides *Web* objects, *Site* objects, and *List* objects. These objects are similar to work with as the server-side objects.

Figure 7-25 shows the client object model architecture. The client-side models are provided through proxy.js and managed assembly files, which can be referenced in custom applications just as other object models. The object models are implemented as a Windows Communication Foundation (WCF) service. All the operations are inherently asynchronous; commands are serialized to XML and sent to the server in a single HTTP request. On the server side, for every command, a corresponding server object model call is made and the server responses are compacted into JavaScript Object Notation (JSON) format, which is parsed by the proxy and associated with the appropriate client-side objects.

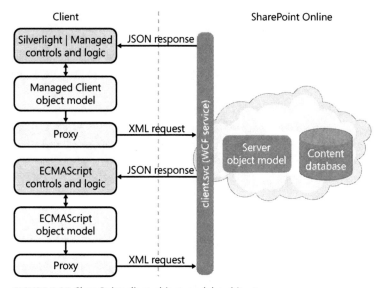

FIGURE 7-25 SharePoint client object model architecture.

Key traits of client object models are that they are consistent with server-side object models, as well as consistent with one another. So, if you learn one of the client object models, you will be able to get up to speed on the others rapidly, as the other two are very similar in functionality.

Even with the client-side object models, the browser must first make a synchronous call to the web server to render the page and download associated resources, such as the Silverlight XAP and any JavaScript files. The Silverlight application can then use a variety of data access mechanisms to communicate asynchronously with the SharePoint server.

Client Object Model: What Works and What Doesn't

In the client-side object model, code runs remotely on the client and thus is not subjected to the same restrictions as sandboxed solutions. Here are a few key operations that can be performed with the client-side object model:

- **Access to web services in SharePoint Online**   Using the client object model, you can access all the ASMX and WCF web services by using the REST interface in SharePoint Online. Examples of these include the Lists web service and User Profile service.

- **Access to a different site collection than the one in which the application is hosted**   In a Visual Studio sandboxed Web Part that uses the SharePoint server-side object model, you can only access objects in the current site collection. With client object model code, you can access objects in different site collections.

- **Access to external web services and data not hosted in SharePoint Online**   Using the client object model, you can access external web services that are hosted externally. Examples of these could include a weather service to show weather forecasts, or connecting to a service hosted in Windows Azure.

Here are some examples of operations that cannot be performed with client-side object models:

- Create a web application or a site collection.

- Read/write from/write to the server-side hard disk.

- Make farm configuration changes.

Using the Silverlight Client Object Model

With Visual Studio 2010, it is quite easy to create a Silverlight application and target it for deployment into SharePoint as part of the deployment package. You build the Silverlight application just as you would normally in Visual Studio 2010, although you can write code in this Silverlight application to make client-side calls to the SharePoint object model. This application can then be bundled into a .xap file and deployed to the document library in SharePoint Online. SharePoint has an out-of-box (OOB) Silverlight Web Part that is specifically designed to host .xaps on a SharePoint page. So you can add that Web Part on the page and just point it to the .xap file in the document library and the application will run.

Another approach is to build the Silverlight application in Visual Studio 2010, but deploy it as part of a sandboxed Web Part solution. Even though the sandboxed Web Part is prohibited from performing certain functions, the Silverlight application can perform them because it runs on the client side after the page has been downloaded from the server, and thus circumvents the limitations inherent to sandboxed solutions. To develop Silverlight solutions that use the SharePoint 2010 client object model, the following Dynamic Link Libraries (DLLs) must be included in your project:

```
Microsoft.SharePoint.Client.Silverlight.dll
Microsoft.SharePoint.Client.Runtime.Silverlight.dll
```

These DLLs are located in the path C:\Program Files\Common Files\Microsoft Shared\Web Server Extensions\14\TEMPLATE\LAYOUTS\ClientBin.

Note These DLLs are built specifically for Silverlight applications. They are already included in the .xap file, so you do not need to distribute them.

For more information on how to build Silverlight applications and integrate them with SharePoint 2010 using Visual Studio 2010, go to *http://bit.ly/fEh6fr.*

Using the .NET Client Object Model

The .NET client object model works similarly to the Silverlight client object model. The difference is that with the .NET client object model, you can build client applications that communicate with SharePoint Online remotely in any .NET application. To develop .NET applications that use the SharePoint 2010 client object model, the following DLLs need to be referenced in the project:

```
Microsoft.SharePoint.Client.dll
Microsoft.SharePoint.Client.Runtime.dll
```

These DLLs are located in the path C:\Program Files\Common Files\Microsoft Shared\Web Server Extensions\14\ISAPI.

If you are developing your .NET application on a non-SharePoint server, you can copy the DLLs locally and reference them on your development computer. These DLLs are not automatically included in your solution and will need to be included with your application.

Note For more information on how to use the SharePoint 2010 managed client object model, go to *http://bit.ly/geGGSn.*

Using the JavaScript Client Object Model

The JavaScript client object model implementation in SharePoint 2010 is used mainly for dialog box development, ribbon development, or SharePoint data access with JavaScript through the Content Editor Web Part, for example.

> **Note** To get started with the JavaScript implementation and to understand the classes and library, go to *http://msdn.microsoft.com/en-us/library/ee538253.aspx*.
>
> Although beyond the scope of this chapter, the Patterns & Practices SharePoint Guidance for 2010 provides good documentation on the pros and cons of various client-side approaches from an architectural standpoint. It covers areas such as query efficiency and performance, synchronous and asynchronous operations, security, and use of binary data. See *http://bit.ly/a3u6aK*.

Authentication in the Client Object Model

When you use sandboxed solutions to deploy code that runs on the server side, you do not need to worry about providing any authentication mechanism because the users have already authenticated to the server and the server-side code automatically runs in the context of the logged-on user. However, if you are using the client-side API, you might need to account for authentication because the code runs remotely on the client side. Here are the different authentication scenarios for the three client-side object model implementations.

Authentication in the ECMAScript Object Model

In this scenario, ECMAScript on the SharePoint page runs in the browser after the page has been rendered from the server. Since the browser has already been authenticated, the ECMAScript implementation uses the authentication cookie available in the browser. Therefore, normally there is no need to perform any authentication when using the ECMAScript client object model.

Authentication in the Silverlight Object Model

This scenario is similar to the ECMAScript scenario. If the Silverlight .xap file is located in the same SharePoint Online domain or site, the Silverlight client object model will use the same authentication cookies from the browser session. Therefore, normally there is no need to perform any authentication when using the Silverlight client object model.

Authentication in the .NET Managed Object Model

This scenario is different from the two previous ones. Your .NET Framework code is not automatically authenticated remotely. Therefore, you need to provide a mechanism for the user to log on to SharePoint Online so that you can then use the authentication cookie with your *ClientContext* object.

The user must log on interactively, so you have to include a *WebBrowser* control in your .NET Framework application (such as in a Windows Forms or WPF user interface), and have the user employ that control to log on to SharePoint Online. When the user is authenticated, the *WebBrowser* control will have received the authentication cookie supplied by SharePoint Online. However, these cookies are marked as *HTTPOnly*, and therefore cannot be accessed directly by your .NET Framework code. Instead, you must make a call to the WININET.DLL. The .NET Framework can call COM-based DLL methods through *P/Invoke*, and the method that you need to call is *InternetGetCookieEx*. This can return regular cookies and those with the *HTTPOnly* flag.

After you have retrieved the cookie, you can add the cookie to the *ClientContext* object's request.

SharePoint Online Integration with Azure

Windows Azure and SQL Azure are two cloud-based services offered by Microsoft that let you build, scale, and host applications in Microsoft data centers. With this service, you can host your application and SQL data in the cloud. Fortunately, there are ways to integrate your applications and data stored in Azure with SharePoint Online.

There is a good business case for integrating the two cloud-based services. Azure provides scalable endpoint to cloud-based data and services with SharePoint solutions. This integration also lets your corporation migrate to a cloud-based model completely or in a hybrid scenario and still have those cloud-based services integrated with SharePoint Online. Another possibility is to integrate the Azure services with the core features of SharePoint such as workflow, search, collaboration, Silverlight, or document management.

SharePoint Online and Silverlight Integration with Azure

There are two primary ways to integrate SharePoint Online and Silverlight with Azure. The first is to use an iframe to host an Azure application. This method has the advantages that it's simple and lightweight, and requires no code or deployment to SharePoint. The disadvantages are that the styling and formatting might be off, there is no "deep" integration, and there is no deployment through a SharePoint artifact.

The second approach of Azure integration in SharePoint Online and Silverlight is to use a sandboxed solution to deploy a Silverlight application hosted in SharePoint Online to interact with the Azure application/data. This has the advantage that you can use the existing services/data and a straightforward coding model for the interaction. The disadvantage is that now you have a service dependency on Azure.

Figure 7-26 shows how this interaction between a Silverlight Web Part and Azure can work. Notice that you have a Silverlight Web Part deployed within SharePoint Online. Because Silverlight is a client application, it can call out to an external web service hosted in Azure, even though the Web Part was deployed into the sandbox. The service in Azure then does something with the request, and can call back to SharePoint Online through SharePoint Online's own web services. Perhaps it posts a document to a library, creates a list item, starts a workflow, or creates a subsite. The Silverlight application could be set up to respond to the response from Azure. The Silverlight application could ping a SharePoint list every 60 seconds, waiting for Azure to deposit a new list item. When Azure deposits the new item, the Silverlight application can then update its user interface and present the response to the user.

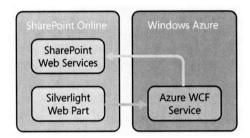

FIGURE 7-26 You can use a Silverlight Web Part to call into an Azure service, send and receive data, as well as receive a response from Azure through the out-of-the-box SharePoint Online web services.

SharePoint Online Dedicated Integration with Azure

The preceding two methods also apply to the SharePoint Online Dedicated model. However, SharePoint Online Dedicated comes with a supported full-trust coded model to connect with Azure. This is done through the use of the CASI (Claims, Azure, and SharePoint Integration) Kit. The CASI Kit is a combination of guidance, base class assemblies, Web Parts, and sample applications. Together, these pieces let you create WCF applications that are claims-aware and host them in the Windows Azure cloud. The kit contains a base class that will be used to provide the Azure and claims glue that connects them with SharePoint. A Web Part that is also included gives you an easy out-of-the-box way to simply plug that data from Azure into your SharePoint site. What is pretty cool about it is that it does this asynchronously with a client-side call so that your website doesn't come to a grinding halt while a bunch of server-side calls are made from your SharePoint pages to a potentially latent cloud-based service. The CASI Kit is a rather advanced topic, and to learn more about it, reference the following webpage: *http://bit.ly/9kLYZL*.

Part III
Deploying SharePoint in the Private Cloud

This final part of the book takes a closer look at what is required to deploy Microsoft SharePoint into a private cloud. Migrating SharePoint to the cloud doesn't necessarily mean you're leaving your data center's walls, and this part helps you frame up what it will take to see the same high-availability, auto-healing, and access-anywhere capabilities offered by the cloud, but in your own data center.

Chapter 8 kicks off this part of the book by introducing the concept of a private cloud. In one sentence, a private cloud is the intersection of virtualization and automation. However, a lot of technologies are involved in helping to make this marriage work, among them Hyper-V, the System Center suite, and the Opalis workflows, all of which are covered in this chapter.

Chapters 9 through 11 carry the cloud conversation forward by discussing a fundamental requirement for a SharePoint cloud: namely, the multitenancy capabilities of SharePoint 2010. Through the multitenancy features, you can support multiple "tenants" in a single web application, which means you can isolate the data, customizations, and performance implications from one tenant to another. This tenant isolation is a key component to the ability to support a private SharePoint cloud.

Chapter 8
Introduction to Creating a Private Cloud

In this chapter, you will learn about:

- The benefits of a private cloud

- Building a private cloud

- Automation in a private cloud with System Center and PowerShell

- What SharePoint roles you should and shouldn't virtualize

- Virtualization performance considerations

- Getting started with Hyper-V

During the past few years, almost every major newspaper and magazine has been advertising, evangelizing, and debating the benefits of the cloud. To understand these benefits, consider the scenario of migrating your company's email to the cloud. Now consider all the physical pieces that make up the email system in the organization. Also consider the physical hardware in the test and production environment. Every time a patch is developed or a new version is released it requires testing and validation. All of this equipment requires specialized training on email systems and hardware. Every new release requires more training. The organization has spam and virus scanning capabilities, which also require even more licensing and training, installation, and maintenance.

As an alternative, consider hosting all your email services directly in Microsoft Exchange Online. To your end users, there is no difference between this scenario and the one just described, because the Microsoft Outlook client's functionality works exactly the same. However, the organization no longer is required to do any installation, patching, or upgrades of Exchange Server. All the support is offloaded to the cloud.

Of course, not all companies can move to the public cloud. This is especially true for larger companies and government organizations because they might have strong ties to internal systems or regulatory compliance concerns. So, what options do these larger companies have? Must they forfeit all the great benefits of the cloud, such as worldwide failover, the ability to self-heal, and the ability to automatically increase or decrease capacity based on ever-changing demand? The answer is an emphatic *no*!

In principal, a private cloud takes all the benefits that are expected in a public cloud scenario and incorporates them into a company's private data center. To do this, a private cloud utilizes the automation benefits of modern monitoring solutions such as Microsoft System Center as well as the virtualization benefits of Microsoft Hyper-V. The benefits of a private cloud become apparent once servers migrate from a Physical to Virtual (P2V) architecture. The capacity of the infrastructure can be flexible to the current demand because of the ease with which it can provision and deprovision new virtual machines. Hardware no longer has to be dedicated to specific applications.

Once an organization has decided to virtualize, however, it cannot assume that it should virtualize everything. Although many software companies are finally approving virtualization as a platform, several issues can complicate this decision. From a Microsoft SharePoint perspective, it is common to virtualize the web front–ends (WFEs). But what if they are hosting the Secure Sockets Layer (SSL) certificate? What if dynamic compression is enabled in Internet Information Server (IIS)? Both of these options increase CPU processing utilization and affect the decision of whether to virtualize or not. Later in this chapter you'll see a breakdown of which roles should and shouldn't be virtualized, and some things to consider along the way.

Hyper-V is Microsoft's hypervisor-based virtualization system for 32-bit and 64-bit systems. At the time of this writing, Hyper-V is in its second release and is available as a standalone product called Microsoft Hyper-V Server 2008. It is also available as an installable role in Windows Server 2008 R2 and Windows Server 2008. Hyper-V is a foundation for Microsoft virtualization technologies and allows multiple operating systems on a single physical server as well as complete isolation of the operating systems from one another. Toward the end of this chapter, you will find an introduction to planning a Hyper-V deployment, as well as some rudimentary step-by-step procedures to help you get started installing and creating virtual machines.

Beyond virtualization, the other main differentiator between a cloud and a typical virtualized infrastructure is the ability to automate tasks. In this scenario, provisioning of new servers becomes part of an automated process rather than a series of manual, project-based initiatives. Specialized monitoring solutions, such as System Center, automatically detect performance issues and can react by self-healing or adding virtual servers to support the increase in demand. Windows PowerShell scripting is also fully supported for both System Center and SharePoint. By creating custom scripts, you can automate myriad, otherwise manual, processes, such as extending System Center Orchestrator (SCO) workflows and creating sites in SharePoint.

Private Cloud Benefits

There are many reasons to incorporate cloud-based technologies into your existing data centers. A private cloud is the implementation of cloud services on resources that are dedicated to your organization, whether the resources are on-premises or off-premises. With a private cloud, you get many of the benefits of public cloud computing—including reliability and predictability, automation (self-healing and self-service), as well as capacity scalability and elasticity.

Ratio of Servers to Administrators

The average number of server administrators to servers in today's typical data center is 50 servers:1 administrator. This sounds pretty good until you consider the average ratio of cloud-based data centers, which is 500:1. The reason for this dramatically increased ratio concerns automation of server maintenance and operation. The "self-healing" capabilities of SCO significantly reduce the burden on IT staff in this regard, and therefore allow a data center the cost-effective capability to support dramatically more servers.

Reliability and Predictability

One of the main differentiators between a cloud-based data center and a typical data center is the focus of a cloud-based data center on making applications highly available and fault-tolerant. Since this is the main priority, private cloud-based data centers are more predictable and reliable. In order to resolve an outage, a data center that isn't cloud-based might require some of the following steps, which could take several hours to complete:

- **Building another server**   This can create hardware issues because most organizations do not have extra physical machines available.

- **Installing a new operating system**   Although most system administrators have streamlined this process, it can still take a very long time to complete.

- **Installing new software**   This requires the expertise of on-call staff and, possibly, support from the software company.

- **Installing patches**   Synchronizing the latest patches in both the operating system and the software can take even more time.

- **Restoring Databases**   Getting the database administrator to start going through transaction logs to get the system close to the last working instance can take even longer.

Conversely, a private cloud is more reliable because it is highly automated, agile, and supports self-service.

Highly Automated, Agile, and Supports Self-Service

Another differentiator between a cloud-based system and a typical system is how much automation is integrated into the environment. If you run the same outage scenario previously mentioned, but include an automated response, the remediation time decreases dramatically, if not to zero.

The outage or issue is picked up and an entirely new virtual server can be provisioned in an automated response. An appropriate host can be selected based on customizable criteria and a snapshot can be imaged onto the virtual machine. The new server can be online in minutes, not hours or days. Microsoft System Center is a suite of products with which you can manage and automate servers and systems in your organization. The following is a list of all the products in the Systems Center suite:

System Center Virtual Machine Manager   Provides central management of virtual machines across the data center.

System Center Data Protection Manager   A complete backup tool with which you can take snapshots of complete virtual machines up to every 15 minutes.

System Center Operations Manager   A comprehensive management and monitoring tool that can detect errors or outages across your data center.

System Center Configuration Manager   Use this to remotely configure resources such as laptops and servers.

System Center Service Manager   A comprehensive service management system that orchestrates people, processes, and technology through an IT service desk/ticketing system. This system allows operations staff to approve automated remedies, as well as tenant self-service requests.

System Center Orchestrator 2012 (formerly Opalis)   An automation platform that allows workflow processes that coordinate System Center and other management tools to automate incident response, change and compliance, and service life-cycle management processes.

Flexibility to Meet Diverse Capacity Patterns

Capacity in a data center is never constant or linear. Rather, it ebbs and flows, and is often quite unpredictable. A private cloud handles diverse capacity patterns much better than typical data centers because of all the virtualization and automation that is baked into a private cloud. This means that as your requirements for applications change, your infrastructure can adapt to the situation without a lengthy hardware procurement process or resolution time frame.

A common capacity application that a private cloud can handle well is the "On and Off" application (see Figure 8-1). This pertains to applications that are only used during certain periods, and are not used during periods of planned inactivity. An example of this is a tax preparation application that is used during certain times of the year, such as tax season. By providing this application in a private cloud, you can turn off the hardware resources that are required or reallocate them to other applications when tax season has ended. A private cloud benefits from being able to relocate those physical resources rather than having them sit idle for six months of the year. Simply turn the virtual machines off, and turn them back on when the system needs to resume.

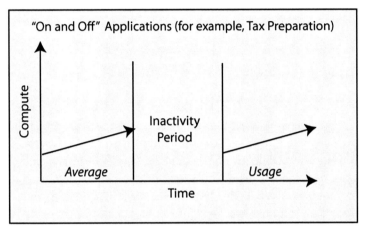

FIGURE 8-1 The cloud benefits from being able to turn services on and off without incurring costs when those services aren't being used.

A second capacity example that benefits from a private cloud is a "Growing Fast" application (see Figure 8-2). This refers to applications that are in their initial launch phase, but are getting busier and are requiring more hardware resources. This sort of fast growth is something that most organizations fail to plan for, largely because it is hard to forecast adoption of an application. Once all the physical resources are allocated, it is very difficult to provision, set up, and deploy computers into a physical production environment to respond to an increased need for capacity. Because of this, many data centers overallocate resources to accommodate a certain level of growth that might be unrealistic (but is needed in order to be safe). So, how do you spend enough without spending too much? A private cloud can automatically allocate more resources as demand changes. Also, a private cloud is not only able to expand during busy times, but also contracts during slower times to reduce power consumption or free up resources for other applications.

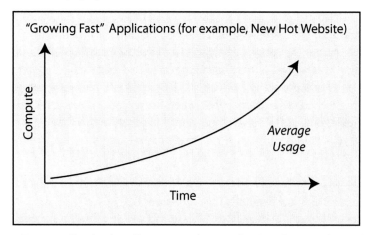

FIGURE 8-2 The cloud readily accommodates applications that grow fast and use an ever-increasing amount of capacity.

A third capacity example that is amenable to a private cloud is a "Random Bursting" application (see Figure 8-3). This refers to applications that have a normal utilization level but experience bursts of activity, thereby requiring more hardware resources. For example, a news site featuring an important company update could generate surges in resource utilization. Without a private cloud, organizations would be forced to overallocate hardware for an application that does not always need it. This creates excess heat, excess expense in terms of hardware cost, excess data-center utilization, and increased administration. Conversely, a private cloud could automatically scale up or down as utilization changes.

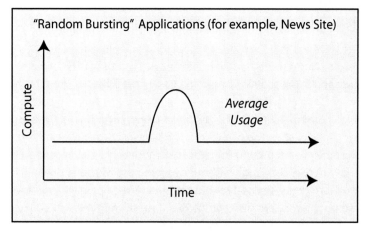

FIGURE 8-3 The cloud can auto-scale to accommodate random bursts of throughput and utilization. In a typical data center, this would result in outages or poor performance.

A fourth capacity type is a "Predictable Bursting" application (see Figure 8-4). This can be an application that has a predictable pattern of increased utilization, such as a state lottery website. People who play the lottery frequently check the website after the numbers are drawn to see if they won. If numbers are drawn on Wednesday evening, Thursday could be a high-load day, whereas the rest of the week would show very low utilization. A private cloud would benefit the data center in this case because resources could be allocated during these bursts, and then reallocated elsewhere during the low-utilization dips.

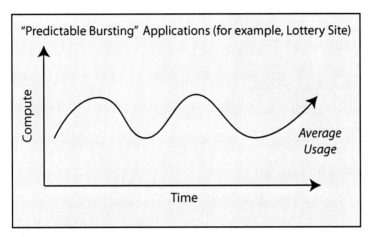

FIGURE 8-4 Similar to unpredictable bursting, the cloud can auto-scale to accommodate predictable bursting, and then deprovision those resources after the capacity demand decreases.

How Do You Build a Private Cloud?

The process of building a private cloud is an extensive study and cannot be exhaustively covered in a single chapter. Two core Microsoft software products facilitate the configuration and management of a private cloud: Hyper-V and System Center Suite. These two products are discussed in great detail in two 800-plus page books:

- *Windows Server 2008 Hyper-V Resource Kit*, by Janique Carbon and Robert Larson (2009, Microsoft Press)

- *Microsoft System Center Configuration Manager 2007*, by Steven D. Kaczmarek with the Microsoft System Center Team (2008, Microsoft Press)

These resources can provide you with a wealth of information on virtualization and automation. Therefore, this chapter will simply give you a primer on these deep areas of study. To help you consider what it takes to build a private cloud, take a look at Figure 8-5.

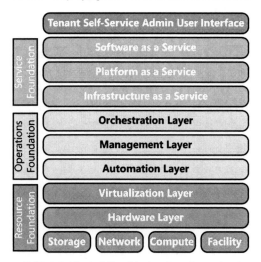

FIGURE 8-5 The building blocks of a private cloud.

The Resource Foundation

The resource foundation is really the foundation upon which a cloud is built. This foundation contains the physical resources that support the cloud. These include storage area networks (SANs), networking tools such as switches and firewalls, physical server hosts for computing (CPU processing), and physical building resources such as electricity, server racks, cables, and so on. This physical layer is what the virtual layer is built on. Virtual machines run on physical host servers running in the Hardware layer. The Virtualization layer rounds out the resource foundation and provides support for the majority of cloud benefits discussed in the previous section.

The Operations Foundation

The operations foundation is composed of three critical layers of a private cloud: the Automation layer, the Management layer, and the Orchestration layer. These layers provide all the core management, monitoring, and automation that are central to a private cloud. Without these components, all you're really left with is a virtualized data center, but you don't have the cloud benefits such as self-healing ability, error reporting, configuration consistency, and capacity auto-scaling.

The Automation Layer

The Automation layer includes technologies that provide the interface between higher-level management systems (the Management layer and above) and the physical/virtual resources they leverage. This includes components such as Windows PowerShell 2.0 for custom scripting and automation, Windows Management Instrumentation (WMI) for remote scripting of cloud technologies and resources such as System Center and operating systems, and WS-Management for remote web service administration.

Automating a Private Cloud with PowerShell

In System Center, anytime you complete an action in the Virtual Machine Manager (VMM), the commands are presented in a PowerShell cmdlet script that you can save and reuse when performing the action at a later date. By scripting these functions, you can easily deploy a large number of virtual machines, for instance, and save time by not having to repeat the action over and over in the GUI.

SharePoint also has hundreds upon hundreds of PowerShell cmdlets that you can use to automate your deployments. These deployments can include the following:

- Creating a farm
- Creating service applications
- Creating web applications
- Creating site collections
- Creating subsites, libraries, and lists
- Upgrading or patching a farm
- Backing up and restoring sites or other content
- Moving site collections from one database to another

The list goes on and on. Often, IT departments will tie these cmdlets to workflows in System Center Orchestrator 2012. This allows automated responses to issues in SharePoint or requests made by end users through System Center Service Manager's self-service portal.

> **Note** A great resource for automating these SharePoint techniques is *Automating SharePoint 2010 with Windows PowerShell 2.0*, by Gary Lapointe and Shannon Bray (2011, Wiley). This is nearly 800 pages of PowerShell goodness!

In subsequent chapters of this book, we will take a closer look at the multitenancy features of SharePoint 2010, which are only configurable with PowerShell. Automation in general is important when it comes to building a private cloud in SharePoint, but multitenancy is an especially critical topic to understand. A key feature of the cloud is that cloud tenants, or subscribers to the cloud's services, cannot be adversely affected by other tenants. This tenant isolation is achievable in SharePoint through the new multitenancy capabilities in SharePoint 2010, as we will discuss in Chapter 9, "Introducing Multitenancy in SharePoint 2010," through Chapter 11, "Configuring Tenant-Aware Site Collections."

The Management Layer

The Management layer uses the System Center Suite to perform core management functions. These functions might include patch compliance checking, patch deployment and installation, patch verification, system monitoring for stability and outages, as well as backup functions. The core System Center products that perform these management services are System Center Operations Manager, System Center Configuration Manager, System Center Virtual Machine Manager, and System Center Data Protection Manager.

Note PowerShell is integrated into the entire System Center Suite. This introduces the ability to script solutions for the virtualized infrastructure. We will discuss in the next chapter the capacity to automatically provision computers and administer them.

System Center Operations Manager System Center Operations Manager (SCOM) is an end-to-end service management tool that works seamlessly with Microsoft software and organizations. SCOM allows you to view reports across your organization and see all state, health, and performance problems that might be present. You can also set alerts to receive email notifications if certain events are generated in your servers or applications, such as degradations of availability, performance, optimal configuration, security, or even custom errors. In short, SCOM allows you to have rapid insight into the overall health of your enterprise's resources and applications.

System Center Configuration Manager System Center Configuration Manager (SCCM) is an enterprise application that remotely configures enterprise assets, such as employee laptops and servers. With thousands of technology resources in an enterprise organization, SCCM reduces the total cost of ownership by automating the maintenance of these systems and also provides consistency across the organization. SCCM provides management tools for IT in the following areas:

- **Asset intelligence** Provides IT administrators with insight into what hardware and software products are deployed across their organization (what they have, who is using the products, and where they are located).

- **Software distribution and update** Used to install and configure software applications across the organization, including laptops, tablets, mobile devices, and servers.

- **Desired configuration management** Helps organizations to define a desired state for their resources with the goal of improving availability, security, and performance across their network.

- **Operating system deployment**   Automates the installation and configuration of operating systems in the enterprise.

- **Power management**   Used to maximize cost savings from energy-saving desktop and laptop systems by enforcing power consumption rules and policies.

System Center Virtual Machine Manager   System Center Virtual Machine Manager (SCVMM) is an ideal tool for managing a private cloud infrastructure. It offers a wide range of scalability across virtual environments including Windows Server Hyper-V, Microsoft Virtual Server, and VMware ESX. It also has support for consolidating physical servers into a virtual infrastructure (for example, P2V). In addition, SCVMM features intelligent placement for workloads on the best-suited physical host servers, as well as a library of functionality that allows the management of predefined images that are ready to be manually or automatically provisioned. Combined with SCOM, SCVMM allows the use of performance and resource optimization (PRO) to allow dynamic and responsive management and dynamic reallocation of virtualized workloads. Figure 8-6 shows an example of a running SCVMM.

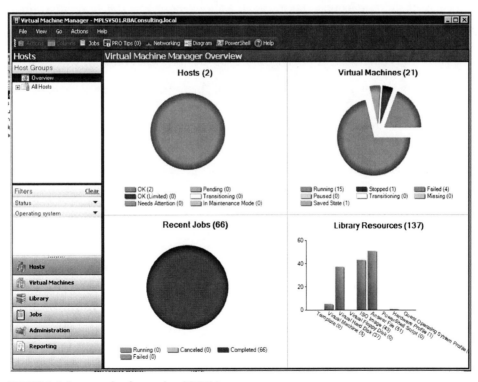

FIGURE 8-6 An example of a running SCVMM.

System Center Data Protection Manager   System Center Data Protection Manager (SCDPM) is a unified data protection manager for the enterprise. Whether you need a backup strategy for SQL Server, Exchange Server, SharePoint, virtual machines, file shares, or employee laptops, SCDPM does it all. SCDPM uses local disk, tape backup, and cloud-based repositories to provide a seamless backup and recovery solution for all the assets in your enterprise.

The Orchestration Layer: System Center Orchestrator 2012

System Center Orchestrator 2012, formerly called System Center Opalis, is an automation platform for orchestrating and integrating IT tools to drive down the cost of data center operations while improving the reliability of IT processes. You could say that System Center Orchestrator is the "brains" behind the automated, "self-healing" responses to things such as system outages or increased capacity demands and auto-scaling.

System Center Orchestrator enables IT organizations to automate recommended practices, such as those found in Microsoft Operations Framework (MOF) and the Information Technology Infrastructure Library (ITIL). This is achieved through workflow processes that coordinate System Center and other management tools to automate incident response, change and compliance, and service life-cycle management processes.

Through its workflow designer, System Center Orchestrator automatically shares data and initiates tasks in SCOM, SCCM, SCSM, VMM, Active Directory, and third-party tools. System Center Orchestrator even has a SharePoint integration pack to help you automate common SharePoint tasks.

System Center Orchestrator automates IT infrastructure tasks, while SCSM automates human workflow tasks. The combined offering ensures repeatable, consistent results by removing the latency associated with manual coordination service delivery. System Center and System Center Orchestrator facilitate integration, efficiency, and business alignment of data-center IT services by:

- Automating cross-silo processes and enforcing best practices for incident, change, and service life-cycle management.

- Reducing unanticipated errors and service delivery time by automating tasks across vendor and organization silos.

- Integrating System Center with non-Microsoft tools to enable interoperability across the data center.

- Orchestrating tasks across systems for consistent, documented, and compliant activity.

For more information on System Center Orchestrator, see the example scenario about orchestrating a business process originating in SharePoint via Opalis. This scenario is discussed at the end of this chapter.

The Service Foundation

Cloud computing is really about managing the different components required for solutions. There are basically three private cloud models, and you'll notice a pattern with regard to benefits and tradeoffs as you compare each model. These models include Infrastructure as a Service, Platform as a Service, and Software as a Service. Services in a private cloud are very important. Often, an IT department will identify key services it provides to the business, as well as a chargeback model to support IT's ability to provide these services.

Infrastructure as a Service

The Infrastructure as a Service (IaaS) model (see Table 8-1) builds upon the resource foundation set up by an enterprise IT department. In this model, the IT department will manage the operating system (including installation and patching), virtualization, storage, and logical server configurations. The tenants or subscribing business-related departments then manage all the software and services they see fit to install on the virtual servers that are provisioned for them. This affords business units the flexibility they need to install and manage their own applications without getting bogged down in IT's red tape, but they still benefit from all the infrastructure and availability guarantees and service level agreements (SLAs) that IT promises them. However, they don't get the support from IT that they would if they went with something such as Platform as a Service or Software as a Service (discussed shortly).

TABLE 8-1 IaaS Abstracts Even More from the Organization

Resource/ Management Foundation	IaaS
Applications	Applications
Development	Development
.NET Runtime	.NET Runtime
Databases	Databases
Security	Security
Management	Management
Load Balancing	Load Balancing
Scaling	Scaling
Backup	Backup
Logical Servers	Logical Servers
Storage	Storage
Virtualization	Virtualization
OS	OS
Server Hardware	Server Hardware
Networking	Networking
Utilities	Utilities
Physical	Physical

▒ Managed by business-related department

░ Managed by IT department

Platform as a Service

The Platform as a Service (PaaS) model (see Table 8-2) abstracts and manages even more solution components than the IaaS model. In a PaaS scenario, the IT department handles everything from backups, scaling, and load balancing, to security, databases, and development platforms. PaaS offers quicker time to market by requiring the tenant or business-related department to only focus on its applications and services, rather than the underlying infrastructure. Microsoft's Windows Azure product is a PaaS offering. With this product, an IT department may build its own proprietary platform service on top of which business units can build their own customized applications. An example could be a centralized warehousing system built by a manufacturing company's IT department, but given to the company's other departments as a platform onto which they can build their own custom views, reports, or applications that utilize the data in a way that is unique to that particular department.

TABLE 8-2 Using PaaS, Organizations Can Build Applications Without Concern for Underlying Infrastructure

Resource/ Management Foundation	IaaS	PaaS
Applications	Applications	Applications
Development	Development	Development
.NET Runtime	.NET Runtime	.NET Runtime
Databases	Databases	Databases
Security	Security	Security
Management	Management	Management
Load Balancing	Load Balancing	Load Balancing
Scaling	Scaling	Scaling
Backup	Backup	Backup
Logical Servers	Logical Servers	Logical Servers
Storage	Storage	Storage
Virtualization	Virtualization	Virtualization
OS	OS	OS
Server Hardware	Server Hardware	Server Hardware
Networking	Networking	Networking
Utilities	Utilities	Utilities
Physical	Physical	Physical

Managed by business-related department

Managed by IT department

Software as a Service

Unlike the previously discussed models, the Software as a Service (SaaS) model (see Table 8-3) removes all application management responsibilities from tenants or business-related departments. Instead, the IT department develops, deploys, and maintains the solution, and the business department simply consumes the solution as a service and configures it to meet its specific needs. SharePoint is a prime example of the SaaS model. With SharePoint, a business department doesn't have to buy any servers or software licenses. It simply signs up and configures its SharePoint tenant sites as it sees fit.

Chapter 10, "Configuring Tenant-Aware Service Applications," introduces multitenancy in SharePoint to support SharePoint as a Service in an enterprise.

TABLE 8-3 Using SaaS, Organizations Can Use and Configure Software with Little Concern for Custom Development or Infrastructure

Resource/ Management Foundation	IaaS	PaaS	SaaS
Applications	Applications	Applications	Applications
Development	Development	Development	Development
.NET Runtime	.NET Runtime	.NET Runtime	.NET Runtime
Databases	Databases	Databases	Databases
Security	Security	Security	Security
Management	Management	Management	Management
Load Balancing	Load Balancing	Load Balancing	Load Balancing
Scaling	Scaling	Scaling	Scaling
Backup	Backup	Backup	Backup
Logical Servers	Logical Servers	Logical Servers	Logical Servers
Storage	Storage	Storage	Storage
Virtualization	Virtualization	Virtualization	Virtualization
OS	OS	OS	OS
Server Hardware	Server Hardware	Server Hardware	Server Hardware
Networking	Networking	Networking	Networking
Utilities	Utilities	Utilities	Utilities
Physical	Physical	Physical	Physical

▓ Managed by business-related department

░ Managed by IT department

The Self-Service Layer: SCSM

A private cloud wouldn't be a private cloud without a self-service portal. Self-service capability is critical to cloud computing. Instead of a business department navigating through months of IT red tape to get the services it needs, that department ought to be able to navigate to a self-service portal and simply start provisioning the services it wants. This might entail the provisioning of new virtual machines, or subscribing to a SaaS model, such as SharePoint as a Service. The portal could feature a request site where the department requests SharePoint sites it wants, as well as the users who need access to them. Then, after it submits the request, an automated process provisions the requested resources as well as updates the chargeback system to ensure that the IT department is compensated for the services the business department is utilizing.

> **Note** SCSM can be tied to System Center Orchestrator, which can, in turn, use custom PowerShell scripts to automate the creation of SharePoint assets, such as site collections and features.

SCSM is a user-centric, self-service, web-based tool designed to facilitate this sort of self-service provisioning. It also has a support or IT help-desk-like component that allows users to create incidents and service tickets as well as view the status of their tickets.

In addition, SCSM works in conjunction with SCOM. When SCOM detects a performance issue, it automatically creates a ticket in SCSM. This ticket could be automatically approved, or it could require human approval. After it receives approval, an automated action could, for example, provision new virtual servers to increase capacity. SCSM also allows users to do the following:

- Reset passwords (requires Microsoft ILM)

- Request or install software with minimal or no IT involvement

- Read IT announcements

- Search company Knowledge Base articles for IT-specific information

- Create service maps from information gathered by System Center

- Identify service dependencies

- Automate workflows and templates to ensure that change management processes are in place

- Integrate with other products

Preparing for Virtualization with Hyper-V

Virtualization with Hyper-V allows multiple operating systems to run on a single physical computer as virtual machines. Virtualization has gone through several phases over the years. Initially, virtualization focused specifically on the IT production environment to lower costs. During this phase, only a handful of tools were available for creating virtual machines and converting P2V machines, and few tools were available that offered specific monitoring capabilities focused on a virtual infrastructure. Also, because of a lack of training, many administrators were expected to just absorb the additional knowledge. In addition, it became difficult to justify virtualizing many of the applications in an environment, because most software vendors were not yet supporting virtualized hardware.

Needless to say, this created a lot of frustration among IT directors and CIOs. One of the primary reasons organizations choose to explore virtualization is to reduce the amount of equipment in their data centers. Additional reasons include the following:

- Lack of air conditioning capacity because the amount of heat generated exceeds the cooling capacity in the data center

- Lack of physical space in the data center

- Desire to reduce the data center footprint (this could be part of a green initiative)

- Desire to reduce cooling requirements in the data center

- Desire to reduce capital expenditures by reducing the amount of hardware procured through consolidation

- Less expensive licensing for virtual equipment:

  - Windows Server 2008 Standard Edition (one physical + one virtual)

  - Windows Server 2008 Enterprise Edition (one physical + four virtual)

  - Windows Server 2008 Datacenter Edition or Itanium-based systems (one physical + unlimited virtual)

> **Note** Licensing information can and does change. See Microsoft's licensing page for virtualization to confirm these figures at *http://bit.ly/anjvPq*.

- Automation and productivity

- Reduced Fiber Channel connections

- More efficient utilization of multicore processors

- Easier to support your servers and data centers

The second phase of virtualization focused on improving SLAs by virtualizing mission-critical applications. During this phase, many companies continued to run into more licensing issues but also started to find problems unique to virtual environments. Training was finally becoming more accessible, but there were far too many virtualized environments compared to trained administrators. Tools to specifically monitor a virtual infrastructure were not considered a priority and most organizations used existing monitoring equipment. Unfortunately, organizations learned some harsh lessons when, instead of one server going down, one host would go down and would take dozens of servers down with it.

At the time of this writing, we are in the phase of providing IaaS, SaaS, and PaaS. The success of this phase is based on cloud-based computing.

Now that companies and organizations are heavily investing in training and utilizing specific monitoring tools, a more flexible, scalable, and reliable architecture is available without introducing unnecessary costs or over-designing an environment. Companies can plan a small launch and easily add capacity as their needs increase. This allows more companies to offer cloud-based services where only a handful of administrators can monitor thousands of virtual machines. Additionally, it creates an opportunity for organizations to create private and hybrid clouds and utilize this powerful and flexible technology.

Lack of training is the biggest factor in building an unsuccessful virtualization deployment. Even though a large number of organizations have deployed mission-critical applications to a virtualized environment, the early adopters faced issues concerning a lack of training and expertise. Therefore, a lack of experts in the field combined with a lack of appropriate training and books made it very difficult for organizations to have a successful deployment.

The proper proactive approach to reducing the perception of a failed implementation is to start by defining your expectations up front and base them on realistic goals. Additionally, it is imperative to include the right tools to monitor and diagnose issues in a virtualized environment. Finally, do not forget about training. Launching a virtualized infrastructure takes a serious training commitment for your IT professionals. Although many talented administrators are available, specific training is required for a virtualized environment.

Virtualizing SharePoint

SharePoint 2010 supports the virtualization of all its roles and components. Even SQL Server can be virtualized. However, before you determine that you want to virtualize 100 percent of the stack, consider Table 8-4, which shows performance implications for several of the most common roles in such a scenario. As you can see, some roles that are resource-intensive are better candidates for physical hardware.

TABLE 8-4 Different SharePoint Roles Have Different Impacts on Overall Resource Load

Role	Memory-Intensive	CPU-Intensive	Network-Intensive	Drive-Intensive
WFE	Potential	Potential	Potential	No
Application	Potential	Potential	Potential	Potential
Query	Yes	Potential	Potential	Yes
Crawl	Yes	Yes	Potential	Yes
Database	Yes	Yes	Yes	Yes
Business Intelligence Stack	Yes	Yes	Yes	Potential

> **Note** When planning the virtual architecture, put all roles and services across at least two physical hosts. This will provide service redundancy if a host ever goes down.

The following subsections discuss these roles in more detail.

Web Server Role

WFEs are generally not memory-intensive and can be ideal candidates for virtualization. Consider WFEs if you plan to utilize dynamic compression (in IIS) because that can require additional processor resources. Run Secure Sockets Layer (SSL) certificates on the WFEs because they can increase processor utilization. Consider offloading the certificates to a certificate authority instead. Disk utilization also tends to not be I/O-intensive. Additional consideration should be made when combining the Query role with the WFE because this will put additional load on the WFE.

Application Server Role

Most services can be virtualized, but planning their utilization and scope will be extremely important when deciding whether to virtualize. Smaller roles such as the Central Administration role or managed metadata role can easily be virtualized, but applications such as Excel services and PowerPivot, which require more processing or memory power, should be carefully monitored if you decide to virtualize them. Watch out for increases in processor utilization, memory, and I/O utilization. Of all the services, PowerPivot in particular stands out as a service you likely do not want to virtualize.

Query Component Role

The Query role can be both I/O and memory-intensive. Processor utilization is increased when combined with a WFE. When combining the Query and Crawl roles, use separate virtual disks to avoid contention, and place the separate virtual disks on separate physical arrays if possible. This is the same kind of best practice used with database servers when separating log and database files.

Crawl Component Role

The Crawl role is often placed on a physical machine unless the deployment is in a nonproduction environment. It is memory, CPU, and I/O-intensive. Also, this role tends to not have the high availability requirements of the other roles, unless fresh search results are part of the company's availability requirements. If freshness is a high-availability requirement, consider creating more than one crawl component and place them across multiple servers (virtual and physical) to achieve service redundancy.

Since the crawl component is so dependent on I/O, pass-through should be used if you do decide to virtualize this role. In addition, this drive has the potential to become extremely large (depending on the number of items crawled). When combining the Query and Index roles, separate the disks to avoid contention.

Database Planning Role

Although Microsoft officially supports virtualizing SQL Server 2008 and SQL Server 2008 R2, the company does not recommend that you virtualize the database layer in a SharePoint environment. SharePoint utilizes a high amount of memory, CPU, and I/O resources, and is network-intensive. A robust SQL Server would approach 32 GB of memory and 12-plus processor cores. This sort of robust configuration is nearly impossible to achieve when virtualized. If a decision is made to virtualize the database layer, it is important to use pass-through for your drives, since I/O is commonly the bottleneck, not necessarily SQL itself.

Storage Planning Role

Virtual machine dynamic drives can be placed in commodity storage such as a SAN. For SQL databases, dedicate at least four separate physical arrays (preferably RAID 10) for tempdb, logs, search databases, and other service databases. These arrays can be direct attached storage, but often they are put on a SAN, as well, with a good fiber connection. Content databases can be placed on a commodity SAN because there is low I/O associated with them (in comparison). Network attached storage (NAS) is a horrible choice.

BI Stack Role

Services such as Performance Point, Excel Services, and PowerPivot can all be virtualized. However, you should virtualize these services with caution. PowerPivot, for example, has huge memory demands. If you have a PowerPivot workbook that is, for example, 1 GB in size, the workflow running in SharePoint will consume approximately 2 GB of server memory. Therefore, if you have five of these documents, you'll need 10 GB of memory! For heavy BI solutions, it might be best to have physical servers on which you can dedicate a larger pool of resources.

Don't Use the Farm Configuration Wizard!

It is not a good practice to install SharePoint in a production environment with the Configuration Wizard and PSConfig. All of the wizards in SharePoint automatically create databases with a GUID attached to the database name (see Figure 8-7). This is more difficult to monitor due to poor naming conventions, and the naming conventions should be inline with your organization's existing patterns.

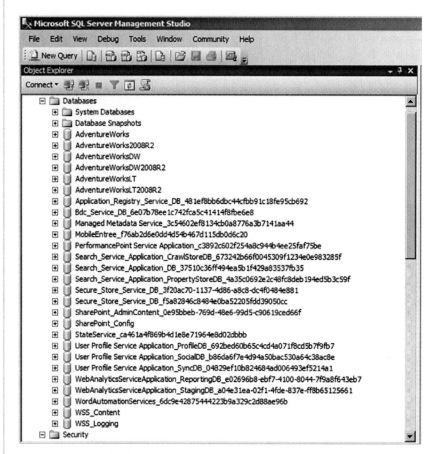

FIGURE 8-7 A sample of database names automatically generated by the SharePoint GUI installers.

Additionally, the automated installation installs and enables too many services by default. This could cause poor performance in a production environment if all the roles are not appropriately planned out.

Microsoft Assessment and Planning Toolkit

Virtualization planning starts with the Microsoft Assessment and Planning (MAP) Toolkit 5.5. MAP performs three functions when installed in your environment. The first function performs a secure, agentless, and network-wide inventory that scales from small businesses to large enterprises. From a single networked computer, MAP collects and organizes device information. The MAP Toolkit uses WMI, the Remote Registry Service, Active Directory Domain Services (ADDS), and the Computer Browser service.

The second function of MAP is compatibility analysis. This is a form of hardware analysis that looks at devices installed on a computer and reports the availability of drivers for those devices. Device assessment can be used for migration and consolidation scenarios for Windows 7, Windows Server 2008 R2, and SQL Server 2008 R2. MAP recognizes both Windows Server and Linux operating systems, including those running in a virtual environment. Additionally, the VMware discovery feature in MAP identifies already virtualized servers running VMware that can be managed with the SCVMM platform, or can be migrated to the Hyper-V hypervisor.

Finally, MAP generates reports containing both a summary and detailed assessment results for each migration scenario. The results are provided in Microsoft Office Excel workbooks (see Figures 8-8 and 8-9) and Microsoft Office Word documents. Reports are generated to identify currently installed Windows client operating systems as well as their hardware recommendations for migration. MAP also identifies all deployed browsers as well as anti-virus and antimalware programs. It can also identify Linux, VMware, and Windows Server operating systems and currently installed Office software. Additionally, it performs complete web application and database discovery as well as a Windows Azure platform capacity assessment.

	A	B	C	D
1	**Windows Azure Platform Capacity Estimates Summary**			
2	This worksheet provides a summary of the type and quantity of Windows Azure compute instances, estimated monthly compute hours, SQL Azure Databases, and estimated network bandwidth required to migrate the selected web applications and databases to the Windows Azure Platform using this assessment.			
3				
4	**Summary Item**	**Count**		
5	Web Applications included in Assessment	310		
6	Databases included in Assessment	121		
7	Small Windows Azure compute instances required	271		
8	Medium Windows Azure compute instances required	16		
9	Large Windows Azure compute instances required	15		
10	Web Applications that cannot be sized	8		
11	Windows Azure monthly small compute hours	261360		
12	Windows Azure monthly network bandwidth (GB)	1655.04		
13	Windows Azure monthly storage (GB)	726		
14	1 GB SQL Azure Web databases required	108		
15	5 GB SQL Azure Web databases required	1		
16	Databases that cannot be sized	12		
17	SQL Azure monthly network bandwidth (GB)	888.44		

FIGURE 8-8 A sample generated Excel spreadsheet from MAP.

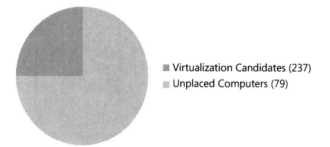

■ Virtualization Candidates (237)
■ Unplaced Computers (79)

FIGURE 8-9 A sample chart generated in a Word document from MAP.

Server Virtualization Validation Program

Before beginning a virtualization exercise, it is important to understand that Microsoft has a support policy on virtualization. At the time of this writing, SharePoint Server 2010 is certified by Microsoft through the Server Virtualization Validation Program (SVVP). Windows SharePoint Services 3.0 virtualization is supported for production when you use Virtual Server 2005 R2, Windows Server 2008 Hyper-V, and third-party virtualization providers certified by Microsoft through SVVP. Microsoft Office SharePoint Server 2007 virtualization is supported for production use when you use Virtual Server 2005 R2, Windows Server 2008 Hyper-V, and third-party virtualization providers certified by Microsoft through SVVP.

When you begin to decide what components in a SharePoint installation should be included in a virtualization solution, it is important to follow Microsoft's recommendation for a phased-in approach for a Hyper-V infrastructure. Microsoft recommends the following virtualization phases.

Planning

When you are planning a Hyper-V implementation, the planning phase should involve the CIO, since virtualization is not an inexpensive venture. This should include high-level discussions about the company's strategy; the CIO will provide the business priorities and plans. Next, the organization's strategic initiatives should be considered, and then a high-level application workload assessment should be determined. Finally, it is important to look at the workload of the following systems:

- Messaging (email)
- Collaboration (information sharing and document management; for example, SharePoint)
- Unified communications (includes instant messaging, web conferencing, telephony, and voice mail)
- Customer Relationship Management (CRM)
- Line of Business (LoB) applications

Evaluation

This is where the IT department evaluates the technology on a small scale. This involves getting support personnel trained on the technology and planning a small Proof of Concept (PoC). For example, this could include deploying a small SharePoint private cloud and creating the PowerShell scripts required to automate the installation.

Proof of Concept

This is the first official release of the virtualized environment to a small subset of IT users that run various system integration tests to validate functionality. Feedback is generally informal. But it is important to monitor the farm. Virtualization PoCs typically get thrown away after the PoC has been completed, rather than being promoted to production, for example.

User Acceptance Test

This release is a larger-scale deployment. The deployment is more formalized and uses the rehearsed steps in the previous stages. To better track the larger user acceptance tests, a quality assurance tracking system is the best way to assign tests to users and issues to IT.

Pilot

This is a larger rollout that is still contained within the IT organization. Depending on the relationship with the business partner(s) involved, they might also participate in testing the pilot. The system integration tests should be provided to the larger user base. To adequately document issues, a dedicated issue tracking system should be implemented. This prevents multiple requests on the same issue from being tracked. A team should be dedicated to resolving the issues in a timely manner before beginning user acceptance testing.

Production

This is the final deployment to the production environment.

Virtualization Performance Considerations

When building a virtualized system, you must consider some very important performance factors: integration components, patching, proper host roles, processors, memory, network, storage, and scaling. These factors are discussed in the following subsections.

Integration Components

Hyper-V has integration components that help virtual machines to achieve a more consistent state and better performance by enabling the guest to use synthetic devices. Some examples of integration components include the VMBus, time sync, video driver, network driver, and storage driver.

Patching

It is important to ensure that Hyper-V is patched to the most recent level for Windows Server 2008 on guests and hosts. This provides improvements in security, stability, performance, user experience, forward compatibility of configurations, and the programming model.

Proper Host Roles

When building the guest and host environments, avoid unnecessary host roles. The host should only have Hyper-V running as a role. The guest should be running the minimum required roles for complete functionality.

Processors

Hyper-V on Windows Server 2008 SP1 (or Windows Server 2008 R2) supports the ability of a 12:1 ratio of virtual processor cores to physical processor cores when all guest operating systems are running Windows 7. If you're not running Windows 7, the supported ratio is 8:1 (for Windows Server, for example). However, SharePoint requires a 1:1 ratio. This means that SharePoint *does not* support overallocating processor cores by assigning more cores to virtual machines than are physically available.

> **Note** Hyper-V separates the host-installed operating system from virtual operating systems. Therefore, save at least two cores for the host/parent. Again, overallocating cores is not supported for SharePoint.
>
> Look for host servers that have CPUs that support EPT (Intel) or RVI (AMD). You'll experience around 5 percent greater throughput with these configurations (for example, Intel's Nehalem architecture). This increase can be as much as 16 percent with hyperthreading.

Memory

It is important to not only allocate minimum and recommended amounts of memory for each virtual machine, but also to be cautious to not exceed the Non-Uniform Memory Access (NUMA) memory guidelines. These guidelines exist at the hardware level in multiprocessor environments. NUMA creates boundaries in a virtualized environment, and you can encounter a performance hit each time you cross a boundary. For example, if you have a host with 24 GB of memory and four processor sockets (sockets, not cores), your NUMA boundary would be 6 GB (24/4). Therefore, it is advisable that you keep your virtual machines at or less than 6 GB of memory for that particular host.

> **Note** The host operating system does not have the ability to detect which pages should be prioritized, so it is important to use memory instead of paging.

If you do allocate more memory than the boundary, you'll experience an approximate 8 percent performance hit each time a boundary is crossed. This is because each socket has its own dedicated memory space. When you go past the boundary, the virtual machine has to be extended across two different memory spaces. This is often called "split brain."

> **Note** In the previous 24 GB example with a 6 GB NUMA boundary, if you have a virtual machine with 22 GB of dedicated memory, you will cross the boundary four times, and you could see a performance degradation of nearly 30 percent!

Figure 8-10 illustrates the split brain concept. This figure shows a virtual machine that has two virtual processors, but since the memory allocated is greater than the NUMA boundary, the virtual machine is split across the two physical CPUs. Conversely, Figure 8-11 shows a virtual machine that is within the NUMA boundary and therefore is running on just a single physical processor; as such, it is achieving a higher level of performance and throughput.

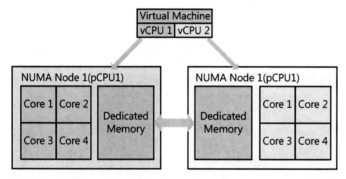

FIGURE 8-10 When you allocate too much memory, you run the risk of your virtual machines crossing a NUMA boundary, and the performance hit that comes with it.

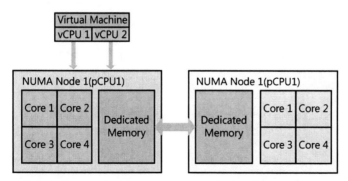

FIGURE 8-11 Instead, allocate memory in multiples of the NUMA boundary value to ensure that your virtual machines never cross the boundary and only run on (preferably) a single physical CPU.

Allocate Memory in Multiples of the NUMA Boundary

To achieve maximum memory utilization, allocate memory in multiples of the NUMA boundary. For example, if you have a NUMA boundary of 6 GB, it would be not advisable to allocate three virtual machines 4 GB of memory each. This is because at least one of the three virtual machines will be a split brain machine, as shown in Figure 8-12.

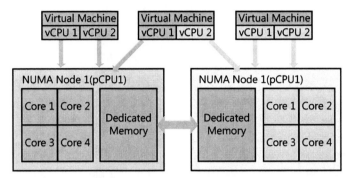

FIGURE 8-12 Simply allocating less than the NUMA boundary value doesn't guarantee that a virtual machine won't cross the boundary. As this example shows, if the memory isn't a multiple of the NUMA value, it could cross the boundary.

In this example, it would be better to allocate 6 GB to each virtual machine to keep any of the virtual machines from crossing the NUMA boundary. Another option would be to go down to 3 GB each (rather than 4 GB), because 3 is a multiple of 6 and thus would again keep any of the virtual machines from crossing the boundary.

Network

In terms of network, you should focus on only utilizing the IPv4 network protocol for Hyper-V guests. It has been observed that you get better performance when IPv4 is used exclusively. IPv6 should be disabled (see Figure 8-13) on both the Hyper-V host and guest virtual machines. IPv6 is a newer packet format for networks, and is designed to minimize packet header processing.

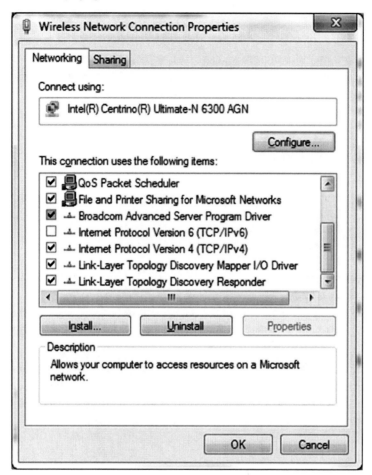

FIGURE 8-13 A normal network panel with IPv6 disabled.

Storage

Disk performance is important to consider when hosting the Crawl role or SQL Server database. WFE and Query servers do not typically require such high disk utilization. Most virtual machines use a virtual disk for their C drive, and for other drives, for that matter. Virtual drives are nice because they are portable and you can take snapshots of the drive for point-in-time recoverability purposes.

Note Fixed-size virtual disks provide better performance than dynamically sized disks.

On the other hand, you can also select pass-through for your virtual machines (see Figure 8-14). By selecting pass-through, you lose the benefits of a virtual hard drive. However, you can dedicate a physical disk or array to a given virtual machine. This might be advisable if there is a serious I/O requirement on that machine. SQL Server is the most likely candidate for pass-through because of how I/O-intensive the SharePoint databases can be.

 Note Two options are available for disk drivers: SCSI and IDE. SCSI is more efficient than IDE and offers RAID configuration and a higher speed.

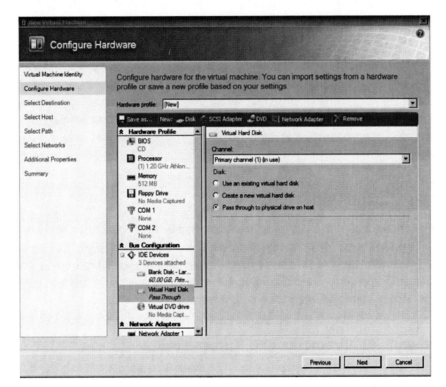

FIGURE 8-14 Creating a new virtual machine in SCVMM with the pass-through option.

Scaling

At some point, you're going to experience diminishing returns on scaling WFEs on a single host. In fact, you might even see diminishing returns as your start to add too many WFEs. A good rule of thumb is to have no more than three WFEs on any given host. However, this is just a rule of thumb, and you should load-test varying configurations to determine exactly how your unique hardware stacks up.

Another scaling metric to watch out for is the ratio of WFEs to SQL servers. A rule of thumb here is that if you plan to add a fifth WFE, you really ought to also add a second SQL server; otherwise, you will have little added throughput (if not diminishing throughput). SQL is often limited by your I/O performance, so consider running performance on your disks and watch your reads, writes, and queue depths to monitor I/O throughput. You might need to simultaneously dedicate new RAID 10 arrays as part of your SQL scaling strategy. Again, note that dedicated arrays are recommended, in the following priority: tempdb, logs, search databases, other service databases, and finally, content databases on commodity storage.

You have a lot of flexibility when planning how to scale service applications. You can add new virtual servers and dedicate one or more services to run on that virtual server. As you see CPU and memory bottlenecks on that server, you can scale out and add more servers to support the service load. A key recommendation is to have each service running on at least two virtual machines across at least two physical hosts to provide redundancy and high availability.

Getting Started with Hyper-V

There are literally dozens of 1,000-page books on Hyper-V that go into infinitely more detail than what we can cover in this chapter. However, this section can help you get started with Hyper-V without the need to take on so much reading. Herein you'll see step-by-step procedures to install Hyper-V, create and configure a virtual machine, and install and configure a guest operating system and integration components.

Hardware Requirements and Known Issues

Hyper-V requires an x64-based processor, hardware-assisted virtualization, and hardware data execution protection. Hardware requirements and known issues are included in the release notes. We recommend that you review the release notes before you install Hyper-V.

To download the release notes for the latest release of Hyper-V, go to *http://go.microsoft.com/FWLink/?Linkid=98821*. To review the release notes, go to *http://go.microsoft.com/FWLink/?Linkid=102060*.

Install Hyper-V

You can use Server Manager to install Hyper-V. To install Hyper-V, perform the following steps:

1. Log on to the host server, click Start, and then click Server Manager.

2. In the Roles Summary area of the Server Manager main window, click Add Roles.

3. On the Select Server Roles page, click Hyper-V.

4. On the Create Virtual Networks page, click one or more network adapters if you want to make their network connection available to virtual machines.

5. On the Confirm Installation Selections page, click Install.

6. You must restart your computer to complete the installation. Click Close to finish the wizard, and then click Yes to restart the computer.

7. After the server restarts, log on with the same account the administrator used to install the role. After the Resume Configuration Wizard completes the installation, click Close to close the wizard.

Create and Set Up a Virtual Machine

After the administrator has installed Hyper-V, it is available to create a virtual machine and set up an operating system on it. Before creating the virtual machine, it will be helpful to consider the following questions. Answering these questions will make it easier to create the virtual machine.

- Is the installation media available for the operating system you want to install on the virtual machine? It is possible to use physical media, a remote image server, or a .iso file. The method you use will determine how the virtual machine is configured.

- How much memory will be allocated to the virtual machine?

- Where will you store the virtual hard disks for the virtual machine and what naming convention is required?

The following steps will help you create and set up a virtual machine:

1. To open Hyper-V Manager, click Start, and then under Administrative Tools, click Hyper-V Manager.

2. From the Action pane, click New, and then click Virtual Machine.

3. From the New Virtual Machine Wizard, click Next.

4. On the Specify Name And Location page, specify the name of virtual machine and where the virtual hard disk should be stored.

5. On the Memory page, specify enough memory to run the guest operating system required for use on the virtual machine (again, consider NUMA boundaries).

6. On the Networking page, connect the network adapter to an existing virtual network if the installation requires network connectivity.

> **Note** If a remote image server is available to install an operating system on the virtual machine, use an external network if one has been created.

7. On the Connect Virtual Hard Disk page, specify a name, location, and size to create a virtual hard disk so that an installation of an operating system can begin on it.

8. On the Installation Options page, choose the desired method to install the operating system:

   - Install an operating system from a boot CD/DVD-ROM. You can use either physical media or an image file (.iso file).

   - Install an operating system from a boot floppy disk.

   - Install an operating system from a network-based installation server. To use this option, you must configure the virtual machine with a network adapter connected to the same network as the image server.

9. Click Finish.

After you create the virtual machine, you can start the virtual machine and install the operating system, which we will discuss next.

Install the Operating System and Integration Services

In the final step of this process, you connect to the virtual machine to set up the operating system. As part of the setup, you install a software package that improves integration between the virtualization server and the virtual machine.

> **Note** The instructions in this step assume that you specified the location of the installation media when you created the virtual machine. The instructions also assume that you are installing an operating system for which integration services are available.

To install the operating system and integration services, follow these steps:

1. From the Virtual Machines section of the Results pane, right-click the name of the virtual machine that you created in the preceding section, and then click Connect.

   The Virtual Machine Connection tool opens.

2. From the Action menu in the Virtual Machine Connection window, click Start.

3. Proceed through the OS Installation Wizard.

4. After the operating system is set up, you are ready to install the integration services. From the Action menu of the Virtual Machine Connection window, click Insert Integration Services Setup Disk.

   If Autorun does not start the installation automatically, you can start it manually. From a command prompt, type [Drive letter to DVD drive]:\support\amd64\setup.exe.

Capturing the Screen and Using the Keyboard and Mouse

When you are at the point where you need to provide input to complete the process, move the mouse cursor over the image of the setup window. After the mouse pointer changes to a small dot, click anywhere in the Virtual Machine Connection window. This action "captures" the mouse so that keyboard and mouse input is sent to the virtual machine. To return the input to the physical computer, press Ctrl+Alt+Left Arrow key and then move the mouse pointer outside the Virtual Machine Connection window.

After you have completed the setup and integration services are installed, you can proceed to test the virtual machine by customizing it to suit your testing goals. For example, you can view or modify the virtual hardware that is configured for the virtual machine. From the Virtual Machines pane, right-click the name of the virtual machine you created in the preceding section, and then click Settings. From the Settings window, click the name of the hardware to view or change it, such as allocating more memory or virtual processors.

Automating SharePoint in a Private Cloud Using Opalis

As we discussed previously in this chapter, Opalis is an automation platform for orchestrating and integrating IT tools and systems. This orchestration and integration is achieved through workflow processes that coordinate System Center and other management tools to automate incident response, change and compliance, and service life-cycle management processes.

> **Note** At the time of this writing, Microsoft is in the process of renaming Opalis to System Center Orchestrator. As of summer 2011, the product is currently in beta testing. The scenarios described in this section use Opalis, not System Center Orchestrator, as the backdrop.

Through its workflow designer, Opalis automatically shares data and initiates tasks in SCOM, SCCM, SCSM, VMM, Active Directory, and third-party tools. SharePoint is also another area where Opalis has strong integration features.

A SharePoint integration pack is available that you can install into Opalis; it offers a nice suite of integration points with SharePoint. For example, you can use the *Monitor List Item* object in an Opalis workflow to create the workflow site and wait for a new list item to be created in SharePoint, or possibly to wait for an existing item to be updated. Once the *Monitor List Item* object fires, you can use custom PowerShell scripts, or objects from other integration packs (such as other System Center packs or third-party packs) to automate a slew of associated business processes or IT functions.

Opalis has the following main components:

- **Client**   This is the application that creates, modifies, deploys, tests, and manages policies (see Figure 8-15). A policy is the workflow designer surface whereby you can drop and configure your objects to model and create the necessary automation.

- **Action Server**   Policies are executed on the Action Servers and more than one Action Server can be created. It is possible to dedicate Action Servers for policies requiring a lot of disk space.

- **Operator Console**   This is a web-based application that provides real-time information about metrics such as policy state, duration, and capacity utilization, as well as other helpful reporting capabilities.

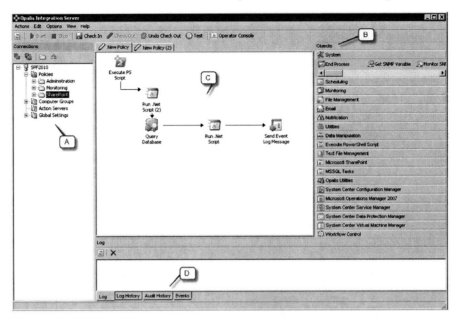

FIGURE 8-15 The Opalis Policy Designer is the "brains" of System Center. This is where you can configure your custom workflows to automate just about any IT function imaginable.

Figure 8-15 shows the Opalis client connected to the Opalis Integration Server. Four sections are available in the client:

- **Section A**   Displays the current server connection and the Policies, Computer Groups, Action Servers, and Global Settings.

- **Section B**   Displays the default and all the integration pack objects that are available for development.

- **Section C**   Displays the current policies that are available: Groups are available under Computer Groups, Action Servers are available under Action Servers, and Settings are available under Global Settings.

- **Section D**   Displays the Log, Log History, Audit History, and Events.

Example Scenario: Solving Real-World SharePoint Problems with Opalis

One of the more troublesome issues in SharePoint concerns creating new site collections. This is because this task usually requires someone with farm administrator access or the ability to enable self-service site creation (which isn't advisable because that is a common cause for site sprawl). Site collection administration does not tend to have a high priority in a typical administrator's daily role, which causes delays and frustration.

There are many ways to create a system whereby users can request new site collections, and after they are approved, the site collections are automatically provisioned on the users' behalf. A common technique to facilitate this request process is to use a Visual Studio workflow that facilitates the approval, and thereafter provisions the new site. One downfall of this approach, however, is that it requires custom .NET code to be deployed to the server farm. Often, a farm will have strong no-code requirements because the operations team wants to keep the environment clean and not risk outages, or unforeseen performance problems.

Surprisingly, Opalis is a pretty compelling platform in which to build this solution, especially because of the SharePoint farm's no customizations requirement. You can use the Monitor List Item object to watch for a new "request" to be added into a SharePoint list. When a user adds the new list item, Opalis can respond by creating a service ticket in SCSM. A person on the operations team, or perhaps someone on the information architecture team, can approve or reject this new site collection request.

> **Note** The *Monitor List Item* object comes with the SharePoint integration pack.

When the request is approved, Opalis can respond and provision the site collection by using the *Execute PowerShell Script* object. When you drop this object on the designer surface, you can easily type in your PowerShell code that provisions the new site.

Then you can update the SharePoint list item that originally kicked off the process to show that the request has been completed. You would use the *Update List Item* object in Opalis to update the list item in SharePoint. At this point, the SCSM ticket will be closed automatically so that there is a record of the change and a record of the new site. You can use the *Get Activity* object to get the service ticket in SCSM, and the *Update Activity* object to close down the ticket. Figure 8-16 shows how this Opalis policy would look.

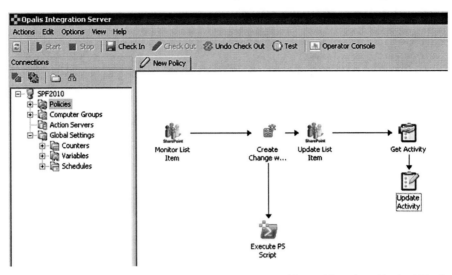

FIGURE 8-16 In the case of the site request process, you would use objects found in the SCSM integration pack, SharePoint integration pack, and PowerShell integration pack for Opalis.

> **Note** The following integration packs are necessary for this scenario:
>
> - SCSM integration pack
> - SharePoint integration pack
> - Execute PowerShell Script integration pack

To understand how this Opalis policy works, let's look at each object individually.

The Monitor List Item Object

When you drop the Monitor List Item on the designer, you can configure it to watch for new items and/or watch for item updates. In the case of the site request process, we only care about when a new request is made. Notice in Figure 8-17 how the Include New Items property is set to True and the Include Updated Items property is set to False. Also notice the Polling Interval property. The polling interval tells Opalis how often to check the list for new requests.

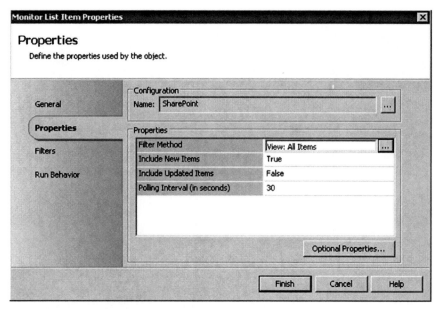

FIGURE 8-17 The Monitor List Item object pings a SharePoint list, waiting for new list items to be created and/or existing items to be updated.

The *Create Change with Template* Object

When you view the properties of the *Create Change with Template* object, you'll want to set the Connection property to the name of the SCSM instance in which you want to create the ticket. Then, for Class, choose Change Request, and for Template, choose Standard Change Request. The fields need to be added to, so click Select Optional Fields and set the Status, Impact, Title, and Actual Start Date fields. Notice in Figure 8-18 that the status of the new ticket is set to New and the impact is set to Minor.

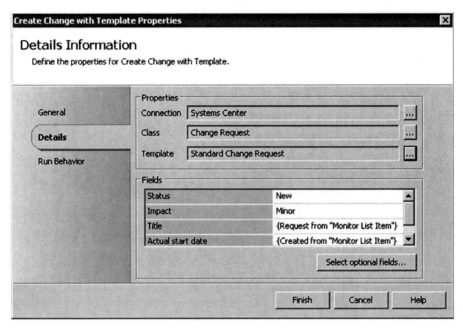

FIGURE 8-18 The *Create Change with Template* object creates service tickets in SCSM to help facilitate system change approval/rejection, as well as create a log of changes and new sites.

The Execute PowerShell Script Object

The Execute PowerShell Script object is probably one of the most important objects in Opalis, given its unlimited potential to script whatever your heart desires. In the case of the site collection request, we want to provision a new site collection when the ticket is approved. We need the *New-SPSite* PowerShell cmdlet to do this.

Notice in Figure 8-19 how you can configure this object. The first property (*PS Script 01*) simply stores the script itself. You can click the Expand button to expand and edit the script's code (see Figure 8-20). The other properties are equally important. Since your Opalis server likely will not be running on your SharePoint server, you're going to need to connect remotely to the SharePoint farm to run the *New-SPSite* cmdlet. The Execute PowerShell Object helps you do this by offering options to configure the remote PowerShell call. Notice the Host Name, Port Number, Domain/User Name, and Password properties.

Execute PS Script Properties
Properties
Define the properties used by the object.
General
Properties
Filters
Run Behavior
Input Properties
PS Script 01
Authentication Method
Default
Host Name
spf2010
Port Number
5985
Domain Name
ad2008r2
User Name
scom
Password
****
Connection Timeout (min)
1
Script Timeout (min)
4
Subscribe
Cut
Copy
Paste
Delete
Select All
Expand...
Optional Properties...
Finish
Cancel
Help

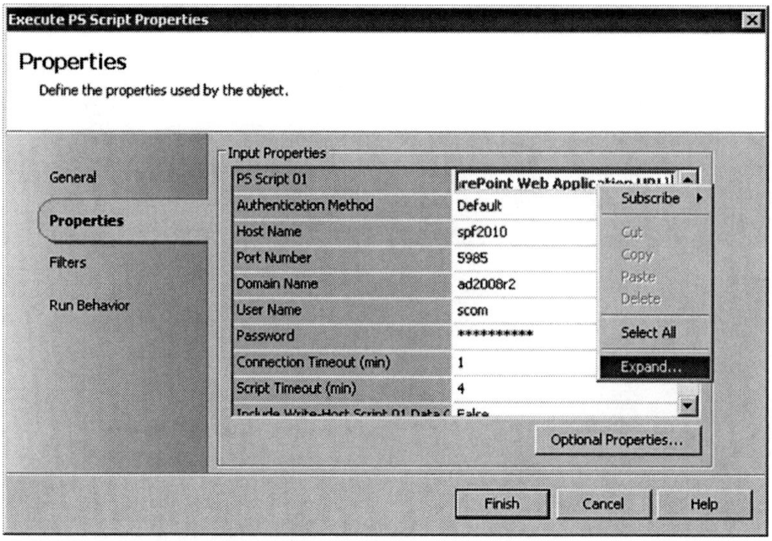

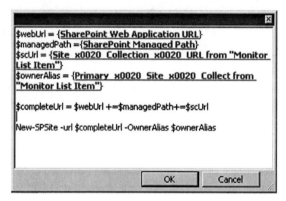

FIGURE 8-19 You can use the Execute PowerShell Script object to execute just about any custom PowerShell script imaginable. Its properties allow Opalis to connect to a server to execute the script remotely.

$webUrl = {SharePoint Web Application URL}
$managedPath ={SharePoint Managed Path}
$scUrl = {Site_x0020_Collection_x0020_URL from "Monitor List Item"}
$ownerAlias = {Primary_x0020_Site_x0020_Collect from "Monitor List Item"}
$completeUrl = $webUrl +=$managedPath+=$scUrl
New-SPSite -url $completeUrl -OwnerAlias $ownerAlias
OK
Cancel

FIGURE 8-20 When you expand the script property, you can start coding your script. You can share variables between scripts by defining the variables under Global Settings (see Figure 8-16 and Figure 8-22).

This PowerShell script contains five variables. You can define variables in the Global Settings section, under Variables, as shown in Figure 8-16 and Figure 8-21. The script in Figure 8-20 concatenates the variables and then creates a new site collection with the URL and primary site collection administrator passed in as dynamic variables.

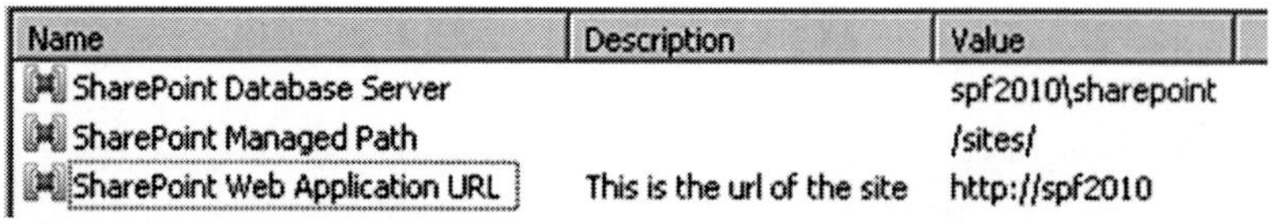

Name
Description
Value
SharePoint Database Server
spf2010\sharepoint
SharePoint Managed Path
/sites/
SharePoint Web Application URL
This is the url of the site
http://spf2010

FIGURE 8-21 Global variables can be used to share variables among your various scripts.

The Update List Item Object

The objective of the Update List Item object in this scenario is to demonstrate automated completion of the operation without the complexity of creating a SharePoint workflow. This object takes in the ID of the list item from the Monitor List Item object and updates the Status column to Complete.

Open the Configuration section of this object and select the SharePoint configuration that points to the Site Collection Request list. Two properties are set up in this object, as listed here and shown in Figure 8-22:

- **ID**   This is subscribed to from the Monitor List Item object.

- **Status**   This is set to the value of Complete.

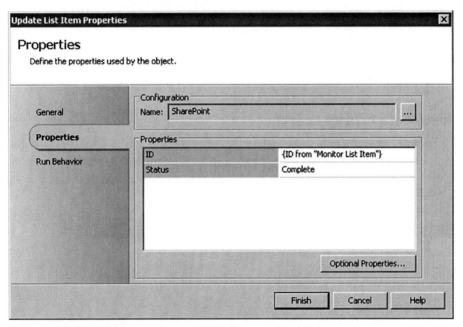

FIGURE 8-22 You use the Update List Item object to update a list item in a SharePoint list. Simply set the ID property to the ID of the list item you want to update, and then set the other fields of the item you want to change.

The *Get Activity* Object

The *Get Activity* object loads the SCSM ticket created earlier with the *Create Change with Template* object. The Source Object Guid property simply points to the *Create Change with Template* object, as shown in Figure 8-23.

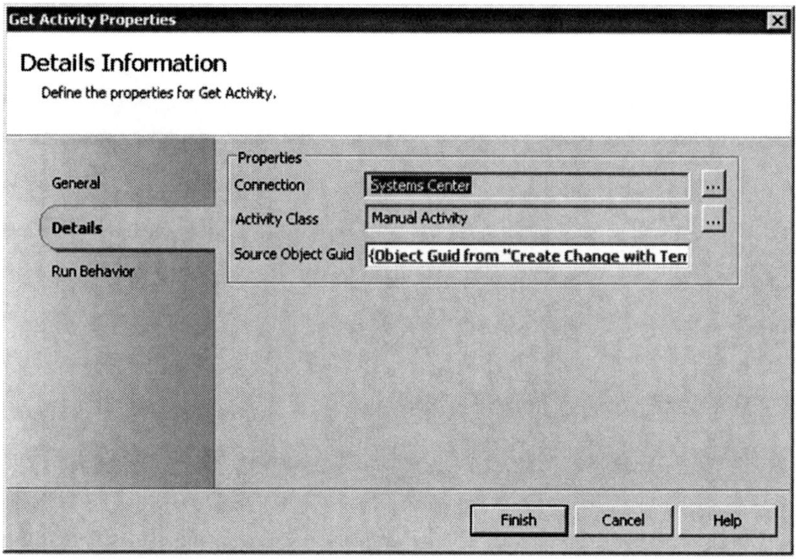

FIGURE 8-23 You use the *Get Activity* object to fetch a ticket in SCSM.

The *Update Activity* Object

The final object in the policy, the *Update Activity* object, updates SCSM and changes the status of the ticket to Completed. Set the Object Guid property to that of the *Get Activity* object. The only field utilized is the Status field and in this example, you'd set it to Completed, as shown in Figure 8-24.

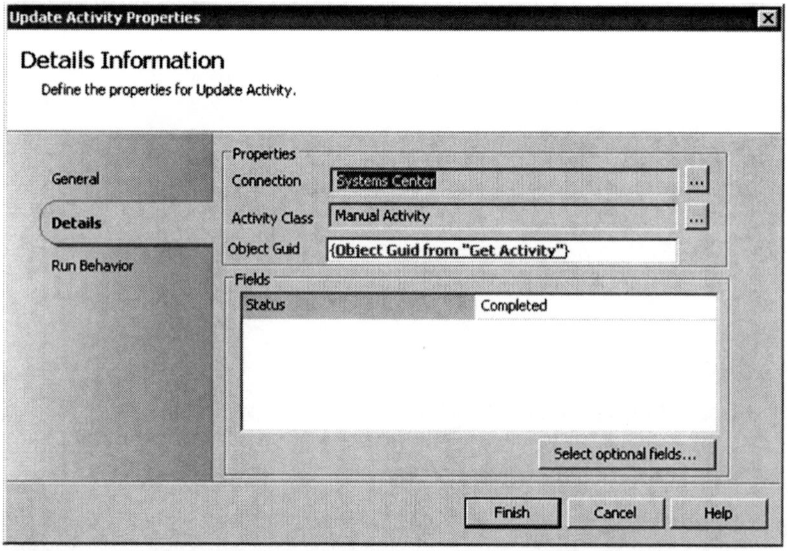

FIGURE 8-24 You use the *Update Activity* object to make updates to existing service tickets in SCSM.

Chapter 9
Introducing Multitenancy in SharePoint 2010

In this chapter, you will learn about:

- The benefits of multitenancy to an internal IT organization

- The multitenancy data architecture

- The pros and cons of multiple web applications versus site collections for tenancy

- What site subscriptions, tenant administration sites, and feature packs are

- The ten easy steps to configuring multitenancy

A *tenant* in a traditional sense is a person who occupies a residence that contains more than one family living independently of one another, but who has a right to use a common set of services that other tenants share. For example, each tenant in an apartment complex has his or her own private living quarters, but shares services such as elevators and stairs, hallways, parking spaces, yard care, and trash pickup with other tenants.

Multitenancy in Microsoft SharePoint takes this idea of shared services and independent living, but more accurately describes them as data isolation, delegated administration, and delegated configuration. This sense of isolation and delegation is where the multitenancy features of SharePoint 2010 shine so brightly.

By taking advantage of these features, you "host" multiple department or customer sites, for example, within the same infrastructure and farm, whereby you can guarantee autonomy and isolation among those "tenants" of your SharePoint farm. Each department has its own set of site collections that they can centrally manage and administrate.

What's more, from a customization perspective, tenants are isolated from one another because of the introduction of sandboxed solutions. As we discussed in Chapter 7, "Introduction to Customizing and Developing in SharePoint Online," *sandboxed solutions* isolate customizations in the sense that one tenant's customizations can never negatively impact those of another tenant, even though both tenants reside in the same farm and hardware.

Delegation is another key benefit of multitenancy. Only a few key individuals have access to Central Administration in a typical SharePoint farm. However, departments often would appreciate having more control over such things as key services and configurations. With multitenancy, a department can create these services in "partitioned mode" whereby, through a tenant administration site, each tenant can configure the services as the department sees fit.

A good example of this is the managed metadata service application. Each department tenant would likely have its own set of terms and vocabulary, and with the service application in partitioned mode, the tenant can have its own dedicated term store and not be relegated to share terms with other business units or customers.

Some of the multitenancy features of SharePoint 2010 include site subscriptions, host header site collections, feature packs, service application provisioning, and tenant administration sites. Most of these features never existed in earlier versions of SharePoint, and Microsoft is making great strides in supporting isolated groups of SharePoint sites and services.

Why Multitenancy for On-Premises IT?

When you think about what multitenancy is, the term *hosting* jumps out at you. Why go through all this rigmarole if you're just a plain-vanilla IT department? The truth is that multitenancy isn't for all organizations; however, more would stand to benefit than you might think. The following subsections discuss the key benefits of multitenancy.

Enables Easier Chargeback

Many IT organizations use a chargeback program to charge their company's other departments for IT services. From a SharePoint perspective, sometimes departments are charged based on the number of sites or perhaps the total disk space utilized. With multitenancy, it is easier to track which sites are associated with the different payers because the sites are tracked with a subscription ID. Therefore, it is easier to query and calculate chargeable metrics by using this ID.

You can also use the new feature pack capability to group features together and sell them as units back to your businesses. Those features will not show up in the user interface if the feature pack is not associated with the tenant.

Supports Multiple Licensing SKUs in the Same Farm

Feature packs can also be used to group the features associated with SharePoint Foundation, SharePoint Standard, and SharePoint Enterprise edition capabilities. Therefore, you could have one tenant that purchases user licenses for the Standard edition, but not for the Enterprise edition, and thus would not see the enterprise features in its sites.

> **Note** The farm itself must be licensed with the SharePoint Enterprise SKU, even if some tenants only have SharePoint Server Standard client access licenses assigned to them.

Alternatively, you could have a tenant that does have user licenses for the SharePoint Enterprise edition, and if you associate a feature pack with those features, the tenant would see the enterprise capabilities. Without feature packs, the features associated with SharePoint Foundation, SharePoint Standard, and SharePoint Enterprise are only configurable at the web application level. If two site collections are in the same web application, both must have enterprise features. This will help IT departments to better segregate users who are licensed differently, which means IT departments won't need as many expensive licenses when those departments won't be using the functionality.

Accommodate "Vanity URLs" en Masse

Everybody wants a unique URL. Some examples within a company might be:

- *http://sales.litware.com*
- *http://news.litware.com*
- *http://hrbenefits*
- *http://teamXYZ*

The preceding list could go on and on, and that is precisely the problem. Without the multitenancy features of SharePoint 2010, you really can't support hundreds of unique URLs per farm. This is because SharePoint wasn't designed to support scaling of web applications, and you might find yourself suffering performance issues if you have too many (depending on configuration, hardware, and so on). The situation becomes even more troublesome if you have hundreds of site collections, each preferring its own URL, or perhaps not a URL that is so deep in the chain, such as *http://teamA* over *http://intranet/sites/teamA*.

Fortunately, it's easily to accommodate this with multitenancy. Essentially, each tenant can have its own URL. So if you have 1,000 site collections in a given web application, you could technically have more than 1,000 unique URLs by which users access those sites.

Delegates Site Collection Creation and Management

People love being able to create and delete their own site collections. Through the tenant administration site, your departments have this ability. Without the tenant administration site, you'll need someone with farm administrator privileges creating your site collections, or you can rely on self-service site creation.

Delegates Service Application Administration

The administration of service applications is typically not opened up to a broad set of individuals. Usually only a small group of people has such a high level of access. What's more, these service applications are often shared across most, if not all, the sites in a farm. This can be a problem because a given site collection might need different settings compared to others in the group.

A great example of this is the managed metadata service application. The term store for the sales department will likely be different from the term store for the HR department. It's possible to create more than one managed metadata service application, but what if you have 50 departments? The application doesn't scale that far, unless you partition the service application, or relegate yourself to putting security on each term set and opening up access to Central Administration to configure them. In the case of partitioning, you can have one instance of the managed metadata service application; however, it's created in partitioned mode. With the service application in partitioned mode, you have a unique partition for each tenant, and thus each tenant gets its own term store that it has full administrative privileges to manage through its tenant administration site.

Options for Tenant Sites in SharePoint

Multitenancy isn't necessarily new for SharePoint 2010. You've always been able to support more than one tenant per farm. Either you can have a new web application for each tenant, or you can have a new site collection(s) for each. It's in the latter case where SharePoint 2010 has made significant strides, but the former, a web application for each tenant, remains a viable option for some. The following subsections discuss each option in turn.

Give Each Tenant Its Own Dedicated Web Application

The first approach to multitenancy in SharePoint is to give each tenant its own dedicated web application. Table 9-1 lists the pros and cons of this option.

TABLE 9-1 Pros and Cons of Giving Each Tenant Its Own Web Application

Pros	Cons
Easiest configuration	Doesn't scale well
Able to isolate authentication mechanisms	No tenant administrator site
Unique web.config for each tenant	
Natural data isolation	

One of the most compelling reasons why someone would create a new web application for each tenant is that it's likely the easiest approach. Using the multitenancy features of SharePoint 2010 requires a fair amount of Windows PowerShell expertise, but you can create web applications right through the Central Administration page. This is much more straight-forward for beginners.

Another significant benefit to creating new web applications is authentication. It is a best practice to have different authentication mechanisms running on different web applications, thus keeping them isolated. This isn't always possible, but it remains desirable. A good example would be anonymous access and authenticated access. You'd typically expect to have two web applications for this: one would host Internet-facing content, and the other intranet collaboration content.

A less obvious benefit to each tenant having its own web application is the fact that a web application gets its own dedicated web.config file. A web.config file is the XML configuration file for the web application/ASP.NET site. It stores all sorts of important settings, such as authentication mechanisms, trusted and not-trusted custom code, trusted Web Parts, and connection strings to external databases. All the site collections in the web application share the same web.config file, so if your web application hosts many tenants, ensure that these settings are applicable to everyone. If each tenant had its own web application, it would be easier to specify unique settings for each tenant.

For many companies, data isolation is very important. With this model, data isolation is very natural. All the databases in this web application are only used for one single tenant. The only trouble point would perhaps be service applications that are shared with this tenant's web application and other web applications for other tenants. Those shared service applications might have shared data, but it would be easy enough to create multiple shared service applications for each tenant such that you could guarantee data independence.

However, this brings us to the limitations of this approach, the biggest of which is scale, because your infrastructure can't support hundreds of web applications and service applications if it gets to the point where you want everybody to have dedicated services. Most IT departments are going to need to support many dozens of discrete groups in a business that needs to collaborate. It wouldn't be good to architect a solution that uses dedicated web applications, only to discover that a year later you're running into scaling problems.

Note Having a maximum of 20 web applications per farm is just a rule of thumb. Performance implications actually depend on the farm's configuration, hardware, and so forth.

Another limitation is the fact that your tenants won't benefit from having their own tenant administration site. This means they can't administer SharePoint services as they see fit. Also, you don't get the benefit of service application partitioning. Therefore, if you don't want the settings of the various service applications to be the same for each tenant, you're going to need to create multiple copies of each service application for each tenant. It is much easier to partition the services, and it results in much less overhead on the infrastructure as well.

The next option for hosting multiple tenants in a farm is to create site collections in one web application for each tenant. So, rather than have one web application for each tenant, you would have only one that is shared among all tenants. There are two ways you can do this. One way is to use the multitenancy features of SharePoint 2010, such as service application partitioning, tenant administration sites, and host header site collections. Another way is to simply provision site collections in "normal mode" without using the multitenancy features. The following subsection details the latter approach.

Give Each Tenant One or More Site Collections in a Shared Web Application

As noted in the preceding section, this approach hosts multiple tenants in a farm through the creation of site collections in one web application for each tenant, yet it does not require the use of multitenancy features. Table 9-2 lists the pros and cons of this approach.

TABLE 9-2 **Pros and Cons of Giving Each Tenant Its Own Site Collection**

Pros	Cons
Very simple to configure	All tenants share the same service settings
Scales very well, can support thousands of tenants	Tenants can't create/delete their own site collections
	No vanity URLs
	Can easily hit managed path boundaries
	Harder reporting/diagnosing
	People Picker hard to control; no security isolation

This approach is even easier to configure than creating a unique web application for each tenant. All you need to do is to create one web application and start filling it up with site collections for your tenants. This is a significant benefit over a unique web application for each tenant, because you can easily scale this model to thousands of tenants. This is possible since a given web application can house tens of thousands of site collections.

But quickly you'll notice a problem, and that again goes back to isolation and delegation. Isolation is immediately a problem if you don't want one tenant to be able to see the content of another tenant. How can you prevent tenant A from adding tenant B users into its sites? If this is an important business requirement for you, consider using the multitenancy features because you can lock down the People Picker for a given tenant to only be able to search users in a given Active Directory organizational unit. Another isolation concern has to do with search results, because you don't want tenant A to see search results for content in tenant B's sites.

Chapter 11, "Configuring Tenant-Aware Site Collections," describes how to create site subscriptions and associate them to a given organizational unit to filter out who shows up in the People Picker when assigning permissions.

Another significant concern with this model is that service application settings are shared among all the tenants in the web application. Again, consider the managed metadata service application. In this model, all the tenants will share the same term store(s). If the sales department is not permitted to see the terms and metadata of the HR department, this wouldn't be achievable in this model. All the sites and all the tenants will share the same term store. They'll all share the same content type hub. They'll all share the same connections to external data sources, as with the case of the business data catalog service application (unless security is placed on the individual models), and so on and so forth.

The basic premise here is that tenants don't have their own tenant administration site with which they can administer their partitioned services. Most IT departments won't be allowing access for tenants to administer services other tenants are using. This also plays into a tenant's ability to create and delete new or existing site collections. In this traditional model, the creation of new site collections must be done through Central Administration, which would likely require a service ticket to the help desk and a significant turnaround time. Again, with tenant administration sites, tenants can manage their sites without the need to get IT involved.

Note You could rely on self-service site creation to let users create site collections. But with multitenancy, this can very easily be configured on a tenant-by-tenant basis, and can guarantee that new site collections always correspond to a given tenant.

From a URL perspective, a limitation of this model is that all site collections and tenants will access their content through the same root URL, such as http://intranet.litware.com. If it's preferred to have unique URLs for each tenant, such as http://ABC.litware.com and http://TeamA, this model would not support that. If unique URLs are needed, you'll want tenant-aware site collections that are provisioned by using host headers.

In addition, you can easily run into boundaries with managed paths in this model. Most SharePoint administrators like to bucket their site collections under appropriate managed paths, such as http://intranet.litware.com/HR or http://intranet.litware.com/Sales. This provides a nice URL where the entire HR tenant site would fall under the HR managed path. But if you have hundreds or thousands of tenants or site collections, this isn't possible because of Microsoft's recommended limit of 20 managed paths per web application—so again we have a scale problem. To get around this, a lot of times people place all their site collections in the "sites" managed path, but again, this isn't as desirable because it's harder to differentiate what sites belong to which tenants, based on URL—in fact, it's impossible.

The last significant disadvantage of this model concerns reporting. If one tenant has 100 site collections and another has 200, how can you determine which site collections belong to which tenant? Well, if you bucket them in intelligible managed paths, you can distinguish them visually. But if you have an automated chargeback program, you'd benefit from the concept of subscription IDs. Essentially, a site collection's subscription ID maps that site collection to a particular tenant, and thus programmatic reporting on tenant usage and charges is easier. With this model, it's just a grab bag of site collections, and there's no apparent programmatic way to tell what sites belong to whom.

Give Each Tenant One or More Site Collections Associated with a Unique Site Subscription in a Shared Web Application

This option for hosting multiple tenants is very similar to the preceding option, except that the site collections are *tenant-aware*, meaning they were created with site subscriptions, partitioned service applications, and, likely, host headers. Table 9-3 lists the pros and cons of this option.

TABLE 9-3 **Pros and Cons of Giving Each Tenant a Site Subscription**

Pros	Cons
Scales very well, can support thousands of tenants	All site collections and service applications must be created with PowerShell if they are to be tenant-aware
Security boundaries more enforceable	Requires a fairly deep understanding of PowerShell
Each tenant has its own tenant administration site	
Service application settings are configurable on a tenant-by-tenant basis	
Each tenant can have its own unique URL	

In a nutshell, this model affords you the benefits of data isolation, security boundaries, service setting independency, and unique URLs; the only limitation is the relative configuration complexity when compared to the other approaches. The complexity is really from a PowerShell perspective. If you're familiar with PowerShell, you'll find it to be very natural and easy to learn the new commands. If you're new to PowerShell, it'll take some getting used to. However, in the next two chapters, you'll see full walkthroughs on how to configure everything in PowerShell, so get your Ctrl+C and Ctrl+P warmed up!

Multitenancy Architecture

From an architecture perspective, tenants are grouped together in one web application by their respective subscription ID. Whenever a new site collection is created, it is assigned the same ID as the other site collections in the tenancy. In addition to site collections for collaboration, a given tenant will also have a site collection used for tenant administration. The tenant uses its tenant administration site to configure settings such as service application settings, site collection creation and deletion, and so on.

All the data for these site collections is stored in a content database, just like regular site collections. However, when the site collections are associated with a subscription ID, they're stored in a partition of the database that is separate from the other tenants. This guarantees that any SQL query performed from within the context of that tenant will never return data from another tenant.

Scaling Content Databases

Despite the fact that the data in the databases is partitioned, you'll still need to watch out for content databases becoming too large. The current guideline is to keep content databases less than 100 GB in size (200 GB if there's only one site collection in the database). A part of your monitoring strategy should be to watch the growth of your databases and utilize the *Move-SPSite* PowerShell command to move the site from one database to another to keep the size within the recommended level.

Note The *New-SPSite* PowerShell command now features a *–ContentDatabase* parameter. This is helpful when trying to keep tenant site collections in their own database, or perhaps when keeping site collections that are expected to be very large in their own databases. When you use this in conjunction with the *New-SPContentDatabase* command, you can first create the new database, and then start to put the new site collections into it. This is easier than configuring the "Online"/"Offline" settings in Central Administration.

This same partitioning is also done for service application databases. As shown in Figure 9-1, the web application is associated to two service applications, but since those service applications are created in partitioned mode, the data is stored in tenant partitions and is isolated from other tenant data. This gives you the main benefit of only needing one service application for all your tenants. So rather than having, say, three managed metadata service applications, you could just have one that is partitioned. This brings a great benefit to your infrastructure from a scaling perspective.

When a service application is partitioned, most of the settings for the service application are configured in the tenant administration sites. This lets the tenants configure the settings as they see fit, and it guarantees that the settings in one tenant can never negatively affect the settings of another tenant.

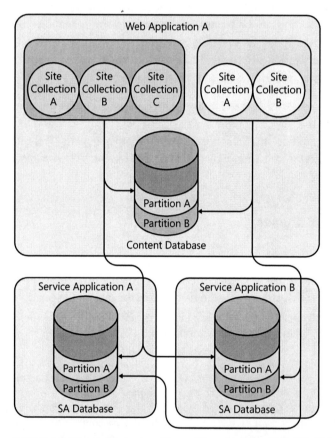

FIGURE 9-1 Tenant data is stored in partitioned tables within SQL. This isolates the data from one tenant to another, and includes the data within content databases as well as service application data.

Service Application Partitioning

With service application partitioning, you create a service application that is to be used and shared across multiple tenants. Rather than creating one instance of the service application for each tenant, you can create a service application in partitioned mode and thereby leverage it across all your tenants, and still maintain tenant isolation.

When a service application is in partitioned mode, the databases themselves are partitioned with a database partition for each tenant. This guarantees data isolation, because a given tenant will not be permitted to query data outside its own partition of the database.

When the data is partitioned like this, it is easy to delegate the administration of the service application down to the tenants themselves. A tenant can specify its service application settings and not impact the services used by other tenants. The managed metadata service application benefits from partitioning because each tenant gets its term store and term set. The business data connectivity service application benefits because a tenant can upload its own models and connections to external systems, and not run the risk of other tenants being able to access its external data. The secure store service application benefits from partitioned mode because all the credentials used by the tenant to access external systems can't be retrieved by other tenants. The user profile service application benefits because a tenant won't be able to browse the profiles of another tenant. The SharePoint search service application benefits because a tenant can specify its own managed properties, content sources, crawl rates, and so on, which might be totally irrelevant to a different tenant. If you didn't have service application partitioning, it would be much harder to share these services across many tenants, and in many cases it would be impossible because of data security concerns.

 Note FAST search cannot be partitioned, only SharePoint Search.

The unfortunate thing about creating service applications in partitioned mode is that the only way to do it is through PowerShell. Whereas in normal mode, you could've used the Central Administration user interface, for partitioned mode, you're stuck with PowerShell. Many of you might use PowerShell already for most of the SharePoint administration you do; therefore, this will be straightforward for you. The only difference when creating these service applications is that you must add the *–PartitionedMode* flag onto the *New-ServiceApplication* PowerShell cmdlet. With this flag in place, the service application will be created in partitioned mode after execution.

> **Note** Some service applications use the *–Partitioned* flag rather than the *–PartitionedMode* flag.

Chapter 10, "Configuring Tenant-Aware Service Applications," provides full PowerShell examples of how to create all the service applications with PowerShell.

> **Note** The team that built the Microsoft Word Automation Services application must not have gotten the memo to enable the creation of the service application only by PowerShell. Conveniently enough, when in Central Administration, there's a check box in the new service application UI that you can select to create it in partitioned mode. Perhaps someday it will be this easy for the rest of the service applications, but alas, not today.

An important thing to note is that once a service application has been created in partitioned mode, it is impossible to change it back to normal mode later (and vice versa). After the service application has been created in partitioned mode, most of the service settings will only be available in the tenant's tenant administration site. For example, all the managed metadata service application settings are delegated down to the tenant. This means the term store is configured on a tenant-by-tenant basis, as is defining the content type hub for the tenant. Some service applications still have settings that are managed in Central Administration, whereas only a portion of the settings are delegated down. The user profile service application is an example of this, where management of the profiles and properties is delegated down, but configuring the synchronization process is still managed in Central Administration.

Notice that not all service applications store tenant-specific data. Managed metadata, Business Connectivity Services (BCS), and user profiles are examples of service applications that do store tenant data. However, Access Services, Excel Calculation, and State are examples that do not. In fact, some service applications cannot even be created in partitioned mode. Table 9-4 shows which service applications store tenant data and which can't be created in partitioned mode.

TABLE 9-4 Service Applications That Can Be Partitioned and Store Tenant Data

Service application name	Can be partitioned	Stores tenant data
Access Services	No	No
BCS	Yes	Yes
Excel Calculation	No	No
FAST for SP	No	No
Managed Metadata	Yes	Yes
Performance Point	No	No
PowerPoint	No	No
Project Server	Yes	Yes
Usage and Health	No	No
User Profiles	Yes	Yes
Search	Yes	Yes
Secure Store	Yes	Yes
Subscriptions Settings	Yes	Yes
State	Yes	No
Web Analytics	No	Yes
Word Conversions	Yes	No
Word Viewing	Yes	No
Visio Graphics	Yes	No

Support for FAST for SharePoint and Performance Point

FAST for SharePoint and Performance Point are two services that actually *do not work* in a multitenant environment! If your tenants must use these services, you'll likely need dedicated web applications for each tenant. Hopefully, in future releases of the product, we'll see these services become fully tenable.

Site Subscriptions

The Subscription Settings service application keeps track of globally unique identifiers (GUIDs) that are associated to site collections signifying which tenant the site collection belongs to. Each unique ID is akin to a single tenant. All site collections associated with the same subscription ID make up the tenancy for that particular tenant. At the time of this writing, subscriptions can only be managed through PowerShell or the object model, and once a site collection is associated with a given subscription ID, it cannot be changed later.

> **Note** Site collections associated with a subscription ID can span more than one web application. However, this is not recommended.

> ## Important! Sites Cannot Change Their Subscription ID After the Fact
>
> This is worth repeating. After a site collection is provisioned and associated to a given site subscription (tenant), it cannot be changed later. You need to delete and re-create the site! The bottom line is that you must associate a site to a subscription with care. Confirm the ID of the subscription before you proceed.

The user profile service application also uses subscription IDs by mapping them to organizational units within an Active Directory domain. This will configure which users the user profile service application should crawl and import for each tenant. Additionally, with this configuration, the People Picker will only show users in that organizational unit when managing security and authorization within the tenant sites. Chapter 11 provides more detail on how to configure this, but for now, consider the following PowerShell script:

```
$sub = New-SPSiteSubscription
$site = Get-SPSite -Identity http://intranet.litware.com/tenant1/somesite
$sub.Add($site)
```

Notice that the first thing the code does is to create a new site subscription. You manage this subscription through the Subscriptions Settings service application, and you can use it later by retrieving it with the *Get-SPSiteSubscription* PowerShell cmdlet. After you have a handle to your subscription, you can associate a site collection to it. First get the site by using the *Get-SPSite* cmdlet, and then call the *Add* method on the subscription. Thereafter, that site will always be associated to that subscription and tenant.

Figure 9-2 shows the PowerShell output after you create a new site subscription. You can see that this is a new site subscription with no sites in the tenancy. Additionally, Figure 9-3 shows how you can tell which tenant a particular site collection belongs to.

PowerShell Console
PS C:\Users\administrator.PDD\Documents> $sub = New-SPSiteSubscription
PS C:\Users\administrator.PDD\Documents> $sub
Id Sites
-- -----
fe74b451-51de-4b5b-ba26-15f3884d1c9d {}
PS C:\Users\administrator.PDD\Documents>
Script execution completed.

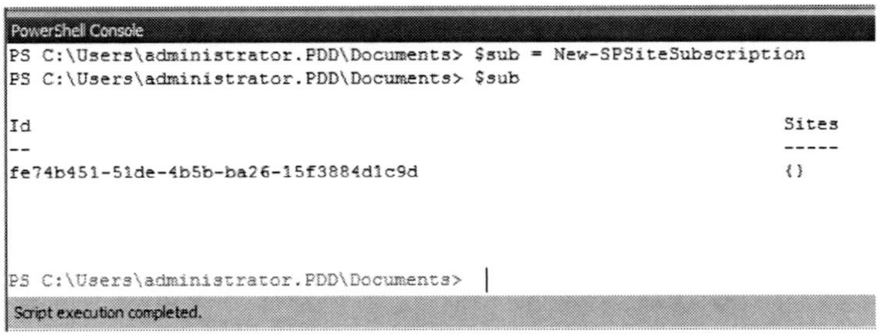

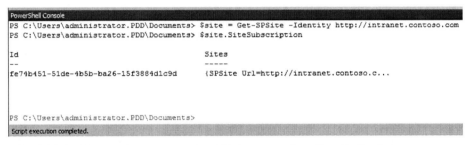

FIGURE 9-2 Through PowerShell, you can see the ID of a given tenant as well as the sites that make up that tenancy.

PowerShell Console
PS C:\Users\administrator.PDD\Documents> $site = Get-SPSite -Identity http://intranet.contoso.com
PS C:\Users\administrator.PDD\Documents> $site.SiteSubscription
Id Sites
-- -----
fe74b451-51de-4b5b-ba26-15f3884d1c9d {SPSite Url=http://intranet.contoso.c...
PS C:\Users\administrator.PDD\Documents>
Script execution completed.

FIGURE 9-3 In this example, you can see to which tenancy a given site collection belongs.

Tenant Administration

Tenants can administer their site collections and service application settings through their own, dedicated tenant administration sites. A *tenant administration site* is simply another site collection in the tenancy that uses the "tenantadmin#0" site template. This site template automatically knows which partitioned service applications are associated with the current web application. As it detects which service applications are available, it will render appropriate settings to the tenant to configure as it sees fit. Figure 9-4 shows an example of what a tenant administration site looks like.

FIGURE 9-4 A tenant can administer its site collections and service application settings through its tenant administration site.

Since the tenant administration site template is not visible in the user interface, you will need to create this site with PowerShell. The following is a sample command that will provision a tenant administration site:

```
New-SPSite -Url http://intranet.litware.com/tenant1/admin -OwnerAlias litware\jdoe
-OwnerEmail john.doe@litware.com -Template tenantadmin#0 -SiteSubscription $sub
-AdministrationSiteType TenantAdministration
```

> **Note** The *$sub* variable is a handle on the site subscription (tenant) into which the new site collection will be provisioned.

The following is a list of common activities that you can perform from the tenant administration site:

- Create and delete site collections
- Configure the managed metadata term store
- Upload BCS models to external data
- Configure connection credentials to external systems
- Configure search
- Configure user profiles and profile properties

Host Header Site Collections

Host header site collections let each tenant have a dedicated URL. Typically when two site collections are in the same web application, this is not possible. This is because all site collections in a given web application share the URL that is defined in the web application settings as well as the binding on the Internet Information Server (IIS) site. Fortunately, however, with this new feature of host header site collections, we can circumvent this historically frustrating condition. Now every site collection in the web application can have its own URL.

For example, a site collection found under the "sites" managed path, such as http://intranet .litware.com/sites/HR, can be accessible through something totally different, such as http:// HR. In the past, this sort of business requirement would automatically necessitate a new web application; however, that's no longer the case.

Host header site collections are very easy to create, but it requires the use of PowerShell. The first thing you would do is to create the Domain Name System (DNS) entry for the host header. Then you provision the site collection again with the *New-SPSite* command, but in addition to the *-Url* parameter, add the *-HostHeaderWebApplication* parameter. The following serves as an example where the default host header of hosting.cotoso.com is being superseded with litwareinc.com:

```
New-SPSite -Template STS#0 -SiteSubscription $sub -Url http://litwareinc.com
-HostHeaderWebApplication http://hosting.contoso.com -OwnerAlias litware\jdoe -OwnerEmail
jdoe@litwareinc.com
```

> **Note** Remember that a DNS entry on your DNS server is required to make the site browseable. Ask a domain administrator to help configure this entry. Additionally, a new binding must exist on the IIS site itself for the host header URL to be resolved in IIS. See Chapter 11 for steps showing how to configure this binding.

Feature Packs

Feature packs are the best way to show or hide features within a tenant-aware site collection or collections. One of the most common circumstances for which people would want to configure feature packs is to limit tenants to the Foundation, Server, or Enterprise edition features of SharePoint. You might do this if you have one tenant that owns client access licenses (CALs) for the Enterprise edition, but another tenant that doesn't. In this scenario, you won't need two separate farms, or you wouldn't need to make that second tenant purchase Enterprise CALs (nobody wants to pay for something he won't use!). All you need to do is to associate the Foundation tenant to a feature pack with foundation features within it, and associate the Enterprise tenant with a second feature pack that contains enterprise features. It's that easy!

Another business case for feature packs would be if you created a custom feature for a particular tenant. If you install that feature in the farm, it will be available to be activated in every single site collection in the farm. This might not be desirable. Instead, you can create a dedicated feature pack for that particular tenant and add all the features into the pack to which you want the tenant to have access, including the custom feature you wrote just for the tenant.

Another great outcome of feature packs is site template trimming. By default, a tenant will be able to create a site off all the out-of-the-box site templates. However, you might not want the tenant to be able to use all the site templates. For example, if you have a chargeback model, you might charge a tenant to use the Business Intelligence (BI) features of SharePoint, which comes with a site template called the BI Center. You don't want the tenant creating BI sites if the tenant has not purchased that module in your chargeback scheme. This is possible with feature packs because if a site template is dependent on features that are not within the tenant's feature pack, that site template will not show up in the template picker when the tenant goes to create a new site. In the case of the BI features, all you'd need to do is to not include the *BICenterDashboardsLib* feature in the pack and the BI Center site template will not be available.

A Chargeback Model Loves Feature Packs

As just mentioned, feature packs are great for IT departments that need to support chargeback. Some IT departments charge their business units a fee for the services IT provides, such as SharePoint services. The SKU is a great mechanism for chargeback (Foundation, Server, and Enterprise editions), and feature packs are a great way to mechanize that approach.

You can even get more granular than SKUs, such as charging for particular features, as in the example given with the BI features. This can be useful because some features are much more server resource–intensive than others. BI is a great example of a resource-intensive set of features, especially when compared to less intensive features such as managed metadata services.

Creating feature packs is simple. Just use the *New-SPSiteSubscriptionFeaturePack* PowerShell cmdlet to create the pack. Then add features to the pack until you have all the features in the pack that you want the tenant to be able to use. You can do this with the *Add-SPSite SubscriptionFeaturePackMember* cmdlet. The following code block shows how to create a pack with one feature inside it that would let you use document libraries for that tenant, and then shows how to associate that feature pack to the tenant whose ID is stored in the *$subId* variable:

```
$pack = New-SPSiteSubscriptionFeaturePack
Add-SPSiteSubscriptionFeaturePackMember -Identity $pack -FeatureDefinition DocumentLibrary
Set-SPSiteSubscriptionConfig -Identity $subId -FeaturePack $pack
```

> **Note** Chapter 10 discusses how to create the *$sub* variable.

Ten Easy Steps to Tenant-Aware SharePoint

Chapters 10 and 11 go into detail about how to implement all the high-level concepts described in this chapter. This means that you will be seeing a lot of PowerShell in the subsequent chapters.

The process to set up a multitenant SharePoint environment follows a specific order. Fortunately, you can break down the process into the following 10 steps:

1. Create the Site Subscription Service Application
2. Create other partitioned service applications
3. Create feature packs
4. Create new site subscription
5. Assign feature pack to a tenant to filter featuers
6. Assign Active Directory OU to tenant to filter people picker
7. Create necessary managed paths
8. Create new root, tenant admin, and my site host site collections
9. Associate tenant to User Profile service application to filter profiles
10. Create content type hub for content type syndication

The first two steps create the necessary service applications. You at least need the site subscription service application because multitenancy isn't possible without it. Thereafter, you can choose the service applications you need, such as managed metadata and user profiles. The process for setting up these service applications encompasses steps 1 and 2 and is covered in Chapter 10.

Chapter 11 covers steps 3 and 4, which are prerequisites for creating tenants. Feature packs can be assigned after a tenant has existed for a while, but usually they are set up first. Managed paths really must be set up first because you need a place to install your site collections.

Chapter 11 also covers the other 6 steps. Essentially, these pertain to how you set up a tenant. You must create a new site subscription, obviously. Then you create the root site collection, tenant administration site collection, and My Site Host, if necessary. Thereafter, you assign the tenant a feature pack as well as associate it to an organizational unit in Active Directory so that the People Picker and profiles are filtered to only show those that belong to the tenant. Finally, you might want to specify a content type hub for content type syndication across all the tenants' site collections. This will keep all their content types consistent.

Chapter 10
Configuring Tenant-Aware Service Applications

In this chapter, you will learn about:

- What a service application is and its basic architecture

- Associating web applications to proxy groups

- Creating custom proxy groups

- Servicing applications are administered in Central Administration

- Creating all the service applications in SharePoint with PowerShell

Show me the PowerShell!

If that is what you were thinking when you read Chapter 9, "Introducing Multitenancy in SharePoint 2010," and you were feeling increasingly anxious to see all this Windows PowerShell business in action, this chapter is for you. After a brief introduction to service application architecture and basic user interface actions, you'll dive right in to the PowerShell goodness.

PowerShell is an important topic with regard to multitenancy, for two reasons. First, the word *automation* comes to mind. Private clouds are all about virtualization and automation. How do you automate Microsoft SharePoint administration? Through PowerShell. This is true when it comes to managing services, as well. Take the search service application as an example. You can configure hundreds of settings in that service application. Using PowerShell to configure the search service application is a great way to achieve consistency and automation when building up and tearing down environments, and it also works well as a disaster recovery mechanism.

The second reason PowerShell is a pertinent topic regarding multitenancy is that many of these service applications can only be created in PowerShell. Nope, there's no user interface for this stuff. So whether you wanted to or not, it's time to get your PowerShell hat and gloves on, and dig in!

Introduction to Service Applications

One last introduction, I promise.

Before digging into the code, you should know what you're creating. What is a service application? How do you manage a service application in Central Administration? How do you configure SharePoint sites to use services? These answers and more introductory concepts are covered in this section.

Shared Service Basics

Service applications are services that can be shared across many sites, web applications, and even farms. Search, for example, is a feature of SharePoint that is consumed within SharePoint sites via its service application endpoint. This endpoint is essentially a Windows Communication Foundation (WCF) web service that is consumed, and it is called a "service application proxy," in SharePoint lingo.

What's nice about service applications is that they are entirely independent from one another. A web application simply associates itself to a group of service applications that it wants to consume. That group can be composed of any services an administrator wants to throw in the bucket. The only limitation is the SKU that is purchased, because some service applications are only available in SharePoint Server Standard or Enterprise edition, as opposed to what you get for free with SharePoint Foundation edition.

This is very different from how services worked in SharePoint 2007. In that version, instead of associating a web application to a group of configurable service applications, you associated it to a Shared Services Provider (SSP). An SSP was a special site collection in which you configured *all* the services. Thus, even if you only wanted two of the services, you still got all of them. Additionally, all the settings configured in the SSP were in effect for all the sites in all the web applications associated to the SSP. There was no individual "tenant" customization of these services, as is the case with SharePoint 2010 tenant-aware service applications.

One of the significant ways that this lack of individual customization manifested itself was through the inability to specify unique permissions on each service and for each tenant. You couldn't say that so-and-so has access to administer Search, but not the Business Data Catalog, for example. Nor could you say tenant A can't see the profiles of tenant B (without creating two separate SSPs). Additionally, the SSP was considered a single point of failure for multiple services, whereas in SharePoint 2010, each service is its own WCF endpoint, and therefore a failure in one won't impact another.

Creating Service Applications

Creating service applications is pretty easy. You can do it either through the Central Administration user interface or via PowerShell. Central Administration is easier for most, but PowerShell is nice when you want to automate the creation of service applications, such as when you're building up and tearing down test and sandbox environments. Additionally, PowerShell is nice if you want to have finer control over the naming of the associated databases. In either case, you must use PowerShell when creating tenant-aware service applications. So it's good to know how to create them in both ways.

Claims-Based Authentication for Multitenancy

Although it's possible to use classic mode authentication, you'll save yourself a lot of trouble if you configure all your web applications to use claims. If you use classic authentication, you'll be required to use the farm account when creating tenant sites; otherwise, you'll get an Access Denied error. Switching to claims will let you use your own account (granted, you still need permissions on the web application, PowerShell scripting permissions, and so on). Additionally, when using claims, you must go through some hoops to get Search to work. You'll need a dedicated search crawl account and crawl rule for each tenant. To avoid the hassle, upgrade to claims.

To create a service application through the Central Administration user interface, select Application Management | Manage Service Applications; this brings you to a page where you can see all the service applications that have been configured on your farm. To create a new service application, simply select the New drop-down list, and then choose the service application that you'd like to create, as depicted in Figure 10-1.

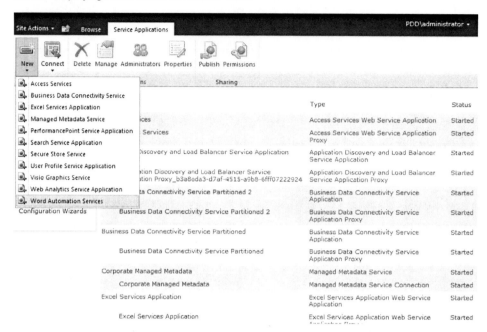

FIGURE 10-1 You can configure a service application in Central Administration or through PowerShell, but you must create tenant-aware services in PowerShell.

After you click the service application that you want to create, you'll be prompted to enter the service application name, the database server name, the app pool identity, and other pertinent information. When you click OK, the service application is provisioned, and you'll see it in the list of available service applications.

To create a service application through PowerShell, you'll use the *New-SPServiceApplication* and *New-SPServiceApplicationProxy* cmdlets. After you've provisioned the service application, you must start the service instance by using the *Start-SPServiceInstance* cmdlet.

Note The *New-SPServiceApplication* and *New-SPServiceApplication* cmdlets actually don't exist. Each service application has its own command to provision itself. For instance, the managed metadata service application's command is *New-SPMetadataServiceApplication*. The next two sections in this chapter cover how to provision each service application with PowerShell.

Remember that the proxy is the WCF endpoint that the web front-end (WFE) is going to talk through to get at the service application, so you must create both the service application and the proxy. Also remember that you might want to start the service on more than one server so that you get some redundancy, depending on your server capacity, recovery time objective (RTO)/recovery point objective (RPO), and so forth. Be sure to run the *Start-SPServiceInstance* cmdlet for each service application on all your application servers in your farm.

> **Note** Each service application has its own degree of performance impact to the servers on which it's running. It's good to have each service application running on at least two servers in the farm. However, you want to balance the number of services running on a given server with the server's size and the current load being placed on the server. Otherwise, you might end up with a performance bottleneck.

If you don't use PowerShell to start the services, you can (fortunately) use the user interface. From the Central Administration user interface, select System Settings, and then click Services On Server. You can then select the server that you want to start the service on, and then click the Start button to start the service (see Figure 10-2). Remember to have a given service running on at least two servers so that you achieve service redundancy.

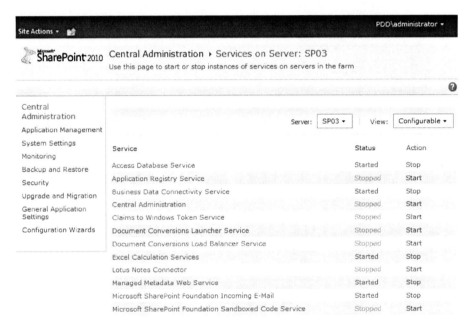

FIGURE 10-2 Ensure that you start a service application instance on at least two servers in the farm to achieve service redundancy. You can do this through Central Administration or through PowerShell.

As mentioned earlier, the service application proxy is simply a WCF endpoint. You can see the endpoint when you look at Internet Information Server (IIS). If you open IIS, you'll notice a site called SharePoint Web Services, and under this site is a slew of virtual directories. Each virtual directory points to a subdirectory within the 14 Root folder (c:\program files\common files\microsoft shared\web server extensions\14). This is where the service endpoint is deployed. You can't differentiate each service when you look at the virtual directory name because it's a globally unique identifier (GUID). However, if you click a directory and then click the Content View button, you'll notice the .svc endpoint with a descriptive name, as shown in Figure 10-3.

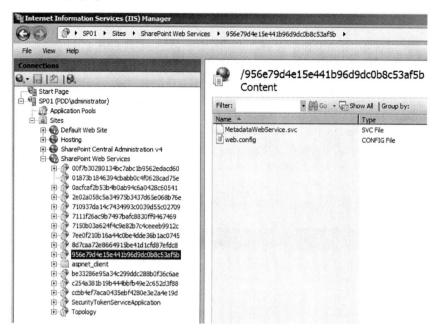

FIGURE 10-3 Service applications deploy themselves as a WCF endpoint. SharePoint sites talk through the endpoint's proxy to communicate with the service.

Consuming Service Applications

A service application is consumed by a web application when you associate that web application to a group of proxies that contains the proxy for your service application. By default, there is one proxy group that contains all the proxies. The name of the group is Default, and you can add and remove proxies from this group if you wish. Another option is to create custom groups that have a more appropriate name that signifies their purpose. Figure 10-4 shows the Default proxy group with a few service applications associated to the intranet web application. There's also a custom group called Tenant-Aware. This group contains additional services that only work for tenant sites. As we will discuss later, when a service application is partitioned, it only works for tenant-aware sites, and thus it wouldn't apply to normal sites. This is a good example where you'd want at least two groups of service applications in which you segregate those that are partitioned from those that are not partitioned.

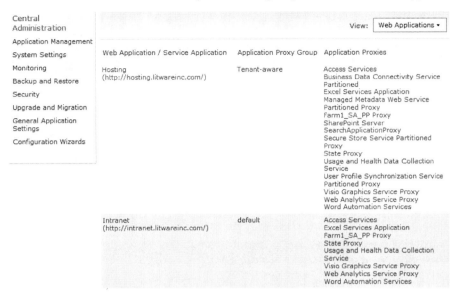

FIGURE 10-4 Web applications are associated to a proxy group that contains all the service applications the web application can consume.

Mixed-Mode Service Applications

In some cases, you might want to mix partitioned service applications with those that are not partitioned. These are referred to as *mixed-mode service applications.*

Consider the managed metadata service application. You would want this service application partitioned such that each tenant or department could configure its own terms and vocabulary to be used within its sites. However, what if you want a shared set of terms, such as a corporate-sanctioned vocabulary of product names, for example? You wouldn't want to manage this list of product names in each and every tenant term store.

Instead, you can create a second managed metadata service application, but this time not in partitioned mode. Then you can add that service application to the proxy group that the other, partitioned service application is in. Thus, the tenant sites will be able to utilize both their custom terms and the terms that are centrally published and managed.

Unfortunately, you can only give a custom proxy group an identifiable name through PowerShell. The command you use to do this is the *New-SPServiceApplicationProxyGroup* command, as seen here:

```
New-SPServiceApplicationProxyGroup -Name "Tenant-aware"
```

To add proxies to the group, you can use the *Add-SPServiceApplicationProxyGroupMember* cmdlet, or you can do this through the user interface. To configure this through the Central Administration user interface, click Application Management, and then click Service Application Associations. Next, click the name of your custom proxy group. A dialog box opens from which you can select the proxies that you want to add to the group (see Figure 10-5). Thereafter, you can click the web application name and toggle which proxy group and service that web application ought to consume (see Figure 10-6).

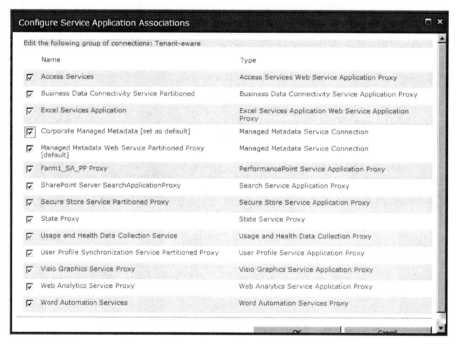

FIGURE 10-5 You can configure which proxies are in a proxy group either through Central Administration or through the *Add-SPServiceApplicationProxyGroupMember* cmdlet.

FIGURE 10-6 After you have your proxy configured, you can associate it to a web application and make those services available to its sites.

Service Application Federation

Thus far, you've seen how to create service applications on the same farm from which the web application is consuming those services. However, there's an important architectural concept called "service application federation" that handles this task differently. Instead of the services being on the same farm as the sites and content, the services are on a different, shared services farm. This is nice when you have multiple farms in your organization that all want to consume the same services.

Search is a great example of this. Why have every farm crawl and serve queries for the same content? It would be better and cheaper to do this in only one place, because then you'd have less load on those consuming farms. This will increase the responsiveness of those farms.

To set up federation, you first need to exchange certificates between the publishing farm and the consuming farms. This informs those farms that they trust one another. Then you publish the services from the services farm, and connect to those published services on the consumers. This is a very extensive and technical process, so for more information, see the article at *http://bit.ly/dXZxEc*.

Step 1: Configuring the Site Subscription Service

With a basic introduction to service applications under your belt, it's time to start building one. The preceding section demonstrated how to create service applications through the user interface. That is easy enough, and we won't discuss it further in this book. The real value is in learning how to create service applications through PowerShell, because again, PowerShell is the only way to create tenant-aware service applications.

Referring back to the 10 steps listed at the end of Chapter 9, step 1 shows you how to create the site subscription service application. This is the foundation on which tenant sites are built in SharePoint. This service tracks all subscription IDs and the sites to which they are assigned. But before we jump in and create this service application, we must ensure that an application pool is available in which to host the service application.

Configuring Prerequisites

All service applications need to execute within an application pool in IIS. Before we can start creating our service application, we need to provision a new application pool, or get a handle on an existing one.

> ### Getting Started with PowerShell
>
> If you're new to PowerShell, you'll need to learn how to execute the following cmdlets. You can execute PowerShell cmdlets in several ways, but the author's personal recommendation is to download a free editor called PowerGUI from *http://www.PowerGui.com*. You can download the scripts from *http://www.sharepoint-in-the-cloud.com* and simply select the code you want to execute; then press Ctrl+F7 to run the commands.
>
> Without PowerGUI or a similar editor, you'll be relegated to entering the following cmdlets and pressing the Enter key in between each command. Pressing Ctrl+F7 is much faster.
>
>
>
> > **Note** After you install PowerGUI, you'll either need to add the SharePoint PowerShell library or run the following command to load the SharePoint cmdlets:
> >
> > ```
> > Add-PSSnapin Microsoft.SharePoint.PowerShell
> > ```
> >
> > Be sure to use the 64-bit version of your editor or none of the commands will work.

The first thing you want to do is to set some global variables that all the following scripts in this chapter will use. With these variables, you'll get some much needed reuse; otherwise, you'll need to enter this information over and over again. The first thing to set is the SQL server name. All the service application databases will be stored on this SQL server, so ensure that the user running the script has Db_Creator permissions to that server. The farm name variable is used as a database prefix on all the databases created in the subsequent commands. The next two variables store the application pool identity and the application pool name, as shown in the following:

```
$databaseServerName = "SQL01"                 #Database Server
$FarmName = "HostingFarm"                      #Database Prefix
$appPoolUserName = "litwareinc\spservice"      #App pool identity
$saAppPoolName = "SharePoint Services Apps"     #App pool name
```

With those variables in place, the next step is to get or create the application pool. The *Get-SPServiceApplicationPool* cmdlet will retrieve the pool, and then a check is made to determine if the pool is null, meaning it doesn't exist. If it doesn't exist yet, the script will create it by using the *New-SPServiceApplicationPool* cmdlet.

However, before the script can create the application pool, it first needs to ensure that the identity provided is set up as a managed account in SharePoint. If not, it creates a new managed account by using the *New-SPManagedAccount* cmdlet and will prompt the user running the cmdlet for the password, as demonstrated here:

```
$saAppPool = Get-SPServiceApplicationPool -Identity $saAppPoolName -EA 0
if($saAppPool -eq $null)
{
    Write-Host "Creating Service Application Pool..."

    # Check to see if identity is already a SP managed account
    # if not, create it as a managed account
    $appPoolAccount = Get-SPManagedAccount -Identity $appPoolUserName -EA 0
    if($appPoolAccount -eq $null)
    {
        Write-Host "Please supply the password for the Service Account..."
        $appPoolCred = Get-Credential $appPoolUserName
        $appPoolAccount = New-SPManagedAccount -Credential $appPoolCred -EA 0
    }

    $appPoolAccount = Get-SPManagedAccount -Identity $appPoolUserName -EA 0

    # Create the app pool
    New-SPServiceApplicationPool -Name $saAppPoolName -Account $appPoolAccount -EA 0 > $null
    $saAppPool = Get-SPServiceApplicationPool -Identity $saAppPoolName -EA 0

    if($saAppPool -eq $null)
    { Write-Host "ERROR: Could not create app pool" }
    else { Write-Host "App Pool Created Successfully
" }
}
```

Note "-EA 0" stands for –ErrorAction SilentlyContinue.

Configuring the Site Subscription Service

With the *$saAppPool* variable successfully storing the desired application pool, it's time to start provisioning service applications and assigning them to use that application pool, the first of which is the site subscription service application. This service application stores all the tenant subscription IDs and which site collections are associated to which tenant. It is the first of many service applications you'll create, and is required before you can provision any tenant site collections.

```
$subsInstanceName = "SPSubscriptionSettingsServiceInstance"
$subsName = "Hosting Subscription Settings"
$subsDBName = "Hosting_SubscriptionSettings"

Write-Host "Creating $subsName Application and Proxy..."
$subs = New-SPSubscriptionSettingsServiceApplication -ApplicationPool $saAppPool
    -Name $subsName -DatabaseName $subsDBName
$proxy = New-SPSubscriptionSettingsServiceApplicationProxy -ServiceApplication $subs

Write-Host "Starting subsInstanceName..."
Get-SPServiceInstance | where{$_.GetType().Name -eq $subsInstanceName} |
    Start-SPServiceInstance
```

In the preceding example, notice the *subsName* and *subsDBName* variables. These variables store the service application display name and the database name, respectively. Then the script provisions the service application by running the *New-SPSubscriptionSettingsService Application* cmdlet and creates the needed proxy by calling *New-SPSubscriptionSettingsService ApplicationProxy*. With the proxy in place, the last thing to do is to start the service instance by first getting the service and then calling *Start-SPServiceInstance*. Note that you will want to start the service on more than one server for the sake of redundancy.

Step 2: Creating Tenant-Aware Service Applications

With the subscription settings service application in place, you're now ready to start cranking out the other service applications you want available to your tenants. For the most part, there's no particular order in which to do this, so simply execute the scripts as you see fit. Just remember the dependency on the application pool you created earlier as well as the *$saAppPoolName* variable.

> **Note** Order does matter for Search, Microsoft Visio, and Web Analytics service applications. Search depends on the Usage and Health service application, and the Visio and Web Analytics applications depend on the State service application.

Creating the Business Connectivity Service

With the Business Connectivity Service (BCS) application, you can connect to external data sources from within your sites. You can connect to those data sources from within SharePoint Designer, and save those connections, called models, in the BCS, as illustrated in the following:

```
$bcsSAName = "Business Data Connectivity Service Partitioned"
Write-Host "Creating BCS Service and Proxy..."
$BCSDBName = ("{0}_SA_BCS" -f $FarmName)
New-SPBusinessDataCatalogServiceApplication -PartitionMode -Name $bcsSAName
    -ApplicationPool $saAppPoolName -DatabaseServer $databaseServerName
    -DatabaseName $BCSDBName > $null
Get-SPServiceInstance |
    Where-Object {$_.TypeName -eq "Business Data Connectivity Service"} |
    Start-SPServiceInstance > $null
```

> **Note** Interestingly, the *New-SPBusinessDataCatalogServiceApplication* cmdlet also configures the proxy for you, so you actually don't need to run the *New-SPBusinessDataCatalogService ApplicationProxy* cmdlet.
>
> As a general rule, the BCS application should be contained in its own dedicated application pool, since it connects to external data.

Just as is the case for all service applications, the first step is to create it. Next, create the proxy (in the case of BCS this is done automatically), and then start the service on at least two servers in the farm so that there's no single point of failure. This script has two variables that you might want to configure: the *$bcsSAName* variable stores the service application display name, and the *$BCSDBName* stores the database name.

Creating the Secure Store Service

When BCS connects to data, it can either use the user's credentials to connect to that data, or share credentials stored in the secure store service. In the example that follows, you can use the secure store service to enter credentials that other users can use to connect to data so that they don't have access to the data, nor can they be prompted for credentials.

```
$secureStoreSAName = "Secure Store Service Partitioned"
Write-Host "Creating Secure Store Service and Proxy..."
$storeDB = ("{0}_SA_SecureStore" -f $FarmName)
New-SPSecureStoreServiceapplication -PartitionMode -Name $secureStoreSAName
    -Sharing:$false -DatabaseServer $databaseServerName -DatabaseName $storeDB
    -ApplicationPool $saAppPoolName -AuditingEnabled:$true -AuditlogMaxSize 30 |
    New-SPSecureStoreServiceApplicationProxy -Name "$secureStoreSAName Proxy"
    -DefaultProxygroup > $null
Get-SPServiceInstance | Where-Object {$_.TypeName -eq "Secure Store Service"} |
    Start-SPServiceInstance > $null
```

Note As a general rule, the Secure Store service application should be contained in its own dedicated application pool, because it holds credential information.

This service application requires some follow-up configuration. When a tenant goes to configure the service, it will see an error stating that a key has not been generated, as shown in Figure 10-7.

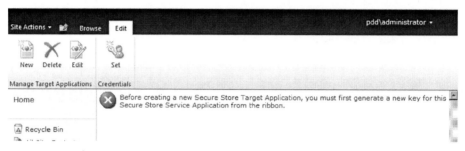

FIGURE 10-7 Before tenants can use the secure store service, a farm administrator must generate an encryption key.

To resolve this message, a farm administrator must manage the service from within Central Administration. When the farm administrator browses to the service application from Central Administration, she will see an error showing that the service must be administered at the tenant level (see Figure 10-8). However, that's not 100 percent true. Before tenants can manage the service application, the farm administrator must click the Generate New Key button to generate the key (this can be scripted, as well). To generate the key, the farm administrator needs to enter the farm passphrase she used when she installed and configured the farm. Thereafter, tenants can start adding credentials into the secure store (see Figure 10-9).

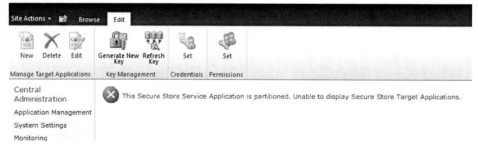

FIGURE 10-8 To generate a key, a farm administrator must manage the application from Central Administration, and then click the Generate New Key button.

FIGURE 10-9 After the key has been generated, tenants can begin storing their encrypted credentials.

Creating the Managed Metadata Service

The managed metadata service application is used to manage a hierarchy of terms and vocabulary that you can use to tag documents within SharePoint. This tagging of documents increases the discoverability of information because users can sort, filter, and group the content; therefore, search results are greatly improved when a document is tagged appropriately. The following script shows how to provision this important service application:

```
$metadataSAName = "Managed Metadata Web Service Partitioned"
Write-Host "Creating Metadata Service and Proxy..."
$metadataDB = ("{0}_SA_MetaData_Partitioned" -f $FarmName)
New-SPMetadataServiceApplication -PartitionMode -Name $metadataSAName
    -ApplicationPool $saAppPoolName -DatabaseServer $databaseServerName
    -DatabaseName $metadataDB > $null
New-SPMetadataServiceApplicationProxy -PartitionMode -Name "$metadataSAName Proxy"
    -DefaultProxyGroup -ServiceApplication $metadataSAName > $null
Get-SPServiceInstance | Where-Object {$_.TypeName -eq "Managed Metadata Web Service"} |
    Start-SPServiceInstance > $null
```

After you've provisioned the service application, ensure that term store administrators have been designated (see Figure 10-10). This can be done by a tenant user who has site collection administrator rights to the tenant administration site, or it can be done by the farm administrator. Regardless of who handles this, this designation is necessary; otherwise, no users will be able to create groups, term sets, or terms. After you create term sets, you can add permissions onto them individually as well.

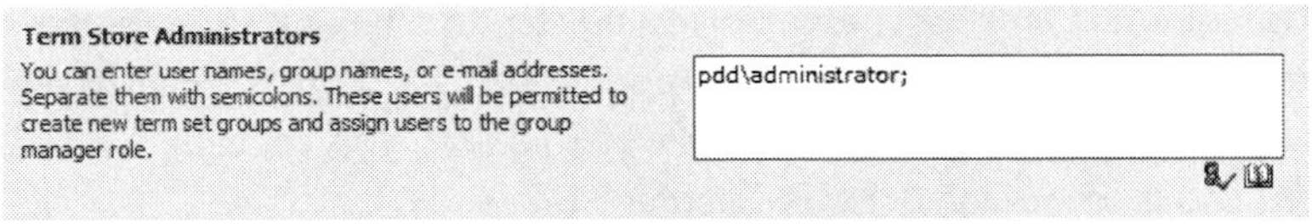

Term Store Administrators

You can enter user names, group names, or e-mail addresses. Separate them with semicolons. These users will be permitted to create new term set groups and assign users to the group manager role.

`pdd\administrator;`

FIGURE 10-10 Before a tenant can start administering its term store, someone must be configured as a term store administrator who can grant other tenant users permissions to the term sets.

Also of consequence are settings on the proxy. These settings can only be configured by a farm administrator. To configure these settings, select the proxy from within the Manage Service Applications page in Central Administration. Then, on the ribbon, click Properties (see Figure 10-11).

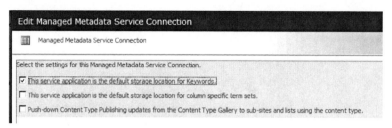

FIGURE 10-11 Not all settings are delegated down to the tenant administrator sites, as is the case for these three managed metadata settings.

The first two settings are there for when you have more than one service application of a given type. If you have two service applications of the same type associated in the same proxy group, you need to choose which one is the default. The default is where all the user-defined keywords and terms are placed.

The third setting controls whether content types should be overridden when their parent, published content type changes. A feature of the managed metadata service application is the ability to define a content type hub. Typically, content types are defined on a site collection-by-site collection basis. However, with the hub, you can share content types across many site collections. This setting then lets you specify what happens when the content type changes, but the child content type has been modified. See Chapter 11, "Configuring Tenant-Aware Site Collections," for more information on content type hubs. Each tenant needs to have its own hub defined to take advantage of this functionality.

Creating the User Profile Service

The user profile service application handles most of the social features of SharePoint. This includes profile pages, profile properties, My Sites, and social tagging and rating. Provisioning this service application is rather straightforward; however, a massive amount of configuration must be performed after you've completed the provisioning. There are two parts to this configuration. The first part involves registering a tenant with the user profile service application. This ensures that only the appropriate user profiles are retrieved so that a tenant can't see or modify the profiles of other tenants. This concept is also relatively straightforward and is covered in detail in Chapter 11.

The second part, however, is not covered in much detail in this book, and it revolves around setting up profile synchronization. This is a very detailed process that requires changing settings in SQL and in Active Directory. This process has changed considerably since SharePoint 2010 was released, so the best and most up-to-date resource is the TechNet article at *http://bit.ly/dcQcsX*.

The multitenancy pieces of this service application are covered in this chapter, and in Chapter 11. You can use the following script to create the service application:

```
$userProfileSAName = "User Profile Synchronization Service Partitioned"
Write-Host "Creating User Profile Service and Proxy..."
$profileDB = ("{0}_SA_Profile_Partitioned" -f $FarmName)
$socialDB = ("{0}_SA_ProfileSocial_Partitioned" -f $FarmName)
$syncDB = ("{0}_SA_ProfileSync_Partitioned" -f $FarmName)
$script = {
    Add-PSSnapin Microsoft.SharePoint.PowerShell
    $pool = Get-SPServiceApplicationPool "Service Applications"
    $userProfileService = New-SPProfileServiceApplication -PartitionMode
        -Name $userProfileSAName -ApplicationPool $saAppPoolName
        -ProfileDBServer $databaseServerName -ProfileDBName $profileDB
        -SocialDBServer $databaseServerName -SocialDBName $socialDB
        -ProfileSyncDBServer $databaseServerName -ProfileSyncDBName $syncDB
    New-SPProfileServiceApplicationProxy -PartitionMode -Name "$userProfileSAName Proxy"
        -ServiceApplication $userProfileService -DefaultProxyGroup > $null
    Get-SPServiceInstance | Where-Object {$_.TypeName -eq "User Profile Service"} |
        Start-SPServiceInstance > $null

}
$farmAccount = Get-Credential "<Farm Account>"
$job = Start-Job -Credential $farmAccount -ScriptBlock $script | Wait-Job
$results = Receive-Job -job $job
```

> **Note** The string "`<Farm Account>`" corresponds to your farm's service account. There's a known issue with the *New-SPProfileServiceApplication* cmdlet that will cause the User Profile Synch Service to fail when provisioning because it doesn't set the correct database owner set on the Synch Table. The only supported way to set these database permissions is to run the command as the farm account, which has the necessary permissions.

After you provision the service application, you can view the settings of the service application in either Central Administration or the tenant administration site. The biggest difference between the two is that profiles are managed in the tenant, and profile properties and synchronization are managed in Central Administration. You can manage profile properties in the tenant, but only those properties allowed in Central Administration. Figure 10-12 shows the administration screen when in Central Administration. You can see that no tenants have yet been associated to this service application.

People
Manage User Properties |
Schedule Audience Compilation | Compile Audiences

Synchronization
Configure Synchronization Connections |
Configure Synchronization Timer Job |
Configure Synchronization Settings |
Start Profile Synchronization

Organizations
Manage Organization Properties

Profiles	
Number of Tenants	0
Number of User Profiles	0
Number of Organization Profiles	1
Audiences	
Number of Audiences	1
Uncompiled Audiences	0
Audience Compilation Status	Idle
Audience Compilation Schedule	Every Saturday at 01:00 AM Ended at
Last Compilation Time	6/5/2011 8:46 AM

Profile Synchronization Settings
User Profile Sync is not currently provisioned.
Synchronization Schedule (Incremental)   Disabled

FIGURE 10-12 The user profile service application is configured in the tenant administration site as well as from within Central Administration.

Creating the Word Conversion Service

The Word conversion service is used to convert Microsoft Word documents from one document type to another. For example, you could use this service to convert a Word document to a PDF, as shown here:

```
$WordAutomationSAName = "Word Automation Services Partitioned"
Write-Host "Creating Word Conversion Service and Proxy..."
$wordDB = ("{0}_SA_WordAutomation_Partitioned" -f $FarmName)
 New-SPWordConversionServiceApplication -PartitionMode -Name $WordAutomationSAName
   -ApplicationPool $saAppPoolName -DatabaseServer $databaseServerName -DatabaseName $wordDB
   -Default > $null
 Get-SPServiceInstance | Where-Object {$_.TypeName -eq "Word Automation Services"} |
   Start-SPServiceInstance > $null
```

Note Interestingly, the *New-SPWordConversionServiceApplication* cmdlet also configures the proxy for you, so you actually don't need to run the *New-SPWordConversionServiceApplication Proxy* cmdlet.

For some reason or another, this service application is the exception to the rule. Figure 10-13 shows that when creating this service application through Central Administration, you can select a check box to create the application in partitioned mode. How convenient!

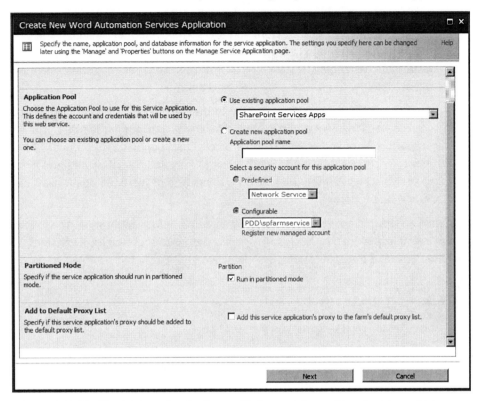

FIGURE 10-13 The Word Automation Service was kind enough to provide a check box, which you can select to specify that it should be created in partitioned mode.

Creating the Search Service

The search service application is by far the most complicated service application to configure with PowerShell, primarily because you need to create so many components, including the following:

- **Admin component and database** This component keeps track of the search topology and performs topology changes such as adding new components.

- **Crawl components and database** The crawl component is used to crawl content and build the index. Typically, you need more crawl components if you have a large amount of content across more than one content source (only one crawl component can crawl a source at a given time), and you have high index freshness requirements.

- **Query components, property databases, and index partitions** The query component handles search queries from end users. The component searches the index file and the properties stored in the property database, and the query processor merges the results and generates the search results. You can configure this component in an active/passive manner to provide a failover mechanism.

  An *index partition* is simply a partition of the total index. So if you have two partitions, you'd have 50 percent of the index in one and 50 percent in the other. This is helpful for performance and scaling reasons, since a partition has a maximum of 10 million items. Processing time in the 50:50 scenario is essentially halved because it only needs to search across half the total content. Likewise, a property database has a capacity of 50 million properties.

So, you can see that a lot goes into creating a search service application. The following is a great example, provided by Microsoft. The first step is to set some local variables, such as the service name and the application pool identity:

```
Write-Host Setting up some initial variables.
$SSAName = "SharePoint Server Search"
$SVCAcct = $appPoolUserName
$SSI = Get-SPEnterpriseSearchServiceInstance -Local
$err = $null
```

After you've set up those variables, you must start the search service instance and create an application pool in which to run the service. This will start the service on the server on which you're running:

```
Write-Host Start Services search services for SSI
Start-SPEnterpriseSearchServiceInstance -Identity $SSI

Write-Host Creating an Application Pool.
$AppPool = New-SPServiceApplicationPool -Name $SSAName"-AppPool" -Account $SVCAcct
```

Next you'll create the search service application in partitioned mode. Just as with the other service applications, you'll want to create the proxy in partitioned mode as well.

> **Note** Whereas other service applications use the flag *-PartitionMode*, the search service application uses the flag *-Partitioned*.

```
Write-Host Create the SearchApplication and set it to a variable
$searchDB = ("{0}_SA_Search" -f $FarmName)
$SearchApp = New-SPEnterpriseSearchServiceApplication -Partitioned -Name $SSAName
    -ApplicationPool $AppPool -DatabaseName $searchDB

Write-Host Create search service application proxy
$SSAProxy = New-SPEnterpriseSearchServiceApplicationProxy -Partitioned
    -Name $SSAName"ApplicationProxy" -Uri $SearchApp.Uri.AbsoluteURI
```

With the service application in place, you can start provisioning the search components. The first component to create must be the admin component, as follows:

```
Write-Host Provision Search Admin Component.
Set-SPEnterpriseSearchAdministrationComponent -SearchApplication $SearchApp
    -SearchServiceInstance $SSI
```

With the admin component in place, you can go ahead and provision the rest of the components, such as the crawl and query components. To create the crawl component, you first need to create the crawl topology, crawl component, and crawl database. Then you must activate the crawl component. Notice how the script uses a loop to keep looping until the topology is activated. It can take several minutes to activate, so the loop locks the person running the script until it's completely finished with the provisioning.

> **Note** This script is just an example. It creates all of these components on a single server in the farm. It's a best practice to create more than one component or failover components so that you have redundancy. To accomplish this, you might run bits and pieces of this script on various servers in your farm to specify which component will run in the various locations.

```
Write-Host Create a new Crawl Topology.
$CrawlTopo = $SearchApp | New-SPEnterpriseSearchCrawlTopology

Write-Host Create a new Crawl Store.
$CrawlStore = $SearchApp | Get-SPEnterpriseSearchCrawlDatabase

Write-Host Create a new Crawl Component.
New-SPEnterpriseSearchCrawlComponent -CrawlTopology $CrawlTopo -CrawlDatabase $CrawlStore
    -SearchServiceInstance $SSI

Write-Host Activate the Crawl Topology.
Do
{
    $err = $null
    $CrawlTopo | Set-SPEnterpriseSearchCrawlTopology -Active -ErrorVariable err
    if ($CrawlTopo.State -eq "Active")
    {
        $err = $null
    }
    Start-Sleep -Seconds 10
}
Until ($err -eq $null)
```

With the crawl components complete, you can now turn your attention to the query components. The first thing you need to do is to get the query topology and add a partition, query component, and property database. And just like before, you can use a loop to wait for the topology to finish provisioning, as demonstrated in the code that follows.

```
write-host Create a new Query Topology.
$QueryTopo = $SearchApp | New-SPenterpriseSEarchQueryTopology -Partitions 1

Write-Host Create a variable for the Query Partition
$Partition1 = ($QueryTopo | Get-SPEnterpriseSearchIndexPartition)

Write-Host Create a Query Component.
New-SPEnterpriseSearchQueryComponent -IndexPartition $Partition1 -QueryTopology $QueryTopo
    -SearchServiceInstance $SSI

Write-Host Create a variable for the Property Store DB.
$PropDB = $SearchApp | Get-SPEnterpriseSearchPropertyDatabase


Write-Host Set the Query Partition to use the Property Store DB.
$Partition1 | Set-SPEnterpriseSearchIndexPartition -PropertyDatabase $PropDB

Write-Host Activate the Query Topology.
Do
{

    $err = $null
    $QueryTopo | Set-SPEnterpriseSearchQueryTopology -Active -ErrorVariable err
        -ErrorAction SilentlyContinue
    Start-Sleep -Seconds 5
    if ($QueryTopo.State -eq "Active")
    {
        $err = $null
    }
}
Until ($err -eq $null)
Write-Host "Your search application $SSAName is now ready"
Creating Other Service Applications
```

The rest of the service applications don't store tenant data, and thus are not created in partitioned mode. Additionally, all of them except the state service and usage service can be created right from the user interface from within Central Administration. Despite this, it seems best to include them in this chapter because a private cloud favors automation, which can only be done through PowerShell. Plus, if you're configuring all your other service applications by using PowerShell to get the tenancy features, you might as well create all of them in a consistent manner.

Creating the State Service

The state service helps SharePoint to manage state, such as workflow state and the state for InfoPath Forms Services. This service application is required on a farm and is used for basic collaboration in form libraries and workflows. However, it is not created automatically unless you use the Farm Configuration Wizard (which isn't recommended). So having this simple script on hand is quite important.

```
$stateSAName = "State Service"
Write-Host "Creating State Service and Proxy..."
$stateDB = ("{0}_SA_State" -f $FarmName)
New-SPStateServiceDatabase -Name $stateDB -DatabaseServer $databaseServerName |
    New-SPStateServiceApplication -Name $stateSAName | New-SPStateServiceApplicationProxy
    -Name "$stateSAName Proxy" -DefaultProxyGroup > $null
```

Creating the Usage Service

The usage service is simply a logging service. It creates a database that gets loaded with all kinds of great information that you can mine. Some examples of things you can do with the data include checking to see if your load balancer is working, checking your most active users, and logging specific performance counters such as CPU, memory, and queue depth to watch server utilization grow over time. Because the data, by default, only lasts 14 days, many organizations build a warehouse from this data so that they can see their environments trending over time.

> **Note** This is arguably the most resource-intensive service application. Only use this if you have specific method to handle the load it will put on your servers, in particular your database servers. For most large farms, a dedicated physical SQL server is required to handle the load.

```
$usageSAName = "Usage and Health Data Collection Service"
Write-Host "Creating Usage Service and Proxy..."
$serviceInstance = Get-SPUsageService
$usageDBName = ("{0}_SA_Usage" -f $FarmName)
New-SPUsageApplication -Name $usageSAName -DatabaseServer $databaseServerName
    -DatabaseName $usageDBName -UsageService $serviceInstance > $null
```

Creating the Access Service

Using the Access service application, you can edit Microsoft Access workbooks from within the browser. It also performs server-side calculations of data within those workbooks.

```
$accesssSAName = "Access Services"
Write-Host "Creating Access Services and Proxy..."
New-SPAccessServiceApplication -Name $accesssSAName -ApplicationPool $saAppPoolName > $null
Get-SPServiceInstance | Where-Object {$_.TypeName -eq "Access Database Service"} |
    Start-SPServiceInstance > $null
```

Creating the Excel Calculation Service

Similar to Access services, you can use Excel services to edit Microsoft Excel documents from within the browser. Again, because Excel uses calculations to render and format the data, this service also is used to handle those calculations on the server side. Excel services are also required for PowerPivot for SharePoint.

```
$excelSAName = "Excel Services Application"
Write-Host "Creating Excel Service..."
New-SPExcelServiceApplication -Name $excelSAName -ApplicationPool $saAppPoolName > $null
Set-SPExcelFileLocation -Identity "http://" -ExcelServiceApplication $excelSAName
   -ExternalDataAllowed 2 -WorkbookSizeMax 10 -WarnOnDataRefresh:$true
Get-SPServiceInstance | Where-Object {$_.TypeName -eq "Excel Calculation Services"} |
   Start-SPServiceInstance > $null
```

Creating the Visio Graphics Service

The Visio graphics service is similar to the Access and Excel services, in that you can view Visio diagrams from within the browser. A lot of people use this service to create dashboards, since the diagrams can have intelligence for querying external data and using conditional formatting from within the diagram. Such querying and formatting is performed via this service application.

```
$visioSAName = "Visio Graphics Service"
Write-Host "Creating Visio Graphics Service and Proxy..."
New-SPVisioServiceApplication -Name $visioSAName -ApplicationPool $saAppPoolName > $null
New-SPVisioServiceApplicationProxy -Name "$visioSAName Proxy"
   -ServiceApplication $visioSAName > $null
Get-SPServiceInstance | Where-Object {$_.TypeName -eq "Visio Graphics Service"} |
   Start-SPServiceInstance > $null
```

Creating the Performance Point Service

This service takes dashboards to a new level. You can point performance point dashboards to a multitude of data sources, and through a drag-and-drop experience, users can build rich dashboards.

```
$performancePointSAName = $FarmName+"_SA_PP"
Write-Host "Creating Performance Point Service and Proxy..."
New-SPPerformancePointServiceApplication -Name $performancePointSAName
   -ApplicationPool $saAppPoolName > $null
New-SPPerformancePointServiceApplicationProxy -Default -Name "$performancePointSAName Proxy"
   -ServiceApplication $performancePointSAName > $null
Get-SPServiceInstance | where-object {$_.TypeName -eq "PerformancePoint Service"} |
   Start-SPServiceInstance > $null
```

Creating the Web Analytics Service

The web analytics service is used to create reports regarding user traffic within site collections. For example, you can see hit counts on pages and sites, visitor information, and search reports such as top queries and queries that don't return results.

```
$WebAnalyticsSAName = "Web Analytics Service"
Write-Host "Creating Web Analytics Service and Proxy..."
$analyticsStageDB = ("{0}_SA_AnalyticsStage" -f $FarmName)
$analyticsWareDB = ("{0}_SA_AnalyticsWarehouse" -f $FarmName)
$stagerSubscription = "<StagingDatabases><StagingDatabase ServerName='$databaseServerName'
    DatabaseName='$analyticsStageDB'/></StagingDatabases>"
$reportingSubscription = "<ReportingDatabases><ReportingDatabase
    ServerName='$databaseServerName' DatabaseName='$analyticsWareDB'/></ReportingDatabases>"
New-SPWebAnalyticsServiceApplication -Name $WebAnalyticsSAName
    -ApplicationPool $saAppPoolName -ReportingDataRetention 20 -SamplingRate 100
    -ListOfReportingDatabases $reportingSubscription
    -ListOfStagingDatabases $stagerSubscription > $null
New-SPWebAnalyticsServiceApplicationProxy -Name "$WebAnalyticsSAName Proxy"
    -ServiceApplication $WebAnalyticsSAName > $null
Get-SPServiceInstance | Where-Object {$_.TypeName -eq "Web Analytics Web Service"} |
    Start-SPServiceInstance > $null
Get-SPServiceInstance |
    Where-Object {$_.TypeName -eq "Web Analytics Data Processing Service"} |
    Start-SPServiceInstance > $null
```

Chapter 11

Configuring Tenant-Aware Site Collections

In this chapter, you will learn:

- How to create tenant site subscriptions
- How to configure tenant services such as managed metadata service
- How to associate the user profile service to a tenant
- PowerShell code that creates tenant site collections

Steps 1 and 2 of the 10-step process that was proposed in Chapter 10, "Configuring Tenant-Aware Service Applications," are concerned with provisioning the necessary service applications that support the multitenancy features of Microsoft SharePoint 2010. Chapter 10 covered steps 1 and 2 at length; in this chapter, you will start building on this foundation using the remaining steps as your guide.

Steps 3 through 10 deal with provisioning individual tenants, along with all the dependencies that are needed to support each tenant. Step 3 covers feature packs and techniques to show or hide SharePoint functionality on a tenant-by-tenant basis. Step 4 describes how to create a tenant by setting up the tenant's subscription ID. This ID is correlated to all the tenant's site collections and features, and thus represents the tenancy's "building blocks." With the tenant established, step 5 details how to associate the feature packs created in step 3 to the new tenant created in step 4.

Step 8 is where the tenant begins to come to life, because in that step you'll start provisioning the tenant's site collections. However, before you start doing that, you must work through a few more foundational steps, including trimming the People Picker in step 6, and setting up the necessary managed paths in step 7.

The final two steps involve configuring user profiles (step 9) and setting up the content type hub (step 10). When you complete step 10, you have a "fully-baked" tenant in SharePoint. Understand that it will take a lot of PowerShell code to get through these remaining eight steps. You can download this code from the book's website to save time (*http://go.microsoft.com/FWLink/?Linkid=227001*). Look for references within each step to its corresponding PowerShell code file.

Step 3: Creating Feature Packs

As described in Chapter 9, "Introducing Multitenancy in SharePoint 2010" (step 3 in the 10 steps to multitenancy), feature packs give you control over what features are available to your tenants. What's nice is that you can configure this on a tenant-by-tenant basis, such that you can easily charge a tenant based on the features it wants, such as Business Intelligence (BI) features or managed metadata features.

A common chargeback is around SKU (as in SharePoint Foundation, SharePoint Server Standard, and SharePoint Server Enterprise editions). Since Microsoft requires differing user licenses for each SKU, you can use feature packs to only allow the features in each SKU for those tenants who own licenses for that SKU. Thus, you can host multiple SKUs in the same farm. Without feature packs, you're relegated to an all-or-nothing model, where if you have 100 users who need the enterprise features, you either need to build them their own farm or buy Enterprise licenses for all your users.

So, to get around this, you can create a unique feature pack either for each tenant or for each chargeback model, such as SKU. You can then assign that feature pack to one or more tenants to allow the features in that pack for that tenant. You can create a new feature pack via PowerShell through the *New-SPSiteSubscriptionFeaturePack* cmdlet, and you can add features to that pack with the *Add-SPSiteSubscriptionFeaturePackMember* cmdlet. After you have added all the features you want into the pack, you can assign the pack to a tenant with the *Set-SPSiteSubscriptionConfig* cmdlet. We will discuss assigning in more detail later, because first you need to create the tenant. So, to get started, take a look at the following script that creates three new feature packs, one for each SKU.

> **Note** Kudos to the folks at Microsoft for providing this long script and saving us all the tedious task of creating it from scratch. The following is just a truncated copy. For the full copy, see the SharePoint 2010 white paper for hosters (*http://bit.ly/Lo4z8q*) or go to the book's website to download the script by itself.

```
Set-Alias AddFeature Add-SPSiteSubscriptionFeaturePackMember
#Foundation Feature Pack
$ffp = New-SPSiteSubscriptionFeaturePack
AddFeature -identity $ffp -FeatureDefinition AdminLinks -EA 0-EA 0
AddFeature -identity $ffp -FeatureDefinition AnnouncementsList -EA 0
AddFeature -identity $ffp -FeatureDefinition BasicWebParts -EA 0
AddFeature -identity $ffp -FeatureDefinition CallTrackList -EA 0
AddFeature -identity $ffp -FeatureDefinition CirculationList -EA 0
AddFeature -identity $ffp -FeatureDefinition ContactsList -EA 0
AddFeature -identity $ffp -FeatureDefinition CTypes -EA 0
AddFeature -identity $ffp -FeatureDefinition CustomList -EA 0
AddFeature -identity $ffp -FeatureDefinition DataSourceLibrary -EA 0
AddFeature -identity $ffp -FeatureDefinition DiscussionsList -EA 0
# ... truncated due to length. Download full script from sharepoint-in-the-cloud.com
```

```
#Standard Feature Pack
$sfp = New-SPSiteSubscriptionFeaturePack
AddFeature -identity $sfp -FeatureDefinition AccSrvRestrictedList -EA 0
AddFeature -identity $sfp -FeatureDefinition AdminLinks -EA 0
AddFeature -identity $sfp -FeatureDefinition AdminReportCore -EA 0
AddFeature -identity $sfp -FeatureDefinition AnnouncementsList -EA 0
AddFeature -identity $sfp -FeatureDefinition AssetLibrary -EA 0
AddFeature -identity $sfp -FeatureDefinition BaseSite -EA 0
AddFeature -identity $sfp -FeatureDefinition BaseWeb -EA 0
AddFeature -identity $sfp -FeatureDefinition BasicWebParts -EA 0
AddFeature -identity $sfp -FeatureDefinition BDR -EA 0
AddFeature -identity $sfp -FeatureDefinition CallTrackList -EA 0
# ... truncated due to length. Download full script from sharepoint-in-the-cloud.com

#Enterprise Feature Pack
$efp = New-SPSiteSubscriptionFeaturePack
AddFeature -identity $efp -FeatureDefinition AccSrvMSysAso -EA 0
AddFeature -identity $efp -FeatureDefinition AccSrvRestrictedList -EA 0
AddFeature -identity $efp -FeatureDefinition AccSrvShell -EA 0
AddFeature -identity $efp -FeatureDefinition AccSrvSolutionGallery -EA 0
AddFeature -identity $efp -FeatureDefinition AccSrvUserTemplate -EA 0
AddFeature -identity $efp -FeatureDefinition AccSrvUSysAppLog -EA 0
AddFeature -identity $efp -FeatureDefinition AddDashboard -EA 0
AddFeature -identity $efp -FeatureDefinition AdminLinks -EA 0
AddFeature -identity $efp -FeatureDefinition AdminReportCore -EA 0
AddFeature -identity $efp -FeatureDefinition AnnouncementsList -EA 0
# ... truncated due to length. Download full script from sharepoint-in-the-cloud.com
```

With the feature packs ready to go, you should make note of the feature pack's IDs. These IDs are important because you need the ID when you're assigning feature packs to tenants. You can always tell which tenant is assigned which feature pack, but you'll want to keep a dictionary of IDs and their descriptions. You can access the ID of the newly created feature packs by using the following script:

```
"Foundation Features: "+$ffp.ID
"Standard Features: "+$sfp.ID
"Enterprise Features: "+$efp.ID
```

After a feature pack has been created and features have been added, you can use the *Get-SPSiteSubscriptionFeaturePack* cmdlet's *FeatureDefinitions* property to print the list of features that are in the pack. You can use this cmdlet if you forget what the pack is being used for. If you want to access all the feature packs that are currently registered, you can use the *Get-SPSiteSubscriptionFeaturePack* cmdlet.

Create a Feature Pack Dictionary

It is very helpful to keep a feature pack dictionary somewhere (such as in Microsoft Excel or in a SharePoint list) that helps you correlate a globally unique identifier (GUID) to a commonly understood display name. For example, if you want the ID of the enterprise features feature pack (previous script used the *$efp* variable), simply running the *Get-SPSiteSubscriptionFeaturePack* cmdlet won't tell you which feature pack contains the enterprise features. It'll simply render the IDs of all the packs.

If you do not create a dictionary, or if you simply forget what features are in a particular ID, you can always inspect the feature pack members. Figure 11-1 shows how you can use the *FeatureDefinitions* property of a feature pack to see the feature members in case you forget.

```
PowerShell Console
PS C:\Users\administrator.PDD\Documents> $ffp.FeatureDefinitions

DisplayName                    Id                                        Scope
-----------                    --                                        -----
AdminLinks                     fead7313-ae6d-45dd-8260-13b563cb4c71      Web
AnnouncementsList              00bfea71-d1ce-42de-9c63-a44004ce0104      Web
BasicWebParts                  00bfea71-1c5e-4a24-b310-ba51c3eb7a57      Site
CallTrackList                  239650e3-ee0b-44a0-a22a-48292402b8d8      Web
CirculationList                a568770a-50ba-4052-ab48-37d8029b3f47      Web
ContactsList                   00bfea71-7e6d-4186-9ba8-c047ac750105      Web
CTypes                         695b6570-a48b-4a8e-8ea5-26ea7fc1d162      Site
CustomList                     00bfea71-de22-43b2-a848-c05709900100      Web
DataSourceLibrary              00bfea71-f381-423d-b9d1-da7a54c50110      Web
DiscussionsList                00bfea71-6a49-43fa-b535-d15c05500108      Web
DocumentLibrary                00bfea71-e717-4e80-aa17-d0c71b360101      Web
EventsList                     00bfea71-ec85-4903-972d-ebe475780106      Web
ExternalList                   00bfea71-9549-43f8-b978-e47e54a10600      Web
FacilityList                   58160a6b-4396-4d6e-867c-65381fb5fbc9      Web
FCGroupsList                   08386d3d-7cc0-486b-a730-3b4cfe1b5509      Web
Fields                         ca7bd552-10b1-4563-85b9-5ed1d39c962a      Site
GanttTasksList                 00bfea71-513d-4ca0-96c2-6a47775c0119      Web
GBWProvision                   6e8a2add-ed09-4592-978e-8fa71e6f117c      Web
GBWWebParts                    3d25bd73-7cd4-4425-b8fb-8899977f73de      Web
GridList                       00bfea71-3a1d-41d3-a0ee-651d11570120      Web
GroupWork                      9c03e124-eef7-4dc6-b5eb-86ccd207cb87      Web
HelpLibrary                    071de60d-4b02-4076-b001-b456e93146fe      Site
PS C:\Users\adm...\Documents>
```

FIGURE 11-1 You can always check to see which features are in a given feature pack by inspecting the *FeatureDefinitions* property of the feature pack.

Step 4: Creating a New Site Subscription

Finally! With all the dependencies out of the way, you can start creating tenants. Creating a tenant is actually so easy, it's dangerous. All you need to do is to run the *New-SPSiteSubscription* cmdlet. As you can see in Figure 11-2, when you run the cmdlet and assign it to a variable, a new tenant is created that's represented by a unique ID (a GUID).

FIGURE 11-2 To create a new tenant, simply run the *New-SPSiteSubscription* PowerShell cmdlet. Thereafter, you can start associating the ID to site collections, and thereby form the tenancy.

You'll need to run the *New-SPSiteSubscription* cmdlet for each tenant that you want created. After you have a site subscription, you can start adding site collections to the tenancy. Alternatively, you can add them as you create them when using the *New-SPSite* cmdlet, by passing the *site* subscription as a parameter. You can tell that in Figure 11-2, the newly created tenant does not have any site collections in it.

As noted earlier, the best way to identify what GUID is associated with what tenant is to keep a tenant dictionary in an Excel document or SharePoint list. That way, you can more easily look up the tenant name and gather its GUID. If you don't have a dictionary of tenants, you can try to identify who the tenant is by inspecting all the site collections associated with the site subscription. Figure 11-3 shows how you can use the *Get-SPSiteSubscription* command to first get all the subscriptions, and then get a particular subscription, and thereafter display all the site collections in that subscription.

```
PowerShell Console
PS C:\Users\administrator.PDD\Documents> Get-SPSiteSubscription

Id                                                   Sites
--                                                   -----
c4cd9df8-dc12-4302-8c4f-03e7261348b9                 {SPSite Url=http://fulfillment.litware}
83322539-132f-4dc0-b8d6-221ce6a674fd                 {SPSite Url=http://hr.litwareinc.com, S
d4b08002-3d68-484d-a62c-69c0dd76acca                 {SPSite Url=http://marketing.litwareinc
9d78e16e-5ded-4760-a7d5-7ac5edce4795                 {SPSite Url=http://sales.litwareinc.com
8303fb17-f311-4024-8f33-890b302f2ea2                 {SPSite Url=http://manufacturing.litwar


PS C:\Users\administrator.PDD\Documents> $subs = Get-SPSiteSubscription
PS C:\Users\administrator.PDD\Documents> $subs

Id                                                   Sites
--                                                   -----
c4cd9df8-dc12-4302-8c4f-03e7261348b9                 {SPSite Url=http://fulfillment.litware}
83322539-132f-4dc0-b8d6-221ce6a674fd                 {SPSite Url=http://hr.litwareinc.com, S
d4b08002-3d68-484d-a62c-69c0dd76acca                 {SPSite Url=http://marketing.litwareinc
9d78e16e-5ded-4760-a7d5-7ac5edce4795                 {SPSite Url=http://sales.litwareinc.com
8303fb17-f311-4024-8f33-890b302f2ea2                 {SPSite Url=http://manufacturing.litwar


PS C:\Users\administrator.PDD\Documents> $sub2 = $subs[2]
PS C:\Users\administrator.PDD\Documents> $sub2.Sites

Url
---
http://marketing.litwareinc.com
http://marketing.litwareinc.com/admin
http://marketing.litwareinc.com/mysitehost


PS C:\Users\administrator.PDD\Documents>
```

FIGURE 11-3 You can use the *Get-SPSiteSubscription* cmdlet to get a list of all your tenants' subscription IDs. Thereafter, you can inspect the *Sites* property of a given tenant to see which site collections make up that tenancy.

You can see in Figure 11-3 how to access all the subscriptions, and then how to grab a particular tenant and display all the site collections in that tenancy. Just by looking at the URL, you can tell this tenant is the marketing department.

If you're new to PowerShell, it might be helpful to know there's another way to get at the subscription you want. If you have hundreds of tenants, counting them in order to find the index to put in the brackets ([]) is arduous. Rather, you can substitute a *where-object* cmdlet to only get the subscription that matches the ID you're looking for. Alternatively, you can use the *Get-SPSiteSubscription* cmdlet and pass the ID (that is, *$sub = Get-SPSiteSubscription <GUID>*). You can see this in action in Figure 11-4, where the subscription ID for the Sales tenant is retrieved.

```
PowerShell Console
PS C:\Users\administrator.PDD\Documents> $sub3 = $subs | Where-Object { $_.Id.ToString()
-eq "9d78e16e-5ded-4760-a7d5-7ac5edce4795" }
PS C:\Users\administrator.PDD\Documents> $sub3.Sites

Url
---
http://sales.litwareinc.com
http://sales.litwareinc.com/admin
http://sales.litwareinc.com/mysitehost


PS C:\Users\adm...\Documents>
```

FIGURE 11-4 If you know your tenant's subscription ID, you can retrieve just that tenant by searching for that ID in the collection of subscription IDs. You can do this by using the *where-object* cmdlet.

A third way to identify a tenant's site subscription is to first get a site collection that you know is in the tenancy and then inspect the *SiteSubscription* property. This property will contain the ID of the site subscription you're looking for, as you can see in Figure 11-5.

```
PowerShell Console
PS C:\Users\administrator.PDD\Documents> $salesSite = Get-SPSite
http://sales.litwareinc.com

PS C:\Users\administrator.PDD\Documents> $salesSite.SiteSubscription

Id                                        Sites
--                                        -----
9d78e16e-5ded-4760-a7d5-7ac5edce4795      {SPSite Url=http://sales.litwareinc.com,...


PS C:\Users\adm...\Documents>
```

FIGURE 11-5 Sometimes you might have a site collection, but you might not remember which tenant that site belongs to. To find out, you can inspect the *SiteSubscription* property of the site itself.

Step 5: Assigning a Feature Pack to a Tenant

With your feature packs and tenant site subscriptions created, you can now start to associate those tenants to feature packs. After you assign a feature pack to a particular tenant's site subscription, the tenant will only see the features that are in the pack. To configure this association, use the *Set-SPSiteSubscriptionConfig* PowerShell cmdlet. There is currently no user interface to associate a tenant to a feature pack.

When you run the *Set-SPSiteSubscriptionConfig* cmdlet, you'll want a handle to the site subscription to which you're associating the feature pack. In previous sections, you used the *$sub* variable, and in this case you'll pass that variable into the *–Id* parameter. The only other parameter you need to pass is the *–FeaturePack* parameter.

In step 3, you saw how to create new feature packs with the *New-SPSiteSubscriptionFeaturePack* cmdlet. You can also use the *Get-SPSiteSubscriptionFeaturePack* cmdlet to get the feature pack you want to assign to the tenant. You pass both the site subscription and the feature pack into the *Set-SPSiteSubscriptionConfig* cmdlet, as you can see in the following code:

```
Set-SPSiteSubscriptionConfig -id $sub -FeaturePack $efp
```

The following script shows first how to get a handle to a site subscription with the *Get-SP SiteSubscription* cmdlet, and then how to associate that site subscription to a feature pack with the *Set-SPSiteSubscriptionConfig* cmdlet:

```
$marketing = Get-SPSiteSubscription "d4b08002-3d68-484d-a62c-69c0dd76acca"
Set-SPSiteSubscriptionConfig -Id $marketing -FeaturePack $ffp

$sales = Get-SPSiteSubscription "9d78e16e-5ded-4760-a7d5-7ac5edce4795"
Set-SPSiteSubscriptionConfig -Id $sales -FeaturePack $sfp
Set-SPSiteSubscriptionConfig -Id $sales -FeaturePack $efp

$hr = Get-SPSiteSubscription "83322539-132f-4dc0-b8d6-221ce6a674fd"
Set-SPSiteSubscriptionConfig -Id $hr -FeaturePack $sfp
```

Changing the Assigned Feature Pack After Sites Are Created

Notice in the preceding code how the *$sales* site subscription's feature pack was set twice. You can always change the assigned feature pack at a later date. However, you cannot assign more than one feature pack to a given tenant at the same time. At first the Sales site was set to the Standard SKU feature pack, but thereafter it was set to the Enterprise SKU feature pack (packs defined in step 3).

Note It is very important to understand that when you change the assigned feature pack, the currently active features on any existing sites are not deactivated. If you want them deactivated, you'll want to run the *Disable-SPFeature* cmdlet for each feature you took out of the feature pack. New sites, however, will not have those features active if they are not active in the new feature pack. The same is true for newly added features to the feature pack. Those features won't be available to existing site collections until you run the *Enable-SPFeature* cmdlet.

Another helpful example is shown in Figure 11-6. This figure shows how you can determine which feature pack you want to assign to a tenant. When you run *Get-SPSiteSubscription FeaturePack*, you get a list of all the feature pack IDs. This list isn't terribly helpful in identifying the one you want unless you happen to have the ID memorized. However, when you look into the *FeatureDefinitions* property of a given feature pack, you can easily see which features are in the pack, and thus determine whether that pack is the one that you want to assign to the tenant. You can see in the figure that this feature pack contains the BI features of SharePoint, so you can conclude that this feature pack is the pack containing all the features for the Enterprise SKU of SharePoint, as was defined in step 3.

```
PowerShell Console
PS C:\Users\administrator.PDD\Documents> $fpacks = Get-SPSiteSubscriptionFeaturePack
PS C:\Users\administrator.PDD\Documents> $fpacks

FeatureDefinitions                        Id
------------------                        --
{FeatureDefinition/29ea7495-fca1-4dc6-8ac... 19d20401-9c8b-40a5-a38c-601c8802132f
{FeatureDefinition/fead7313-ae6d-45dd-826... 4118906d-0de1-4684-a42d-bf66599e9177
{FeatureDefinition/a4d4ee2c-a6cb-4191-ab0... 18793a23-dd0a-4cf3-8528-f64003901f32


PS C:\Users\administrator.PDD\Documents> $fpacks[0].FeatureDefinitions

DisplayName                Id                                    Scope
-----------                --                                    -----
AccSrvMSysAso              29ea7495-fca1-4dc6-8ac1-500c247a036e  Web
AccSrvRestrictedList       a4d4ee2c-a6cb-4191-ab0a-21bb5bde92fb  Web
AccSrvShell                bcf89eb7-bca1-4468-bdb4-ca27f61a2292  Web
AccSrvSolutionGallery      744b5fd3-3b09-4da6-9bd1-de18315b045d  Site
AccSrvUserTemplate         1a8251a0-47ab-453d-95d4-07d7ca4f8166  Web
AccSrvUSysAppLog           28101b19-b896-44f4-9264-db028f307a62  Web
AddDashboard               d250636f-0a26-4019-8425-a5232d592c09  Web
AdminLinks                 fead7313-ae6d-45dd-8260-13b563cb4c71  Web
AdminReportCore            b8f36433-367d-49f3-ae11-f7d76b51d251  Site
AnnouncementsList          00bfea71-d1ce-42de-9c63-a44004ce0104  Web
AssetLibrary               4bcccd62-dcaf-46dc-a7d4-e38277ef33f4  Site
BaseSite                   b21b090c-c796-4b0f-ac0f-7ef1659c20ae  Site
BaseWeb                    99fe402e-89a0-45aa-9163-85342e865dc8  Web
BasicWebParts              00bfea71-1c5e-4a24-b310-ba51c3eb7a57  Site
BDR                        3f59333f-4ce1-406d-8a97-9ecb0ff0337f  Web
BICenterDashboardsLib      f979e4dc-1852-4f26-ab92-d1b2a190afc9  Web
BICenterDataconnectionsLib 26676156-91a0-49f7-87aa-37b1d5f0c4d0  Web
BICenterSampleData         3992d4ab-fa9e-4791-9158-5ee32178e88a  Web
BizAppsCTypes              43f41342-1a37-4372-8ca0-b44d881e4434  Site
BizAppsFields              5a979115-6b71-45a5-9881-cdc872051a69  Site
PS C:\Users\adm...\Documents>
```

FIGURE 11-6 A feature pack is essentially just a GUID, but it's not easy to remember. If you forget what a given pack is meant to be used for, you can check which features are in the pack by inspecting the *FeatureDefinitions* property.

For one final example, what if you know a site subscription but do not know which feature pack is assigned to it? In this case, you can call the *Get-SPSiteSubscriptionConfig* cmdlet and pass in the subscription ID. Thereafter, you can call the *FeaturePack* parameter to get a handle on the feature pack, and then call *FeatureDefinitions* to see the features in the pack, as illustrated in Figure 11-7.

```
PowerShell Console                                                         ▼ ₽ X
PS C:\Users\administrator.PDD\Documents> $config = Get-SPSiteSubscriptionConfig  ▲
-Identity $marketing
PS C:\Users\administrator.PDD\Documents> $config.FeaturePack.FeatureDefinitions

DisplayName                   Id                                    Scope
-----------                   --                                    -----
AdminLinks                    fead7313-ae6d-45dd-8260-13b563cb4c71  Web
AnnouncementsList             00bfea71-d1ce-42de-9c63-a44004ce0104  Web
BasicWebParts                 00bfea71-1c5e-4a24-b310-ba51c3eb7a57  Site
CallTrackList                 239650e3-ee0b-44a0-a22a-48292402b8d8  Web
CirculationList               a568770a-50ba-4052-ab48-37d8029b3f47  Web
ContactsList                  00bfea71-7e6d-4186-9ba8-c047ac750105  Web
CTypes                        695b6570-a48b-4a8e-8ea5-26ea7fc1d162  Site
CustomList                    00bfea71-de22-43b2-a848-c05709900100  Web
DataSourceLibrary             00bfea71-f381-423d-b9d1-da7a54c50110  Web
DiscussionsList               00bfea71-6a49-43fa-b535-d15c05500108  Web
DocumentLibrary               00bfea71-e717-4e80-aa17-d0c71b360101  Web
EventsList                    00bfea71-ec85-4903-972d-ebe475780106  Web
ExternalList                  00bfea71-9549-43f8-b978-e47e54a10600  Web
FacilityList                  58160a6b-4396-4d6e-867c-65381fb5fbc9  Web
FCGroupsList                  08386d3d-7cc0-486b-a730-3b4cfe1b5509  Web
Fields                        ca7bd552-10b1-4563-85b9-5ed1d39c962a  Site
GanttTasksList                00bfea71-513d-4ca0-96c2-6a47775c0119  Web
GBWProvision                  6e8a2add-ed09-4592-978e-8fa71e6f117c  Web
GBWWebParts                   3d25bd73-7cd4-4425-b8fb-8899977f73de  Web
GridList                      00bfea71-3a1d-41d3-a0ee-651d11570120  Web
PS C:\Users\...\Documents>
```

FIGURE 11-7 If you forget which feature pack is assigned to a particular tenant, you can get the tenant's subscription and inspect the *FeaturePack* property to see what features are available to it.

In the previous example, you saw how the Marketing tenant was assigned the Foundation features through the *$ffp* feature pack, the HR tenant was assigned the Server Standard features with the *$sfp* feature pack, and the Sales tenant was assigned the Server Enterprise features through the *$efp* feature pack (variables defined in step 3). To demonstrate how these features are trimmed out of the user interface, look at the following figures. Figure 11-8 shows the Marketing tenant administration site, where the only features available to be configured are the Foundation features. This is much different from the Sales tenant administration site with the Enterprise features enabled. Figure 11-9 shows the Sales tenant administration site, and you'll quickly notice a lot more functionality that isn't available to the Marketing tenant administrators.

FIGURE 11-8 When a tenant is assigned just the foundation features through a custom feature pack, its site does not show the features to which it doesn't have access.

FIGURE 11-9 Alternatively, if the tenant has a feature pack with more features, those features are available in the interface. This site has far more features available than the one found in Figure 11-8.

Step 6: Filtering the People Picker to an Active Directory Organizational Unit

Similar to how you associated a feature pack to a tenant's site subscription, you can also associate a tenant to an organizational unit in Active Directory (AD). This is handy because when a tenant is associated to an organizational unit (OU) in AD, the People Picker will only show users in that OU. For example, if a tenant wants to let users have contribute rights to one of its sites, the only users it can add are users in its own OU. So, if you have sensitive data in your Human Resources sites, for example, you could lock those sites down to just users in the Human Resources OU. You would do this with the *Set-SPSiteSubscriptionConfig* cmdlet, similar to how you associated the tenant to a feature pack. The following script shows how to associate a tenant's site subscription to an OU:

```
Set-SPSiteSubscriptionConfig -Id $hr
    -UserAccountDirectoryPath "OU=Human Resources,OU=Tenants,DC=pdd,DC=com"
```

> **Note** In the previous section, the variable *$hr* was created by using the *Get-SPSiteSubscription* PowerShell cmdlet.

The *UserAccountDirectoryPath* parameter corresponds exactly to the OU structure in AD. For example, notice in Figure 11-10 that there is an AD domain called pdd (Phil's Dev Domain), and underneath it there is an OU called Tenants, and below that there's an OU called Human Resources. This OU structure is what dictates the parameter value of *OU=Human Resources, OU=Tenants,DC=pdd,DC=com.*

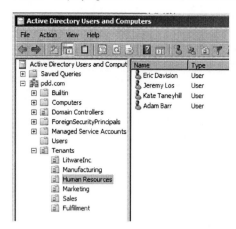

FIGURE 11-10 The *–UserAccountDirectoryPath* parameter must be mapped to your AD domain's OU structure.

After the *Set-SPSiteSubscriptionConfig* cmdlet has been run and is targeting the correct OU, the People Picker is trimmed to just those users. For example, in Figure 11-10, there's a user named Adam Barr. Notice also in Figure 11-11 that there is a separate OU called Marketing with two users with "b" in their name, Brad and Ben. When a user in the Human Resources tenancy searches for "b", the user only sees Adam Barr because the results are filtered, as you can see in Figure 11-12.

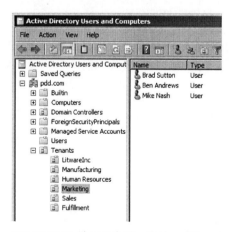

FIGURE 11-11 The Marketing OU has different users in it than the Human Resources OU, and thus the People Picker for these two tenants will only show users in their assigned OU.

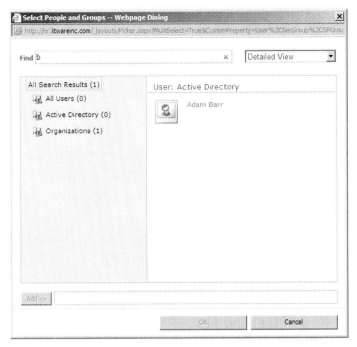

FIGURE 11-12 When searching for "b", despite there being users in the Marketing OU who would match this search, only users in the Human Resources OU are returned because this is the OU that is associated with the tenant.

Step 7: Configuring Tenant-Aware Managed Paths

Managed paths in SharePoint are the URL locations, where site collections are installed. There are two kinds of managed paths: explicit managed paths, where only one site collection is installed, and wildcard managed paths. Wildcard managed paths support one or more site collections. For example, consider the "root" managed path of a given web application, where the managed path URL is "/". If the web application's URL is http://litwareinc.com, the root site collection is installed into the "/" managed path. This is considered an explicit managed path because only one site collection is found at http://litwareinc.com. This doesn't have to only be the root; for instance, you could have a managed path with the URL "Sales", such that you'd have one and only one site collection found at http://litwareinc.com/sales.

However, consider a wildcard managed path with a URL of "sites". This managed path can hold multiple site collections—for example, http://litwareinc.com/sites/HR, http://litwareinc.com/sites/Marketing, and so on.

Before you can create your tenant site collections, you need to create the managed paths into which you want to install your site collections. With tenants, one common approach is to create a wildcard managed path for each tenant, such as http://litwareinc.com/tenant1 and http://litwareinc.com/tenant2. This approach works and makes it easy to remember the tenant by its URL, but it has the following shortcomings:

- Users can "mine" the URLs and guess the locations of sites they perhaps wouldn't otherwise know were there.

- After 20 managed paths per web application, SharePoint might take a performance hit, and it is a Microsoft-recommended practice not to exceed this supported boundary.

- Obviously, with only 20 managed paths, you're not going to be able to support more than 20 tenants per web application.

- Vanity URLs wouldn't make sense, such as the URL http://humanresources/human resources/home, where http://humanresources is the vanity URL and "/humanresources" is the managed path.

Instead, a better approach is to create a few "shared" managed paths, but to create them in tenant mode such that vanity URLs can share them. To accomplish this, you must create the managed paths in PowerShell. You can create managed paths through the Central Administration interface, but those managed paths will not work for vanity URLs (also called *host header site collections*).

The cmdlet you'll use is the *New-SPManagedPath* cmdlet, where you specify the URL, the *–HostHeader* to configure support for vanity URLs, and the *–Explicit* tag to designate the managed path as an explicit managed path. If you leave *–Explicit* off, the managed path will be configured as a wildcard managed path.

> **Note** Typically, you must specify the *–WebApplication* parameter, where you enter the URL of the web application for which this managed path is created. However, since you're specifying the *–HostHeader* parameter, this isn't required because host header managed paths are available farm-wide when used in conjunction with host header site collections.

Use the following script to configure the most common managed paths. Five managed paths are created in total—the first one contains the tenant administration site, one holds the My Site Host, followed by a wildcard managed path that holds the My Sites themselves. Next, there are two more managed paths, one holds a content type hub and one holds other generic sites. With these five managed paths in place, you're now ready to start creating site collections.

```
New-SPManagedPath admin -HostHeader -Explicit
New-SPManagedPath mysitehost -HostHeader -Explicit
New-SPManagedPath mysites/personal -HostHeader
New-SPManagedPath ctypehub -HostHeader -Explicit
New-SPManagedPath sites -HostHeader
```

Step 8: Creating Tenant Site Collections

With your new tenant created via the *New-SPSiteSubscription* cmdlet, it's time to start provisioning site collections to be a part of that tenant. You'll likely be creating quite a few different types of site collections. This includes a root site collection, which is a must before other site collections can be created. Then, you'll most certainly want a tenant administrator site, as well as a My Site Host if your tenant wishes to give its users their own My Site. Lastly, you'll want a site collection to serve as the content type hub if you wish to enable content type syndication.

Create the Root Site Collection

The first site you create must be the root site collection. This is necessary when you're using host header site collections. If you're not using host header site collections, you don't need to worry as much about the order. To create a new site collection for a tenant, first get a handle to the tenant's site subscription and store it in a variable. See step 5 for instructions on how to do this. Then, you'll execute the *New-SPSite* cmdlet and pass the subscription ID in as a parameter. In addition to the site subscription parameter, notice the other variables that the *New-SPSite* cmdlet requires:

```
$user = "litware\phil"
$email = phil@litwareinc.com
$hostUrl = http://Manufacturing.litwareinc.com
$hostWebApp = http://hosting.litwareinc.com
$sub = Get-SPSiteSubscription "9d78e16e-5ded-4760-a7d5-7ac5edce4795"
```

The *$hostUrl* parameter is the only parameter you won't need if you're not using host header site collections. All the others are required. The *$user* and *$email* properties specify the site collection administrator. The *$hostUrl* property specifies your tenant's vanity URL. The *$hostWebApp* property specifies the actual URL of the web application in which the new site should be created. All of this appears in the following command, which shows the completed *New-SPSite* cmdlet.

> **Note** If you're not creating a host header site collection, simply take out the *–HostHeaderWeb Application* parameter and replace the *–Url* parameter with the URL of the web application, plus the location where you want the site created, such as -Url `http://intranet.litware.com/ sites/newsite`.

```
New-SPSite -Template STS#0 -SiteSubscription $sub -Url $hostUrl
-HostHeaderWebApplication $hostWebApp -OwnerAlias $user -OwnerEmail $email
```

> **Note** If you're getting an Access Denied error when you run the *New-SPSite* cmdlet, it might be because you're not using claims-based authentication or you're not a SharePoint Shell administrator (*Add-SPShellAdmin*). Switch to claims-based authentication (from classic mode authentication) or use the farm account when running the command.

STS#0: Template ID

The string STS#0 corresponds to a particular site template definition found in the 14 Root folder, c:\program files\common files\microsoft shared\web server extensions\14\TEMPLATE\SiteTemplates. "STS" represents the standard team site template, and "#0" represents configuration number 0, which translates to "Blank Site" when looking at the site template picker when creating new sites. Some other site template IDs are listed in Table 11-1.

TABLE 11-1 Site Templates and Their Corresponding IDs

Value	Site definition
STS#0	Team Site
STS#1	Blank Site
STS#2	Document Workspace
MPS#0	Basic Meeting Workspace
MPS#1	Blank Meeting Workspace
MPS#2	Decision Meeting Workspace
MPS#3	Social Meeting Workspace
MPS#4	Multipage Meeting Workspace
BLOG#0	Blog
SGS#0	Basic Group Work Site
SGS#1	Blank Group Work Site
tenantadmin#0	Tenant administration Site
SPSMSITEHOST#0	My Site Host Site
WIKI#0	Wiki

Create the Tenant Administration Site

With the root site now in place, it's time to start creating the other necessary site collections, the first of which is the tenant administration site collection. Again, this site collection lets the tenant administer its own site collections, such as creating new sites or deleting existing sites. What's more, the tenant can administer its partitions of the available shared services, such as managed metadata and secure store.

To create a new tenant administration site, you'll use the same process described in the previous section. The only variable you'll want to change is the *$hostUrl* variable. Instead, point it to the new tenant administration site's URL, as in the following:

```
$adminUrl = $hostUrl+"/admin"
```

> **Note** You've probably already surmised that the "/admin" corresponds to the "admin" explicit managed path that is created in step 7.

Then, substitute the *$hostUrl* variable for the *$adminUrl* variable and run the *New-SPSite* cmdlet again, as shown in the code following this paragraph. You'll notice the only difference from the cmdlet run in the previous section is the introduction of a new parameter: *–AdministrationSiteType*. This tells the site subscription service application that this site collection is the designated tenant administration site for the tenant found in the *$sub* parameter.

```
New-SPSite -Template tenantadmin#0 -SiteSubscription $sub -Url $adminUrl
    -HostHeaderWebApplication $hostWebApp -OwnerAlias $user -OwnerEmail $email
    -AdministrationSiteType TenantAdministration
```

> **Note** The *$sub*, *$hostWebApp*, *$user*, and *$email* variables were created in the previous section.

Create the My Site Host

If you want your tenant to be able to create My Sites, you'll need to create a My Site Host site collection in an explicit managed path. You would do this in the same way that you created the tenant administration site, but you'd use a different URL and template. For starters, create a new variable to store the updated URL:

```
$mhost = $hostUrl+"/mysitehost"
```

Then, run the *New-SPSite* cmdlet again, but instead, use the *$mhost* variable for the URL property. Also, ensure that you use the My Site Host template ID (SPSMSITEHOST#0), as you can see in the following code:

```
New-SPSite -Template SPSMSITEHOST#0 -SiteSubscription $sub -Url $mhost
    -HostHeaderWebApplication $hostWebApp -OwnerAlias $user -OwnerEmail $email
```

> **Note** Again, note that the *$sub*, *$hostWebApp*, *$user*, and *$email* variables were created in the "Create the Root Site Collection" section.

It's important to note again that /mysitehost corresponds to the mysitehost explicit managed path. Also, My Sites will not be functional until you associate this My Site Host site collection as well as the mysites/personal wildcard managed path to the user profile service application. See step 9 for guidance on how to associate this My Site Host.

Enable Self-Service Site Creation

The next step is to enable self-service site creation. This is required if you want your tenants to create and delete site collections through the tenant administration user interface. You can enable self-service site creation either through the Central Administration user interface or through the following *stsadm* command where the *–url* parameter is the URL of the web application:

```
stsadm -o enablessc -url $hostingMainURL
```

> **Note** Unfortunately, you cannot configure this on a tenant-by-tenant basis. It's all or nothing. Every tenant in the web application either can create site collections, or cannot. Also, you unfortunately cannot change this setting with PowerShell.

To enable self-service site creation through the Central Administration interface, click Application Management | Manage Web Applications, and then select the web application on which you want to enable self-service site creation. On the ribbon, select Self-Service Site Creation, as shown in Figure 11-13. Thereafter, a dialog box appears, in which you can simply turn self-service site creation on or off.

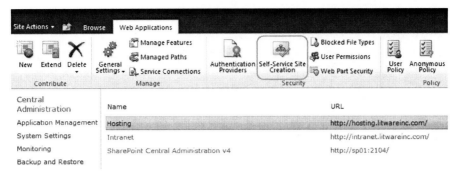

FIGURE 11-13 You can enable self-service site creation through Central Administration.

Create the Host Named Sites by Using SSL

Thus far, you have not seen any examples of creating new site collections using HTTPS/SSL. All the examples shown were created over HTTP. If you want to use HTTPS, or just HTTP, for that matter, ensure that the public URL in the default zone on the web application is set to HTTPS, as shown in Figure 11-14. By default, all host header site collections will use the protocol as defined in the public URL of the default zone. So, if you want HTTP, enter HTTP, and vice versa for HTTPS (SSL).

Alternate Access Mapping Collection

Select an Alternate Access Mapping Collection.

Alternate Access Mapping Collection: **Hosting ▾**

Public URLs

Enter the public URL protocol, host, and port to use for this resource in any or all of the zones listed. The Default Zone URL must be defined. It will be used if needed where the public URL for the zone is blank and for administrative actions such as the URLs in Quota e-mail.
http://go.microsoft.com/fwlink/?LinkId=114854

Default
`https://hosting.litwareinc.com`

Intranet

Internet

Custom

Extranet

| Save | Delete | Cancel |

FIGURE 11-14 For a host header site collection to run on SSL, you must configure the public URL of the default zone to run on HTTPS.

To configure the public URL of the default zone, you must access alternate access mappings while in Central Administration. Click Application Management | Configure Alternate Access Mappings, and then click the Edit Public URLs link on the toolbar to edit the default URL.

Need Both HTTP and HTTPS?

To have host header site collections use HTTP and HTTPS in the same web application, you are required to create at least two web applications, one running HTTP in the public URL of the default zone, and the other running HTTPS for secure traffic.

Beyond simply configuring the public URL of the default zone, you must also install a wildcard certificate in Internet Information Server (IIS). For instance, if you purchase the wildcard certificate for *.litwareinc.com, all host header site collections must be subdomains of litware inc.com, such as https://marketing.litwareinc.com and https://sales.litwareinc.com. This is where you might have a problem. If you want a host header for https://contoso.com in the same web application as https://marketing.litwareinc.com, this will not be possible because it won't match the format of the certificate. Instead, you'll need a separate web application and certificate for that site.

Use Host-Named Site Collections with Off-Box SSL Termination

If you have traffic coming in from the Internet, you are most likely going to use SSL to secure that traffic. In some cases, people like to use off-box SSL termination to change the protocol from HTTPS to HTTP after the request gets inside the firewall. This SSL termination is usually performed on a proxy server in a perimeter network as it forwards the request to the SharePoint farm. To configure your web application to support off-box SSL termination, you configure it the same way that you would if you were not going to terminate, where all traffic would remain over HTTPS. This essentially just means to again specify HTTPS in the public URL of the default zone as well as configuring your certificates as you normally would.

> **Note** The reverse proxy or terminator cannot change the host header to something else. It must maintain the same host header that the client requested—for example, https://sales.litwareinc.com.
>
> If the client request is sent to the default SSL port of 443, the reverse proxy or terminator must forward the request to port 80. If the client request was on a nonstandard SSL port, the forward request must still use that same nonstandard port.

Step 9: Associating the Tenant to the User Profile Service Application

User profiles are an important feature of SharePoint. People use them to create a "social" experience in their business. You can share personal information such as hobbies, and you can share work-related information such as your skills and where they fit in the organizational structure.

To enable the profile features to be available to your tenants, you first must create a user profile service application in partitioned mode via PowerShell. This process was described in Chapter 10. After you have created the service application, you can start importing users from your AD. However, a particular tenant will not be able to see its profiles until you associate the tenant's subscription ID with the user profile service application. Additionally, you must specify which OU in AD contains the users for the particular tenant. Thus, after this association and OU are configured, the tenant will see the profiles for its users that reside in that particular OU.

This process is separate from the process by which you specified the same OU to filter the People Picker search results. If you remember from a few sections earlier, the People Picker for a given tenant can be trimmed to only show users in a particular OU. Although this is similar to what you need to do with user profiles, it requires a different cmdlet. Instead of the *Set-SPSiteSubscriptionConfig* cmdlet (where you filtered the People Picker), you must use the *Set-SPSiteSubscriptionProfileConfig* cmdlet to associate the tenant's site subscription to the user profile service application and an OU.

In addition to setting up the import of the correct user profiles, this cmdlet is also used to tell the user profile service application which site collection is the My Site Host. When a user clicks the ribbon to navigate to her My Site, SharePoint needs to know the location of the tenant's My Site Host, which does the redirection to the user's My Site. The *Set-SPSite SubscriptionProfileConfig* cmdlet sets up this association, as well as which managed path in which the My Sites resides (for example, /mysites/personal). The My Sites managed path also must be specified so that the My Site Host knows in which wildcard managed path to create the new My Site site collections.

To use the *Set-SPSiteSubscriptionProfileConfig* cmdlet, first you must get a handle to the user profile service application's proxy. You can do this with the *Get-SPServiceApplicationProxy* cmdlet, as shown here:

```
$UPSProxy = Get-SPServiceApplicationProxy |
    where-object {$_.DisplayName -eq "Partitioned User Profile Service Proxy"}
```

> **Note** *Partitioned User Profile Service Proxy* is the display name of the UPSA proxy, which you can see while in Central Administration.

With a variable storing a handle to the proxy, you're almost ready to configure the association. First, look at the other variables that will all be passed as parameters into the *Set-SP SiteSubscriptionProfileConfig* cmdlet:

```
$OUName = "Human Resources"
$mySiteHostURL = http://marketing.litwareinc.com/mysitehost
$mySiteMP = "/mysites/personal"
$sub = $marketing
```

The *$OUName* variable stores the name of the OU in AD (see Figure 11-15). The *$mSiteHostURL* variable stores the full URL to the My Site Host site collection. The *$mySiteMP* variable stores the name of the wildcard managed path that houses the My Sites. Finally, you need a handle to your tenant's site subscription's ID.

> **Note** The *$marketing* variable was defined a few sections earlier, but you can use the *Get-SPSiteSubscription* cmdlet to get your tenant's site subscription's ID.

FIGURE 11-15 When associating a tenant to the user profile service application, you must specify the name of an OU that it should import profiles from, such as "Human Resources."

With those variables in place, you can now execute the *Set-SPSiteSubscriptionProfileConfig* cmdlet. The following is an example showing the parameters and the variables in use:

```
Add-SPSiteSubscriptionProfileConfig -id $sub -MySiteHostLocation $mySiteHostURL
  -MySiteManagedPath $mySiteMP -SynchronizationOU $OUName
  -ProfileServiceApplicationProxy $UPSProxy
```

Profiles won't immediately start to appear after you run the *Set-SPSiteSubscriptionProfile Config* cmdlet. You must first configure profile synchronization in Central Administration. (See the TechNet article at *http://bit.ly/dcQcsX* for more information.) However, you can see if the tenant was registered successfully. If you open Central Administration and click the user profile service application, you should see the Number Of Tenants report increase by one (see Figure 11-16). This number will remain at zero until you run the *Set-SPSiteSubscriptionProfile Config* cmdlet for a tenant.

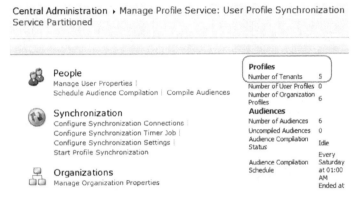

FIGURE 11-16 After you start associating tenants to the user profile service application, you'll notice that the number of tenants the service application is aware of is increasing.

Object Not Set To An Instance Of An Object Error

If you get an Object Not Set To An Instance Of An Object error when you execute the *Set-SPSiteSubscriptionProfileConfig* cmdlet, you likely do not have permissions on the user profile service application's proxy. To fix this error, open Central Administration, select Application Management | Manage Service Applications, and then click the partitioned user profile service application's proxy. After you have the proxy selected, on the ribbon, click the Permissions button. Thereafter, enter your user ID as a full control user, and then click OK (see Figure 11-17).

FIGURE 11-17 You might receive an error when running the *Set-SPSiteSubscriptionProfileConfig* cmdlet because you don't have permission to use the user profile service application's proxy.

Step 10: Configuring a Content Type Hub

The last step in this process is to designate a site collection as the content type hub. This lets you syndicate your content types across all your site collections, and thus have a consistent content type experience no matter which site you're in. The hub is where you define your content types, and all other sites can be configured to "subscribe" to the content types in the hub and receive updates when the content types in the hub change.

The first thing to do is to create a new site collection in the tenancy. You can do this through the tenant administration interface or through PowerShell. The following cmdlet creates a new "Blank Site" in the "ctypehub" explicit managed path:

```
New-SPSite -url "http://marketing.litwareinc.com/ctypehub" -SiteSubscription $marketing
   -HostHeaderWebApplication $hostWebApp -owneralias $user
   -owneremail $email -template sts#0
```

Note The *$marketing*, *$hostWebApp*, *$user*, and *$email* variables were created in examples in previous sections of this chapter. *$marketing* corresponds to a site subscription, *$hostWebApp* is the URL to the web application, *$user* is the user's logon (domain\principal), and *$email* is the user's email address.

With a site collection available, you now need to associate this site collection to the managed metadata service application. To make this association, you must get a handle to the managed metadata service application that you created in Chapter 10, and if you haven't created one yet, ensure that you create it in partitioned mode. Specifically, you must get the service application proxy with the *Get-SPServiceApplicationProxy* PowerShell cmdlet. The following cmdlet shows how you can do this:

```
$mmsProxy = Get-SPServiceApplicationProxy | where-object {$_.DisplayName -eq "Managed
Metadata Web Service Partitioned Proxy"}
```

Note Managed Metadata Web Service Partitioned Proxy is the display name of your managed metadata service application's proxy, as shown in Figure 11-18.

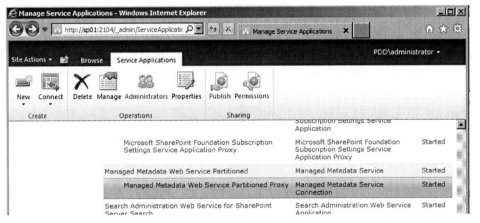

FIGURE 11-18 When retrieving the proxy with PowerShell, you'll use the proxy's display name in conjunction with the *where-object* cmdlet.

With the *$mmsProxy* variable storing your proxy, the next step is to run the *Set-SPSiteSub scriptionMetadataConfig* cmdlet to make the association between the tenant site collection and the service application proxy. The following example passes the tenant's site subscription in the *–identity* parameter, the proxy in the *–serviceProxy* parameter, and the URL to the content type hub in the *–huburi* parameter. The *SyndicationErrorReportEnabled* parameter, if present, sends emails to site collection administrators when a syndication error occurs.

```
Set-SPSiteSubscriptionMetadataConfig -identity $sub -ServiceProxy $mmsProxy
    -HubUri "http://marketing.sharepoint.com/cthub" -SyndicationErrorReportEnabled
```

With the content type hub associated to the service application proxy, you can now start syndicating your content types. To get started, you must first enable the Content Type Syndication Hub feature. You can do this either with the following PowerShell cmdlet or through the user interface by navigating to Site Settings | Site Collection Features, and then clicking the Activate button (see Figure 11-19).

```
Enable-SPFeature -Identity ContentTypeHub -url http://marketing.litwareinc.com/ctypehub
```

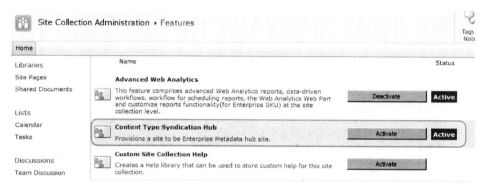

FIGURE 11-19 You can also enable the Content Type Syndication Hub feature through the user interface via Site Settings | Site Collection Features. Just ensure that you activate the feature on the same site you associated to the user profile service application.

With the Content Type Syndication Hub feature activated on your hub, the next step is to start creating and modifying your content types. After you have a new content type as you want it, you must configure that content type for publishing. By default, it will not be published. To publish it, click the Manage Publishing For This Content Type link on the content type's setting page (see Figure 11-20). Next, select the Publish option to configure this content type for publishing (see Figure 11-21), and then click the OK button.

Note After you've configured a content type to be published, you might want to check its status to see if any errors occurred during publishing, or to kick off a manual publish. To perform these actions, go to the content type hub and navigate to Site Settings | Site Collection Administration | Content Type Publishing. This interface renders the status of your hub as well as all the content types that are marked to be published. Content types are published via a timer job, so if you don't see it published, you might need to wait for the timer job to run.

Site Content Type Information

Name: Document

Description: Create a new document.

Parent: Item

Group: Document Content Types

Settings

- Name, description, and group
- Advanced settings
- Workflow settings
- Delete this site content type
- Document Information Panel settings
- Manage publishing for this content type

FIGURE 11-20 To configure a content type for publishing, go to the content type settings, and then click Manage Publishing For This Content Type.

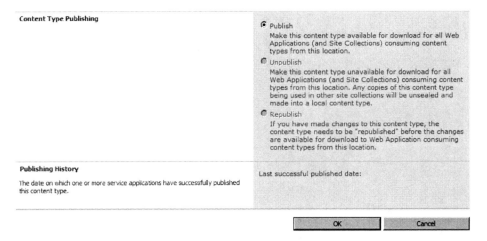

Content Type Publishing

- Publish

  Make this content type available for download for all Web Applications (and Site Collections) consuming content types from this location.

- Unpublish

  Make this content type unavailable for download for all Web Applications (and Site Collections) consuming content types from this location. Any copies of this content type being used in other site collections will be unsealed and made into a local content type.

- Republish

  If you have made changes to this content type, the content type needs to be "republished" before the changes are available for download to Web Application consuming content types from this location.

Publishing History

The date on which one or more service applications have successfully published this content type.

Last successful published date:

[OK]   [Cancel]

FIGURE 11-21 Select the Publish option, and then click OK. Thereafter, the content type syndicates across all your tenant's site collections.

Appendix

Server, Online SharePoint, and Online Dedicated Compared

It's crucial for you to know the differences between the Microsoft Server, Microsoft SharePoint Online, and Microsoft SharePoint Online Dedicated editions, and which platform is best suited for your business needs. The main differences fall into four categories: capacities, available services and service applications, different ways to customize SharePoint, and the different out-of-the-box features available to users.

> ### Refer to the SharePoint Online Service Descriptions
>
> This appendix shows comparisons that might change frequently. Microsoft is continually working toward parity with on-premises SharePoint Server and SharePoint Online. Refer to the SharePoint Online Standard and Dedicated service descriptions to see the most up-to-date reference for what does and does not work with these versions.

SharePoint Online Capacities

The following table shows how SharePoint Online Standard and Dedicated editions compare from a capacity perspective. There's no point in listing SharePoint on-premises here, because when you deploy SharePoint yourself, these are "guidelines" and not "boundaries," as they are with Microsoft Online.

Feature	Online Standard edition	Online Dedicated edition
Base storage	10 GB	0 GB
Per-user storage	500 MB	250 MB
Storage per kiosk or partner user	0 MB	0 MB
Additional storage	$2.50/GB/month	Variable (1 TB increments)
Site collection storage quotas	Up to 100 GB	Up to 200 GB
My Site storage allocation (does not count against tenant's overall storage pool)	Up to 500 MB	Up to 5 GB
Site collections (#) per tenant	Up to 300 (non-My Site site collections)	Unlimited
Total storage per tenant	Up to 5 TB	Up to 30 TB
Additional web applications	Not supported	Supported

Services and Service Applications in SharePoint Online

SharePoint Online takes advantage of shared service applications to provide common functionality across multiple site collections, web applications, and even farms. In SharePoint Online, not all service applications are available between the Standard and Dedicated editions. Obviously, all are available for on-premises solutions, so those are left out of this equation. The following table specifies which service applications are available to the Standard and Dedicated models:

Feature	Online Standard edition	Online Dedicated edition
Access Services	Not supported	Supported
Business Connectivity Services	Not supported	Supported
Excel Calculation	Supported	Supported
FAST for SharePoint	Not supported	Not supported
Forms Services	Supported	Supported
Managed Metadata	Supported	Supported
Performance Point	Not supported	Not supported
PowerPoint	Supported	Supported
Project Server	Not supported	Not supported
Usage Processing	Not supported	Supported

Feature	Online Standard edition	Online Dedicated edition
User Profiles	Supported	Supported
Search	Not supported (local search is supported)	Supported
Secure Store	Not supported	Not supported
State	Not supported	Supported
Web Analytics	Not supported	Supported
Word Conversions	Not supported	Supported
Word Viewing	Supported	Supported
Visio Graphics	Supported	Supported

Customizations in SharePoint Online

There are many differences between the Standard and Dedicated editions with regard to what can and cannot be customized. Chapter 7, "Introduction to Customizing and Developing in SharePoint Online," provides the most detail about this, but the following table presents a high-level view of some of the key differences:

Feature	Online Standard edition	Online Dedicated edition
SharePoint Designer	Supported	Supported
Master pages and page layouts	Supported	Supported
Content types/taxonomy	Supported	Supported
Web Templates	Supported	Supported
Data form Web Parts	Supported	Supported
SharePoint web services and REST APIs	Supported	Supported
Client object model	Supported	Supported
InfoPath forms	Supported	Supported
Declarative workflows	Supported	Supported
.NET workflows	Not supported	Supported
Custom features	Supported (Web and Site scopes)	Supported (all scopes)
Custom Web Parts	Supported (partial trust only)	Supported (full trust supported)
Web.config changes	Not supported	Supported (rare)
Azure integration	Not supported	Supported
Line of Business data	Not supported	Supported

Regarding multitenancy, the main difference between customization in the Standard and Dedicated editions is that the Standard edition requires all customizations to be deployed as sandboxed solution. Any code in the sandbox is partially trusted, governed by resource quotas, and cannot access data outside the site collection to which the code is deployed. With the Dedicated edition, you have a lot more flexibility because you can deploy full-trust solutions at the farm level. Note, however, that Microsoft has a strict approval and analysis process to ensure that your code is stable. See Chapter 7 for more details about how this process works.

SharePoint Online Features and Capabilities

SharePoint 2010 has literally hundreds of out-of-the-box features. The trouble is that some of these features are not available in SharePoint Online. The series of tables that follow outline all the features, and where they are enabled across the SharePoint on-premises and online options. Note that the Online Dedicated edition can be deployed as either a SharePoint Server Standard edition or an Enterprise client access license (CAL). So check the "Standard CAL" and "Enterprise CAL" columns to see if the "Yes" in the dedicated column is actually a yes for the CAL you purchased.

Communities

Feature	Standard CAL	Enterprise CAL	Online Standard	Online Dedicated
Ask Me About	Yes	Yes	Yes	Yes
Blogs	Yes	Yes	Yes	Yes
Colleague Suggestions	Yes	Yes	Yes	Yes
Colleagues Network	Yes	Yes	Yes	Yes
Discussions	Yes	Yes	Yes	Yes
Enterprise Wikis	Yes	Yes	Yes	Yes
Keyword Suggestions	Yes	Yes	Yes	Yes
Memberships	Yes	Yes	Yes	Yes
My Site: My Content	Yes	Yes	Yes	Yes
My Site: My Newsfeed	Yes	Yes	Yes	Yes
My Site: My Profile	Yes	Yes	Yes	Yes
Note Board	Yes	Yes	Yes	Yes

Feature	Standard CAL	Enterprise CAL	Online Standard	Online Dedicated
Organization Browser	Yes	Yes	Yes	Yes
Photos and Presence	Yes	Yes	Yes	Yes
Ratings	Yes	Yes	Yes	Yes
Recent Activities	Yes	Yes	Yes	Yes
Status Updates	Yes	Yes	Yes	Yes
Tag Clouds	Yes	Yes	Yes	Yes
Tag Profiles	Yes	Yes	Yes	Yes
Tags	Yes	Yes	Yes	Yes
Tags and Notes Tool	Yes	Yes	Yes	Yes
Wikis	Yes	Yes	Yes	Yes

Composites

Feature	Standard CAL	Enterprise CAL	Online Standard	Online Dedicated
Client Object Model	Yes	Yes	Yes	Yes
Developer Dashboard	Yes	Yes	Yes	Yes
Event Receivers	Yes	Yes	Yes	Yes
Language-Integrated Query (LINQ) for SharePoint	Yes	Yes	Yes	Yes
Solution Packages	Yes	Yes	Yes	Yes
REST and ATOM Data Feeds	Yes	Yes	Yes	Yes
Ribbon and Dialog Framework	Yes	Yes	Yes	Yes
SharePoint Timer Jobs	Yes	Yes	No	Yes
Silverlight Web Part	Yes	Yes	Yes	Yes
Workflow Models	Yes	Yes	Yes	Yes
Access Services	No	Yes	Yes	Yes
Browser-Based Customizations	Yes	Yes	Yes	Yes
Business Data Connectivity Service	Yes	Yes	No	Yes
External Data Column	Yes	Yes	No	Yes
Business Data Web Parts	No	Yes	No	Yes
External Lists	Yes	Yes	No	Yes

Feature	Standard CAL	Enterprise CAL	Online Standard	Online Dedicated
Business Data Integration with the Office Client	No	Yes	No	Yes
Business Connectivity Services Profile Page	Yes	Yes	No	Yes
SharePoint Designer	Yes	Yes	Yes	Yes
Forms: Out-of-Box workflows and customization through SharePoint Designer	Yes	Yes	Yes	Yes
InfoPath Forms Services	No	Yes	Yes	Yes
Sandboxed Solutions	Yes	Yes	Yes	Yes
Workflow	Yes	Yes	Yes	Yes
Microsoft Visual Studio 2010 SharePoint Developer Tools	Yes	Yes	Yes	Yes
Workflow Templates	Yes	Yes	Yes	Yes
SharePoint Service Architecture	Yes	Yes	Yes	Yes

Content

Feature	Standard CAL	Enterprise CAL	Online Standard	Online Dedicated
Records Center	Yes	Yes	No	No
In-Place Legal Holds	Yes	Yes	Yes	Yes
Document Sets	Yes	Yes	Yes	Yes
Metadata-driven Navigation	Yes	Yes	Yes	Yes
Multi-Stage Disposition	Yes	Yes	Yes	Yes
Rich Media Management	Yes	Yes	Yes	Yes
Shared Content Types	Yes	Yes	Yes	Yes
Support for Accessibility Standards	Yes	Yes	Yes	Yes
Content Organizer	Yes	Yes	Yes	Yes

Feature	Standard CAL	Enterprise CAL	Online Standard	Online Dedicated
Unique Document IDs	Yes	Yes	Yes	Yes
Microsoft Word Automation Services	Yes	Yes	No	Yes
Managed Metadata Service	Yes	Yes	Yes	Yes

Insights

Feature	Standard CAL	Enterprise CAL	Online Standard	Online Dedicated
Business Intelligence Center	No	Yes	No	No
Chart Web Parts	No	Yes	No	Yes
Data Connection Library	No	Yes	No	Yes
Excel Services	No	Yes	Yes	Yes
Microsoft Office PerformancePoint Services	No	Yes	No	No
Visio Services	No	Yes	Yes	Yes
Calculated KPIs	No	Yes	No	Yes
Dashboards	No	Yes	No	Yes
Decomposition Tree	No	Yes	No	No
Microsoft Excel Services and PowerPivot for SharePoint	No	Yes	No	No

Search

Feature	Standard CAL	Enterprise CAL	Online Standard	Online Dedicated
Advanced Content Processing	No	Yes—FAST	No	Yes
Best Bets	Yes	Yes	Yes	Yes
Tunable Relevance with Multiple Rank Profiles	No	Yes—FAST	No	Yes
Extensible Search Platform	No	Yes—FAST	No	Yes

Feature	Standard CAL	Enterprise CAL	Online Standard	Online Dedicated
Business Intelligence Indexing Connector	No	Yes—FAST	No	No
SharePoint 2010 Search Connector Framework	Yes	Yes	No	Yes
Contextual Search	No	Yes—FAST	No	No
Deep Refinement	No	Yes—FAST	No	No
Duplicate Detection	Yes	Yes	Yes	Yes
Federated Search	Yes	Yes	No	Yes
Metadata-Driven Refinement	Yes	Yes	Yes	Yes
Mobile Search Experience	Yes	Yes	Yes	Yes
People and Expertise Search	Yes	Yes	Yes	Yes
Phonetics and Nickname Search	Yes	Yes	Yes	Yes
Public Search Scopes (cross-site)	Yes	Yes	No (private only)	Yes
Query Suggestions, "Did You Mean?" and Related Queries	Yes	Yes	Yes	Yes
Recently Authored Content	Yes	Yes	Yes	Yes
Relevancy Tuning	Yes	Yes	No	Yes
Rich Web Indexing	No	Yes—FAST	No	No
Extreme Scale Search	No	Yes—FAST	No	No
Enterprise Scale Search	Yes	No	No	No
Windows 7 Search	Yes	Yes	Yes	Yes
Similar Results	No	Yes—FAST	No	Yes
Single Site Collection Search	No	No	Yes	Yes
Site Search	Yes	Yes	Yes	Yes
Click Through Relevancy	Yes	Yes	Yes	Yes
Thumbnails and Previews	No	Yes—FAST	No	No
View in Browser	Yes	Yes	Yes	Yes
Visual Best Bets	No	Yes—FAST	No	No
Basic Sorting	Yes	Yes	Yes	Yes
Advanced Sorting	No	Yes	No	Yes

Sites

Feature	Standard CAL	Enterprise CAL	Online Standard	Online Dedicated
SharePoint Lists	Yes	Yes	Yes	Yes
Web Parts	Yes	Yes	Yes	Yes
Improved Governance	Yes	Yes	Yes	Yes
Large List Scalability and Management	Yes	Yes	Yes	Yes
Multi-Lingual User Interface	Yes	Yes	Yes	Yes
Permissions Management	Yes	Yes	Yes	Yes
Quota Templates	Yes	Yes	Yes	Yes
Secure Store Service	Yes	Yes	No	No
Connections to Microsoft Office Clients	Yes	Yes	Yes	Yes
Web Analytics	No	Yes	No	Yes
Lightweight Public-Facing site	No	No	Yes	Yes
Audience Targeting	Yes	Yes	Yes	Yes
Cross-Browser Support	Yes	Yes	Yes	Yes
External sharing	No	No	Yes	Yes
SharePoint Ribbon	Yes	Yes	Yes	Yes
Mobile Connectivity	Yes	Yes	Yes	Yes
Office Web Apps	No	No	Yes	Yes
SharePoint Workspace	Yes	Yes	Yes	Yes
Out-of-the-Box Web Parts	Yes	Yes	Yes	Yes
Scalability	Yes	Yes	Yes	Yes
Support for Office Web Applications	Yes	Yes	n/a	n/a
Templates	Yes	Yes	Yes	Yes
Accessibility	Yes	Yes	Yes	Yes
Configuration Wizards	Yes	Yes	Yes	Yes

Index

Symbols

A

D

About the Author

Phil Wicklund is the author of *SharePoint 2010 Workflows in Action* (Manning Publications), in addition to this book. He has more than seven years of SharePoint experience and is a frequent blogger, speaker, and author around SharePoint products and technologies. He began working with SharePoint in 2003 and has since architected and administered many dozens of enterprise SharePoint environments. He started as a SharePoint development instructor, and has since moved into consulting with RBA Consulting, where he shares real-world insights and in-depth best practices with his clients. You can find Phil's blog at *www.philwicklund.com*.

About the Technical Editor

Wayne Ewington is a principal consultant for Microsoft Consulting Services, based in Auckland, New Zealand. He focuses primarily on technologies such as SharePoint (MSS, MSF, MOSS, and WSS) as well as development tools such as Microsoft Visual Studio Team System (VSTS) and Team Foundation Server (TFS). He is a Microsoft Certified Master on SharePoint 2010 and was one of the first to obtain this certification in Australasia. As a principal consultant, he works with clients and partners, assisting them with the successful deployment and use of Microsoft technologies. During his spare time, he enjoys renovating his 105-year-old house and spending time with his wife and two daughters.

About the Contributing Authors

Eric Hanes (Chapter 2) is an information architect and business analyst with more than 15 years of experience designing and building solutions that address complex business problems. He has been particularly focused on SharePoint over the past seven years, utilizing Microsoft's most popular software as a major point of countless solutions for many well-known Fortune 500 companies. At the intersection of business acumen and technical depth, he is a high-powered liaison within customer organizations who can problem-solve while working with technical design.

Brian Wilson (Chapter 3) is a consultant with RBA Consulting in Dallas, Texas. With more than 10 years of experience in the IT industry, he has worked on various large Internet, intranet, and extranet projects that involve all aspects of SharePoint, from architecture to development. He uses creative methods to solve tough business problems, which allows for flexibility and easy customization for business users. He started working with SharePoint 2007, but has also worked with older versions such as WSS 2.0. Now focused on SharePoint 2010 and SharePoint Online, he spends time helping companies brand their different environments to provide a look and feel that follows current market trends.

Faraz Khan (Chapter 7) is a senior consultant with RBA Consulting in Denver, Colorado. He has worked in IT for the past seven years and has been consulting since 2008. He is a Certified Technical Specialist in SharePoint 2010 configuration and a Virtual TS. He was on the advisory board of the patterns & practices group at Microsoft, which has been developing new versions of the SharePoint guidance for developers every few months. Faraz has been working on SharePoint since the 2003 release and has been an integral part of several enterprise (intranet, extranet, and Internet) implementations of SharePoint. He also has experience with the complete feature set and has been a speaker at the last two SharePoint Fest conferences in Denver.

Brian Nielsen (Chapter 8) has been working in IT for more than 15 years. During this time, he has designed and developed applications for a wide variety of industries, including insurance, accounting, corporate, health care, and oil and gas. Initially, he started replacing mainframe applications with applications built with Lotus Notes. Those skills continued to develop and grow to include SharePoint, virtualization, and cloud-based systems. He is a very pragmatic developer and always strives to consider the implications of technology decisions on the entire enterprise. Brian's background includes pivotal roles at Fortune 500 companies for high-profile projects, and he has worked with SharePoint since its initial release. He is currently a senior consultant in the Dallas office of RBA. He has been a contributor to CodePlex and a presenter at SharePoint TechFest.

What do you think of this book?

We want to hear from you!
To participate in a brief online survey, please visit:

microsoft.com/learning/booksurvey

Tell us how well this book meets your needs—what works effectively, and what we can do better. Your feedback will help us continually improve our books and learning resources for you.

Thank you in advance for your input!

CPSIA information can be obtained at www.ICGtesting.com
Printed in the USA
LVOW050309261011

252126LV00003B/21/P

9 780735 662100